THE COUNT OF MONTE-CRISTO

WITH THESE WORDS ON A SMALL SLIP OF PARCHMENT: "JULIE'S DOWRY."

THE COUNT
OF
MONTE - CRISTO

BY

ALEXANDRE DUMAS

EDITED BY

G. E. MITTON

CONTAINING EIGHT FULL-PAGE
ILLUSTRATIONS IN COLOUR BY

SYBIL TAWSE

A. & C. BLACK, LTD.
4, 5 & 6 SOHO SQUARE, LONDON, W. 1
1926

This edition first published in 1920

Printed in Great Britain

NOTE

" MONTE-CRISTO " is a splendid story ; nearly everyone
has attempted to read it, but few have ever penetrated
the labyrinth of the second part ! Dumas was paid for
quantity, and nobly he responded. The first part, however, telling of the unjust imprisonment of the young
sailor, Edmond Dantès, of his thrilling escape from the
Château d'If, and his reappearance in the world as the
Count of Monte-Cristo, is fairly straightforward. It is
the second part, recounting his revenge on the trio who
had wrecked his life, that becomes insufferably tedious
and complicated. In the present book an attempt has
been made to cut away all that is redundant and allow
the story to stand out clearly. It would have been
impossible otherwise to bring the matter within the
compass of a single volume of reasonable type. The
slightly archaic and conventional wording of the transla-
tion of 1846 has been used, as it accords with the
atmosphere of the time in which the story is placed, and
nothing has been altered unnecessarily, only a few
words being interpolated to link up the points where
cuts have been made.

G. E. MITTON.

v

CONTENTS

CHAPTER   PAGE

I. MARSEILLES—THE ARRIVAL - - - 1

II. FATHER AND SON - - - - 8

III. THE CATALANS - - - - - 13

IV. CONSPIRACY - - - - - 23

V. THE MARRIAGE-FEAST - - - - 28

VI. THE DEPUTY PROCUREUR DU ROI - - 41

VII. THE EXAMINATION - - - - 45

VIII. THE CHÂTEAU D'IF - - - - 53

IX. THE OGRE OF CORSICA - - - - 61

X. THE HUNDRED DAYS - - - - 69

XI. THE TWO PRISONERS - - - - 73

XII. A LEARNED ITALIAN - - - - 86

XIII. THE ABBÉ'S CHAMBER - - - - 93

XIV. IN PLACE OF THE DEAD - - - - 106

XV. THE ISLE OF TIBOULEN - - - - 111

XVI. THE SECRET CAVE - - - - 126

XVII. THE AUBERGE OF PONT DU GARD - - 138

XVIII. THE PRISON REGISTER - - - - 151

XIX. THE FIFTH OF SEPTEMBER - - - 163

XX. ITALY: SINBAD THE SAILOR - - - 169

XXI. THE CARNIVAL AT ROME - - - - 178

XXII. VAMPA THE BRIGAND - - - - 186

XXIII. THE GUESTS - - - - - 195

XXIV. UNLIMITED CREDIT - - - - 211

XXV. THE DAPPLED GREYS - - - - 222

XXVI. HAYDÉE - - - - - - 225

Contents

CHAPTER		PAGE
XXVII.	TOXICOLOGY	233
XXVIII.	AT THE OPERA	243
XXIX.	THE RISE AND FALL OF THE STOCKS	252
XXX.	THE TRYSTING PLACE	254
XXXI.	M. NOIRTIER DE VILLEFORT	257
XXXII.	A CONJUGAL SCENE	260
XXXIII.	THE BALL	268
XXXIV.	MADAME DE SAINT-MÉRAN	276
XXXV.	M. NOIRTIER TELLS THE TRUTH	289
XXXVI.	ALBERT AND HAYDÉE	295
XXXVII.	A NEWSPAPER PARAGRAPH	306
XXXVIII.	THE LEMONADE	313
XXXIX.	THE BURGLARY	321
XL.	BEAUCHAMP	330
XLI.	ALBERT CHALLENGES THE COUNT	341
XLII.	THE NIGHT	352
XLIII.	THE MEETING	360
XLIV.	THE SUICIDE	372
XLV.	VALENTINE	376
XLVI.	DEPARTURE FOR BELGIUM	383
XLVII.	THE APPARITION	388
XLVIII.	DANGLARS' SIGNATURE	395
XLIX.	THE CEMETERY OF PÈRE-LA-CHAISE	400
L.	THE DIVISION	404
LI.	THE JUDGE	410
LII.	THE DEPARTURE	419
LIII.	THE FIFTH OF OCTOBER	433

LIST OF ILLUSTRATIONS

IN COLOUR

WITH THESE WORDS ON A SMALL SLIP OF PARCHMENT: "JULIE'S DOWRY" - - *Frontispiece*

FACING PAGE

"YES!" SAID EDMUND, AND HE EXTENDED HIS HAND TO THE CATALAN WITH A CORDIAL AIR - 18

"ONE! TWO! THREE, AND AWAY!" - - - 110

"AH, HERE IS MY MOTHER!" CRIED ALBERT - - 204

"DEAR GRANDPAPA," CRIED SHE, "WHAT HAS HAPPENED?" 258

"EDMUND, YOU WILL NOT KILL MY SON?" - - 352

"YES, COME AT TWELVE O'CLOCK; I SHALL THEN BE FAR AWAY!" - - - - - 400

JACOPO POINTED TOWARDS THE HORIZON - - 440

THE COUNT OF MONTE-CRISTO

CHAPTER I

MARSEILLES—THE ARRIVAL

On the 28th of February, 1815, the watch-tower of Notre-Dame de la Garde, signalled the three-master, the Pharaon, from Smyrna, Trieste, and Naples.

As usual, a pilot put off immediately, and, rounding the Château d'If, got on board the vessel between Cape Morgion and the Isle of Rion.

Immediately, and according to custom, the platform of Fort Saint-Jean was covered with lookers-on ; it is always an event at Marseilles for a ship to come into port, especially when this ship, like the Pharaon, had been built, rigged, and laden on the stocks of the old Phocée, and belonged to an owner of the city.

The ship drew on : it had safely passed the strait, which some volcanic shock has made between the Isle of Calasareigne and the Isle of Jaros : had doubled Pomègue, and approached the harbour under topsails, jib, and foresail, but so slowly and sedately that the idlers, with that instinct which misfortune sends before it, asked one another what misfortune could have happened on board. However, those experienced in navigation saw plainly that if any accident had occurred, it was not to the vessel herself, for she bore down with all the evidence of being skilfully handled, the anchor ready to be dropped, the bowsprit-shrouds loose, and beside the pilot, who was steering the Pharaon by the narrow entrance of the port of Marseilles, was a young man, who, with an active and vigilant eye, watched every motion of the ship, and repeated each direction of the pilot.

The vague disquietude which prevailed amongst the spectators

1

had so much affected one of the crowd that he did not await the arrival of the vessel in harbour, but jumping into a small skiff, desired to be pulled alongside the Pharaon, which he reached as she rounded the creek of La Réserve.

When the young man on board saw this individual approach he left his station by the pilot, and came, hat in hand, to the side of the ship's bulwarks.

He was a fine tall, slim, young fellow, with black eyes, and hair as dark as the raven's wing; and his whole appearance bespoke that calmness and resolution peculiar to men accustomed from their cradle to contend with danger.

"Ah! is it you, Dantès?" cried the man in the skiff. "What's the matter? and why have you such an air of sadness aboard?"

"A great misfortune, M. Morrel!" replied the young man,— "a great misfortune, for me especially! Off Civita Vecchia we lost our brave Captain Leclere."

"And the cargo?" inquired the owner eagerly.

"Is all safe, M. Morrel; and I think you will be satisfied on that head. But poor Captain Leclere——"

"What happened to him?" asked the owner, with an air of considerable resignation.

"He died of the brain-fever in dreadful agony." Then turning to the crew, he said—

"Look out there! all ready to drop anchor!"

All hands obeyed. At the same moment the eight or ten seamen, who composed the crew, sprang, some to the main sheets, others to the braces, others to the halliards, others to the jib-ropes, and others to the topsail brails.

The young sailor gave a look to see his orders were promptly and accurately obeyed, and then turned again to the owner.

"And how did this misfortune occur?" inquired he, resuming the inquiry suspended for a moment.

"Alas! sir, in the most unexpected manner. After a long conversation with the harbour-master, Captain Leclere left Naples greatly disturbed in his mind. At the end of twenty-four hours he was attacked by a fever, and died three days afterwards. We performed the usual burial-service, and he is at his rest sewn up in his hammock, with two bullets of thirty-six pounds each at his head and heels, off the Island of El Giglio. We bring to his widow his sword and cross of honour. It was worth while, truly," added the young man, with a melancholy smile, "to make war against the English for ten years, and to die in his bed at last, like every body else."

"Why, you see, Edmond," replied the owner, who appeared more comforted at every moment, "we are all mortal, and the old must make way for the young. If not, why, there would be no promotion ; and as you have assured me that the cargo——"

"Is all safe and sound, M. Morrel, take my word for it ; and I advise you not to take 1,000*l.* for the profits of the voyage."

Then, as they were just passing the Round Tower the young man shouted out, "Ready, there, to lower topsails, foresail, and jib!"

The order was executed as promptly as if on board a man-of-war.

"Let go ! and brail all !"

At this last word all the sails were lowered, and the bark moved almost imperceptibly onwards.

"Now, if you will come on board, M. Morrel," said Dantès, observing the owner's impatience, "here is your supercargo, M. Danglars, coming out of his cabin, who will furnish you with every particular. As for me, I must look after the anchoring, and dress the ship in mourning."

The owner did not wait to be twice invited. He seized a rope which Dantès flung to him, and, with an activity that would have done credit to a sailor, climbed up the side of the ship, whilst the young man, going to his task, left the conversation to the individual whom he had announced under the name of Danglars, who now came towards the owner. He was a man of twenty-five or twenty-six years of age, of unprepossessing countenance, obsequious to his superiors, insolent to his inferiors ; and then, besides his position as responsible agent on board, which is always obnoxious to the sailors, he was as much disliked by the crew as Edmond Dantès was beloved by them.

"Well, M. Morrel," said Danglars, "you have heard of the misfortune that has befallen us ?"

"Yes—yes ! poor Captain Leclere ! He was a brave and an honest man !"

"And a first-rate seaman, grown old between sky and ocean, as should a man charged with the interests of a house so important as that of Morrel and Son," replied Danglars.

"But," replied the owner, following with his look Dantès, who was watching the anchoring of his vessel, "it seems to me that a sailor needs not be so old as you say, Danglars, to understand his business ; for our friend Edmond seems to understand it thoroughly, and not to require instruction from anyone."

" Yes," said Danglars, casting towards Edmond a look in which a feeling of envy was strongly visible.   " Yes, he is young, and youth is invariably self-confident.   Scarcely was the captain's breath out of his body than he assumed the command without consulting anyone, and he caused us to lose a day and a half at the Isle of Elba, instead of making for Marseilles direct."

" As to taking the command of the vessel," replied Morrel, " that was his duty as captain's mate ; as to losing a day and a half off the Isle of Elba he was wrong, unless the ship wanted some repair."

" The ship was as well as I am, and as, I hope, you are, M. Morrel, and this day and a half was lost from pure whim, for the pleasure of going ashore, and nothing else."

" Dantès !" said the shipowner, turning towards the young man, " come this way !"

" In a moment, sir," answered Dantès, " and I'm with you !" Then, calling to the crew, he said—

" Let go !"

The anchor was instantly dropped, and the chain ran rattling through the port-hole.   Dantès continued at his post, in spite of the presence of the pilot, until this manœuvre was completed, and then he added, " Lower the pennant half-mast high—put the ensign in a weft, and slope the yards !"

" You see," said Danglars, " he fancies himself captain already, upon my word."

" And so, in fact, he is," said the owner.

" Except your signature and your partner's, M. Morrel."

" And why should he not have this ?" asked the owner ; " he is young it is true, but he seems to me a thorough seaman, and of full experience."

A cloud passed over Danglars' brow.

" Your pardon, M. Morrel," said Dantès, approaching, " the ship now rides at anchor, and I am at your service.   You hailed me, I think ?"

Danglars retreated a step or two.

" I wished to inquire why you stopped at the Isle of Elba ?"

" I do not know, sir ; it was to fulfil a last instruction of Captain Leclere, who, when dying, gave me a packet for the Maréchal Bertrand."

Morrel looked around him, and then, drawing Dantès on one
side, he said suddenly—

"And how is the emperor?"

"Very well, as far as I could judge from my eyes."

"You saw the emperor, then?"

"He entered the maréchal's apartment whilst I was there."

"And you spoke to him?"

"He asked me questions about the ship, the time it left
Marseilles, the course she had taken, and what was her cargo. I
believe, if she had not been laden, and I had been master, he
would have bought her. But I told him I was only mate, and
that she belonged to the firm of Morrel and Son. 'Ah! ah!'
he said, 'I know them! The Morrels have been shipowners
from father to son; and there was a Morrel who served in the
same regiment with me when I was in garrison at Valence.'"

"*Pardieu!* and that is true!" cried the owner, greatly delighted. "And that was Policar Morrel, my uncle, who was
afterwards a captain. Dantès, you must tell my uncle that the
emperor remembered him, and you will see it will bring tears
into the old soldier's eyes. Come, come!" continued he, patting
Edmond's shoulder kindly. "You did very right, Dantès, to
follow Captain Leclere's instruction, and touch at the Isle of
Elba, although, if it were known, that you had conveyed a
packet to the maréchal, and had conversed with the emperor, it
might bring you into trouble."

"How could that bring me into trouble, sir?" asked Dantès.

"Your pardon; here are the officers of health and the customs
coming alongside!" and the young man went to the gangway.
As he departed Danglars approached and said—

"Well, it appears that he has given you satisfactory reasons
for his landing at Porto-Ferrajo?"

"Yes, most satisfactory, my dear Danglars."

"Well, so much the better," said the supercargo; "for it is
always painful to see a comrade who does not do his duty."

"Dantès has done his," replied the owner, "and that is not
saying much. It was Captain Leclere who gave orders for this
delay."

"Talking of Captain Leclere, has not Dantès given you a
letter from him?"

"To me?—no—was there one?"

"I believe, that besides the packet, Captain Leclere had
confided a letter to his care."

"Of what packet are you speaking, Danglars?"

"Why, that which Dantès left at Porto-Ferrajo."

"How do you know he had a packet to leave at Porto-Ferrajo?"

Danglars turned very red.

"I was passing close to the door of the captain's cabin, which was half open, and I saw him give the packet and letter to Dantès."

"He did not speak to me of it," replied the shipowner; "but if there be any letter he will give it to me."

Danglars reflected for a moment.

"Then, M. Morrel, I beg of you," said he, "not to say a word to Dantès on the subject, I may have been mistaken."

At this moment the young man returned, and Danglars retreated as before.

"All is arranged now," said he.

"Then, you can come and dine with me?"

"Excuse me, M. Morrel, excuse me, if you please: but my first visit is due to my father, though I am not the less grateful for the honour you have done me."

"Right, Dantès, quite right.   I always knew you were a good son."

"And," inquired Dantès, with some hesitation, "do you know how my father is?"

"Well, I believe, my dear Edmond, although I have not seen him lately."

"Yes, he likes to keep himself shut up in his little room."

"That proves, at least, that he has wanted for nothing during your absence."

Dantès smiled.

"My father is proud, sir; and if he had not a meal left I doubt if he would have asked anything from anyone, except God."

"Well, then, after this first visit has been made we rely on you."

"I must again excuse myself, M. Morrel; for after this first visit has been paid I have another, which I am most anxious to pay."

"True, Dantès, I forgot that there was at the Catalans someone who expects you no less impatiently than your father—the lovely Mercédès."

Dantès blushed.

"Then I have your leave to go, sir?"

"Yes, if you have nothing more to say to me."

"Nothing."

"Captain Leclere did not, before he died, give you a letter for me?"

"He was unable to write, sir. But that reminds me that I must ask your leave of absence for some days."

"To get married?"

"Yes, first, and then to go to Paris."

"Very good; have what time you require, Dantès. It will take quite six weeks to unload the cargo, and we cannot get you ready for sea until three months after that; only be back again in three months, for the Pharaon," added the owner, patting the young sailor on the back, "cannot sail without her captain."

"Without her captain!" cried Dantès, his eyes sparkling with animation; "pray mind what you say, for you are touching on the most secret wishes of my heart. Is it really your intention to nominate me captain of the Pharaon?"

"If I were sole owner I would nominate you this moment, my dear Dantès, and say it is settled; but I have a partner, and you know the Italian proverb—*Che a compagno a padrone*— 'He who has a partner has a master.' But the thing is at least half done, as you have one out of two voices. Rely on me to procure you the other; I will do my best."

"Ah! M. Morrel," exclaimed the young seaman, with tears in his eyes, and grasping the owner's hand, "M. Morrel, I thank you in the name of my father and of Mercédès."

"Tell me, Dantès, if you had the command of the Pharaon, should you have pleasure in retaining Danglars?"

"Captain or mate, M. Morrel," replied Dantès, "I shall always have the greatest respect for those who possess our owners' confidence."

"Good! good! Dantès. I see you are a thorough good fellow, and will detain you no longer. Go, for I see how impatient you are. Good luck to you!"

The young sailor jumped into the skiff, and sat down in the stern, desiring to be put ashore at the Canebière. The two rowers bent to their work, and the little boat glided away as rapidly as possible in the midst of the thousand vessels which choke up the narrow way which leads between the two rows of ships from the mouth of the harbour to the Quai d'Orléans.

CHAPTER II

DANTÈS, after having traversed the Canebière, took the Rue de Noailles, and entering into a small house, situated on the left side of the Allées de Meillan, rapidly ascended four stories of a dark staircase, holding the baluster in his hand, whilst with the other he repressed the beatings of his heart, and paused before a half-opened door, which revealed all the interior of a small apartment.

This apartment was occupied by Dantès' father.

The news of the arrival of the Pharaon had not yet reached the old man, who, mounted on a chair, was amusing himself with staking with tremulous hand some nasturtiums which, mingled with clematis, formed a kind of trellis at his window.

Suddenly he felt an arm thrown round his body, and a well-known voice behind him exclaimed, " Father ! dear father !"

The old man uttered a cry, and turned round ; then, seeing his son, he fell into his arms, pale and trembling.

" What ails you, my dearest father ? Are you ill ?" inquired the young man much alarmed.

" No, no, my dear Edmond—my boy—my son !—no; but I did not expect you ; and joy, the surprise of seeing you so suddenly—— Ah ! I really seem as if I were going to die !"

" Come, come, cheer up, my dear father ! 'Tis I—really I ! They say joy never hurts. The good Captain Leclere is dead, father, and it is probable that, with the aid of M. Morrel, I shall have his place. Do you understand father ? Only imagine me a captain at twenty, with a hundred louis pay, and a share in the profits ! Is this not more than a poor sailor, like me, could have hoped for ?"

" Yes, my dear boy," replied the old man, " and much more than you could have expected."

" Come, come," said the young man, " a glass of wine, father, will revive you. Where do you keep your wine ?"

" No, no; thank ye. You need not look for it ; I do not want it," said the old man.

"Yes, yes, father, tell me where it is;" and he opened two or three cupboards.

"It is no use," said the old man ; "there is no wine."

"What! no wine ?" said Dantès, turning pale, and looking alternately at the hollow cheeks of the old man and the empty cupboards. "What! no wine ? Have you wanted money, father ?"

"I wanted nothing since I see you," said the old man.

"Yet," stammered Dantès, wiping the perspiration from his brow,—"yet I gave you two hundred francs when I left three months ago."

"Yes, yes, Edmond, that is true, but you forgot at that time a little debt to our neighbour, Caderousse. He reminded me of it, telling me if I did not pay for you, he would be paid by M. Morrel ; and so, you see, lest he might do you an injury, I paid him——"

"But," cried Dantès, "it was a hundred and forty francs I owed Caderousse. So that you have lived for three months on sixty francs ?"

"You know how little I require," said the old man.

"Here, father! here !" said Edmond, "take this—take it, and send for something immediately."

And he emptied his pockets on the table, whose contents consisted of a dozen pieces of gold, five or six crowns, and some smaller coin.

The countenance of old Dantès brightened.

"Whom does this belong to ?" he inquired.

"To me! to you! to us! Take it ; buy some provisions ; be happy, and to-morrow we shall have more. I have some smuggled coffee, and most capital tobacco, in a small chest in the hold, which you shall have to-morrow. But, hush ! here comes somebody."

"'Tis Caderousse, who has heard of your arrival, and, no doubt, comes to congratulate you on your fortunate return."

There appeared at the door at that moment the black and shock head of Caderousse. He was a man of twenty-five or twenty-six years of age, and held in his hand a morsel of cloth, which, in his capacity as a tailor, he was about to turn into the lining of a coat.

"What! is it you, Edmond, returned ?" said he, with a broad Marseillaise accent, and a grin that displayed his teeth as white as ivory.

"Yes, as you see, neighbour Caderousse; and ready to be agreeable to you in any and every way," replied Dantès, but ill concealing his feeling under this appearance of civility.

"Thanks—thanks; but, fortunately, I do not want for any thing; and it chances that at times there are others who have need of me." Dantès made a gesture. "I do not allude to you, my boy. No!—no! I lent you money, and you returned it; that's like good neighbours, and we are quits."

"We are never quits with those who oblige us," was Dantès' reply; "for when we do not owe them money, we owe them gratitude."

"What's the use of mentioning that? What is done is done. Let us talk of your happy return, my boy. It seems you have come back rich," continued the tailor, looking askance at the handful of gold and silver which Dantès had thrown on the table.

The young man remarked the greedy glance which shone in the dark eyes of his neighbour.

"Eh!" he said, negligently, "this money is not mine: I was expressing to my father my fears that he had wanted many things in my absence, and to convince me, he emptied his purse on the table. Come, father," added Dantès, "put this money back in your box—unless neighbour Caderousse wants anything, and in that case it is at his service."

"No, my boy, no," said Caderousse. "I am not in any want, thank God! the state nourishes me. Keep your money—keep it, I say;—one never has too much;—but at the same time, my boy, I am as much obliged by your offer as if I took advantage of it."

"It was offered with good-will," said Dantès.

"No doubt, my boy; no doubt. Well, you stand well with M. Morrel, I hear,—you insinuating dog, you!"

"M. Morrel has always been exceedingly kind to me," replied Dantès.

"So much the better—so much the better! Nothing will give greater pleasure to all your old friends; and I know one down there behind the citadel of Saint Nicolas, who will not be sorry to hear it."

"Mercédès?" said the old man.

"Yes, my dear father, and with your permission, now I have seen you, and know you are well, and have all you require, I will ask your consent to go and pay a visit to the Catalans."

"Go, my dear boy," said old Dantès; "and Heaven bless you in your wife, as it has blessed me in my son!"

"His wife!" said Caderousse; "why, how fast you go on, father Dantès; she is not his wife yet, it appears."

"No, but according to all probability she soon will be," replied Edmond.

"Yes—yes," said Caderousse; "but you were right to return as soon as possible, my boy."

"And why?"

"Because Mercédès is a very fine girl, and fine girls never lack lovers; she, particularly, has them by dozens."

"Really?" answered Edmond, with a smile which had in it traces of slight uneasiness.

"Ah, yes," continued Caderousse, "and capital offers too; but you know you will be captain, and who could refuse you then?"

"Meaning to say," replied Dantès, with a smile which but ill concealed his trouble, "that if I were not a captain——"

"Eh—eh!" said Caderousse, shaking his head.

"Come, come," said the sailor, "I have a better opinion than you of women in general, and of Mercédès in particular; and I am certain that, captain or not, she will remain ever faithful to me."

"So much the better—so much the better," said Caderousse. "When one is going to be married, there is nothing like implicit confidence; but never mind that, my boy,—but go and announce your arrival, and let her know all your hopes and prospects."

"I will go directly," was Edmond's reply; and, embracing his father, and saluting Caderousse, he left the apartment.

Caderousse lingered for a moment, then taking leave of old Dantès, he went down stairs to rejoin Danglars, who awaited him at the corner of the Rue Senac.

"Well," said Danglars, "did you see him?"

"I have just left him," answered Caderousse.

"Did he allude to his hope of being captain?"

"He spoke of it as a thing already decided."

"Patience!" said Danglars, "he is in too much hurry, it appears to me."

"Why, it seems M. Morrel has promised him the thing."

"So that he is quite elate about it."

"That is to say, he is actually insolent on the matter—has already offered me his patronage, as if he were a grand personage, and proffered me a loan of money, as though he were a banker."

"Which you refused."

"Most assuredly; although I might easily have accepted, for it was I who put into his hands the first silver he ever earned; but now M. Dantès has no longer any occasion for assistance—he is about to become a captain."

"Pooh!" said Danglars, "he is not one yet."

"*Ma foi!*—and it will be as well he never should be," answered Caderousse; "for if he should be, there will be really no speaking to him."

"If we choose," replied Danglars, "he will remain what he is, and, perhaps, become even less than he is."

"What do you mean?"

"Nothing—I was speaking to myself. And is he still in love with the Catalane?"

"Over head and ears: but unless I am much mistaken, there will be a storm in that quarter."

"What do you know?—come, tell me!"

"Well, every time I have seen Mercédès come into the city, she has been accompanied by a tall, strapping, black-eyed Catalan, with a red complexion, brown skin, and fierce air, whom she calls cousin."

"And you say Dantès has gone to the Catalans?"

"He went before I came down."

"Let us go the same way; we will stop at La Réserve, and we can drink a glass of La Malgue, whilst we wait for news."

"Come along," said Caderousse; "but mind you pay the shot."

"Certainly," replied Danglars; and going quickly to the spot alluded to, they called for a bottle of wine and two glasses.

Père Pamphile had seen Dantès pass not ten minutes before; and, assured that he was at the Catalans, they sat down under the budding foliage of the planes and sycamores, in the branches of which the birds were joyously singing on a lovely day in early spring.

CHAPTER III

ABOUT a hundred paces from the spot where the two friends were, with their looks fixed on the distance, and their ears attentive, whilst they imbibed the sparkling wine of La Malgue, behind a bare, and torn, and weather-worn wall, was the small village of the Catalans.

One day a mysterious colony quitted Spain, and settled on the tongue of land on which it is to this day. It arrived from no one knew where, and spoke an unknown tongue. One of its chiefs, who understood Provençal, begged the commune of Marseilles to give them this bare and barren promontory, on which, like the sailors of the ancient times, they had run their boats ashore. The request was granted, and three months afterwards, around the twelve or fifteen small vessels which had brought these gipsies of the sea, a small village sprang up.

This village, constructed in a singular and picturesque manner, half Moorish, half Spanish, is that we behold at the present day inhabited by the descendants of those men who speak the language of their fathers. For three or four centuries they remained faithful to this small promontory, on which they had settled like a flight of seabirds, without mixing with the Marseillaise population, intermarrying, and preserving their original customs and the costume of their mother country, as they have preserved its language.

In the only street of this little village, there was in one of the houses, on which the sun had stamped that beautiful colour of the dead leaf peculiar to the buildings of the country, a young and beautiful girl, with hair as black as jet, her eyes as velvety as the gazelle's, who was leaning with her back against the wainscot, rubbing in her slender fingers, moulded after the antique, a bunch of heath-blossoms, the flowers of which she was picking off and strewing on the floor; her arms, bare to the elbow, embrowned, and resembling those of the Venus at Arles,

13

moved with a kind of restless impatience, and she tapped the earth with her pliant and well-formed foot so as to display the pure and full shape of her well-turned leg, in its red cotton stocking with grey and blue clocks.

At three paces from her, seated in a chair which he balanced on two legs, leaning his elbow on an old worm-eaten table, was a tall young man of twenty or two-and-twenty, who was looking at her with an air in which vexation and uneasiness were mingled. He questioned her with his eyes, but the firm and steady gaze of the young girl controlled his look.

"You see, Mercédès," said the young man, "here is Easter come round again, tell me, is not this the moment for a wedding?"

"I have answered you a hundred times, Fernand, and really you must be your own enemy to ask me again."

"Well, repeat it,—repeat it, I beg of you, that I may at last believe it! Tell me for the hundredth time that you refuse my love, which had your mother's sanction. Make me fully comprehend that you are trifling with my happiness, that my life or death are immaterial to you. Ah! to have dreamed for ten years of being your husband, Mercédès, and to lose that hope, which was the only stay of my existence!"

"At least it was not I who ever encouraged you in that shape, Fernand," replied Mercédès; "you cannot reproach me with the slightest coquetry. I have always said to you, I love you as a brother, but do not ask from me more than sisterly affection, for my heart is another's. Is not this true, Fernand?"

"Yes, I know it well, Mercédès," replied the young man. 'Yes, you have been cruelly frank with me; but do you forget that it is among the Catalans a sacred law to intermarry?"

"You mistake, Fernand, it is not a law, but merely a custom; and, I pray of you, do not cite this custom in your favour. You are included in the conscription, Fernand, and are only at liberty on sufferance, liable at any moment to be called upon to take up arms. Once a soldier, what would you do with me, a poor orphan, forlorn, without fortune, with nothing but a hut, half in ruins, containing some ragged nets, a miserable inheritance left by my father to my mother, and by my mother to me? She has been dead a year, and, you know, Fernand, I have subsisted almost entirely on public charity. Sometimes you pretend I am useful to you, and that is an excuse to share with me the produce of your fishing, and I accept it, Fernand, because you are the son of my father's brother, because we were brought up together, and still more because it would give you so much pain if I refuse. But I feel very deeply that this fish which I go and sell, and with the produce of which I buy the flax I spin, — I feel very keenly, Fernand, that this is charity!"

"And if it were, Mercédès, poor and lone as you are, you suit me as well as the daughter of the first shipowner, or the richest banker of Marseilles! What do such as we desire but a good wife and careful housekeeper, and where can I look for these better than in you?"

"Fernand," answered Mercédès, shaking her head, "a woman becomes a bad manager, and who shall say she will remain an honest woman, when she loves another man better than her husband? Rest content with my friendship, for I repeat to you that is all I can promise, and I will promise no more than I can bestow."

"I understand," replied Fernand, "you can endure your own wretchedness patiently, but you are afraid of mine. Well, Mercédès, beloved by you I would tempt fortune; you would bring me good luck, and I should become rich. I could extend my occupation as a fisherman, might get a place as clerk in a warehouse, and become myself a dealer in time."

"You could do no such thing, Fernand; you are a soldier, and if you remain at the Catalans it is because there is not a war; so remain a fisherman, and contented with my friendship, as I cannot give you more."

"Well, you are right, Mercédès. I will be a sailor; instead of the costume of our fathers, which you despise, I will wear a varnished hat, a striped shirt, and a blue jacket with an anchor on the buttons. Would not that dress please you?"

"What do you mean?" asked Mercédès, darting at him an angry glance—"what do you mean? I do not understand you."

"I mean, Mercédès, that you are thus harsh and cruel with me because you are expecting someone who is thus attired; but, perhaps, he you await is inconstant, or, if he is not, the sea is so to him."

"Fernand!" cried Mercédès, "I believed you were good-hearted, and I was mistaken! Fernand, you are wicked to call to your aid jealousy and the anger of God! Yes, I will not deny it, I do await, and I do love him to whom you allude; and, if he does not return, instead of accusing him of the inconstancy which you insinuate, I will tell you that he died loving me and me only."

The young Catalan made a gesture of rage.

"I understand you, Fernand ; you would be revenged on him because I do not love you ; you would cross your Catalan knife with his dirk.   What end would that answer ?   To lose you my friendship if he were conquered, and see that friendship changed into hate if you were conqueror.   Believe me, to seek a quarrel with a man is a bad method of pleasing the woman who loves that man.   No, Fernand, you will not thus give way to evil thoughts.   Unable to have me for your wife, you will content yourself with having me for your friend and sister ; and besides," she added, her eyes troubled and moistened with tears, "wait, wait, Fernand, you said just now that the sea was treacherous, and he has been gone four months, and during these four months we have had some terrible storms."

Fernand made no reply, nor did he attempt to check the tears which flowed down the cheeks of Mércèdes, although for each of these tears he would have shed his heart's blood ; but these tears flowed for another.   He arose, paced awhile up and down the hut, and then, suddenly stopping before Mércédès, with his eyes glowing and his hands clenched—

"Say, Mércédès," he said, "once for all, is this your final determination ?"

"I love Edmond Dantès," the young girl calmly replied, "and none but Edmond shall ever be my husband."

"And you will always love him !"

"As long as I live."

Fernand let fall his head like a defeated man, heaved a sigh which resembled a groan, and then, suddenly looking her full in the face, with clenched teeth and expanded nostrils, said—

"But if he is dead——"

"If he is dead, I shall die too."

"If he has forgotten you——"

"Mércédès !" cried a voice, joyously, outside the house— "Mércédès !"

"Ah !" exclaimed the young girl, blushing with delight, and springing up with love, "you see he has not forgotten me, for here he is !"   And, rushing towards the door, she opened it, saying, "Here, Edmond, here I am !"

Fernand, pale and trembling, receded like a traveller at the sight of a serpent, and fell into a chair beside him.

Edmond and Mércèdes were clasped in each other's arms The burning sun of Marseilles, which penetrated the room by the open door, covered them with a flood of light. At first they saw nothing around them. Their intense happiness isolated them from all the rest of the world, and they only spoke in broken words, which are the tokens of a joy so extreme that they seem rather the expression of sorrow.

Suddenly Edmond saw the gloomy countenance of Fernand, as it was defined in the shadow, pale and threatening, and by a movement, for which he could scarcely account to himself, the young Catalan placed his hands on the knife at his belt.

" Ah! your pardon," said Dantès, frowning in his turn. " I did not perceive that there were three of us." Then, turning to Mercédès, he inquired, " Who is this gentleman ?"

"One who will be your best friend, Dantès, for he is my friend, my cousin, my brother—it is Fernand—the man whom, after you, Edmond, I love the most in the world. Do you not remember him ?"

" Yes !" said Edmond, and without relinquishing Mercédès' hand clasped in one of his own, he extended the other to the Catalan with a cordial air.

But Fernand, instead of responding to this amicable gesture, remained mute and trembling.

Edmond then looked scrutinisingly at Mércèdes, agitated and embarrassed, and then again at Fernand, gloomy and menacing.

This look told him all, and his brow became suffused and angry.

" I did not know, when I came with such haste to you, that I was to meet an enemy here."

" An enemy !" cried Mércèdes, with an angry look at her cousin. " An enemy in my house, do you say, Edmond! If I believed that I would place my arm under yours and go with you to Marseilles, leaving the house to return to it no more."

Fernand's eye darted lightning.

" And, should any misfortune occur to you, dear Edmond," she continued, with the same calmness, which proved to Fernand that the young girl had read the very innermost depths of his sinister thought, "if misfortune should occur to you I would ascend the highest point of the Cape de Morgion, and cast myself headlong from it."

Fernand became deadly pale.

" But you are deceived, Edmond," she continued. " You

have no enemy here—there is no one but Fernand, my brother, who will grasp your hand as a devoted friend."

And at these words the young girl fixed her imperious look on the Catalan, who, as if fascinated by it, came slowly towards Edmond, and offered him his hand.

His hatred, like a powerless though furious wave, was broken against the strong ascendancy which Mercédès exercised over him.

Scarcely, however, had he touched Edmond's hand than he felt he had done all he could do, and rushed hastily out of the house.

" Oh !" he exclaimed, running furiously and tearing his hair— " Oh ! who will deliver me from this man ?   Wretched—wretched that I am !"

" Hallo ! Catalan !   Hallo, Fernand ! where are you running to ?" exclaimed a voice.

The young man stopped suddenly, looked around him, and perceived Caderousse sitting at table with Danglars under an arbour.

" Well," said Caderousse, " why don't you come ?   Are you really in such a hurry that you have not time to say ' how do ' to your friends ?"

" Particularly when they have still a full bottle before them," added Danglars.   Fernand looked at them both with a stupefied air, but did not say a word.

" He seems besotted," said Danglars, pushing Caderousse with his knee.   " Are we mistaken, and is Dantès triumphant in spite of all we have believed ?"

" Why, we must inquire into that," was Caderousse's reply ; and turning towards the young man, said, " Well, Catalan, can't you make up your mind ?"

Fernand wiped away the perspiration streaming from his brow, and slowly entered the arbour, whose shade seemed to restore some calmness to his senses, and the coolness, something of refreshment to his exhausted body.

" Good day," said he.   " You called me, didn't you ?"   And he fell rather than sat down on one of the seats which surrounded the table.

" I called you because you were running like a madman ; and I was afraid you would throw yourself into the sea," said Caderousse, laughing.   " Why, when a man has friends, they are there not only to offer him a glass of wine, but to prevent his swallowing three or four pints of water unnecessarily !"

"YES!" SAID EDMUND, AND HE EXTENDED HIS HAND TO THE CATALAN WITH A
CORDIAL AIR. *Page* 18.

Fernand gave a groan, which resembled a sob, and dropped his head into his hands, his elbows leaning on the table.

" Well, Fernand, I must say," said Caderousse, beginning the conversation with that brutality of the common people, in which curiosity destroys all diplomacy, " you look uncommonly like a rejected lover ;" and he burst into a hoarse laugh.

" Bah !" said Danglars, " a lad of his make was not born to be unhappy in love. You are laughing at him, Caderousse !"

" No," he replied, " only hark how he sighs ! Come, come, Fernand !" said Caderousse, " hold up your head and answer us. It's not polite not to reply to friends who ask news of your health."

" My health is well enough," said Fernand, clenching his hands without raising his head.

" Ah ! you see, Danglars," said Caderousse, winking at his friend, " this it is, Fernand whom you see here is a good and brave Catalan, one of the best fishermen in Marseilles, and he is in love with a very fine girl, named Mércèdes ; but it appears, unfortunately, that the fine girl is in love with the second in command on board the Pharaon ; and, as the Pharaon arrived to-day—why, you understand !"

" No, I do not understand," said Danglars.

" Poor Fernand has been dismissed," continued Caderousse.

" Well, and what then ?" said Fernand, lifting up his head, and looking at Caderousse like a man who looks for someone on whom to vent his anger; " Mercédès is not accountable to any person, is she ? Is she not free to love whomsoever she will?"

" Oh ! if you take it in that sense," said Caderousse, " it is another thing ! But I thought you were a Catalan, and they told me the Catalans were not men to allow themselves to be supplanted by a rival. It was even told me that Fernand, especially, was terrible in his vengeance."

Fernand smiled piteously. " A lover is never terrible," he said.

" Poor fellow !" remarked Danglars, affecting to pity the young man from the bottom of his heart. " Why, you see, he did not expect to see Dantès return so suddenly ! he thought he was dead, perhaps ; or, perchance, faithless ! These things always come on us more severely when they come suddenly."

" Ah, *ma foi*, under any circumstances !" said Caderousse, who drank as he spoke, and on whom the fumes of the wine of La Malgue began to take effect—" under any circumstances

Fernand is not the only person put out by the fortunate arrival of Dantès; is he, Danglars?"

"No, you are right—and I should say that would bring him il! luck."

"Well, never mind," answered Caderousse, pouring out a glass of wine for Fernand, and filling his own for the eighth or ninth time, whilst Danglars had merely sipped his. "Never mind — in the meantime he marries Mercédès — the lovely Mercédès—at least, he returns to do that."

During this time Danglars fixed his piercing glance on the young man, on whose heart Caderousse's words fell like molten lead.

"And when is the wedding to be?" he asked.

"Oh, it is not yet fixed!" murmured Fernand.

"No, but it will be," said Caderousse, "as surely as Dantès will be captain of the Pharaon—eh, Danglars?"

Danglars shuddered at this unexpected attack, and turned to Caderousse, whose countenance he scrutinised to try and detect whether the blow was premeditated; but he read nothing but envy in a countenance already rendered brutal and stupid by drunkenness.

"Well," said he, filling the glasses, "let us drink to Captain Edmond Dantès, husband of the beautiful Catalane!"

Caderousse raised his glass to his mouth with unsteady hand, and swallowed the contents at a gulp. Fernand dashed his on the ground.

"Eh! eh! eh!" stammered Caderousse. "What do I see down there by the wall in the direction of the Catalans? Look, Fernand! your eyes are better than mine. I believe I see double. You know wine is a deceiver: but I should say it was two lovers walking side by side, and hand in hand. Heaven forgive me! they do not know that we can see them, and they are actually embracing!"

Danglars did not lose one pang that Fernand endured.

"Do you know them, M. Fernand?" he said.

"Yes," was the reply, in a low voice. "It is M. Edmond and Mademoiselle Mercédès!"

"Ah! see there, now!" said Caderousse; "and I did not recognise them! Holloa, Dantès! holloa, lovely damsel! Come this way, and let us know when the wedding is to be, for M. Fernand here is so obstinate he will not tell us!"

"Hold your tongue! will you?" said Danglars, pretending to

restrain Caderousse, who, with the tenacity of drunkards, leaned out of the arbour. " Try to stand upright, and let the lovers make love without interruption. See, look at M. Fernand, and follow his example—he is well behaved !"

Fernand, probably excited beyond bearing, pricked by Danglars, as the bull is by the bandilleros, was about to rush out; for he had risen from his seat, and seemed to be collecting himself to dash headlong upon his rival, when Mercédès, smiling and graceful, lifted up her lovely head, and shewed her clear and bright eye. At this Fernand recollected her threat of dying if Edmond died, and dropped again heavily on his seat.

Danglars looked at the two men, one after the other, the one brutalised by liquor, the other overwhelmed with love. "I shall extract nothing from these fools," he muttered ; " and I am very much afraid of being here between a drunkard and a coward. Yet this Catalan has eyes that glisten like the Spaniards, Sicilians, and Calabrians, who practise revenge so well. Unquestionably, Edmond's star is in the ascendant, and he will marry the splendid girl—he will be captain, too, and laugh at us all, unless——" a sinister smile passed over Danglars' lips—" unless I mingle in the affair," he added.

"Hallo !" continued Caderousse, half rising, and with his fist on the table, " hallo, Edmond ! do you not see your friends, or are you too proud to speak to them ?"

"No ! my dear fellow," replied Dantès, " I am not proud, but I am happy ; and happiness blinds, I think, more than pride."

" Ah ! very well, that's an explanation !" said Caderousse. " Well, good day, Madame Dantès !"

Mercédès curtseyed gravely, and said,—

" That is not my name, and in my country it bodes ill fortune, they say, to call young girls by the name of their betrothed before he becomes their husband. Call me, then, Mercédès, if you please."

" We must excuse our worthy neighbour, Caderousse," said Dantès, " he is so easily mistaken."

" So, then, the wedding is to take place immediately, M. Dantès," said Danglars, bowing to the young couple.

" As soon as possible, M. Danglars ; to-day all preliminaries will be arranged at my father's, and to-morrow, or next day at latest, the wedding festival here at La Réserve. My friends will be there, I hope; that is to say, you are invited, M. Danglars, and you Caderousse."

"And Fernand," said Caderousse, with a chuckle, "Fernand, too, is invited!"

"My wife's brother is my brother," said Edmond; "and we, Mercédès and I, should be very sorry if he were absent at such a time."

Fernand opened his mouth to reply, but his voice died on his lips, and he could not utter a word.

"To-day the preliminaries, to-morrow or next day the ceremony! you are in a hurry, captain!"

"Danglars," said Edmond, smiling, "I will say to you as Mercédès said just now to Caderousse, 'Do not give me a title which does not belong to me;' that may bring me bad luck."

"Your pardon," replied Danglars, "I merely said you seemed in a hurry, and we have lots of time, the Pharaon cannot be under weigh again in less than three months."

"We are always in a hurry to be happy, M. Danglars; for when we have suffered a long time, we have great difficulty in believing in good fortune. But it is not selfishness alone that makes me thus in haste; I must go to Paris."

"To Paris! really! and will it be the first time you have ever been there, Dantès?"

"Yes."

"Have you business there?"

"Not of my own; the last commission of poor Captain Leclere; you know to what I allude, Danglars, it is sacred. Besides, I shall only take the time to go and return."

"Yes, yes, I understand," said Danglars, and then in a low tone he added,—

"To Paris, no doubt to deliver the letter which the Grand Marshal gave him. Ah! this letter gives me an idea,—a capital idea! Ah! Dantès, my friend, you are not yet registered number One on board the good ship Pharaon," then turning towards Edmond, who was walking away, "Good journey," he cried.

"Thank you," said Edmond, with a friendly nod, and the two lovers continued their route, calm and joyous.

CHAPTER IV

CONSPIRACY

DANGLARS followed Edmond and Mercédès with his eyes until the two lovers disappeared behind one of the angles of Fort Saint-Nicolas, then turning round, he perceived Fernand, who had fallen pale and trembling into his chair, whilst Caderousse stammered out the words of a drinking song.

" Well, my dear sir," said Danglars to Fernand, " here is a marriage which does not appear to make everybody happy."

" It drives me to despair," said Fernand.

" Come," said Danglars, " you appear to me a good sort of fellow, and, hang me! I should like to help you, but——"

" Yes," said Caderousse, " but how ?"

" My dear fellow," replied Danglars, " you are three parts drunk ; finish the bottle and you will be completely so. Drink, then, and do not meddle with what we are discussing, for that requires all one's wit and cool judgment."

" I—drunk ?" said Caderousse, " well, that's a good one ! I could drink four more such bottles ; they are no bigger than Eau-de-Cologne flasks. Père Pamphile, more wine !" and Caderousse rattled his glass upon the table.

" You were saying, sir——" said Fernand, awaiting with great anxiety the end of this interrupted remark.

" What was I saying ? I forget. This drunken Caderousse has made me lose the thread of my sentence."

" Drunk, if you like ; so much the worse for those who fear wine, for it is because they have some bad thoughts which they are afraid the liquor will extract from their hearts."

" You said, sir, you would like to help me, but——"

" Yes ; but, I added, to help you it would be sufficient that Dantès did not marry her you love ; and the marriage may easily be thwarted, methinks, and yet Dantès need not die."

" Death alone can separate them," remarked Fernand.

" You talk like a noodle, my friend," said Caderousse, " and

23

here is Danglars, who is a wide-awake, clever, deep fellow, who
will prove to you that you are wrong.   Prove it, Danglars.   I
have answered for you.   Say there is no need why Dantès should
die : it would indeed be a pity he should.   Dantès is a good
fellow ; I like Dantès ; Dantès, your health !"
    Fernand rose impatiently.
    " Let him run on," said Danglars, restraining the young man ;
" drunk as he is he is not much out in what he says.   Absence
severs as well as death, and if the walls of a prison were between
Edmond and Mercédès they would be as effectually separated as
if they lay under a tombstone."
    " Yes ; only people get out of prison," said Caderousse, who,
with what sense was left him, listened eagerly to the conversation, "and when they get out, and their names are Edmond
Dantès, they revenge——"
    " What matters that ?" muttered Fernand.
    " And why, I should like to know," persisted Caderousse,
" should they put Dantès in prison ; he has neither robbed,
nor killed, nor murdered."
    " Hold your tongue !" said Danglars.
    " I won't hold my tongue !" replied Caderousse, " I say I want
to know why they should put Dantès in prison ; I like Dantès ;
Dantès, your health !"   And he swallowed another glass of wine.
    Danglars saw in the muddled look of the tailor the progress
of his intoxication, and turning towards Fernand, said,—
    " Well, you understand there is no need to kill him."
    " Certainly not, if, as you said just now, you have the means
of having Dantès arrested.   Have you that means ?"
    " It is to be found for the searching.   But, why should I
meddle in the matter ? it is no affair of mine."
    " I know not why you meddle," said Fernand, seizing his arm,
" but this I know, you have some motive of personal hatred
against Dantès, for he who himself hates is never mistaken in the
sentiments of others."
    " I ! motives of hatred against Dantès ?   None, on my word !
I saw you were unhappy, and your unhappiness interested me ;
that's all ; but the moment you believe I act for my own
account, adieu, my dear friend, get out of the affair as best you
may ;" and Danglars rose as if he meant to depart.
    " No, no," said Fernand, restraining him, " stay ! It is of very
little consequence to me at the end of the matter whether you
have any angry feeling or not against Dantès.   I hate him ! I

confess it openly. Do you find the means, I will execute it provided it is not to kill the man, for Mercédès has declared she will kill herself if Dantès is killed."

Caderousse, who had let his head drop on the table, now raised it, and looking at Fernand with his dull and fishy eyes, he said,—

"Kill Dantès! who talks of killing Dantès? I won't have him killed—I won't! He's my friend, and this morning offered to share his money with me, as I shared mine with him. I won't have Dantès killed—I won't!"

"And who has said a word about killing him, muddlehead?" replied Danglars. "We were merely joking: drink to his health," he added, filling Caderousse's glass, "and do not interfere with us."

"Yes, yes, Dantès, good health!" said Caderousse, emptying his glass. "Here's to his health! his health!—hurrah!"

"Waiter," said Danglars, "pen, ink, and paper."

The waiter fetched them as he was desired.

"When one thinks," said Caderousse, letting his hand drop on the paper, "there is here wherewithal to kill a man more surely than if we waited at the corner of a wood to assassinate him, I have always had more dread of a pen, a bottle of ink, and a sheet of paper, than of a sword or pistol."

"The fellow is not so drunk as he appears to be," said Danglars. "Give him some more wine, Fernand." Fernand filled Caderousse's glass, who, toper as he was, lifted his hand from the paper and seized it.

The Catalan watched him until Caderousse, almost overcome by this fresh assault on his senses, rested, or rather allowed his glass to fall, upon the table.

"Well!" resumed the Catalan, as he saw the final glimmer of Caderousse's reason vanishing before the last glass of wine.

"Well, then; I should say, for instance," resumed Danglars, "that if after a voyage such as Dantès has just made, and in which he touched the Isle of Elba, someone were to denounce him to the king's procureur as a Bonapartist agent——"

"I will denounce him!" exclaimed the young man hastily.

"Yes, but they will make you then sign your declaration, and confront you with him you have denounced. I will supply you with the means of supporting your accusation, for I know the fact well. But Dantès cannot remain for ever in prison, and one day or other he will leave it, and the day when he comes out, woe betide him who was the cause of his incarceration!

" Oh, I should wish nothing better than that he would come and seek a quarrel with me."

" Yes, and Mercédès! Mercédès, who will detest you if you have only the misfortune to scratch the skin of her dearly beloved Edmond!"

" True!" said Fernand.

" No! no!" continued Danglars, " if we resolve on such a step, it would be much better to take, as I now do, this pen, dip it into this ink, and write with the left hand (that the writing may not be recognised) the denunciation we propose." And Danglars, uniting practice with theory, wrote with his left hand, and in a writing reversed from his usual style, and totally unlike it, the following lines which he handed to Fernand, and which Fernand read in an under tone :—

" Monsieur,—The procureur du roi is informed by a friend of the throne and religion, that one Edmond Dantès, mate of the ship Pharaon, arrived this morning from Smyrna, after having touched at Naples and Porto-Ferrajo, has been intrusted by Murat with a letter for the usurper, and by the usurper with a letter for the Bonapartist committee in Paris.

" Proof of this crime will be found on arresting him, for the letter will be either upon him, or at his father's, or in his cabin on board the Pharaon."

" Very good," resumed Danglars : " now your revenge looks like common sense, for in no way can it revert to yourself, and the matter will thus work its own way ; there is nothing to do now but fold the letter as I am doing, and write upon it, ' To M. le Procureur Royal,' and that's all settled."

And Danglars wrote the address as he spoke.

" Yes, and that's all settled," exclaimed Caderousse, who, by a last effort of intellect, had followed the reading of the letter, and instinctively comprehended all the misery which such a denunciation must entail. " Yes, and that's all settled : only it will be an infamous shame ;" and he stretched out his hand to reach the letter.

" Yes," said Danglars, taking it beyond his reach ; " and as what I say and do is merely in jest, and I amongst the first and foremost should be sorry if any thing happened to Dantès— the worthy Dantès—Look here !"

And taking the letter he squeezed it up in his hands, and threw it into a corner of the arbour.

" All right!" said Caderousse. " Dantès is my friend, and I won't have him ill-used."

"And who thinks of using him ill? Certainly neither I nor Fernand!" said Danglars, rising, and looking at the young man, who still remained seated, but whose eye was fixed on the denunciatory sheet of paper flung into the corner.

"In this case," replied Caderousse, "let's have some more wine. I wish to drink to the health of Edmond and the lovely Mercédès."

"You have had too much already, drunkard," said Danglars; "and if you continue you will be compelled to sleep here, because unable to stand on your legs."

"I?" said Caderousse, rising with all the offended dignity of a drunken man, "I can't keep on my legs! Why, I'll bet a wager I go up into the belfry of the Accoules, and without staggering, too!"

"Well done!" said Danglars, "I'll take your bet; but to-morrow—to-day it is time to return. Give me your arm, and let us go."

"Very well, let us go," said Caderousse; "but I don't want your arm at all. Come, Fernand, won't you return to Marseilles with us?"

"No," said Fernand; "I shall return to the Catalans."

"You're wrong. Come with us to Marseilles—come along."

"I will not."

"What do you mean? you will not? Well, just as you like, my prince; there's liberty for all the world. Come along, Danglars, and let the young gentleman return to the Catalans if he chooses."

Danglars took advantage of Caderousse's temper at the moment, to take him off towards Marseilles by the Porte-Saint-Victor, staggering as he went.

When they had advanced about twenty yards, Danglars looked back and saw Fernand stoop, pick up the crumpled paper, and, putting it into his pocket, then rush out of the arbour towards Pillon.

"Come, come," said Danglars to himself, "now the thing is at work, and it will effect its purpose unassisted."

CHAPTER V

THE morning's sun rose clear and resplendent, gilding the heavens, and even the foamy waves with its bright refulgent beams.

The plenteous feast had been prepared at La Réserve. The apartment destined for the purpose was spacious, and lighted by a number of windows, over each of which was written in golden letters the name of one of the principal cities of France ; beneath these windows a wooden balcony extended the entire length of the house. And although the entertainment was fixed for twelve o'clock at noon, an hour previous to that time the balcony was filled with impatient and expectant guests, consisting of the favoured part of the crew of the Pharaon, and other personal friends of the bridegroom, the whole of whom had arrayed themselves in their choicest costumes, in order to do greater honour to the day.

Various rumours were afloat, to the effect that the owners of the Pharaon had promised to attend the nuptial feast ; but all seemed unanimous in doubting that an act of such rare and exceeding condescension could possibly be intended.

Danglars, however, who now made his appearance, accompanied by Caderousse, effectually confirmed the report, stating, that he had recently conversed with M. Morrel, who had himself assured him he intended joining the festive party upon the occasion of their second officer's marriage.

Even while relating this aloud, an enthusiastic burst of applause from the crew of the Pharaon announced the presence of M. Morrel, who hailed the visit of the shipowner as a sure indication that the man whose wedding-feast he thus delighted to honour would ere long be first in command of the Pharaon ; and as Dantès was universally beloved on board his vessel, the sailors put no restraint on the tumultuous joy at finding the opinion and choice of their superiors so exactly coincide with their own.

This noisy though hearty welcome over, Danglars and Caderousse were despatched to the residence of the bridegroom to convey to him the intelligence of the arrival of the important personage who had recently joined them, and to desire he would hasten to receive his honourable guest.

The above-mentioned individuals started off upon their errand at full speed ; but ere they had gone many steps they perceived a group advancing towards them, composed of the betrothed pair, a party of young girls in attendance on the bride, by whose side walked Dantès' father ; the whole brought up by Fernand, whose lips wore their usual sinister smile.

Neither Mercédès nor Edmond observed the strange expression of his countenance ; basking in the sunshine of each other's love they heeded not the dark lowering look that scowled on their innocent felicity.

Having acquitted themselves of their errand, and exchanged a hearty shake of the hand with Edmond, Danglars and Caderousse took their places beside Fernand and old Dantès,— the latter of whom attracted universal notice. The old man was attired in a suit of black, trimmed with steel buttons, beautifully cut and polished. His thin but still powerful legs were arrayed in a pair of richly embroidered clocked stockings, evidently of English manufacture ; while from his three-cornered hat depended a long streaming knot of white and blue ribands. Thus he came along, supporting himself on a curiously carved stick, his aged countenance lit up with happiness, while beside him crept Caderousse, whose desire to partake of the good things provided for the wedding party had induced him to become reconciled to the Dantès, father and son, although there still lingered in his mind a faint and imperfect recollection of the events of the preceding night ; just as the brain retains on waking the dim and misty outline of the dream that has " murdered sleep."

Dantès himself was simply, though becomingly, clad in the dress peculiar to the merchant-service,—a costume somewhat between a military and a civil garb ; and with his fine countenance, radiant with joy and happiness, a more perfect specimen of manly beauty could scarcely be imagined.

Lovely as the Greeks of Cyprus or Chios, Mercédès boasted the same bright flashing eyes of jet, and ripe, round, coral lips. One more practised in the arts of great cities would have hid her blushes beneath a veil, or, at least, have cast down her

thickly fringed lashes, so as to have concealed the liquid lustre
of her animated eyes ; but, on the contrary, the delighted girl
looked around her with a smile that seemed to invite all who
saw her to behold, and beholding, to rejoice with her in her exceeding happiness.

Immediately the bridal *cortège* came in sight of La Réserve,
M. Morrel came forth to meet it, followed by the soldiers and
sailors there assembled, to whom he had repeated the promise
already given, that Dantès should be the successor to the late
Captain Leclere.   Edmond, at the approach of his patron,
respectfully placed the arm of his affianced bride within that of
M. Morrel, who forthwith conducting her up the flight of
wooden steps leading to the chamber in which the feast was
prepared, was gaily followed by the guests, beneath whose
thronging numbers the slight structure creaked and groaned as
though alarmed at the unusual pressure.

" Father," said Mercédès, stopping when she had reached the
centre of the table, " sit, I pray you, on my right hand ; on my
left I will place him who has ever been a brother to me," pointing with a soft and gentle smile to Fernand ; but her words and
look seemed to inflict the direst torture on him, for his lips
became ghastly pale, and even beneath the dark hue of his
complexion the blood might be seen retreating as though some
sudden pang drove it back to the heart.

During this time, Dantès, at the opposite side of the table,
had been occupied in similarly placing his most honoured guests.
M. Morrel was seated at his right hand, Danglars at his left,
while at a sign from Edmond, the rest of the company arranged
themselves as they found it most agreeable.

And now commenced the work of devastation upon the many
good things with which the table was loaded.   Sausages of
Arles, with their delicate seasoning and piquant flavour, lobsters
in their dazzling red cuirasses, prawns of large size and brilliant
colour, the echinus, with its prickly outside and dainty morsel
within ; the clovis, esteemed by the epicures of the south as
more than rivalling the exquisite flavour of the oyster.   All
these, in conjunction with the numerous delicacies cast up by
the wash of waters on the sandy beach, and styled by the grateful fishermen " sea fruits," served to furnish forth this marriage-
table.

" A pretty silence, truly !" said the old father of the bridegroom, as he carried to his lips a glass of wine of the hue and

brightness of the topaz, which had just been placed before Mercédès herself. " Now, would anybody think that this room contained a happy, merry party, who desire nothing better than to laugh and dance the hours away ?"

" Ah !" sighed Caderousse, " a man cannot always feel happy because he is about to be married !"

" The truth is," replied Dantès, " that I am too happy for noisy mirth ; if that is what you meant by your observation, my worthy friend, you were right ; joy takes a strange effect at times, it seems to oppress us almost the same as sorrow."

Danglars looked towards Fernand, whose excitable nature received and betrayed each fresh impression.

" Why, what ails you ?" asked he of Edmond. " Do you fear any approaching evil ? I should say that you were the happiest man alive at this instant."

" And that is the very thing that alarms me," returned Dantès. " Man does not appear to me to be intended to enjoy felicity so unmixed ; happiness is like the enchanted palaces we read of in our childhood, where fierce, fiery dragons defend the entrance and approach ; and monsters of all shapes and kinds, requiring to be overcome ere victory is ours. I own that I am lost in wonder to find myself promoted to an honour of which I feel myself unworthy—that of being the husband of Mercédès."

" Nay, nay !" cried Caderousse, smiling, " you have not attained that honour yet. Mercédès is not yet your wife. Just assume the tone and manner of a husband, and see how she will remind you that your hour has not yet come !"

The bride blushed and seemed half inclined to be angry, while Fernand, restless and uneasy, seemed to start at every fresh sound, occasionally applying his handkerchief to his brow to wipe away the large drops of perspiration that gathered again, almost as soon as they were removed.

" Well, never mind that, neighbour Caderousse, it is not worth while to contradict me for such a trifle as that. 'Tis true that Mercédès is not actually my wife ; but," added he, drawing out his watch, " in an hour and a half from this she will be as fast and firm as holy church can make her."

A general exclamation of surprise ran round the table, with the exception of the elder Dantès, whose laugh displayed the still perfect beauty of his large white teeth. Mercédès looked pleased and gratified, while Fernand grasped the handle of his knife with a convulsive clutch.

"In an hour?" inquired Danglars, turning pale. "How is that, my friend!"

"Why, thus it is," replied Dantès. "Thanks to the influence of M. Morrel, to whom, next to my father, I owe every blessing I enjoy, every difficulty has been removed. We have purchased permission to waive the usual delay; and at half-past two o'clock the mayor of Marseilles will be waiting for us at the Hôtel-de-Ville. Now, as a quarter-past one has already struck, I do not consider I have asserted too much in saying that in another hour and thirty minutes Mercédès will have become Madame Dantès."

Fernand closed his eyes, a burning sensation passed across his brow, and he was compelled to support himself by the table to prevent his falling from his chair; but in spite of all his efforts, he could not refrain from uttering a deep groan, which, however, was lost amid the noisy felicitations of the company.

"Upon my word," cried the old man, "you make short work of this kind of affair. Arrived here only yesterday morning, and married to-day at three o'clock! Commend me to a sailor for going the quick way to work!"

"But," asked Danglars, in a timid tone, "how did you manage about the other formalities—the contract—the settlement?"

"Oh, bless you!" answered Dantès, laughingly, "our papers were soon drawn up. Mercédès has no fortune; I have none to settle on her. So, you see, our papers were quickly written out, and certainly do not come very expensive."

This joke elicited a fresh burst of applause.

"So that what we presumed to be merely the betrothed feast turns out to be the actual wedding-dinner!" said Danglars.

"No, no!" answered Dantès; "don't imagine I am going to put you off in that shabby manner. To-morrow morning I start for Paris: five days to go, and the same to return, with one day to discharge the commission intrusted to me, is all the time I shall be absent. I shall be back here by the twelfth of March, and the next day I give my real marriage-feast."

"Upon my word," said Caderousse to Danglars, from whose mind the friendly treatment of Dantès, united with the effect of the excellent wine he had partaken of, had effaced every feeling of envy or jealousy at Dantès' good fortune—"upon my word, Dantès is a downright good fellow, and when I see him sitting there beside his pretty wife that is so soon to be, I cannot help thinking it would have been a great pity to have served him that trick you were planning yesterday."

"Oh, there was no harm meant!" answered Danglars; "at first I certainly did feel somewhat uneasy as regarded what Fernand might be tempted to do, but when I saw how completely he had mastered his feelings, even so far as to become one of his rival's bride's-men, I knew there was no further cause for apprehension."

Caderousse looked full at Fernand—he was ghastly pale.

"Certainly," continued Danglars, "the sacrifice was no trifling one when the beauty of the bride is considered. Upon my soul that future captain of mine is a lucky dog! Gad! I only wish he would let me take his place!"

"Shall we not set forth?" asked the sweet, silvery voice of Mercédès; "two o'clock has just struck, and you know we are expected at the Hôtel-de-Ville in a quarter of an hour."

"To be sure!—to be sure!" cried Dantès, eagerly quitting the table; "let us go directly!"

His words were re-echoed by the whole party, who rose with a simultaneous cheer, and commenced forming themselves into procession.

At this moment Danglars, who had been incessantly observing every change in Fernand's look and manner, perceived him stagger and fall back, with an almost convulsive spasm, against a seat placed near one of the open windows. At the same instant the ear caught a sort of indistinct sound on the stairs, followed by the measured tread of soldiery, with the clanking of swords and military accoutrements; then came a hum and buzz as of many voices, so as to deaden even the noisy mirth of the bridal party, among whom a vague feeling of curiosity and apprehension quelled every disposition to talk, and almost instantaneously the most deathlike stillness prevailed.

Nearer and nearer came those sounds of terror. Three distinct knocks, as though from the hilt of a sword, against the door, increased the fears of the before gay party. Each looked inquiringly in the countenance of his neighbour, while all wished themselves quietly and safely at home.

"I demand admittance," said a loud voice outside the room, "in the name of the law!"

As no attempt was made to prevent it, the door was opened, and a magistrate, wearing his official scarf, presented himself, followed by four soldiers and a corporal. Uneasiness now yielded to the most extreme dread on the part of those present.

" May I venture to inquire the reason of this unexpected visit ?" said M. Morrel, addressing the magistrate, whom he evidently knew; " there is doubtless some mistake easily explained."

" If it be so," replied the magistrate, " rely upon every reparation being made; meanwhile, I am the bearer of an order of arrest, and although I most reluctantly perform the task assigned me, it must, nevertheless, be fulfilled. Who among the persons here assembled answers to the name of Edmond Dantès ?"

Every eye was turned towards the individual so described, who, spite of the agitation he could not but feel, advanced with dignity, and said in a firm voice, " I am he! what is your pleasure with me ?"

" Edmond Dantès," replied the magistrate, " I arrest you in the name of the law !"

" Me !" repeated Edmond, slightly changing colour, " and wherefore, I pray ?"

" I cannot inform you, but you will be duly acquainted with the reasons that have rendered such a step necessary at your first examination."

M. Morrel felt that further resistance or remonstrance was useless. He saw before him an officer delegated to enforce the law, and perfectly well knew that it would be as unavailing to seek pity from a magistrate decked with his official scarf as to address a petition to some cold, marble effigy. Old Dantès, however, saw not all this. His paternal heart could not contemplate the idea of such an outrage as consigned his beloved child to prison amid the joys of his wedding-feast. Rushing forward, therefore, he threw himself at the magistrate's feet, and prayed and supplicated in terms so moving, that even the officer was touched; and although firm to his duty, he kindly said, " My worthy friend, let me beg of you to calm your apprehensions. Your son has probably neglected some proscribed form or attention in registering his cargo, and it is more than probable he will be set at liberty directly he has given the information required, whether touching the health of his crew, or the value of his freight."

" What is the meaning of all this," inquired Caderousse, frowningly, of Danglars, who had assumed an air of utter surprise.

"How can I tell you?" replied he; "I am, like yourself, utterly bewildered at all that is going on, not a word of which do I understand."

Caderousse then looked around for Fernand, but he had disappeared.

The scene of the previous night now came back to his mind with startling accuracy. The painful catastrophe he had just witnessed appeared effectually to have rent away the veil which the intoxication of the evening before had raised between himself and his memory.

"So! so!" said he, in a hoarse and choking voice, to Danglars, "this, then, I suppose, is a part of the trick you were concerting yesterday? All I can say is, that if it be so, 'tis an ill turn, and well deserves to bring double evil on those who have projected it."

"Nonsense!" returned Danglars, "I tell you again I have nothing whatever to do with it; besides, you know very well that I tore the paper to pieces."

"No, you did not!" answered Caderousse, "you merely threw it by—I saw it lying in a corner."

"Hold your tongue, you fool!—what should you know about it?—why, you were drunk!"

"Where is Fernand?" inquired Caderousse.

"How do I know?" replied Danglars; "gone, as every prudent man ought to do, to look after his own affairs, most likely. Never mind where he is, let us go and see what is to be done for our poor friends in this, their affliction."

During this conversation, Dantès, after having exchanged a cheerful shake of the hand with all his sympathising friends, had surrendered himself to the officer sent to arrest him, merely saying, "Make yourselves quite easy, my good fellows, there is some little mistake to clear up, that's all, depend upon it! and very likely I may not have to go so far as the prison to effect that."

"Oh, to be sure!" responded Danglars, who had now approached the group, "nothing more than a mistake, I feel quite certain."

Dantès descended the staircase, preceded by the magistrate, and followed by the soldiers. A carriage awaited him at the door; he got in, followed by two soldiers and the magistrate, and the vehicle drove off towards Marseilles.

"Adieu! adieu! dearest Edmond!" cried Mercédès, stretching out her arms to him from the balcony.

The prisoner, whose ready ear caught the despairing accents of his betrothed, felt as though the chill hand of death pressed on his heart, as leaning from the coach he tried to reply in cheerful tones.

" Good-bye, my sweet Mercédès !—we shall soon meet again !"

The rapid progress of the vehicle, which disappeared round one of the turnings of Fort Saint-Nicolas, prevented his adding more.

" Wait for me, here, all of you !" cried M. Morrel ; " I will take the first conveyance I find, and hurry to Marseilles, whence I will bring you word how all is going on."

" That's right !" exclaimed a multitude of voices, " go, and return as quickly as you can !"

This second departure was followed by a long and fearful state of terrified silence on the part of those who were left behind. The old father and Mercédès remained for some time apart, each absorbed in their separate griefs ; but at length the two poor victims of the same blow raised their eyes, and with a simultaneous burst of feeling rushed into each other's arms.

Meanwhile Fernand made his reappearance, poured out for himself a glass of water with a trembling hand ; then hastily swallowing it, went to sit down on the first vacant chair he perceived, and this was, by mere chance, placed next to the seat on which poor Mercédès had fallen, half fainting, when released from the warm and affectionate embrace of old Dantès. Instinctively Fernand drew back his chair.

" He is the cause of all this misery—I am quite sure of it," whispered Caderousse, who had never taken his eyes off Fernand, to Danglars.

" I really do not think so," answered the other ; " he is too stupid to imagine such a scheme. I only hope the mischief will fall upon the head of whoever wrought it."

" You don't mention those who aided and abetted the cruel deed, any more than those who advised it," said Caderousse.

" Surely," answered Danglars, " one cannot be expected to become responsible for all the idle words one may have been obliged to listen to in the course of our lives."

Meantime the subject of the arrest was being canvassed in every different form.

" What think you, Danglars," said one of the party, turning towards him, " of the late unfortunate event ?"

" Why, upon my word, I know not what to say," replied

he. " I think, however, that it is just possible Dantès may have been detected with some trifling article on board ship considered here as contraband."

" But how could he have done so without your knowledge, Danglars, who was the ship's supercargo?"

" Why, as for that, I could only know what I was told respecting the merchandise with which the vessel was laden. I know she was loaded with cotton, and that she took in her freight at Alexandria from the magazine of M. Pastret, and at Smyrna from M. Pascal; that is all I was obliged to know, and I beg I may not be asked for any further particulars."

" Now, I recollect!" cried the afflicted old father; " my poor boy told me yesterday he had got a small case of coffee, and another of tobacco for me!"

" There you see!" exclaimed Danglars. " Now the mischief is out; depend upon it the custom-house people went rummaging about the ship in our absence, and discovered poor Dantès' hidden treasures."

Mercédès, however, paid no heed to this explanation of her lover's arrest. Her grief, which she had hitherto tried to restrain, now burst out in a violent fit of hysterical sobbing.

" Come, come!" said the old man, " be comforted, my poor child; there is still hope!"

" Hope!" repeated Danglars.

" Hope!" faintly murmured Fernand; but the word seemed to die away on his pale agitated lips, and a convulsive spasm passed over his countenance.

" Good news! good news!" shouted forth one of the party stationed in the balcony on the look-out. " Here comes M. Morrel back. No doubt, now, we shall hear that our friend is released!"

Mercédès and the old man rushed to meet the person from whom they hoped so much; but the first glance at the pale desponding countenance of M. Morrel prepared them for evil tidings.

" What news?" exclaimed a general burst of voices.

" Alas! my friends," replied M. Morrel, with a mournful shake of his head, " the thing has assumed a more serious aspect than I expected."

" Oh! indeed—indeed, sir, he is innocent!" sobbed forth Mercédès.

" That I believe!" answered M. Morrel; " but still he is charged——"

" With what ?" inquired the elder Dantès.

" With being an agent of the Bonapartist faction !"

A despairing cry escaped the pale lips of Mercédès, while the heart-stricken father fell listlessly into a chair, kindly placed for him by one of the pitying guests.

" Ah, Danglars !" whispered Caderousse, " you have deceived me—the trick you spoke of last night has been played off, I see ; but I cannot suffer a poor old man or an innocent girl to die of grief through your fault. I am determined to tell them all about it."

" Be silent, you simpleton !" cried Danglars, grasping him by the arm, " or I will not answer even for your own safety. Who can tell whether Dantès be innocent or guilty ? The vessel did touch at Elba, where he quitted it, and passed a whole day in the island. Now, should any letters or other documents of a compromising character be found upon him, will it not be taken for granted that all who uphold him are his accomplices ?"

With the rapid instinct of selfishness, Caderousse readily perceived the solidity of this mode of reasoning ; he gazed doubtfully, wistfully on Danglars, and then insensibly continued to retreat from the dangerous proximity in which he found himself.

" Suppose we wait awhile, and see what comes of it !" said he, casting a bewildered look on his companion.

" To be sure !" answered Danglars. " Let us wait, by all means. If he be innocent, of course he will be set at liberty ; if guilty, why, it is no use involving ourselves in his conspiracy."

" Then let us go hence. I cannot stay to endure the sight of that old man's distress."

" With all my heart !" replied Danglars, but too pleased to find a partner in his retreat. " Let us take ourselves out of the way, and leave every one else to do the same thing if they please."

After their departure, Fernand, who had now again become the only friend and protector poor Mercédès could find in this trying hour, led the weeping girl back to her home, which she had quitted with such different hopes and feelings in the morning, while some friends of Dantès conducted the poor heart-broken parent to his childless and dreary abode.

The rumour of Edmond's arrest as a Bonapartist agent was not slow in circulating throughout the city.

" Could you ever have credited such a thing, my dear Danglars ?" asked M. Morrel, as on his return to the port for the purpose of gleaning fresh tidings of Dantès, he overtook his supercargo and Caderousse. "Could you have believed such a thing possible?"

"Why, you know I told you," replied Danglars, "that I considered the circumstance of his having anchored in the Isle of Elba as a very suspicious circumstance."

"And did you mention these suspicions to any person besides myself?"

"Certainly not!" returned Danglars. Then added in a low whisper, "You understand that, on account of your uncle, M. Policar Morrel, who served under the other government, and who does not altogether conceal what he thinks on the subject, you are strongly suspected of regretting the abdication of Napoleon. I should have feared to injure both Edmond and yourself, had I divulged my own apprehensions to a soul. I am too well aware that though a subordinate, like myself, is bound to acquaint the shipowner with everything that occurs, there are many things that he ought most carefully to conceal from all else."

"'Tis well, Danglars—'tis well!" replied M. Morrel. "You are a worthy fellow. But in the midst of all our trouble," continued M. Morrel, "we must not forget that the Pharaon has at present no captain."

"Oh!" replied Danglars, "since we cannot leave this port for the next three months, let us hope that long before that Dantès will be set at liberty."

"Of that I entertain no doubt; but in the meantime what are we to do?"

"I am entirely at your service, M. Morrel," answered Danglars. "You know that I am as capable of managing a ship as the most experienced captain in the service; and it will be so far advantageous to you to accept my services, that upon Edmond's release from prison no further change will be requisite on board the Pharaon than for Dantès and myself each to resume our respective posts."

"Thanks! thanks! my good friend, for your excellent idea and acceptable proposition—that will smooth all difficulties. I fully authorise you at once to assume the command of the Pharaon, and look carefully to the unloading of her freight. Private misfortunes must never induce us to neglect public affairs."

"Depend upon my zeal and attention, M. Morrel; but when

do you think it likely we may be permitted to visit our poor friend in his prison?"

"I will let you know that directly. I have seen M. de Villefort, whom I shall endeavour to interest in Edmond's favour. I am aware he is a furious royalist; but, in spite of that, and of his being the 'king's procureur,' he is a man like ourselves, and I fancy not a bad sort of one!"

"So far, then," said Danglars to himself, "all has gone as I would have it! I am temporarily commander of the Pharaon, with the certainty of being permanently so, if that fool of a Caderousse can be persuaded to hold his tongue. My only fear is the chance of Dantès being released. But bah! he is in the hands of justice; and," added he, with a smile, "she will take her own."

CHAPTER VI

THE DEPUTY PROCUREUR DU ROI

In one of the large aristocratic mansions, situated in the Rue du Grand Cours, opposite the fountain of Medusa, a second marriage-feast was being celebrated, almost at the same hour as the ill-fated repast given by Dantès.

In this case, however, although the occasion of the entertainment was similar, the company assembled were strikingly different. Instead of a rude mixture of sailors, soldiers, and those belonging to the humblest grade of life, the present *ré-union* was composed of the very flower and *élite* of Marseilles society. Magistrates who had resigned their office during the usurper's reign ; officers who, scorning to fight under his banners, had offered their services to foreign powers, with younger members of the family, brought up to hate and execrate the man whom five years of exile would have converted into a martyr, and fifteen of restoration elevated to the rank of a demigod.

The guests were still at table, and the heated and energetic conversation that prevailed betrayed the violent and vindictive passions that then agitated each dweller of the south, where, unhappily, religious strife had long given increased bitterness to the violence of party feeling.

The emperor, now king of the petty Isle of Elba, after having held sovereign sway over one half of the world, was looked upon among the *haute société* of Marseilles as a ruined man, separated for ever from any fresh connexion with France or claim to her throne.

The magistrates freely discussed their political views ; the military part of the company talked unreservedly of Moscow and Leipsic, while the women indulged in open comments upon the divorce of the Empress Josephine.

All seemed to evince that in their royalism it was not over the downfall of one man they rejoiced, but in the bright and cheering prospect of a revivified political existence for themselves.

41

An old man, decorated with the cross of Saint Louis, now rose and proposed the health of King Louis XVIII. This aged individual was the Marquis de Saint-Méran.

This toast, recalling at once the patient exile of Hartwell, and the peace-loving king of France, excited universal enthusiasm; glasses were elevated in the air *à l'Anglais;* and the ladies, snatching their bouquets from their bosoms, strewed the table with their floral treasures. In a word, an almost poetical fervour prevailed.

"Ah!" said the Marquise de Saint-Méran, a woman with a stern, forbidding eye, though still noble and elegant-looking, despite her having reached her fiftieth year—"Ah! these revolutionists, who have driven us from those very possessions they afterwards purchased for a mere trifle during the Reign of Terror, would be compelled to own, were they here, that all true devotion was on our side, since we were content to follow the fortunes of a falling monarch, while they, on the contrary, made their fortune by worshipping the rising sun;—yes, yes, they could not help admitting that the king, for whom we sacrificed rank, wealth, and station, was truly our 'Louis the Well-beloved!' while their wretched usurper has been, and ever will be, to them their evil genius, their 'Napoleon the Accursed!' Am I not right, Villefort? but, pardon me, I forgot your father!"

"Suffer me, madame," said the King's Deputy-Procureur M. de Villefort, who was betrothed to her charming daughter Renée, "to add my earnest request that you will kindly allow the veil of oblivion to cover and conceal the past. What avails retrospection and recrimination touching circumstances wholly past recall? I have laid aside even the name of my father, and altogether disown his political principles. He was—nay, probably may still be—a Bonapartist, and is called Noirtier; I, on the contrary, am a staunch royalist, and style myself de Villefort. Let what may remain of revolutionary sap exhaust itself and die away with the old trunk, and condescend only to regard the young shoot which has started up at a distance from the parent tree, without having the power, any more than the wish, to separate entirely from the stock from which it sprung."

"Bravo, Villefort!" cried the marquis; "excellently well said! Come, now, I have hopes of obtaining what I have been for years endeavouring to persuade the marquise to promise—namely, a perfect amnesty and forgetfulness of the past."

Having made his well-turned speech, Villefort looked carefully round to mark the effect of his oratory, much as he would have done had he been addressing the bench in open court.

" That is right," cried the marquise. " I love to see you thus. Now, then, were a conspirator to fall into your hands he would be most welcome."

" For my part, dear mother," interposed Renée, " I trust your wishes will not prosper, and that Providence will only permit petty offenders, poor debtors, and miserable cheats, to fall into M. de Villefort's hands, then I shall be contented."

" Just the same as though you prayed that a physician might only be called upon to prescribe for headaches, measles, and the stings of wasps, or any other slight affection of the epidermis. If you wish to see me the king's procureur, you must desire for me some of those violent and dangerous diseases from the cure of which so much honour redounds to the physician."

At this moment, and as though the utterance of Villefort's wish had sufficed to effect its accomplishment, a servant entered the room and whispered a few words in his ear. Villefort immediately rose from table and quitted the room upon the plea of urgent business : he soon, however, returned, his whole face beaming with delight.

Renée regarded him with fond affection ; and certainly his handsome features, lit up as they then were with more than usual fire and animation, seemed formed to excite the innocent admiration with which she gazed on her graceful and intelligent lover.

" You were wishing just now," said Villefort, addressing her, " that I were a doctor instead of a lawyer. Well, I at least resemble a doctor in one thing, that of not being able to call a day my own, not even that of my betrothal."

" And wherefore were you called away just now ?" asked Mademoiselle de Saint-Méran, with an air of deep interest.

" For a very serious affair, which bids well to afford our executioner here some work."

" How dreadful !" exclaimed Renée. Her cheeks, that were before glowing with emotion, becoming pale as marble.

" Is it possible ?" burst simultaneously from all who were near enough to the magistrate to hear his words.

" Why, if my information prove correct, a sort of Bonaparte conspiracy has just been discovered. The procureur du roi being absent the matter comes into my hands."

" Oh, Villefort !" cried Renée, clasping her hands, and looking towards her lover with piteous earnestness, " be merciful on this the day of our betrothal."

The young man passed round to the side of the table where the fair pleader sat, and leaning over her chair said tenderly,—

" To give you pleasure, my sweet Renée, I promise to shew all the lenity in my power ; but if the charges brought against this Bonapartean hero prove correct, why, then, you really must give me leave to order his head to be cut off."

Renée, with an almost convulsive shudder, turned away her head, as though the very mention of killing a fellow-creature in cold blood was more than her tender nature could endure.

" Never mind that foolish girl, Villefort," said the marquise, " she will soon get over these things."

So saying, Madame de Saint-Méran extended her dry bony hand to Villefort, who, while imprinting a son-in-law's respectful salute on it, looked at Renée, as much as to say, " I must try and fancy 'tis your dear hand I kiss, as it should have been."

" These are mournful auspices to accompany a betrothal !" sighed poor Renée.

" Upon my word, child !" exclaimed the angry marquise, " your folly exceeds all bounds. I should be glad to know what connexion there can possibly be between your sickly senti-mentality and the affairs of state !"

" Oh, mother !" murmured Renée.

" Nay, madame, I pray you pardon this little traitor ; I promise you, that to make up for her want of loyalty I will be most inflexibly severe ;" then casting an expressive glance at his betrothed, which seemed to say, " Fear not, for your dear sake my justice shall be tempered with mercy," and receiving a sweet and approving smile in return, Villefort quitted the room.

CHAPTER VII

THE EXAMINATION

No sooner had Villefort left the saloon, than he assumed the grave air of a man who holds the balance of life and death in his hands. Except the recollection of the line of politics his father adopted, which might interfere, unless he acted with the greatest prudence, with his own career, Villefort was as happy as a man could be. Already rich, he held a high official situation, though only twenty-seven. He was about to marry a young and charming woman, and besides her personal attractions, which were very great, Mademoiselle de Saint-Méran's family possessed considerable political influence, which they would of course exert in his favour. The dowry of his wife amounted to six thousand pounds, besides the prospect of inheriting twenty thousand more at her father's death.

At the door he met the commissary of police, who was waiting for him. The sight of this officer recalled Villefort from the third heaven to earth; he composed his face as we have before described, and said, " I have read the letter, monsieur, and you have acted rightly in arresting this man ; now inform me what you have discovered concerning him and the conspiracy."

" We know nothing as yet of the conspiracy, monsieur ; all the papers found have been sealed up and placed on your bureau. The prisoner himself is named Edmond Dantès, mate on board the three-master, the Pharaon, trading in cotton with Alexandria and Smyrna, and belonging to Morrel and Son, of Marseilles,"

" Before he entered the navy had he ever served in the marines ?"

" Oh, no, monsieur, he is very young."

" How old ?"

" Nineteen or twenty at the most."

At this moment, and as Villefort had arrived at the corner of the Rue des Conseils, a man, who seemed to have been waiting for him, approached ; it was M. Morrel.

" Ah, M. de Villefort," cried he, " I am delighted to see you. Some of your people have committed the strangest mistake— they have just arrested Edmond Dantès, the mate of my ship."

" I know it, monsieur," replied Villefort, " and I am now going to examine him."

" Oh," said Morrel, carried away by his friendship, " you do not know him, and I do. He is the most estimable, the most trustworthy fellow in the world, and I will venture to say, there is not a better seaman in all the merchant-service. Oh, M. de Villefort, I beseech your indulgence for him."

Villefort, as we have seen, belonged to the aristocratic party at Marseilles, Morrel to the plebeian ; the first was a royalist, the other suspected of Bonapartism. Villefort looked disdainfully at Morrel, and replied,—

" You are aware, monsieur, that a man may be estimable and trustworthy in private life, and the best seaman in the merchant-service, and yet be, politically speaking, a great criminal. Is it not true ?"

The magistrate laid emphasis on these words, as if he wished to apply them to the owner himself, whilst his eyes seemed to plunge into the heart of him who, whilst he interceded for another, had himself need of indulgence. Morrel reddened, for his own conscience was not quite clear on politics ; besides, what Dantès had told him of his interview with the Grand Marshal, and what the emperor had said to him, embarrassed him. He replied, however,—

" I entreat you, M. de Villefort, be, as you always are, kind and just."

Villefort had now arrived at the door of his own house, which adjoined the Palais de Justice, he entered, after having saluted the shipowner, who stood on the spot where he was left.

The antechamber was full of agents of police and gendarmes, in the midst of whom, carefully watched, but calm and smiling, stood the prisoner. Villefort traversed the antechamber, cast a side glance at Dantès, and taking a packet which a gendarme offered him, disappeared, saying, " Bring in the prisoner."

Rapid as had been Villefort's glance, it had served to give him an idea of the man he was about to interrogate. He had recognised intelligence in the high forehead, courage in the dark eye and bent brow, and frankness in the thick lips that shewed a set of pearly teeth.

Villefort's first impression was favourable, but he had been so often warned to mistrust first impulses that he applied the maxim to the impression, forgetting the difference between the two words. He stifled, therefore, the feelings of compassion that were rising, composed his features, and sat down at his bureau. An instant after Dantès entered.

He was pale, but calm and collected, and saluting his judge with easy politeness, looked round for a seat, as if he had been in the saloon of M. Morrel.

It was then that he encountered, for the first time, Villefort's look, that look peculiar to justice; which, whilst it seems to read the culprit's thoughts, betrays nought of its own.

"Who and what are you?" demanded Villefort, turning over a pile of papers, containing information relative to the prisoner that an agent of police had given to him on his entry.

"My name is Edmond Dantès," replied the young man calmly. "I am mate of the Pharaon, belonging to Messrs. Morrel and Son."

"Your age?" continued Villefort.

"Nineteen," returned Dantès.

"What were you doing at the moment you were arrested?"

"I was at the festival of my marriage, monsieur," said the young man, his voice slightly tremulous, so great was the contrast between that happy moment and the painful ceremony he was now under-going; so great was the contrast between the sombre aspect of M. de Villefort and the radiant face of Mercédès.

"You were at the festival of your marriage?" said the deputy, shuddering in spite of himself.

"Yes, monsieur, I am on the point of marrying a young girl I have been attached to for three years."

Villefort, impassive as he was, was struck with this coincidence; and the tremulous voice of Dantès, surprised in the midst of his happiness, struck a sympathetic chord in his own bosom; he also was on the point of being married, and he was summoned from his own happiness to destroy that of another.

This philosophic reflection, thought he, will make a great sensation at M. de Saint-Méran's, and he arranged mentally, whilst Dantès awaited further questions, the antitheses by which orators often create a reputation for eloquence.

When this speech was arranged, Villefort turned to Dantès.

"Have you served under the usurper?"

" I was about to be incorporated in the royal marines when he fell."

"It is reported your political opinions are extreme," said Villefort, who had never heard anything of the kind, but was not sorry to make this inquiry, as if it were an accusation.

" My political opinions!" replied Dantès. " Alas! sir, I never had any opinions. I am hardly nineteen; I know nothing; I have no part to play. If I obtain the situation I desire, I shall owe it to M. Morrel. Thus all my opinions,—I will not say public, but private, are confined to these three sentiments—I love my father, I respect M. Morrel, and I adore Mercédès. This, sir, is all I can tell you, and you see how uninteresting it is."

As Dantès spoke, Villefort gazed at his ingenuous and open countenance, and recollected the words of Renée, who, without knowing who the culprit was, had besought his indulgence for him. With the deputy's knowledge of crime and criminals, every word the young man uttered convinced him more and more of his innocence.

This lad, for he was scarcely a man, simple, natural, eloquent with that eloquence of the heart, never found when sought for, full of affection for everybody, because he was happy, and because happiness renders even the wicked good, extended his affection even to his judge, spite of Villefort's severe look and stern accent. Dantès seemed full of kindness.

" *Pardieu!* " said Villefort, " he is a noble fellow! I hope I shall gain Renée's favour easily by obeying the first command she ever imposed on me. I shall have at least a pressure of the hand in public, and a sweet kiss in private."

Full of this idea, Villefort's face became so joyous, that when he turned to Dantés, the latter, who had watched the change on his physiognomy, was smiling also.

" Sir," said Villefort, " have you any enemies, at least that you know ?"

" Have I enemies?" replied Dantès ; " my position is not sufficiently elevated for that. As for my character, that is, perhaps, somewhat too hasty, but I have striven to repress it. I have had ten or twelve sailors under me ; and if you question them, they will tell you that they love and respect me, not as a father, for I am too young, but as an elder brother."

" But instead of enemies you may have excited jealousy. You are about to become captain at nineteen, an elevated post :

you are about to marry a pretty girl, who loves you, and these two pieces of good fortune may have excited the envy of some one."

" You are right ; you know men better than I do, and what you say may possibly be the case, I confess ; I prefer not knowing them, because then I should be forced to hate them."

" You are wrong ; you should always strive to see clearly around you. You seem a worthy young man ; I will depart from the strict line of my duty to aid you in discovering the author of this accusation. Here is the paper ; do you know the writing ?"

As he spoke, Villefort drew the letter from his pocket, and presented it to Dantès. Dantès read it. A cloud passed over his brow as he said :—

" No, monsieur, I do not know the writing, and yet it is tolerably plain. Whoever did it writes well. I am very fortunate," added he, looking gratefully at Villefort, " to be examined by such a man as you, for this envious person is a real enemy."

And by the rapid glance that the young man's eyes shot forth, Villefort saw how much energy lay hidden beneath this mildness.

" Now," said the deputy, " answer me frankly, not as a prisoner to a judge, but as one man to another who takes an interest in him, what truth is there in the accusation contained in this anonymous letter ?"

" None at all. I will tell you the real facts. I swear by my honour as a sailor, by my love for Mercédès, by the life of my father. When we quitted Naples, Captain Leclere was attacked with a brain-fever. As we had no doctor on board, and he was so anxious to arrive at Elba, that he would not touch at any other port, his disorder rose to such a height, that at the end of the third day, feeling he was dying, he called me to him. ' My dear Dantès,' said he, ' swear to perform what I am going to tell you, for it is a matter of the deepest importance.'

" ' I swear, captain,' replied I.

" ' Well, as after my death the command devolves on you as mate, assume the command, and bear up for the Isle of Elba, disembark at Porto-Ferrajo, ask for the Grand Marshal, give him this letter, perhaps they will give you another letter, and charge you with a commission. You will accomplish what I was to have done, and derive all the honour and profit from it.'

" ' I will do it, captain ; but, perhaps, I shall not be admitted to the Grand Marshal's presence as easily as you expect ?'

4

"'Here is a ring that will obtain audience of him, and remove every difficulty,' said the captain. Two hours after he was delirious; the next day he died. Every where the last requests of a dying man are sacred; but amongst sailors the last requests of his superior are commands. I sailed for the Isle of Elba, where I arrived the next day; I ordered every body to remain on board, and went on shore alone. As I had expected, I found some difficulty in obtaining access to the Grand Marshal; but I sent the ring I had received from the captain to him, and was instantly admitted. He questioned me concerning Captain Leclere's death; and, as the latter had told me, gave me a letter to carry on to a person in Paris. I undertook it because it was what my captain had bade me do. I landed here, regulated the affairs of the vessel, and hastened to visit my affianced bride, whom I found more lovely than ever. Thanks to M. Morrel, all the forms were got over; in a word, I was, as I told you, at my marriage-feast, and I should have been married in an hour, and to-morrow I intended to start for Paris."

"Ah!" said Villefort, "this seems to me the truth. If you have been culpable, it was imprudence, and this imprudence was legitimised by the orders of your captain. Give up this letter you have brought from Elba, and pass your word you will appear should you be required, and go and rejoin your friends."

"You have it already; for it was taken from me with some others which I see in that packet."

"To whom is it addressed?"

"To Monsieur Noirtier, Rue Coq-Héron, Paris."

Had a thunderbolt fallen into the room, Villefort could not have been more stupefied. He sank into his seat, and hastily turning over the packet, drew forth the fatal letter, at which he glanced with an expression of terror.

"M. Noirtier, Rue Coq-Héron, No. 13," murmured he, growing still paler.

"Yes," said Dantès; "do you then know him?"

"No," replied Villefort; "a faithful servant of the king does not know conspirators."

"It is a conspiracy, then?" asked Dantès, who, after believing himself free, now began to feel a tenfold alarm. "I have already told you, however, sir, I was ignorant of the contents of the letter."

"Yes, but you knew the name of the person to whom it was addressed?" said Villefort.

" I was forced to read the address to know to whom to give it."

" Have you shewn this letter to any one ?" asked Villefort, becoming still more pale.

" To no one, on my honour."

" Every body is ignorant that you are the bearer of a letter from the Isle of Elba, and addressed to M. Noirtier ?"

" Every body, except the person who gave it to me."

" This is too much," murmured Villefort.

Villefort's brow darkened more and more, his white lips and clenched teeth filled Dantès with apprehension.

After reading the letter, Villefort covered his face with his hands.

" Oh !" said Dantès, timidly, " what is the matter ?"

Villefort made no answer, but raised his head at the expiration of a few seconds, and again perused the letter.

" You give me your honour that you are ignorant of the contents of this letter ?"

" I give you my honour, sir," said Dantès ; " but what is the matter ? You are ill ;—shall I ring for assistance ?—shall I call ?"

" No," said Villefort, rising hastily ; " stay where you are. It is for me to give orders here, and not you."

" Monsieur," replied Dantès, proudly, " it was only to summon assistance for you."

" I want none ; it was a temporary indisposition. Attend to yourself ; answer me."

Dantès waited, expecting a question, but in vain. Villefort fell back on his chair, passed his hand over his brow, moist with perspiration, and, for the third time, read the letter.

" If he knows the contents of this !" murmured he, " and that Noirtier is the father of Villefort, I am lost !" And he fixed his eyes upon Edmond as if he would have penetrated his thoughts.

" It is impossible to doubt it," cried he suddenly.

" In Heaven's name !" cried the unhappy young man, " if you doubt me, question me ; I will answer you."

Villefort made a violent effort, and in a tone he strove to render firm,—

" Sir," said he, " I am no longer able, as I had hoped, to restore you immediately to liberty ; before doing so, I must consult the judge of instruction ; but you see how I behave towards you."

"Oh!" cried Dantès, "you have been rather a friend than a judge."

"Well, I must detain you some time longer, but I will strive to make it as short as possible. The principal charge against you is this letter, and you see——"

Villefort approached the fire, cast it in, and waited until it was entirely consumed.

"You see I destroy it?"

"Oh!" exclaimed Dantès, "you are goodness itself."

"I shall detain you until this evening in the Palais de Justice. Should any one else interrogate you, do not breathe a word of this letter."

"I promise."

It was Villefort who seemed to entreat, and the prisoner who reassured him.

"You see," continued he, "the letter is destroyed, you and I alone knew of its existence; should you, therefore, be questioned, deny all knowledge of it."

"Fear nothing, I will deny it."

"It was the only letter you had?"

"It was."

"Swear it."

"I swear it."

Villefort rang. An agent of police entered. Villefort whispered some words in his ear, to which the officer replied by a motion of his head.

"Follow him," said Villefort to Dantès.

Dantès saluted Villefort and retired.

Hardly had the door closed, than Villefort threw himself into a chair.

"Alas! alas!" murmured he, "if the procureur du roi had been at Marseilles, I should have been ruined. This accursed letter would have destroyed all my hopes. My father, must your past career always interfere with my successes?"

Suddenly a light passed over his face, a smile played round his mouth, and his lips became unclenched.

"This will do," said he, "and from this letter, which might have ruined me, I will make my fortune."

And after having assured himself the prisoner was gone, the deputy procureur hastened to the house of his bride.

CHAPTER VIII

THE CHÂTEAU D'IF

THE commissary of police, as he traversed the antechamber, made a sign to two gendarmes, who placed themselves one on Dantès' right and the other on his left. A door that communicated with the Palais de Justice was opened, and they traversed a long range of gloomy corridors, whose appearance might have made even the boldest shudder. The Palais de Justice communicated with the prison,—a sombre edifice, that from its grated windows looks on the clock-tower of the Accoules.

After numberless windings Dantès saw an iron door. The commissary knocked thrice, every blow seeming to Dantès as if struck on his heart. The door opened, the two gendarmes gently pushed him forward, and the door closed with a loud sound behind him. The air he inhaled was no longer pure, but thick and mephitic,—he was in prison. He was conducted to a tolerably neat chamber, but grated and barred, and its appearance, however, did not greatly alarm him; besides, the words of Villefort, who seemed to interest himself so much, resounded still in his ears like a promise of freedom.

It was four o'clock when Dantès was placed in this chamber. It was, as we have said, the 1st of March, and the prisoner was soon buried in darkness. The obscurity augmented the acuteness of his hearing: at the slightest sound he rose and hastened to the door, convinced they were about to liberate him, but the sound died away, and Dantès sank again into his seat.

At last, about ten o'clock, and just as Dantès began to despair, steps were heard in the corridor, a key turned in the lock, the bolts creaked, the massy oaken door flew open, and a flood of light from two torches pervaded the apartment.

By the torchlight Dantès saw the glittering sabres and carbines of four gendarmes.

The conviction that they came from M. de Villefort relieved all Dantès' apprehension, he advanced calmly and placed himself

in the centre of the escort. A carriage waited at the door, the
coachman was on the box, and an exempt seated behind him.

Dantès was about to speak, but feeling himself urged forward,
and having neither the power nor the intention to resist, he
mounted the steps, and was in an instant seated inside between
two gendarmes, the two others took their places opposite, and
the carriage rolled heavily over the stones.   The prisoner
glanced at the windows, they were grated ; he had changed his
prison for another that was conveying him he knew not whither.
Through the grating, however, Dantès saw they were passing
through the Rue Caisserie, and by the quay Saint-Laurent and
the Rue Taramis, to the port.   The carriage stopped, the
exempt descended, approached the guard-house, a dozen soldiers
came out and formed themselves in order, Dantès saw the reflection of their muskets by the light of the lamps on the quay.

" Can all this force be summoned on my account ?" thought he.

The exempt opened the door, which was locked, and without
speaking a word answered Dantès' question, for he saw between
the ranks of the soldiers a passage formed from the carriage to
the port.   The two gendarmes who were opposite to him descended first, then he was ordered to alight, and the gendarmes
on each side of him followed his example.   They advanced
towards a boat, which a custom-house officer held by a chain,
near the quay.   The soldiers looked at Dantès with an air of
stupid curiosity.   In an instant he was placed in the stern-sheets
of the boat between the gendarmes, whilst the exempt stationed
himself at the bow ; a shove sent the boat adrift, and four
sturdy oarsmen impelled it rapidly towards the Pilon.   At a
shout from the boat the chain that closes the mouth of the port
was lowered, and in a second they were outside the harbour.

The prisoner's first feeling was joy at again breathing the
pure air, for air is freedom ; but he soon sighed, for he passed
before La Réserve, where he had that morning been so happy,
and now through the open windows came the laughter and
revelry of a ball.

The boat continued her voyage.   They had passed the Tête
de More, were now in front of the lighthouse, and about to
double the battery ; this manœuvre was incomprehensible to
Dantès.

" Whither are you taking me ?" asked he.

" You will soon know."

" But still——"

" We are forbidden to give you any explanation."

Dantès knew that nothing would be more absurd than to question subordinates, who were forbidden to reply, and remained silent.

The most vague and wild thoughts passed through his mind. The boat they were in could not make a long voyage, there was no vessel at anchor outside the harbour; he thought, perhaps, they were going to leave him on some distant point. He was not bound, nor had they made any attempt to handcuff him; this seemed a good augury. Besides had not the deputy who had been so kind to him told him that provided he did not pronounce the dreaded name of Noirtier, he had nothing to apprehend. Had not Villefort in his presence destroyed the fatal letter, the only proof against him? He waited silently, striving to pierce through the darkness.

They had left the Ile Ratonneau, where the lighthouse stood, on the right, and were now opposite the Point des Catalans. It seemed to the prisoner that he could distinguish a woman on the beach, for it was there Mercédès dwelt. One light alone was visible, and Dantès recognised it as coming from the chamber of Mercédès. A loud cry could be heard by her. He did not utter it. What would his guards think if they heard him shout like a madman? He remained silent, his eyes fixed upon the light; the boat went on, but the prisoner only thought of Mercédès. A rising ground hid the light, Dantès turned and perceived they had got out to sea. Whilst he had been absorbed in thought they had hoisted the sail. In spite of his repugnance to address the guards, Dantès turned to the nearest gendarme, and taking his hand,—

" Comrade," said he, " I adjure you as a Christian and a soldier, to tell me where we are going. I am Captain Dantès, a loyal Frenchman, though accused of treason, tell me where you are conducting me, and I promise you on my honour I will submit to my fate."

The gendarme looked irresolutely at his companion, who returned for answer a sigh that said, " I see no great harm in telling him now," and the gendarme replied,—

" You are a native of Marseilles and a sailor, and yet you do not know where you are going?"

" On my honour I have no idea."

" That is impossible."

" I swear to you it is true. Tell me, I entreat."

" But my orders."

" Your orders do not forbid your telling me what I must
know in ten minutes, in half an hour, or an hour. You see I
cannot escape even if I intended."

" Unless you are blind, or have never been outside the harbour,
you must know."

" I do not."

" Look round you then."

Dantès rose and looked forward, when he saw rise within a
hundred yards of him the black and frowning rock on which
stands the Château d'If. This gloomy fortress, which has for
more than three hundred years furnished food for so many wild
legends, seemed to Dantès like a scaffold to a malefactor.

" The Château d'If!" cried he, " what are we going there
for ?"

The gendarme smiled.

" I am not going there to be imprisoned," said Dantès ; " it
is only used for political prisoners, I have committed no crime.
Are there any magistrates or judges at the Château d'If ?"

" There are only," said the gendarme, " a governor, a garrison,
turnkeys, and good thick walls. Come, come, do not look so
astonished, or you will make me think you are laughing at me
in return for my good nature."

Dantès pressed the gendarme's hand as though he would
crush it.

" You think then," said he, " that I am conducted to the
Château to be imprisoned there ?"

" It is probable ; but there is no occasion to squeeze so hard."

" Without any formality ?"

" All the formalities have been gone through."

" In spite of M. de Villefort's promises ?"

" I do not know what M. de Villefort promised you," said the
gendarme, " but I know we are taking you to the Château d'If.
But what are you doing ? Help ! comrades, help !"

By a rapid movement, which the gendarme's practised eye had
perceived, Dantès sprang forward to precipitate himself into the
sea, but four vigorous arms seized him as his feet quitted the
flooring of the boat. He fell back foaming with rage.

" Good !" said the gendarme, placing his knee on his chest ;
" never believe soft-spoken gentlemen again ! Harkye, my friend,
I have disobeyed my first order, but I will not disobey the second,
and if you move I lodge a bullet in your brain."

And he levelled his carbine at Dantès, who felt the muzzle touch his head.

For a moment the idea of struggling crossed his mind, thus to end the unexpected evil that had overtaken him. But he bethought him of M. de Villefort's promise; and, besides, death in a boat from the hand of a gendarme seemed too terrible. He remained motionless, but gnashing his teeth with fury. At this moment a violent shock made the bark tremble. One of the sailors leaped on shore, a cord creaked as it ran through a pulley, and Dantès guessed they were at the end of the voyage. His guardians, taking hold of his arms, forced him to rise, and dragged him towards the steps that lead to the gate of the fortress, whilst the exempt followed, armed with a carbine and bayonet.

Dantès made no resistance, he was like a man in a dream, he saw soldiers who stationed themselves on the sides, he felt himself forced up fresh stairs, he perceived he passed through a door, and the door closed behind him; but all this as mechanically as through a mist, nothing distinctly. They halted for a minute, during which he strove to collect his thoughts; he looked around; he was in a court surrounded by high walls; he heard the measured tread of sentinels, and as they passed before the light he saw the barrels of their muskets shine. They waited upwards of ten minutes. Certain Dantès could not escape, the gendarmes released him; they seemed awaiting orders. The orders arrived.

"Where is the prisoner?" said a voice.

"Here," replied the gendarmes.

"Let him follow me; I am going to conduct him to his room."

"Go!" said the gendarmes, pushing Dantès.

The prisoner followed his conductor, who led him into a room almost under ground, whose bare and reeking walls seemed as though impregnated with tears; a lamp placed on a stool illumined the apartment faintly, and showed Dantès the features of his conductor, an under-gaoler, ill-clothed, and of sullen appearance.

"Here is your chamber for to-night," said he. "It is late, and Monsieur le Gouverneur is asleep; to-morrow, perhaps, he may change you. In the meantime there is bread, water, and fresh straw, and that is all a prisoner can wish for. Goodnight!"

And before Dantès could open his mouth—before he had noticed where the gaoler placed his bread or the water—before he had glanced towards the corner where the straw was, the gaoler disappeared, taking with him the lamp. Dantès was alone in darkness and in silence: cold as the shadows that he felt breathe on his burning forehead.

With the first dawn of day the gaoler returned, with orders to leave Dantès where he was. He found the prisoner in the same position as if fixed there—his eyes swollen with weeping.

He had passed the night standing and without sleep.

The gaoler advanced; Dantès appeared not to perceive him. He touched him on the shoulder: Edmond started.

" Have you not slept ?" said the gaoler.

" I do not know," replied Dantès.

The gaoler stared.

" Are you hungry ?" continued he.

" I do not know."

" Do you wish for anything ?"

" I wish to see the governor."

The gaoler shrugged his shoulders and left the chamber.

Dantès followed him with his eyes, and stretched forth his hands towards the open door; but the door closed.

All his emotion then burst forth; he cast himself on the ground, weeping bitterly, and asking himself what crime he had committed that he was thus punished.

The day passed thus; he scarcely tasted food, but walked round and round the cell like a wild beast in its cage.

One thought in particular tormented him, namely, that during his journey hither he had sat so still, whereas he might, a dozen times, have plunged into the sea, and thanks to his powers of swimming, for which he was famous, have gained the shore, concealed himself until the arrival of a Genoese or Spanish vessel; escaped to Spain or Italy, where Mercédès and his father could have joined him. He had no fears as to how he should live; good seamen are welcome everywhere; he spoke Italian like a Tuscan, and Spanish like a Castilian; he would have then been happy, whereas he was now confined in the Château d'If, ignorant of the future destiny of his father and Mercédès; and all this because he had trusted to Villefort's promise. The thought was maddening, and Dantès threw himself furiously down on his straw.

The next morning the gaoler made his appearance.

" Well," said the gaoler, " are you more reasonable to-day ?"
Dantès made no reply.

" Come, take courage, do you want anything in my power to
do for you ?"

" I wish to see the governor."

" I have already told you it was impossible."

" Why so ?"

" Because it is not allowed by the rules."

" What is allowed then ?"

" Better fare, if you pay for it, books, and leave to walk
about."

" I do not want books, I am satisfied with my food, and I do
not care to walk about ; but I wish to see the governor."

" If you worry me by repeating the same thing I will not
bring you any more to eat."

" Well, then," said Edmond, " if you do not, I shall die of
famine, that is all."

The gaoler saw by his tone he would be happy to die ; and, as
every prisoner is worth sixpence a day to his gaoler, he replied
in a more subdued tone—

" What you ask is impossible ; but if you are very well
behaved you will be allowed to walk about, and some day you
will meet the governor ; and if he chooses to reply, that is his
affair."

" But," asked Dantès, " how long shall I have to wait ?"

" Ah! a month—six months—a year."

" It is too long a time.   I wish to see him at once."

" Ah !" said the gaoler, " do not always brood over what is
impossible, or you will be mad in a fortnight."

" You think so ?"

" Yes, we have an instance here ; it was by always offering a
million of francs to the governor for his liberty that an abbé
became mad, who was in this chamber before you."

" How long has he left it ?"

Two years."

Was he liberated then ?'

No ; he was put in a dungeon."

Listen !" said Dantès, " I am not an abbé, I am not mad ;
perhaps I shall be ; but at present, unfortunately, I am not.
I will make you another offer."

" What is that ?"

" I do not offer you a million, because I have it not ; but I will give you a hundred crowns if the first time you go to Marseilles you will seek out a young girl, named Mercédès, at the Catalans, and give her two lines from me."

" If I took them, and were detected, I should lose my place, which is worth two thousand francs a year; so that I should be a great fool to run such a risk for three hundred."

" Well," said Dantès, " mark this, if you refuse, at least, to tell Mercédès I am here, I will some day hide myself behind the door, and when you enter I will dash out your brains with this stool."

" Threats !" cried the gaoler, retreating, and putting himself on the defensive, "you are certainly going mad. The abbé began like you; and in three days you will want a strait-waistcoat; but, fortunately, there are dungeons here."

Dantès whirled the stool round his head.

" Oh !" said the gaoler," you shall see the governor at once."

" That is right," returned Dantès, dropping the stool, and sitting on it as if he were in reality mad.

The gaoler went out, and returned in an instant with a corporal and four soldiers.

" By the governor's orders," said he, " conduct the prisoner to the story beneath."

" To the dungeon, then," said the corporal.

" Yes, we must put the madman with the madmen."

The soldiers seized Dantès, who followed passively. He descended fifteen steps, and the door of a dungeon was opened, and he was thrust in. The door closed, and Dantès advanced with outstretched hands until he touched the wall; he then sat down in the corner until his eyes became accustomed to the darkness.

The gaoler was right, Dantès wanted but little of being utterly mad.

CHAPTER IX

THE OGRE OF CORSICA

WE must now enter the small cabinet of the Tuileries with the arched window, so well known as having been the favourite cabinet of Napoleon and Louis XVIII., as also that of Louis Philippe.

There in this closet, seated before a walnut-tree table he had brought with him from Hartwell, and to which, from one of those fancies not uncommon to great people, he was particularly attached, the King Louis XVIII. was carelessly listening to a man of fifty or fifty-two years of age, with grey hairs, aristocratic bearing, and exceedingly gentlemanly attire, whilst he was making a note in a volume of Horace, Gryphius's edition, which was much indebted to the sagacious observations of the philosophical monarch.

There entered M. de Blacas, who entreated his majesty to see M. de Villefort, who had travelled two hundred and twenty leagues from Marseilles in three days to see him on an urgent matter.

" M. de Villefort !" cried the king, " de Villefort ?   He is a man of strong and elevated understanding, ambitious too, and, *pardieu!* you know his father's name !"

" His father ?"

" Yes, Noirtier."

" And your majesty has employed the son of such a man ?"

"Blacas, my friend, you have but limited comprehension.   I told you Villefort was ambitious, and to attain his ambition Villefort would sacrifice everything, even his father.

Turning to M. de Blacas he ordered :

" This instant, count !   Where is he ?"

" Waiting below in my carriage."

" Seek him at once."

" I hasten to do so."

The count left the royal presence with the speed of a young man ; his really sincere royalism made him youthful again.

Louis XVIII. remained alone, and turning his eyes on his half-opened Horace, muttered, " *Justum et tenacem propositi virum.*"

M. de Blacas returned with the same rapidity he had descended, but in the antechamber he was forced to appeal to the king's authority. Villefort's dusty garb, his costume, which was not of courtly cut, excited the susceptibility of M. de Brezé, who was all astonishment at finding that this young man had the pretension to enter before the king in such attire. The count, however, superseded all difficulties with a word—his majesty's order, and, in spite of the observations which the master of the ceremonies made for the honour of his office and principles, Villefort was introduced.

The king was seated in the same place where the count had left him.

"Come in, M. de Villefort," said he, "come in."

Villefort bowed, and, advancing a few steps, waited until the king should interrogate him.

"M. de Villefort," said Louis XVIII., "the Count de Blacas assures me you have some interesting information to communicate."

"Sire, I have come as rapidly to Paris as possible, to inform your majesty that I have discovered, in the exercise of my duties, not a commonplace and insignificant plot, such as is every day got up in the lower ranks of the people and in the army, but an actual conspiracy, a storm which menaces no less than the throne of your majesty. Sire, the usurper is arming three ships, he meditates some project, which, however mad, is yet, perhaps, terrible. At this moment he will have left Elba, to go whither I know not, but assuredly to attempt a landing either at Naples, or on the coast of Tuscany, or, perhaps, on the shore of France. Your majesty is well aware that the sovereign of the Isle of Elba has maintained his relations with Italy and France ?"

" I am, sir," said the king, much agitated ; " and recently we have had information that the Bonapartist clubs have had meetings in the Rue Saint-Jacques. But proceed, I beg of you; how did you obtain these details ?"

" Sire, they are the results of an examination which I have made of a man of Marseilles, whom I have watched for some time, and arrested on the day of my departure. This person, a sailor, of turbulent character, and whom I suspected of Bonapartism, has been secretly to the Isle of Elba. There he saw the

Grand Marshal, who charged him with a verbal mission to a Bonapartist in Paris, whose name I could not extract from him; but this mission was to prepare men's minds for a return (it is the man who says this, sire)—a return which will soon occur."

" And where is this man ?"

" In prison, sire."

" And the matter seems serious to you ?"

" So serious, sire, that when the circumstance surprised me in the midst of a family festival, on the very day of my betrothal, I left my bride and friends, postponing everything, that I might hasten to lay at your majesty's feet the fears which impressed me, and the assurance of my devotion."

" True," said Louis XVIII., "was there not a marriage engagement between you and Mademoiselle de Saint-Méran ?"

" Daughter of one of your majesty's most faithful servants."

At this instant the minister of police appeared at the door, pale, trembling, and as if ready to faint.

Villefort was about to retire, but M. de Blacas, taking his hand, restrained him.

The minister of police was about to throw himself at the feet of Louis XVIII., who retreated a step and frowned.

" Will you speak ?" he said.

" Oh! sire, what a dreadful misfortune! I am, indeed to be pitied. I can never forgive myself!"

" Monsieur," said Louis XVIII., " I command you to speak."

" Well, sire, the usurper left Elba on the 26th February, and landed on the 1st of March in France, at a small port near Antibes, in the Gulf of Juan."

Louis made a gesture of indescribable anger and alarm, and then drew himself up as if this sudden blow had struck him at the same moment in heart and countenance.

" In France!" he cried, " the usurper in France! Then they did not watch over this man. Who knows? they were, perhaps, in league with him."

" Oh, sire!" exclaimed the Comte de Blacas, " M. Dandré is not a man to be accused of treason! Sire, we have all been blind, and the minister of police has shared the general blindness, that is all."

" But——" said Villefort, and suddenly checking himself, he was silent; then he continued, " Your pardon, sire," he said, bowing, " my zeal carried me away. Will your majesty deign to excuse me ?"

"Speak, sir, speak boldly," replied Louis. "You alone fore-warned us of the evil; now try and aid us with the remedy!"

Villefort understood the king. Any other person would, perhaps, have been too much overcome by the intoxication of praise; but he feared to make for himself a mortal enemy of the police minister, although he perceived Dandré was irrevocably lost. In fact, the minister who, in the plenitude of his power, had been unable to penetrate Napoleon's secret, might in the convulsions of his dying throes penetrate his (Villefort's) secret, for which end he had but to interrogate Dantès. He, therefore, came to the rescue of the crestfallen minister, instead of aiding to crush him.

"Sire," said Villefort, "the rapidity of the event must prove to your majesty that God alone can prevent it, by raising a tempest; what your majesty is pleased to attribute to me as profound perspicacity is simply owing to chance; and I have profited by that chance, like a good and devoted servant, that's all. Do not attribute to me more than I deserve, sire, that your majesty may never have occasion to recall the first opinion you have been pleased to form of me."

The minister of police thanked the young man by an eloquent look, and Villefort understood that he had succeeded in his design; that is to say, that without forfeiting the gratitude of the king, he had made a friend of one on whom, in case of necessity, he might rely.

"I came to speak to you, sire, of the mysterious death of General d'Epinay; your majesty doubtless recollects the circumstance," said the minister of police. "All fresh information points to the fact that this death is not the result of a suicide, as we at first believed, but of an assassination. General d'Epinay had quitted, as it appears, a Bonapartist club when he disappeared. An unknown person had been with him that morning, and made an appointment with him in the Rue Saint-Jacques; unfortunately, the general's valet-de-chambre, who was dressing his hair at the moment when the stranger entered, heard the street mentioned, but did not catch the number."

As the police minister related this to the king, Villefort, who seemed as if his very existence hung on his lips, turned alternately red and pale. The king looked towards him.

"Do you not think with me, M. de Villefort, that General d'Epinay, whom they believed attached to the usurper, but who was really entirely devoted to me, has perished, the victim of a Bonapartist ambush?"

" It is probable, sire," replied Villefort. " But is this all that is known ?"

" They are on the traces of the man who appointed the meeting with him."

" On his traces ?" said Villefort.

" Yes, the servant has given his description. He is a man of from fifty to fifty-two years of age, brown, with black eyes, covered with shaggy eyebrows, and a thick moustache. He was dressed in a blue frock-coat, buttoned up to the chin, and wore at his button-hole the rosette of an officer of the Legion of Honour. Yesterday an individual was followed exactly corresponding with this description, but he was lost sight of at the corner of the Rue de la Jussienne and the Rue Coq-Héron."

Villefort leaned on the back of an armchair, for in proportion as the minister of police spoke, he felt his legs bend under him ; but when he learnt that the unknown had escaped the vigilance of the agent who followed him, he breathed again.

Ten minutes afterwards Villefort reached his hotel, ordered his horses in two hours, and desired to have his breakfast brought to him. He was about to commence his repast when the sound of the bell, rung by a free and firm hand, was heard. The valet opened the door, and Villefort heard his name pronounced.

" Who could know that I was here already ?" said the young man.

" Eh, *pardieu !* " said an individual of about fifty years of age, with shaggy eyebrows and a thick moustache, dressed in a blue frock-coat, buttoned up to the chin. " Is it the custom of Marseilles for sons to keep their fathers waiting in their anterooms ?"

" Father !" cried Villefort, " then I was not deceived ; I felt sure it must be you."

M. Noirtier followed with his eyes the servant until he had closed the door, and then, fearing, no doubt, that he might be overheard in the antechamber, he opened the door again, nor was the precaution useless, as appeared from the rapid retreat of Germain.

M. Noirtier then took the trouble to close carefully the door of the antechamber, then that of the bedchamber, and then extended his hand to Villefort, who had followed all his motions with surprise, which he could not conceal.

" Well now, my dear Gérard," said he to the young man, with

a very significant look, " you seem as if you were not very glad to see me ?"

" My dear father," said Villefort, " I am, on the contrary, delighted, but I so little expected your visit that it has some-what overcome me."

" But, my dear fellow," replied M. Noirtier, seating himself, " I might say the same thing to you when you announce to me your wedding for the 28th of February, and on the 4th of March here you are in Paris."

" And if I have come, my dear father," said Gérard, drawing closer to M. Noirtier, " do not complain, for it is for you that I came, and my journey will save you."

" Ah, indeed !" said M. Noirtier, stretching himself out at his ease in the chair. " Really, pray tell me all about it, M. le Magistrat, for it must be interesting."

" Father, you have heard of a certain club of Bonapartists held in the Rue Saint-Jacques ?"

" No. 53 : yes, I am vice-president."

" Father, your coolness makes me shudder."

" Why, my dear boy, when a man has been proscribed by the mountaineers, has escaped from Paris in a hay-cart, been hunted in the *landes* of Bordeaux by M. Robespierre's bloodhounds, he becomes accustomed to most things. But go on, what about the club in the Rue Saint-Jacques ?"

" Why, they induced General d'Epinay to go there, and General d'Epinay, who quitted his own house at nine o'clock in the evening, was found the next day in the Seine."

" Ah, I will tell you something better, have you heard of the landing of the emperor ?"

" Not so loud, father, I entreat of you—for your own sake as well as mine. Yes, I heard this news, and knew it even before you could ; for three days ago I posted from Marseilles to Paris with all possible speed, and half desperate because I could not send with a wish two hundred leagues ahead of me the thought which was agitating my brain."

" Three days ago ? you are crazy. Why three days ago the emperor had not landed."

" But I learned it from a letter addressed to you from the Isle of Elba, which I discovered in the pocket-book of the messenger ; had that letter fallen into the hands of another, you, my dear father, would probably, ere this, have been shot."

Villefort's father laughed.

" Come, come," said he, " it appears that the Restoration has learned from the Empire the mode of settling affairs speedily. Shot, my dear boy! you go ahead with a vengeance. Where is this letter you talk about? I know you too well to suppose you would allow such a thing to pass you."

" I burnt it, for fear that even a fragment should remain; for that letter must have effected your condemnation."

" And the destruction of your future prospects," replied Noirtier; " yes, I can easily comprehend that. But I have nothing to fear whilst I have you to protect me."

" I do better than that, sir—I save you."

" You do?"

" Father, you know very well that General d'Epinay was not a man to drown himself in despair, and people do not bathe in the Seine in the month of January. No, no, do not mistake, this death was a murder in every sense of the word."

" Would you like to know the truth of the matter? well, I will tell you. It was thought reliance might be placed in General d'Epinay, he was recommended to us from the Isle of Elba; one of us went to him and invited him to the Rue Saint-Jacques, where he would find some friends. He came there, and the plan was unfolded to him of the leaving Elba, the projected landing, &c. When he had heard and comprehended all to the fullest extent, he replied that he was a royalist. Then all looked at each other,—he was made to take an oath, and did so, but with such an ill grace that it was really tempting Providence to swear thus, and yet, in spite of that, the general was allowed to depart free—perfectly free. Yet he did not return home. What could that mean? why, my dear fellow, that on leaving us he lost his way, that's all. A murder! really, Villefort, you surprise me. You, a deputy procureur, to found an accusation on such bad premises! Did I ever say to you, when you were fulfilling your character as a royalist, and cut off the head of one of my party, 'My son, you have committed a murder?' No, I said, 'Very well, sir, you have gained the victory, to-morrow, perchance, it will be our turn.' Eh? the thing is simple enough. You who are in power have the means that money produces—we who are in expectation have those which devotion prompts."

" Devotion!" said Villefort, with a sneer.

" Yes, devotion, for that is, I believe, the phrase for hopeful ambition."

' But, father, to return to General d'Epinay; the police have the description of the man who, on the morning of the day when the general disappeared, presented himself at his house."·

" May-be," said Noirtier, looking carelessly around him, " but as this individual is warned; he will consequently change looks and costume."

At these words he rose, and put off his frock-coat and cravat, went towards a table on which lay all the requisites of the toilette for his son, lathered his face, took a razor, and, with a firm hand, cut off the whiskers that might have compromised him and gave the police so decided a trace.   Villefort watched him with alarm, not divested of admiration.

His whiskers cut off, Noirtier gave another turn to his hair, took, instead of his black cravat, a coloured neckerchief, which lay at the top of an open portmanteau, put on in lieu of his blue and high-buttoned frock-coat, a coat of Villefort's, of dark brown, and sloped away in front, tried on before the glass a narrow-brimmed hat of his son's, which appeared to fit him perfectly, and leaving his cane in the corner where he had deposited it, he made to whistle in his powerful hand a small bamboo switch, which the dandy deputy used when he walked, and which aided in giving him that easy swagger, which was one of his principal characteristics.

"Well," he said, turning towards his wondering son, when this disguise was completed,—" well, do you think your police will recognise me now?"

"No, father," stammered Villefort, " at least, I hope not."

" And now, my dear boy," continued Noirtier, " I rely on your prudence to remove all the things which I leave in your care."

Noirtier left the room when he had finished, with the same calmness that had characterised him during the whole of this remarkable and trying conversation.

CHAPTER X

THE HUNDRED DAYS

M. NOIRTIER was a true prophet, and things progressed rapidly as he had predicted. Every one knows the history of the famous return from Elba, a return which, without example in the past, will probably remain without imitation in the future.

Louis XVIII. made but a faint attempt to parry this unexpected blow; the monarchy he had scarcely reconstructed tottered on its precarious foundation, and it needed but a sign of the emperor to hurl to the ground all this edifice composed of ancient prejudices and new ideas. Villefort therefore gained nothing save the king's gratitude (which was rather likely to injure him at the present time), and the cross of the Legion of Honour, which he had the prudence not to wear, although M. de Blacas had duly forwarded the brevet.

Napoleon would, doubtless, have deprived Villefort of his office had it not been for Noirtier, who was all-powerful at the court; and thus the Girondin of '93 and the Senator of 1806 protected him who so lately had been his protector. All Villefort's influence barely enabled him to stifle the secret Dantès had so nearly divulged. The king's procureur alone was deprived of his office, being suspected of royalism.

However, scarcely was the imperial power established, that is, scarcely had the emperor re-entered the Tuileries and issued his numerous orders from that little cabinet into which we have introduced our readers, and on the table of which he found Louis XVIII.'s snuff-box, half full, than Marseilles began to rekindle the flames of civil war, and it required but little to excite the populace to acts of far greater violence than the shouts and insults with which they assailed the royalists whenever they ventured abroad.

Owing to this change, the worthy shipowner became at that moment, we will not say all-powerful—because Morrel was a prudent and rather a timid man, so much so, that many of the

most zealous partisans of Bonaparte accused him of " modera-
tion,"—but sufficiently influential to make a demand in favour
of Dantès.

Villefort retained his place, but his marriage was put off until
a more favourable opportunity.   If the emperor remained on
the throne, Gérard required a different alliance to aid his
career ; if Louis XVIII. returned, the influence of M. Saint-
Méran and himself became double, and the marriage must be
still more suitable.

The deputy-procureur was, therefore, the first magistrate of
Marseilles, when one morning his door opened, and M. Morrel
was announced.

"Monsieur," said Morrel, with assurance, " do you recollect
that a few days before the landing of his majesty the emperor,
I came to intercede for a young man, the mate of my ship,
who was accused of being concerned in a correspondence with
the Isle of Elba, now what was the other day a crime is to-day a
title to favour ; you then served Louis XVIII., and you did not
shew any favour—it was your duty ; to-day you serve Napoleon,
and you ought to protect him—it is equally your duty ; I come,
therefore, to ask what has become of him ?"

Villefort made a violent effort.   " What is his name ?" said
he ; " tell me his name."

"Edmond Dantès."

Villefort would evidently rather have stood opposite the
muzzle of a pistol, at five-and-twenty paces, than have heard
this name pronounced ; but he betrayed no emotion ; he opened
a large register, then went to a table, from the table turned to
his registers, and then turning to Morrel :

" Are you quite sure you are not mistaken, monsieur ?" said
he, in the most natural tone in the world.

Had Morrel been a more quick-sighted man, or better versed
in these matters, he would have been surprised at the king's
procureur answering him on such a subject, instead of referring
him to the governors of the prison or the prefect of the depart-
ment.   But Morrel, disappointed in his expectations of exciting
fear, saw only in its place condescension.   Villefort had calculated rightly.

"No," said Morrel, " I am not mistaken.   I have known him
ten years, and the last four he has been in my service.   Do not
you recollect, I came about six weeks ago to beseech your
clemency, as I come to-day to beseech your justice ; you received

me very coldly ? Oh! the royalists were very severe with the Bonapartists in those days."

"Wait a moment," said Villefort, turning over the leaves of a register. "I have it!—a sailor, who was about to marry a young Catalan girl. I recollect now, it was a very serious charge. When the prisoner left here he was taken to the Palais de Justice, I made my report to the authorities at Paris, and a week after he was carried off, probably to Fenestrelles, to Pignerol, or to the Iles Sainte-Marguerite. Some fine morning he will return to assume the command of your vessel."

"Come when he will, it shall be kept for him. But how is it he has not already returned ? It seems to me the first care of government should be to set at liberty those who have suffered for their adherence to it."

"Do not be too hasty, M. Morrel," replied Villefort. "The order of imprisonment came from high authority, and the order for his liberation must proceed from the same source: and, as Napoleon has scarcely been reinstated a fortnight, the letters have not yet been forwarded."

"Well, M. de Villefort, how would you advise me to act?"

"Petition the minister."

"The minister receives two hundred every day, and does not read three."

"That is true; but he will read a petition countersigned and presented by me."

"And will you undertake to deliver it ?"

"With the greatest pleasure. Dantès was then guilty, and now he is innocent; and it is as much my duty to free him as it was to condemn him."

Villefort dictated a petition, in which, from an excellent intention no doubt, Dantès' services were exaggerated, and he was made out one of the most active agents of Napoleon's return. It was evident that at the sight of this document the minister would instantly release him.

The petition finished, Villefort read it aloud.

"That will do," said he; "leave the rest to me."

This assurance charmed Morrel, who took leave of Villefort, and hastened to announce to old Dantès that he would soon see his son. As for Villefort, instead of sending it to Paris, he carefully preserved the petition that so fearfully compromised Dantès, in the hopes of an event that seemed not unlikely, that is, a second restoration.

After the Battle of Waterloo, Louis XVIII. remounted the throne, Villefort demanded and obtained the situation of king's procureur at Toulouse, and a fortnight afterwards married Renée.

Danglars had comprehended the full extent of the wretched fate that overwhelmed Dantès, and, like all men of small abilities, he had termed this a decree of Providence. But when Napoleon returned to Paris Danglars' heart failed him, and he feared at every instant to behold Dantès eager for vengeance : he therefore informed M. Morrel of his wish to quit the sea, and obtained a recommendation from him to a Spanish merchant, into whose service he entered at the end of March, that is, ten or twelve days after Napoleon's return. He then left for Madrid, and was no more heard of.

Fernand understood nothing except that Dantès was absent. What had become of him ? He cared not to inquire.

During this time every man in France capable of bearing arms rushed to obey the summons of their emperor. Fernand departed with the rest, bearing with him the terrible thought, that perhaps his rival was behind him, and would marry Mercédès.

Caderousse was, like Fernand, enrolled in the army ; but, being married, and eight years older, he was merely sent to the frontier.

Old Dantès, who was only sustained by hope, lost it all at Napoleon's downfall. Five months after he had been separated from his son, and almost at the very hour at which he was arrested, he breathed his last in Mercédès' arms.

M. Morrel paid the expenses of his funeral and the few small debts the poor old man had contracted.

There was more than benevolence in this action ; there was courage ; for to assist, even on his death-bed, the father of so dangerous a Bonapartist as Dantès was stigmatised as a crime.

CHAPTER XI

A YEAR after Louis XVIII.'s restoration a visit was made by the inspector-general of prisons.

Dantès heard from the recesses of his cell the noises made by the preparations for receiving him,—sounds that at the depth where he lay would have been inaudible to any but the ear of a prisoner, who could distinguish the splash of the drop of water that every hour fell from the roof of his dungeon. He guessed something uncommon was passing among the living; but he had so long ceased to have any intercourse with the world that he looked upon himself as dead.

When the inspector had been the usual round, he asked if there were any more prisoners.

"A most dangerous conspirator, a man we are ordered to keep the most strict watch over, as he is daring and resolute; also we have in a dungeon about twenty feet distant, and to which you descend by another stair, an abbé, ancient leader of a party in Italy, who has been here since 1811, and in 1813 he went mad, and the change is astonishing. He used to weep, he now laughs; he grew thin, he now grows fat. You had better see him, for his madness is amusing."

"I will see them both," returned the inspector; "I must conscientiously perform my duty."

At the sound of the key turning in the lock, and the creaking of the hinges, Dantès, who was crouched in a corner of the dungeon, raised his head.

At the sight of a stranger, lighted by two turnkeys, accompanied by two soldiers, and to whom the governor spoke bareheaded, Dantès, who guessed that the moment to address himself to the superior authorities was come, sprang forward with clasped hands.

The soldiers presented their bayonets, for they thought he was about to attack the inspector, and the latter recoiled two or three steps. Dantès saw he was represented as a dangerous prisoner. Then infusing all the humility he possessed into his eyes and voice, he addressed the inspector, and sought to inspire him with pity.

The inspector listened attentively, then turning to the governor, observed, " He will become religious—he is already more gentle ; he is afraid and retreated before the bayonets—madmen are not afraid of anything; I made some curious observations on this at Charenton." Then turning to the prisoner, " What do you demand ?" said he.

" Whatever crime I have committed that I may be tried ; and if I am guilty, I may be shot ; if innocent, I may be set at liberty."

" When were you arrested ?" asked the inspector.

"The 28th of February, 1815, at half-past two in the afternoon."

" To-day is the 30th of June, 1816 ; why, it is but seventeen months.'

" Only seventeen months !" replied Dantès ; " oh, you do not know what is seventeen months in prison !—seventeen ages rather, especially to a man who, like me, had arrived at the summit of his ambition—to a man who, like me, was on the point of marrying a woman he adored, who saw an honourable career open before him, and who loses all in an instant, who sees his prospects destroyed, and is ignorant of the fate of his affianced wife, and whether his aged father be still living ! Seventeen months' captivity to a sailor accustomed to the boundless ocean is a worse punishment than human crime ever merited. Have pity on me, then, and ask for me, not indulgence, but a trial—let me know my crime and my sentence, for incertitude is worse than all."

" We shall see," said the inspector ; then turning to the governor, " On my word, the poor devil touches me ;" turning to Dantès he added, " I can only promise to examine into your case. Who arrested you ?"

" M. Villefort ; see him, and hear what he says."

" M. Villefort is no longer at Marseilles, he is now at Toulouse."

"I am no longer surprised at my detention," murmured Dantès, " since my only protector is removed."

" Had M. de Villefort any cause of personal dislike to you ?"

" None ; on the contrary, he was very kind to me."

" I can then rely on the notes he has left concerning you ?"

" Entirely."

" That is well ; wait patiently, then."

" Will you see the register at once," asked the governor, " or proceed to the other cell ?"

" Let us visit them all," said the inspector ; " if I once mounted the stairs I should never have the courage to descend."

" This one fancies he possesses an immense treasure : the first year he offered government a million of francs (40,000*l*.) for his release, the second two, the third three, and so on progressively, he is now in his fifth year of captivity, he will ask to speak to you in private, and offer you five millions."

They entered the cell. " What is your name ?" the inspector asked the prisoner.

" I am the Abbé Faria, born at Rome. I was for twenty years Cardinal Spada's secretary ; I was arrested, why I know not, in 1811, since then I have demanded my liberty from the Italian and French government."

" I am come to inquire if you have anything to ask or to complain of."

" The food is the same as in other prisons,—that is very bad, the lodging is very unwholesome, but on the whole passable for a dungeon, but it is not that which I speak of, but a secret I have to reveal of the greatest importance. I would speak to you of a large sum amounting to five millions."

" The government does not want your treasures," replied the inspector ; " keep them until you are liberated."

The abbé's eyes glistened ; he seized the inspector's hand.

" But what if I am not liberated," cried he, " and am detained here until my death ? Had not government better profit by it ? I will offer six millions, and I will content myself with the rest."

" On my word," said the inspector, in a low tone, " had I not been told beforehand this man was mad I should believe what he says."

" I am not mad !" replied Faria, with that acuteness of hearing peculiar to prisoners. " The treasure I speak of really exists, and I offer to sign a treaty with you, in which I promise to lead you to the spot you shall dig, and if I deceive you, bring me here again,—I ask no more."

The governor laughed. " Is the spot far from here ?"

" A hundred leagues."

" It is not a bad idea," said the governor.

"If every prisoner took it into his head to travel a hundred leagues, and their guardians consented to accompany them, they would have a capital chance of escaping."

The inspector kept his word with Dantès : he examined the register, and found the following note concerning him,—

EDMOND DANTÈS { Violent Bonapartist ; took an active part in the return from Elba. The greatest watchfulness and care to be exercised.

This note was in a different hand from the rest, which proved it had been added since his confinement.

The inspector could not contend against this accusation ; he simply wrote,—

"Nothing to be done."

This visit had infused new vigour into Dantès ; he had, till then, forgotten the date ; but now, with a fragment of plaster, he wrote the date, 30th July, 1816 ; and made a mark every day, in order not to lose his reckoning again.   Days and weeks passed away, then months, Dantès still waited ; he at first expected to be freed in a fortnight.   This fortnight expired ; he reflected the inspector would do nothing until his return to Paris ; and that he would not reach there until his circuit was finished ; he, therefore, fixed three months : three months passed away, then six more.   During these ten months no favourable change had taken place ; and Dantès began to fancy the inspector's visit was but a dream, an illusion of the brain.

At the expiration of a year the governor was changed ; he had obtained the government of Ham.   He took with him several of his subordinates, and amongst them Dantès' gaoler. A fresh governor arrived ; it would have been too tedious to acquire the names of the prisoners, he learned their numbers instead.

This horrible place consisted of fifty chambers ; their inhabitants were designated by the number of their chamber ; and the unhappy young man was no longer called Edmond Dantès, he was now number 34.

Dantès passed through all the degrees of misfortune that prisoners, forgotten in their dungeon, suffer.   He commenced with pride, a natural consequence of hope, and a consciousness of innocence ; then he began to doubt his own innocence, which justified in some measure the governor's belief in his mental alienation; and then falling into the opposite extreme, he supplicated, not heaven, but his gaoler.

He besought the gaoler one day to let him have a companion, were it even the mad abbé.

The gaoler, though rude and hardened by the constant sight of so much suffering, was yet a man. At the bottom of his heart he had often compassionated the unhappy young man who suffered thus; and he laid the request of number 34 before the governor; but the latter sapiently imagined that Dantès wished to conspire, or attempt an escape, and refused his request.

Rage succeeded to this. Dantès uttered blasphemies that made his gaoler recoil with horror, dashed himself furiously against the walls of his prison, attacked everything, chiefly himself, and the least thing, a grain of sand, a straw, or a breath of air that annoyed him. Then, the letter he had seen that Villefort had shewed to him recurred to his mind, and every line seemed visible in fiery letters on the wall, like the *Mene, Tekel, Upharsin,* of Belshazzar. He said that it was the vengeance of man, and not of heaven, that had thus plunged him into the deepest misery. He consigned these unknown persecutors to the most horrible tortures he could imagine, and found them all insufficient, because, after torture came death, and after death, if not repose, at least that insensibility that resembles it.

By dint of constantly dwelling on the idea that repose was death, and in order to punish, other tortures than death must be invented, he began to reflect on suicide.

"I wish to die," thought he. "When my morning and evening meals are brought," thought he, "I will cast them out of the window, and I shall be believed to have eaten them."

He kept his word; twice a day he cast out, by the barred aperture, the provisions his gaoler brought him, at first gaily, then with deliberation, and at last with regret; nothing but the recollection of his oath gave him strength to proceed. Hunger rendered these viands, once so repugnant, acceptable to him; he held the plate in his hand for an hour at a time, and gazed on the morsel of bad meat, of tainted fish, of black and mouldy bread. It was the last struggle of life, which occasionally vanquished his resolve; then his dungeon seemed less sombre, his prospects less desperate. He was still young, he was only four or five-and-twenty, he had nearly fifty years to live. What unforeseen events might not open his prison-door and restore him to liberty? Thus he raised to his lips the repast that, like a voluntary Tantalus, he refused himself; but he thought of his oath, and he would not break it. He persisted until, at last, he had not sufficient force to cast his supper out of the loophole.

The next morning he could not see or hear; the gaoler feared he was dangerously ill. Edmond hoped he was dying.

The day passed away thus: Edmond felt a species of stupor creeping over him, the gnawing pain at his stomach had ceased, his thirst had abated, when he closed his eyes he saw myriads of lights dancing before them, like the meteors that play about the marshes. It was the twilight of that mysterious country called Death!

Suddenly, about nine o'clock in the evening, Edmond heard a hollow sound in the wall against which he was lying. So many loathsome animals inhabited the prison, that their noise did not, in general, awake him; but whether abstinence had quickened his faculties, or whether the noise was really louder than usual, it was sufficient to make him raise his head and listen. It was a continual scratching, as if made by a huge claw, a powerful tooth, or some iron instrument, attacking the stones.

Although weakened, the young man's brain instantly recurred to the idea that haunts all prisoners—liberty! It seemed to him that Heaven had at length taken pity on him, and had sent this noise to warn him on the very brink of the abyss. Perhaps one of those beloved ones he had so often thought of was thinking of him, and striving to diminish the distance that separated them.

Dantès still heard the sound. It lasted nearly three hours; he then heard a noise of something falling, and all was silent. Some hours afterwards, it began nearer and more distinct; Edmond was immensely interested in that labour, when the gaoler entered.

For the week that he had resolved to die, and for the four days that he put this resolution into execution, Edmond had not spoken to this man, had not answered him when he inquired what was the matter with him, and turned his face to the wall when he looked too curiously at him; but now the gaoler might hear this noise and put an end to it, thus destroying a ray of something like hope that soothed his last moments.

The gaoler brought him his breakfast. Dantès raised himself up, and began to speak on everything; on the bad quality of his food, on the coldness of his dungeon, grumbling and complaining, in order to have an excuse for speaking louder, and wearying the patience of his gaoler, who had solicited some broth and white bread for his prisoner, and had brought it.

Fortunately he fancied Dantès was delirious; and placing his food on the rickety table, he withdrew.

Edmond listened, and the sound became more and more distinct.

"There can be no doubt," thought he, "it is some prisoner who is striving to obtain his freedom."

Suddenly another idea took possession of his mind, so used to misfortune, that it could scarcely understand hope; yet this idea possessed him, that the noise arose from the workmen the governor had ordered to repair the neighbouring dungeon.

He turned his eyes towards the soup his gaoler had brought him, rose, staggered towards it, raised the vessel to his lips and drank off the contents with a feeling of indescribable pleasure. He had often heard that shipwrecked persons had died through having eagerly devoured too much food, so he replaced on the table the bread he was about to devour, and returned to his couch: he did not wish to die. He soon felt that his ideas became again collected, he could think and strengthen his thoughts by reasoning. Then he said to himself, "I must put this to the test, but without compromising anybody. If it is a workman I need but knock against the wall, and he will cease to work in order to find out who is knocking, and why he does so, but as his occupation is sanctioned by the governor, he will soon resume it; if, on the contrary, it is a prisoner the noise I make will alarm him, he will cease and not recommence until he thinks everyone is asleep."

Edmond rose again, but this time his legs did not tremble, and his eyes were free from mists: he advanced to a corner of his dungeon, detached a stone, and with it knocked against the wall where the sound came. He struck thrice.

At the first blow the sound ceased, as if by magic.

Edmond listened intently, an hour passed, two hours passed, and no sound was heard from the wall, all was silent there.

Full of hope, Edmond swallowed a few mouthfuls of bread and water, and thanks to the excellence of his constitution, found himself well-nigh recovered.

In the morning the gaoler brought him fresh provisions, he had already devoured those of the previous day, he ate these, listening anxiously for the sound, walking round and round his cell, shaking the iron bars of the loophole, restoring by exercise vigour and agility to his limbs, and preparing himself thus for his future destiny. At intervals he listened if the noise had not begun again, and grew impatient at the prudence of the prisoner who did not guess he had been disturbed by a captive as anxious for liberty as himself.

Three days passed—seventy-two long tedious hours!

At length one evening as the gaoler was visiting him for the last time that night, Dantès fancied he heard an almost imperceptible movement among the stones. He recoiled from the wall, walked up and down his cell to collect his thoughts, and replaced his ear against the wall. There could be no doubt something was passing on the other side, the prisoner had discovered the danger, and had substituted the lever for the chisel. Encouraged by this discovery, he determined to assist the indefatigable labourer, he began by moving his bed, and sought with his eyes for anything with which he could pierce the wall, penetrate the cement, and displace a stone.

He saw nothing, he had no knife or sharp instrument, the grating of his window alone was of iron, and he had too often assured himself of its solidity. All his furniture consisted of a bed, a chair, a table, a pail, and a jug. The bed had iron clamps, but they were screwed to the wood, and it would have required a screwdriver to take them off. The table and chair had nothing, the pail had had a handle, but that had been removed. He had but one resource, which was to break the jug, and with one of the sharp fragments attack the wall. He let the jug fall on the floor, and it broke in pieces. He concealed two or three of the sharpest fragments in his bed, leaving the rest on the floor. The breaking of his jug was too natural an accident to excite suspicion, he had all the night to work in, but in the darkness he could not do much; and he soon felt his instrument was blunted against something hard, he pushed back his bed and awaited the day. All night he heard the subterranean workman, who continued to mine his way. The day came, the gaoler entered. Dantès told him the jug had fallen from his hands in drinking, and the gaoler went grumblingly to fetch another, without giving himself the trouble to remove the fragments of the broken one. He returned speedily, recommended the prisoner to be more careful, and departed.

Dantès heard joyfully the key grate in the lock, he listened until the sound of steps died away and then hastily displacing his bed, saw by the faint light that penetrated into his cell, that he had laboured uselessly the previous evening in attacking the stone instead of removing the plaster that surrounded it.

The damp had rendered it friable and Dantès saw joyfully the plaster detach itself, in small morsels, it is true, but at the end of half an hour he had scraped off a handful : a mathematician might have calculated that in two years, supposing that the rock was not encountered, a passage twenty feet long and two feet broad might be formed.

The prisoner reproached himself with not having thus employed the hours he had passed in prayers and despair.

In three days he had succeeded, with the utmost precaution, in removing the cement, and exposing the stone ; the wall was formed of rough stones, and to give solidity to them were embedded, at intervals, blocks of hewn stone. It was one of these he had uncovered, and which he must remove from its socket. He strove to do so with his nails, but they were too weak. The fragments of the jug broke, and after an hour of useless toil, Dantès paused. Suddenly an idea occurred to him, he smiled, and the perspiration dried on his forehead.

The gaoler always brought his soup in an iron saucepan, this saucepan contained the soup of a second prisoner, for Dantès had remarked that it was either quite full, or half empty, according as the turnkey gave it to himself or his companion first. The handle of this saucepan was of iron, Dantès would have given ten years of his life in exchange for it. The gaoler poured the contents of this saucepan into his plate. In the evening Dantès placed his plate on the ground near the door, the gaoler as he entered stepped on it and broke it. This time he could not blame the prisoner.

He, therefore, contented himself with grumbling. Then he looked about him for something to pour the soup into ; the whole furniture consisted of one plate, there was no alternative.

" Leave the saucepan," said Dantès, " you can take it away when you bring me my breakfast." This advice was to the gaoler's taste, as it spared him the necessity of ascending, descending, and ascending again. He left the saucepan.

Dantès was beside himself with joy. He rapidly devoured his food, and after waiting an hour lest the gaoler should change his mind and return, he removed his bed, took the handle of the saucepan, inserted the point between the hewn stone and rough stones of the wall, and employed it as a lever. A slight oscillation showed him all went well. At the end of an hour the stone was extricated from the wall, leaving a cavity of a foot and a half in diameter.

Dantès carefully collected the plaster, carried it into the corners of his cell, and covered it with earth. Then wishing to make the best use of this night, in which chance, or rather, his own stratagem, had placed so precious an instrument in his hands, he continued to work without ceasing. At the dawn of day he replaced the stone, pushed his bed against the wall, and lay down. The breakfast consisted of a piece of bread, the gaoler entered and placed the bread on the table.

" You do not bring me another plate ?" said Dantès.

" No," replied the turnkey, " you destroy everything ; first you break your jug, then you make me break your plate ; if all the prisoners followed your example the government would be ruined ; I shall leave you the saucepan and pour your soup into that, so for the future I hope you will not be so destructive to your furniture."

Dantès felt more gratitude for the possession of this piece of iron than he had ever felt for anything ; he had, however, re-marked that the prisoner on the other side had ceased to labour.

All day he toiled on untiringly, and by the evening he had succeeded in extracting ten handfuls of plaster and fragments of stone.

When the hour for his gaoler's visit arrived, Dantès straightened the handle of the saucepan as well as he could and placed it in its accustomed place. The turnkey poured his ration of soup into it, together with the fish, for thrice a week the prisoners were made to abstain from meat : this would have been a method of reckoning time had not Dantès long ceased to do so.

Having poured out the soup, the turnkey retired.

Dantès toiled on all the night, without being discouraged ; but after two or three hours he encountered an obstacle. The iron made no impression, but met with a smooth surface ; he touched it, and found it was a beam. This beam crossed, or rather blocked up, the hole he had made. It was necessary, therefore, to dig above or under it.

The unhappy young man had not thought of this.

" Oh, my God ! my God !" murmured he, " I have so earnestly prayed to you, that I hoped my prayers have been heard. After having deprived me of my liberty, after having deprived me of death, after having recalled me to existence, my God! have pity on me, and do not let me die in despair."

"Who talks of God and despair at the same time?" said a voice that seemed to come from beneath the earth, and, deadened by the distance, sounded hollow and sepulchral in the young man's ears.

Edmond's hair stood on end, and he rose on his knees

"Ah!" said he, "I hear a human voice." He had not heard anyone speak save his gaoler for four or five years, and a gaoler is not a man to a prisoner, he is a living door added to his door of oak, a barrier of flesh and blood added to his barriers of iron.

"In the name of Heaven," cried Dantès, "speak again, though the sound of your voice terrifies me."

"Who are you?" said the voice.

"An unhappy prisoner," replied Dantès, who made no hesitation in answering. "A Frenchman called Edmond Dantès."

"Your profession?"

"A sailor."

"How long have you been here?"

"Since the 28th of February, 1815."

"Of what are you accused?"

"Of having conspired to aid the emperor's return."

"How for the emperor's return? the emperor is no longer on the throne then?"

"He abdicated at Fontainebleau in 1814, and was sent to the island of Elba: but how long have you been here that you are ignorant of all this?"

"Since 1811."

Dantès shuddered, this man had been four years longer than himself in prison.

"Do not dig any more," said the voice; "only tell me how high up is your excavation?"

"On a level with the floor."

"How is it concealed?"

"Behind my bed."

"Has your bed been moved since you have been a prisoner?"

"No."

"What does your chamber open on?"

"A corridor."

"And the corridor?"

"On a court."

"Alas!" murmured the voice.

"Oh, what is the matter?" cried Dantès.

"I am deceived, and the imperfection of my plans has ruined

all.   An error of a line in the plan has been equivalent to fifteen
feet in reality, and I took the wall you are mining for the wall
of the fortress."

"But then you were close to the sea?"

"That is what I hoped."

"And supposing you succeeded?"

"I should have thrown myself into the sea, gained one of the
islands near here,—the Isle de Daume or the Isle de Tiboulen,
and then I was safe."

"Tell me, at least, who you are?"

"I am—I am Number 27."

"You mistrust me, then?" said Dantès.

He fancied he heard a bitter laugh proceed from the unknown.

"Oh! I am a Christian," cried Dantès, guessing instinctively
that this man meant to abandon him.   " I swear to you by Him
who died for us that nought shall induce me to breathe one
syllable to my gaolers, but I conjure you do not abandon me.   If
you do, I swear to you that I will dash my brains out against the
wall, and you will have my death to reproach yourself with."

"How old are you?   Your voice is that of a young man."

"I do not know my age, for I have not counted the years I
have been here.   All I know is, that I was just nineteen when I
was arrested the 28th of February, 1815."

"Not quite twenty-six!" murmured the voice; "at that age
he cannot be a traitor."

"Oh! no, no!" cried Dantès, "I swear to you again, rather
than betray you they shall hew me to pieces!"

"You have done well to speak to me, and entreat me, for I was
about to form another plan, and leave you; but your age reassures
me.   I will not forget you; expect me."

"When?"

"I must calculate our chances; I will give you the signal."

"But you will not leave me; you will come to me, or you will
let me come to you.   We will escape, and if we cannot escape,
we will talk, you of those whom you love, and I of those whom I
love.   You must love somebody?"

"No, I am alone in the world."

"Then you will love me.   If you are young, I will be your
comrade; if you are old, I will be your son.   I have a father, who
is seventy, if he yet lives: I only love him and a young girl called
Mercédès.   My father has not yet forgotten me, I am sure; but
God alone knows if she loves me still: I shall love you as I loved
my father."

"It is well," returned the voice; "to-morrow."

These few words were uttered with an accent that left no doubt of his sincerity; Dantès rose, dispersed the fragments with the same precaution as before, and pushed back his bed against the wall. He then gave himself up to his happiness: he would no longer be alone. He was, perhaps, about to regain his liberty; at the worst, he would have a companion, and captivity that is shared is but half captivity.

All day Dantès walked up and down his cell. He sat down occasionally on his bed, pressing his hand on his heart. At the slightest noise he bounded towards the door. Once or twice the thought crossed his mind that he might be separated from this unknown, whom he loved already, and then his mind was made up,—when the gaoler moved his bed and stooped to examine the opening, he would kill him with his water-jug.

He would be condemned to die, but he was about to die of grief and despair when this miraculous noise recalled him to life.

The gaoler came in the evening; Dantès was on his bed. It seemed to him that thus he better guarded the unfinished opening. Doubtless there was a strange expression in his eyes, for the gaoler said, "Come, are you going mad again?"

Dantès did not answer: he feared that the emotion of his voice would betray him.

The gaoler retired, shaking his head.

The night came; Dantès hoped that his neighbour would profit by the silence to address him, but he was mistaken. The next morning, however, just as he removed his bed from the wall, he heard three knocks; he threw himself on his knees.

"Is it you?" said he, "I am here."

"Is your gaoler gone?"

"Yes," said Dantès, "he will not return until the evening, so that we have twelve hours before us."

"I can work then?" said the voice.

"Oh! yes, yes, this instant, I entreat you."

A moment later the portion of the floor on which Dantès (half buried in the opening) was leaning his two hands gave way: he cast himself back, whilst a mass of stones and earth disappeared in a hole that opened beneath the aperture he himself had formed. Then from the bottom of this passage, the depth of which it was impossible to measure, he saw appear, first, the head, then the shoulders, and lastly the body of a man, who sprang lightly into his cell.

CHAPTER XII.

A LEARNED ITALIAN

RUSHING towards the friend so long and ardently desired, Dantès almost carried him towards the window, in order to obtain a better view of his features by the aid of the imperfect light that struggled through the grating of the prison.

He was a man of small stature, with hair blanched rather by suffering and sorrow than years. A deep-set, penetrating eye, almost buried beneath the thick grey eyebrow, and a long (and still black) beard reaching down to his breast. The meagreness of his limbs, shrunken beneath their covering, joined to the bold outline of his strongly marked features, announced a man more accustomed to exercise his moral faculties than his physical strength. Large drops of perspiration were now standing on his brow, while his garments hung about him in such rags as to render it useless to form a guess as to their primitive description.

The stranger might have numbered sixty, or sixty-five years, but a certain briskness and appearance of vigour in his movements made it probable that he was aged more from captivity than the course of time. He received the enthusiastic greeting of his young acquaintance with evident pleasure, as though his chilled affections seemed re-kindled and invigorated by his contact with one so warm and ardent. He thanked him with grateful cordiality for his kindly welcome, although he must at that moment have been suffering bitterly to find another dungeon where he had fondly reckoned on discovering a means of regaining his liberty.

"Let us first see," said he, "whether it is possible to remove the traces of my entrance here—our future comfort depends upon our gaolers being entirely ignorant of it." Advancing to the opening, he stooped and raised the stone as easily as though it had not weighed an ounce; then fitting it into its place, he said,—

"You removed this stone very carelessly; but I suppose you had no tools to aid you."

"Why!" exclaimed Dantès, with astonishment, "do you possess any?"

" I made myself some; and with the exception of a file, I have all that are necessary—a chisel, pincers, and lever; here is my chisel!"

So saying, he displayed a sharp strong blade, with a handle made of beech-wood.

"I made it with one of the clamps of my bedstead; and this very tool has sufficed to hollow out the road by which I came hither, a distance of at least fifty feet."

" Fifty feet!" re-echoed Dantès, with a species of terror.

"Do not speak so loud, young man!—don't speak so loud! It frequently occurs in a state prison like this, that persons are stationed outside the doors of the cells purposely to overhear the conversation of the prisoners."

" And you say that you penetrated a length of fifty feet to arrive here?" Dantès asked in a lowered voice.

" I do! that is about the distance that separates your chamber from mine—only unfortunately I did not curve aright; for want of the necessary geometrical instruments to calculate my scale of proportion; instead of taking an ellipsis of forty feet, I have made fifty. I expected, as I told you, to reach the outer wall, pierce through it, and throw myself into the sea; I have, however, kept along the corridor on which your chamber opens, instead of going beneath it. My labour is all in vain, for I find that the corridor looks into a court-yard filled with soldiers."

" That's true," said Dantès; "but the corridor you speak of only bounds *one* side of my cell; there are three others—do you know anything of their situation?"

" This one is built against the solid rock, and it would take ten experienced miners, duly furnished with the requisite tools, as many years to perforate it;—this adjoins the lower part of the governor's apartments, and were we to work our way through, we should only get into some lock-up cellars, where we must necessarily be recaptured; the fourth and last side of your cell looks out—looks out—stop a minute, now where does it open to?"

The side which thus excited curiosity was the one where was fixed the loophole through which light was admitted into the chamber. This loophole gradually diminished as it approached the outside, until it ended in an opening through which a child could not have passed, and this was, for better security, furnished with three iron bars, so as to quiet all apprehensions even in the mind of the most suspicious gaoler as to the possibility of a prisoner's escape.

As the stranger finished his self-put question, he dragged the table beneath the window.

"Climb up," said he to Dantès.—The young man obeyed, mounted on the table, and, divining the intentions of his companion, placed his back securely against the wall, and held out both hands. The stranger, whom as yet Dantès knew only by the number of his cell, sprang up with an agility by no means to be expected in a person of his years, and light and steady as the bound of a cat or a lizard, climbed from the table to the outstretched hands of Dantès, and from them to his shoulders; then, almost doubling himself in two, for the ceiling of the dungeon prevented his holding himself erect, he managed to slip his head through the top bar of the window, so as to be able to command a perfect view from top to bottom.

An instant afterwards he hastily drew back his head, saying, "I thought so!" and sliding from the shoulders of Dantès, as dexterously as he had ascended, he nimbly leapt from the table to the ground.

"What made you say those words?" asked the young man, in an anxious tone, in his turn descending from the table.

The elder prisoner appeared to meditate; "Yes," said he at length, "it is so.   This side of your chamber looks out upon a kind of open gallery, where patrols are continually passing, and sentries keep watch day and night."

"Are you quite sure of that?"

"Certain.   I saw the soldier's helmet and the top of his musket; that made me draw my head in so quickly, for I was fearful he might also see me.   Now you see the utter impossibility of escaping through your dungeon?"

"Then," pursued the young man eagerly——

"Then," answered the elder prisoner, "the will of God be done!" and as he slowly pronounced those words, an air of profound resignation spread itself over his care-worn countenance.

Dantès gazed on the individual who could thus philosophically resign hopes so long and ardently nourished with an astonishment mingled with admiration.

"Tell me, I entreat of you, who, and what you are?" said he at length; "never have I met with so remarkable a person as yourself."

The stranger smiled a melancholy smile.   "Then listen,"

said he; "I am the Abbé Faria, and have been imprisoned in this Château d'If since the year 1811; previously to which I had been confined for three years in the fortress of Fenestrelle. In the year 1811 I was transferred to Piedmont in France; I was very far then from expecting the change you have just informed me of, namely, that four years afterwards this colossus of power would be overthrown. Then who reigns in France at this moment? Napoleon II.?"

"No, Louis XVIII.! But why are you here?"

"Because in 1807 I meditated the very scheme Napoleon wished to realise in 1811."

"Excuse my question," said Dantès, "but are you not the priest who is considered throughout the Château d'If—to—be—ill?"

"Mad, you mean, don't you?"

"I did not like to say so," answered Dantès, smiling.

"Well, then," resumed Faria, with a bitter smile, "let me answer your question in full, by acknowledging that I am the poor mad prisoner of the Château d'If, for many years permitted to amuse the different visitors to the prison with what is said to be my insanity."

Dantès remained for a short time mute and motionless; at length he said, "Then you abandon all hope of flight?"

"I perceive its utter impossibility; and I consider it impious to attempt that which the Almighty evidently does not approve."

"Nay be not discouraged. Would it not be expecting too much to hope to succeed at your first attempt? Why not try to find an opening in another direction from that which had so unfortunately failed?"

The abbé sank upon Edmond's bed, while Edmond himself remained standing, lost in a train of deep meditation. Flight had never once occurred to him.—There are, indeed, some things which appear so morally impossible that the mind does not dwell on them for an instant. To undermine the ground for fifty feet—to devote three years to a labour which, if successful, would conduct you to a precipice overhanging the sea—to plunge into the waves at a height of fifty or sixty feet, at the risk of being dashed to pieces against the rocks, should you have been fortunate enough to have escaped the balls from the sentinel's musket; and even, supposing all these perils past, to have to swim for your life a distance of at least three miles ere you could reach the shore—were difficulties so startling and formidable that Dantès had never even dreamed of such a scheme, but resigned himself to his fate. But the sight of an old man clinging to life with so desperate a courage gave a fresh turn to his ideas, and inspired him with new resource and energy.

The young man suddenly exclaimed, " I have found what you were in search of."

Faria started. " Have you, indeed ?" cried he, raising his head with quick anxiety : " pray let me know what it is you have discovered."

" The corridor through which you have bored your way from the cell you occupy here extends in the same direction as the outer gallery. We must pierce through the corridor by forming a side opening about the middle, as it were the top part of a cross. This time you will lay your plans more accurately ; we shall get out into the gallery you have described ; kill the sentinel who guards it, and make our escape."

" One instant, my dear friend," replied the abbé ; " I have thought it no sin to bore through a wall, or destroy a staircase, but I cannot so easily persuade myself to pierce a heart or take away a life."

A slight movement of surprise escaped Dantès. "Is it possible," said he, " that where your liberty is at stake you can allow any such scruple to deter you from obtaining it ?"

" Tell me," replied Faria, " what has hindered you from knocking down your gaoler with a piece of wood torn from your bedstead, dressing yourself in his clothes, and endeavouring to escape ?"

" Simply that I never thought of such a scheme," answered Dantès.

" Because," said the old man, " the natural repugnance to the commission of such a crime prevented its bare idea from occurring to you. Chance, however, frequently affords opportunities we should never ourselves have thought of. Let us, therefore, wait patiently for some favourable moment ; rely upon it, you will not find me more backward than yourself in seizing it."

" Ah !" said Dantès, " you might well endure the tedious delay ; you were constantly occupied in the task you set yourself, and when weary with toil, you had your hopes to refresh and encourage you."

" I assure you," replied the old man, " I did not turn to that source for recreation or support. I wrote or studied."

" Were you then permitted the use of pens, ink, and paper ?"

" Oh, no !" answered the abbé ; " I had none but what I made for myself. When you pay me a visit in my cell, I will show you an entire work, the fruits of the thoughts and reflections of my whole life ; many of them meditated over in the ruins of the Coliseum of Rome, at the foot of St. Mark's Column at Venice, and on the borders of the Arno at Florence, little imagining at the time that they would be arranged in order within the walls of the Château d'If. The work I speak of is called ' *A Treatise on the Practicability of forming Italy into one General Monarchy,*' and will make one large quarto volume."

" And on what have you written all this ?"

" On two of my shirts. I invented a preparation that makes linen as smooth and as easy to write on as parchment."

" But for such a work you must have needed books,—had you any ?"

" I possessed nearly 5,000 volumes in my library at Rome, but after reading them over many times, I found out that with 150 well-chosen books a man possesses a complete analysis of all human knowledge, or at least all that is either useful or desirable to be acquainted with. I devoted three years of my life to reading and studying these 150 volumes, till I knew them nearly by heart. So that since I have been in prison, a very slight effort of memory has enabled me to recall their contents as readily as though the pages were open before me. I could recite you the whole of Thucydides, Xenophon, Plutarch, Titus Livius, Tacitus, Strada, Jornandès, Dante, Montaigne, Shakespeare, Spinosa, Machiavel, and Bossuet. Observe, I merely quote the important names and writers."

" You are, doubtless, acquainted with a variety of languages, so as to have been able to read all these ?"

" Yes ; I speak five of the modern tongues ; that is to say, German, French, Italian, English, and Spanish ; by the aid of ancient Greek I learned modern Greek—I don't speak it so well as I could wish, but I am still trying to improve myself."

" Improve yourself !" repeated Dantès ; " how can you manage to do so ?"

" Why, I made a vocabulary of the words I knew ; turned, returned, and arranged them, so as to enable me to express my thoughts through their medium. I know nearly one thousand words, which is all that is absolutely necessary, although I believe there are nearly one hundred thousand in the dictionaries.

I cannot hope to be very fluent, but I certainly should have no difficulty in explaining my wants and wishes; and that would be quite as much as I should ever require."

Stronger grew the wonder of Dantès, who almost fancied he had to do with one gifted with supernatural powers—still hoping to find some imperfection which might bring him down to a level with human beings, he added, "Then if you were not furnished with pens, how did you manage to write the work you speak of?"

"I made myself some excellent ones, which would be universally preferred to all others, if once known. You are aware what huge whitings are served to us on *maigre* days. Well, I selected the cartilages of the heads of these fishes, and you can scarcely imagine the delight with which I welcomed the arrival of each Wednesday, Friday, and Saturday, as affording me the means of increasing my stock of pens; for I will freely confess that my historical labours have been my greatest solace and relief. While retracing the past, I forget the present; and while following the free and independent course of historical record, I cease to remember that I am myself immured within the gloomy walls of a dungeon."

"But the ink," said Dantès; "how have you procured that?"

"I will tell you," replied Faria; "there was formerly a fire-place in my dungeon, closed up long ere I became an occupant of this prison. Still it must have been many years in use, for it was thickly covered with a coating of soot; this soot I dissolved in a portion of the wine brought to me every Sunday; and I assure you a better ink cannot be desired: for very important notes, for which closer attention is required, I have pricked one of my fingers, and written the facts claiming notice in blood."

"And when," asked Dantès, "will you shew me all this?"

"Whenever you please," replied the abbé.

"Oh, then! let it be directly," exclaimed the young man.

"Follow me, then," said the abbé, as he re-entered the subterraneous passage, in which he soon disappeared, followed by Dantès.

CHAPTER XIII

AFTER having passed with tolerable ease through the subterranean passage, which, however, did not permit of their holding themselves erect, the two friends reached the further end of the corridor, into which the cell of the abbé opened; from that point the opening became much narrower, barely permitting an individual to creep through on his hands and knees. The floor of the abbé's cell was paved, and it had been by raising one of the stones in the most obscure corner that Faria had been able to commence the laborious task of which Dantès had witnessed the completion.

The abbé proceeded to the disused fireplace, raised, by the help of his chisel, a long stone which had doubtless been the hearth, beneath which was a cavity of considerable depth, serving as a safe depository of the articles mentioned to Dantès.

He drew forth from its hiding-place three or four rolls of linen, laid one over the other, like the folds of papyrus found in mummy-cases; these rolls consisted of slips of cloth about four inches wide and eighteen long; they were all carefully numbered and closely covered with writing, so legible that Dantès could easily read it, as well as make out the sense—it being in Italian, a language he, as a Provençal, perfectly understood.

"There!" said he, "there is the work complete—I wrote the word *finis* at the end of the last page about a week ago. I have torn up two of my shirts, and as many handkerchiefs as I was master of, to complete the precious pages. Should I ever get out of prison, and find a printer courageous enough to publish what I have composed, my literary reputation is for ever secured."

"I see," answered Dantès. "Now let me behold the curious pens with which you have written your work."

"Look!" said Faria, shewing to the young man a slender stick about six inches long, and much resembling the handle of a fine painting brush, to the end of which was tied by a piece

93

of thread one of those cartilages of which the abbé had before spoken to Dantès—it was pointed, and divided at the nib like an ordinary pen.

Dantès examined it with intense admiration, then looked around to see the instrument with which it had been shaped so correctly into form.

"Ah, I see!" said Faria, "you are wondering where I found my penknife, are not you? Well, I must confess that I look upon that article of my ingenuity as the very perfection of all my handiwork. I made it, as well as this knife, out of an old iron candlestick."

The penknife was sharp and keen as a razor :—as for the other knife, it possessed the double advantage of being capable of serving as a dagger also.

Dantès laid the different things he had been looking at gently on the table, and stood with his head drooping on his breast, as though overwhelmed by the persevering spirit and strength of character developed in each fresh trait of his new-found friend's conduct.

"You have not seen all yet," continued Faria, "for I did not think it wise to trust all my treasures in the same hiding-place ; let us shut this one up, and then you shall see what else I have to display."

Behind the head of the bed, and concealed by a stone fitting in so closely as to defy all suspicion, was a hollow space, and in this space a ladder of cords between twenty-five and thirty feet in length.

Dantès closely and eagerly examined it—he found it firm, solid, and compact enough to bear any weight.

"Who supplied you with the materials for making this wonderful work?" asked Dantès.

"No one but myself. I tore up several of my shirts, and unravelled the sheets of my bed, during my three years' imprisonment at Fenestrelle ; and when I was removed to the Château d'If, I managed to bring the ravellings with me, so that I have been able to finish my work here."

"And was it not discovered that your sheets were unhemmed?"

"Oh, no! for when I had taken out the thread I required, I hemmed the edges over again."

"With what ?"

"With this needle!" said the abbé, as, opening his ragged vestments, he shewed Dantès a long, sharp fish-bone, with a small perforated eye for the thread, a small portion of which still remained in it.

"Come," said the abbé, closing his hiding-place, and pushing the bed back to its original situation, "let me hear your story."

Dantès obeyed, and commenced what he called his history, which consisted only of the account of a voyage to India, and two or three in the Levant, until he arrived at the recital of his last cruise, with the death of Captain Leclere, and the receipt of a packet to be delivered by himself to the Grand Maréchal; his interview with that personage, and his receiving in place of the packet a letter addressed to M. Noirtier—his arrival at Marseilles and interview with his father—his affection for Mercédès and their nuptial fête—his arrest and subsequent examination in the temporary prison of the Palais de Justice, ending in his final imprisonment in the Château d'If. From the period of his arrival all was a blank to Dantès—he knew nothing, not even the length of time he had been imprisoned. His recital finished, the abbé reflected long and earnestly.

"Could anyone have had an interest in preventing you from being captain of the Pharaon?"

"I cannot believe such was the case. I was generally liked on board; and had the sailors possessed the right of selecting a captain themselves, I feel convinced their choice would have fallen on me. There was only one person among the crew who had any feeling of ill-will towards me. I had quarrelled with him some time previously, and had even challenged him to fight, but he refused."

"What was this man's name?"

"Danglars."

"What rank did he hold on board?"

"He was supercargo."

"And had you been captain, should you have retained him in his employment?"

"Not if the choice had remained with me: for I had frequently observed inaccuracies in his accounts."

"Good again! Now then tell me was any person present during your last conversation with Captain Leclere?"

"No; we were quite alone."

"Could your conversation be overheard by anyone?"

"It might, for the cabin-door was open,—and—stay; now I recollect,—Danglars himself passed by just as Captain Leclere was giving me the packet for the Grand Maréchal."

"That will do," cried the abbé; "now we are on the right scent."

"The thing is clear as day," continued the abbé, "and you must have had a very unsuspecting nature, as well as a good heart, not to have guessed the origin of the whole affair."

"Do you really think so? Ah, that would, indeed, be the treachery of a villain!"

"How did Danglars usually write?"

"Oh! extremely well."

"And how was the anonymous letter written?"

"All the wrong way—backwards, you know."

Again the abbé smiled. "In fact it was a disguised hand? Now as regards the second question. Was there any person whose interest it was to prevent your marriage with Mercédès?"

"Yes, a young Catalan, called Fernand, who loved her."

"Was Danglars acquainted with Fernand?"

"No——yes, he was. Now I recollect having seen them both sitting at table together beneath an arbour at Père Pamphile the evening before the day fixed for my wedding. They were in earnest conversation. Danglars was joking in a friendly way, but Fernand looked pale and agitated."

"Were they alone?"

"There was a third person with them whom I knew perfectly well, and who had, in all probability, made their acquaintance; he was a tailor named Caderousse, but he was quite intoxicated. Stay!—stay!—How strange that it should not have occurred to me before! Now I remember quite well that on the table round which they were sitting were pens, ink, and paper. Oh! the heartless, treacherous scoundrels!" exclaimed Dantès, pressing his hand to his throbbing brows.

"Let us continue. In the first place, then, who examined you—the procureur du roi, his deputy, or a magistrate?"

"The deputy."

"You tell me he burnt the letter in your presence?"

"He did; saying at the same time, 'You see I thus destroy the only proof existing against you.'"

"To whom was this letter addressed?"

"To M. Noirtier, No. 13, Rue Coq-Héron, Paris."

"Now can you conceive any interest your heroic deputy procureur could by possibility have had in the destruction of that letter?"

"Why, it is not altogether impossible he might have had, for he made me promise several times never to speak of that letter

to anyone, assuring me he so advised me for my own interest;
and, more than this, he insisted on my taking a solemn oath
never to utter the name mentioned in the address."

"Noirtier!" repeated the abbé; "Noirtier; I knew a person
of that name at the court of the Queen of Etruria—a Noirtier,
who had been a Girondin during the revolution! What was
your deputy called?"

"De Villefort!"

The abbé burst into a fit of laughter; while Dantès gazed on
him in utter astonishment.

"Noirtier is no other than the father of your sympathetic
deputy procureur."

Had a thunderbolt fallen at the feet of Dantès, or hell
opened its yawning gulf before him, he could not have been
more completely transfixed with horror than at the sound of
words so wholly unexpected, revealing as they did the fiendish
perfidy which had consigned him to wear out his days in the
dark cell of a prison, that was to him as a living grave. Starting up, he clasped his hands around his head as though to
prevent his very brain from bursting, while in a choked and
almost inarticulate voice he exclaimed, "His father! oh, no!
not his father, surely!"

"His own father, I assure you," replied the abbé; "his right
name was Noirtier de Villefort!"

At this instant a bright light shot through the mind of
Dantès, and cleared up all that had been dark and obscure
before. The change that had come over Villefort during the
examination; the destruction of the letter, the exacted promise,
the almost supplicating tones of the magistrate, who seemed
rather to implore mercy than denounce punishment—all returned with a stunning force to his memory. A cry of mental
agony escaped his lips, and he staggered against the wall almost
like a drunken man; then, as the paroxysm passed away, he
hurried to the opening conducting from the abbé's cell to his
own, and said—

"I must be alone to think over all this."

When he regained his dungeon he threw himself on his bed,
where the turnkey found him at his evening visit, sitting with
fixed gaze and contracted features, still and motionless as a
statue; but, during hours of deep meditation, which to him had
seemed but as minutes, he had formed a fearful resolution; and
bound himself to its fulfilment by a solemn oath.

7

Dantès was at length roused from his reverie by the voice of Faria, who, having also been visited by his gaoler, had come to invite his fellow-sufferer to share his supper.

Dantès' whole manner had changed with the revelation of the villainy of which he had been the victim. He was eager now to learn all that the abbé could teach him, so that if ever the chance of freedom came he could revenge himself.

He possessed a prodigious memory, combined with an astonishing quickness and readiness of conception; the mathematical turn of his mind rendered him apt at all kinds of calculation, while his naturally poetical feelings threw a light and pleasing veil over the dry reality of arithmetical computation, or the rigid severity of lines. He already knew Italian, and had also picked up a little of the Romaic dialect during his different voyages to the East, and by the aid of these two languages he easily comprehended the construction of all the others. He now besought the abbé to be his teacher, and set him tasks from day to day. The matter was undertaken seriously, and so many hours were regularly devoted to study. The time passed very quickly, and at the end of six months Dantès began to speak Spanish, English, and German.

It was not until a year later the abbé shewed Dantès a new idea he had made for their escape; it consisted of a plan of his own cell and that of Dantès, with the corridor which united them. In this passage he proposed to form a tunnel, such as is employed in mines; this tunnel would conduct the two prisoners immediately beneath the gallery where the sentry kept watch; once there, a large excavation would be made, and one of the flag-stones with which the gallery was paved be so completely loosened, that at the desired moment it would give way beneath the soldier's feet, who, falling into the excavation below, would be immediately bound and gagged, before he had power to offer any resistance. The prisoners were then to make their way through one of the gallery windows, and to let themselves down from the outer walls by means of the abbé's ladder of cords. The eyes of Dantès sparkled with joy, and he rubbed his hands with delight at the idea of a plan so simple, yet apparently so certain to succeed.

That very day the miners commenced their labours; and that with so much more vigour and alacrity, as they had a long rest from fatigue, and was destined, in all probability, to carry out the dearest wish of the heart of each.

Nothing interrupted the progress of their work except the necessity of returning to their respective cells before the hour their gaoler visited them; they had learned to distinguish the almost imperceptible sound of his footsteps, as he descended towards their dungeons, and by luck were always prepared for his coming.

The fresh earth excavated during their present work, which would have entirely blocked up the old passage, was thrown, by degrees, and with the utmost precaution, out of the window, in either Faria's or Dantès' cell, the rubbish being first pulverised so finely that the night-wind carried it far away without permitting the smallest trace to remain.

More than a year had been consumed in this undertaking; the only tools for which had been a chisel, a knife, and a wooden lever. Faria still continued to instruct Dantès by conversing with him, sometimes in one language, sometimes in another; at others relating to him the history of nations, and great men who from time to time have left behind them one of those bright tracks called glory.

At the end of fifteen months the tunnel was made, and the excavation completed beneath the gallery, and the two workmen could distinctly hear the measured tread of the sentinel as he paced to and fro over their heads.

Compelled, as they were, to await a night sufficiently dark to favour their flight, they were obliged to defer their final attempt till that auspicious moment should arrive; their greatest dread now was lest the stone through which the sentry was doomed to fall should give way before its right time, and this they had in some measure provided against, by placing under it as a kind of prop, a sort of bearer they had discovered among the foundations through which they had worked their way. Dantès was occupied in arranging this piece of wood when he heard Faria, who had remained in his cell for the purpose of cutting a peg to secure their rope ladder, call to him in accents of pain and suffering. Dantès hastened to his dungeon, where he found his friend standing in the middle of the room, pale as death, his forehead streaming with perspiration, and his hands clenched tightly together.

"Quick! quick!" said the abbé; "listen to what I have to say. All is over with me. I am seized with a terrible, perhaps mortal illness; I can feel that the paroxysm is fast approaching: I had a similar attack the year previous to my imprisonment. This malady admits but of one remedy; I will tell **you** what that is; go into my cell as quickly as you can—draw out one of the feet that support the bed, you will find it has been hollowed out for the purpose of containing a small phial you will see there, half-filled with a red-looking fluid, bring it to me —or rather—no, no!—I may be found here, therefore help me back to my room while I have any strength to drag myself along; who knows what may happen? or how long the fit may last?"

Spite of the magnitude of the misfortune which thus suddenly frustrated his hopes, Dantès did not lose his presence of mind, but descended into the corridor dragging his unfortunate companion with him; then, half carrying, half supporting him, he managed to reach the abbé's chamber, when he immediately laid the sufferer on his bed.

"Thanks!" said the poor abbé, shivering as though his veins were filled with ice. "Now that I am safely here, let me explain to you the nature of my attack, and the appearance it will present. I am seized with a fit of catalepsy; when it comes to its height, I may probably lie still and motionless as though dead, uttering neither sigh nor groan. On the other hand, the symptoms may be much more violent, and cause me to fall into fearful convulsions, cover my lips with foaming, and force from me the most piercing shrieks; this last evil you must carefully guard against, for, were my cries to be heard, it is more than probable I should be removed to another part of the prison, and we be separated for ever. When I become quite motionless, cold, and rigid as a corpse, then, and not before—you understand—force open my teeth with a chisel, pour from eight to ten drops of the liquor contained in the phial down my throat, and I may perhaps revive."

"Perhaps!" exclaimed Dantès, in grief-stricken tones.

"Help! help!" cried the abbé; "I—I—die—I——"

So sudden and violent was the fit, that the unfortunate prisoner was unable to complete the sentence began: a violent convulsion shook his whole frame, his eyes started from their sockets, his mouth was drawn on one side, his cheeks became purple, he struggled, foamed, dashed himself about, and uttered the most dreadful cries, which, however, Dantès prevented from being heard by covering his head with the blanket; the fit lasted two hours, then, more helpless than an infant, and colder and paler than marble, more crushed and broken than a reed

trampled under foot, he stretched himself out as though in the
agonies of death, and became of the ghastly hue of the tomb.

Edmond waited till life seemed extinct in the body of his
friend; then taking up the chisel, he with difficulty forced open
the closely fixed jaws, carefully poured the appointed number
of drops down the rigid throat, and anxiously awaited the result.

An hour passed away without the old man's giving the least
sign of returning animation; Dantès began to fear he had
delayed too long ere he administered the remedy, and thrusting
his hands into his hair, continued gazing on the lifeless features
of his friend in an agony of despair. At length a slight colour
tinged the livid cheeks, consciousness returned to the dull open
eyeballs; a faint sigh issued from the lips, and the sufferer
made a feeble effort to move.

"He is saved!—he is saved!" cried Dantès, in a paroxysm of
delight.

"My good Edmond," answered the abbé, "be not deceived.
The attack which has just passed away condemns me for ever to
the walls of a prison. None can fly from their dungeons but
those who can walk."

"It is well," said Dantès. "And now hear my determination
also." Then rising and extending his hand with an air of
solemnity over the old man's head, he slowly added, "Here I
swear to remain with you so long as life is spared to you, and
that death only shall divide us."

Faria gazed fondly on his noble-minded but single-hearted
young friend, and read in his honest open countenance ample
confirmation of truthfulness, as well as sincere, affectionate, and
faithful devotion.

"Thanks, my child," murmured the invalid, extending the
one hand of which he still retained the use. "Thanks for your
generous offer, which I accept as frankly as it is made."

When Dantès returned next morning to the chamber of his
companion in captivity, he found Faria seated and looking composed. In the ray of light which entered by the narrow window
of his cell he held open in his left hand, of which alone, it will
be recollected, he retained the use, a morsel of paper, which,
from being constantly rolled into a small compass, had the form
of a cylinder, and was not easily kept open.

"This paper, my friend," said Faria, "I may now avow to
you, since I have proved you,—this paper is my treasure, of
which, from this day forth, one-half belongs to you."

A cold damp started to Dantès' brow. Until this day,—and what a space of time!—he had avoided talking to the abbé of this treasure, the source whence accusation of madness against the poor abbé was derived. With his instinctive delicacy Edmond had preferred avoiding any touch on this painful chord, and Faria had been equally silent. He had taken the silence of the old man for a return to reason, and now these few words uttered by Faria, after so painful a crisis, seemed to announce a serious relapse of mental alienation.

"You persist in your incredulity, Edmond," continued Faria. "My words have not convinced you. I see you require proofs. Well, then, I will tell you a story I have never told to anyone. You know that I was the secretary and intimate friend of the Cardinal Spada, the last of the princes of that name. I owe to this worthy lord all the happiness I ever knew. He was not rich, although the wealth of his family had passed into a proverb, and I heard the phrase very often, 'As rich as a Spada.' But he, like public rumour, lived on this reputation for wealth; his palace was my paradise. I instructed his nephews, who are dead, and when he was alone in the world I returned to him, by an absolute devotion to his will, all he had done for me during ten years.

"An ancestor of his had died by treachery, and at his death his will consisted in this only, a scrap of paper on which he had written :—

"'I bequeath to my beloved nephew my coffers, my books, and, amongst other, my breviary with the gold corners, which I beg he will preserve in remembrance of his affectionate uncle.'

"The heirs sought everywhere, admired the breviary, laid hands on the furniture, and were greatly astonished that Spada, the rich man, was really the most miserable of uncles—no treasures—unless they were those of science, composed in the library and laboratories.

"The celebrated breviary remained in the family, and was in the cardinals possession. It had been handed down from father to son, for the singular clause of the only will that had been found, had rendered it a real relic, preserved in the family with superstitious veneration. It was an illuminated book with beautiful Gothic characters, and so weighty with gold, that a servant always carried it before the cardinal on days of great solemnity.

"I now come to the last of the family, Cardinal Spada, whose secretary I was. When he died, his library composed of 5,000 volumes, and his famous breviary were bequeathed to me.

" In 1807, a month before I was arrested, and fifteen days after the death of Comte de Spada, on the 25th of December, (you will see presently how the date became fixed in my memory,) I was reading, for the thousandth time, the papers I was arranging, for the palace was sold to a stranger ; and I was going to leave Rome and settle at Florence, when I fell asleep. I awoke in darkness. I rang for a light, but as no one came, I determined to find one for myself. I took a wax-candle in one hand, and with the other groped about for a piece of paper (my matchbox being empty), with which I hoped to produce a light from the small flame still playing on the embers. Fearing, however, to make use of any valuable piece of paper, I hesitated for a moment, then recollected that I had seen in the famous breviary which was on the table beside me, an old paper quite yellow with age, which had served as a marker for centuries, kept there by the request of the heirs. I felt for it, found it, twisted it up together, and putting it to the expiring flame, set light to it.

" But beneath my fingers, as if by magic, in proportion as the fire ascended, I saw yellowish characters appear on the paper, I grasped it in my hand, put out the flame as quickly as I could, lighted my taper in the fire itself, and opened the crumpled paper with inexpressible emotion, recognising, when I had done so, that these characters had been traced in mysterious and sympathetic ink, only appearing when exposed to the fire : nearly one-third of the paper had been consumed by the flame !"

He offered the paper to Dantès, who read the following words traced with an ink of a colour which most nearly resembled rust :—

" This 25th day of April, 1498, be . . .
Alexander VI. and fearing that not . . .
he may desire to become my heir, and re . . .
and Bentivoglio, who were poisoned . . .
my sole heir, that I have bu . . .
and has visited with me, that is in . . .
island of Monte-Cristo all I poss . . .
jewels, diamonds, gems, that I alone . . .
may amount to nearly two mil . . .
will find on raising the twentieth ro . .

creek to the east in a right line.   Two open . . .
in these caves : the treasure is in the furthest a . . .
which treasure I bequeath and leave en . . .
as my sole heir.
    " 25th April, 1494.

                                    " Cæs . . . "

    " And now," said the abbé, " read this other paper ; " and he
presented to Dantès a second leaf with fragments of lines
written on it, which Edmond read as follows :—

    " This 25th day of April, 1498, be . . .
    . . . ing invited to dine by his Holiness
    . . . content with making me pay for my hat
    . . . serves for me the fate of Cardinals Caprara
    . . . I declare to my nephew Guido Spada,
    . . . ried in a place he knows
    . . . the caves of the small
    . . . essed of ingots, gold, money,
    . . . know of the existence of this treasure, which
    . . . lions of Roman crowns, and which he
    . . . ck from the small
    . . . ings have been made
    . . . ngle in the second :
    . . . tire to him

                                    † ar Spada."

    Faria followed him with excited look.
    " It is the declaration of Cardinal Spada, and the will so long
sought for," exclaimed Edmond ; " and who completed it as it
now is ? "
    " I did.   Aided by the remaining fragment I guessed the rest ;
measuring the length of the lines by those of the paper.
    " I resolved to set out, and did set out that very instant,
carrying with me the beginning of my great work on forming
Italy into one kingdom ; but for some time the infernal police
had their eyes on me and my hasty departure aroused their
suspicions.   I was arrested at the very moment I was leaving
Piombino.
    " Now," continued Faria, addressing Dantès with an almost
paternal expression,—" now, my dear fellow, you know as much
as I do myself.   If we ever escape together, half this treasure is

yours; If I die here and you escape alone, the whole belongs to you."

"But," inquired Dantès, hesitating, "has this treasure no more legitimate possessor in this world than ourselves?"

"No, no, be easy on that score; the family is extinct. The last Comte de Spada, moreover, made me his heir; bequeathing to me this symbolic breviary, he bequeathed to me all it contained: no, no, make your mind satisfied on that point. If we lay hands on this fortune, we may enjoy it without remorse."

"And you say this treasure amounts to——"

"Two millions of Roman crowns; nearly thirteen millions of our money."

"Impossible!" said Dantès, staggered at the enormous amount.

"You are my son, Dantès," exclaimed the old man. "You are the child of my captivity. My profession condemns me to celibacy. God has sent you to me to console, at one and the same time, the man who could not be a father, and the prisoner who could not get free."

And Faria extended the arm of which alone the use remained to him to the young man, who threw his own arms around his neck and wept bitterly.

CHAPTER XIV

THE abbé did not know the Isle of Monte-Cristo, but Dantès knew it, and had often passed it, situated twenty-five miles from Pianosa, between Corsica and the Isle of Elba, and he had once touched at it. This island was, always had been, and still is, completely deserted. It is a rock of almost conical form, which seems as though produced by some volcanic effort from the depth of the ocean.

Dantès traced a plan of the island to Faria, and Faria gave him advice as to the means he should employ to recover the treasure.

One night not long after, Edmond awoke suddenly, believing he heard some one calling him. He moved his bed, drew up the stone, rushed into the passage, and reached the opposite extremity; the secret entrance was open.

By the light of the wretched and wavering lamp, of which we have spoken, he saw the old man, pale, but yet erect, clinging to the bedstead. His features were writhing with those horrible symptoms which he already knew, and which had so seriously alarmed him when he saw them for the first time.

Dantès cried, " Oh! I have saved you once, and I will save you a second time !"

And raising the foot of the bed he drew out the phial, still a third filled with the red liquor.

"See!" he exclaimed, "there remains still some of this saving draught. Quick! quick! tell me what I must do this time—are there any fresh instructions? Speak, my friend, I listen."

"There is not a hope," replied Faria, shaking his head. " Monte-Cristo! forget not Monte-Cristo!"

And he fell back in his bed.

Dantès unclosed the teeth, which offered less resistance than before, counted one after the other twelve drops and watched.

Half an hour, an hour, an hour and a half elapsed, and during this time of anguish Edmond leaned over his friend, his hand applied to his heart, and felt the body gradually grow cold, and the heart's pulsation become more and more deep and dull, until at length all stopped : the last movement of the heart ceased, the face became livid, the eyes remained open, but the look was glazed. Faria was dead.

It was six o'clock in the morning, the dawn was just breaking, and its weak ray came into the dungeon and paled the ineffectual light of the lamp.

Dantès extinguished the lamp, carefully concealed it, and then went away, closing as well as he could the entrance to the secret passage by the large stone as he descended. It was time, for the gaoler was coming. On this occasion he began his rounds at Dantès' cell, and on leaving him he went on to Faria's dungeon.

Dantès was then seized with an indescribable desire to know what was going on in the dungeon of his unfortunate friend. He therefore returned by the subterranean gallery, and arrived in time to hear the exclamations of the turnkey, who called out for help.

Other turnkeys came, and then was heard the regular tramp of soldiers, behind them came the governor.

Edmond heard the noise of the bed on which they were moving the corpse, heard the voice of the governor, who desired them to throw water on the face, and seeing that in spite of this application the prisoner did not recover, sent for the doctor. Some words of pity fell on Dantès' listening ears, mingled with brutal laughter.

" Well ! well !" said one, " the madman has gone to look after his treasure. Good journey to him !"

" With all his millions he will not have enough to pay for his shroud !" said another.

" Oh !" added a third voice, " the shrouds of the Château d'If are not dear !"

" Perhaps," said one of the previous speakers, " as he was a churchman, they may go to some expense in his behalf."

" They may give him the honours of the sack."

" Yes, yes ; make your mind easy ; he shall be decently interred in the newest sack we can find."

" Will there be any mass ?" asked one of the attendants.

" That is impossible," replied the governor. " The chaplain

of the Château came to me yesterday to beg for leave of absence in order to take a trip to Hyères for a week. I told him I would attend to the prisoners in his absence. If the poor abbé had not been in such a hurry he might have had his requiem."

During this time the operation of putting the body in the sack was going on.

" This evening," said the governor when the task was ended.

" At what o'clock ?" inquired a turnkey.

"Why, about ten or eleven o'clock."

Then the steps retreated, and the voices died away in the distance ; the noise of the door with its creaking hinges and bolts ceased, and a silence duller than any solitude ensued, the silence of death, which pervaded all, and struck its icy chill through the young man's whole frame.

Dantès, quitting the passage, entered his friend's room.

On the bed, at full length, and faintly lighted by the pale ray that penetrated the window, was visible a sack of coarse cloth, under the large folds of which was stretched a long and stiffened form ; it was Faria's last winding-sheet, a winding-sheet which, as the turnkey said, cost so little.

" I, too," said Dantès, " shall die in my dungeon like Faria."

As he said this, he remained motionless, his eyes fixed like a man struck with a sudden idea. Suddenly he rose, lifted his hand to his brow, as if his brain were giddy, paced twice or thrice round his chamber, and then paused abruptly at the bed. " Why not take the place of the dead ?" he cried to himself.

Without giving himself time to re-consider his decision, and indeed that he might not allow his thoughts to be distracted from his desperate resolution, he bent over the appalling sack, opened it with the knife which Faria had made, drew the corpse from the sack, and transported it along the gallery to his own chamber, laid it on his couch, passed round its head the rag he wore at night round his own, covered it with his counterpane, once again kissed the ice-cold brow, and tried vainly to close the resisting eyes which glared horribly, turned his head towards the wall, so that the gaoler might, when he brought his evening meal, believe that he himself was there asleep, as was his frequent custom ; returned along the gallery, threw the bed against the wall, returned to the other cell, took from the hiding-place the needle and thread, flung off his rags that the men might feel naked flesh only beneath the coarse sack-cloth, and getting into the sack, placed himself in the posture in which the dead body had been laid, and sewed up the mouth of the sack inside.

The beating of his heart might have been heard, if by any mischance the gaolers had entered at that moment.

If they conducted him to the cemetery and laid him in the grave, he would allow himself to be covered with earth, and then, as it was night, the grave-diggers could scarcely have turned their backs, ere he would have worked his way through the soft soil, hoping that the weight would not be too heavy for him to support. If he was deceived in this, and the earth proved too heavy, he would be stifled, and then, so much the better, all would be over.

At length about the hour the governor had appointed, foot-steps were heard on the stairs. Edmond felt that the moment had arrived, and summoning up all his courage, held his breath, wishing at the same time he could have repressed in like manner the quick pulsation of his arteries.

They stopped at the door—there were two men apparently, and Dantès guessed it was the two grave-diggers who came to seek him—this idea was soon converted into certainty, when he heard the noise they made in putting down the hand-bier. The door opened, and a dim light reached Dantès' eyes through the coarse sack that covered him, he saw two shadows approach his bed, a third remaining at the door with a torch in his hand. Each of these two men, approaching the ends of the bed, took the sack by its extremities.

" He's heavy though for an old and thin man," said one, as he raised the head.

" They say every year adds half a pound to the weight of the bones," said another, lifting the feet.

" Have you tied the knot ?" inquired the first speaker.

" What would be the use of carrying so much more weight ?" was the reply ; " I can do that when we get there."

" Yes, you're right," replied his companion.

" What's the knot for ?" thought Dantès.

They deposited the supposed corpse on the bier. Edmond stiffened himself in order to play his part of a dead man, and then the party, lighted by the man with the torch who went first, ascended the stairs.

Suddenly he felt the fresh and sharp night air, and Dantès recognised the *Mistral*. It was a sensation at the same time full of delight and agony.

The bearers advanced twenty paces, then stopped, putting their bier down on the ground.

Edmond heard a heavy and sounding substance laid down beside him, and at the same moment a cord was fastened round his feet with sudden and painful violence.

"Well, have you tied the knot?" inquired the grave-digger, who was looking on.

"Yes, and pretty tight too, I can tell you," was the answer.

"Move on, then."

And the bier was lifted once more, and they proceeded.

They advanced fifty paces farther, and then stopped to open a door, before going forward again. The noise of the waves dashing against the rocks on which the Château is built, reached Dantès' ear distinctly as they progressed.

"Bad weather!" observed one of the bearers; "not a pleasant night for a dip in the sea."

"Why, yes, the abbé runs a chance of being wet," said the other; and then there was a burst of brutal laughter.

Dantès did not comprehend the jest, but his hair stood erect on his head.

"Well, here we are at last," said one of them. "A little farther—a little farther," said the other. "You know very well that the last was stopped on his way, dashed on the rocks, and the governor told us next day that we were careless fellows."

They ascended five or six more steps, and then Dantès felt that they took him one by the head and the other by the heels, and swung him to and fro.

"One!" said the grave-diggers. "Two! Three, and away!"

And at the same instant Dantès felt himself flung into the air like a wounded bird falling, falling with a rapidity that made his blood curdle. Although drawn downwards by some heavy weight which hastened his rapid descent, it seemed to him as if the time were a century. At last, with a terrific dash, he entered the ice-cold water, and as he did so he uttered a shrill cry, stifled in a moment by his immersion beneath the waves.

Dantès had been flung into the sea, and dragged into its depths by a thirty-six pound shot tied to his feet.

The sea is the Cemetery of Château d'If.

"ONE! TWO! THREE, AND AWAY!"
Page 110.

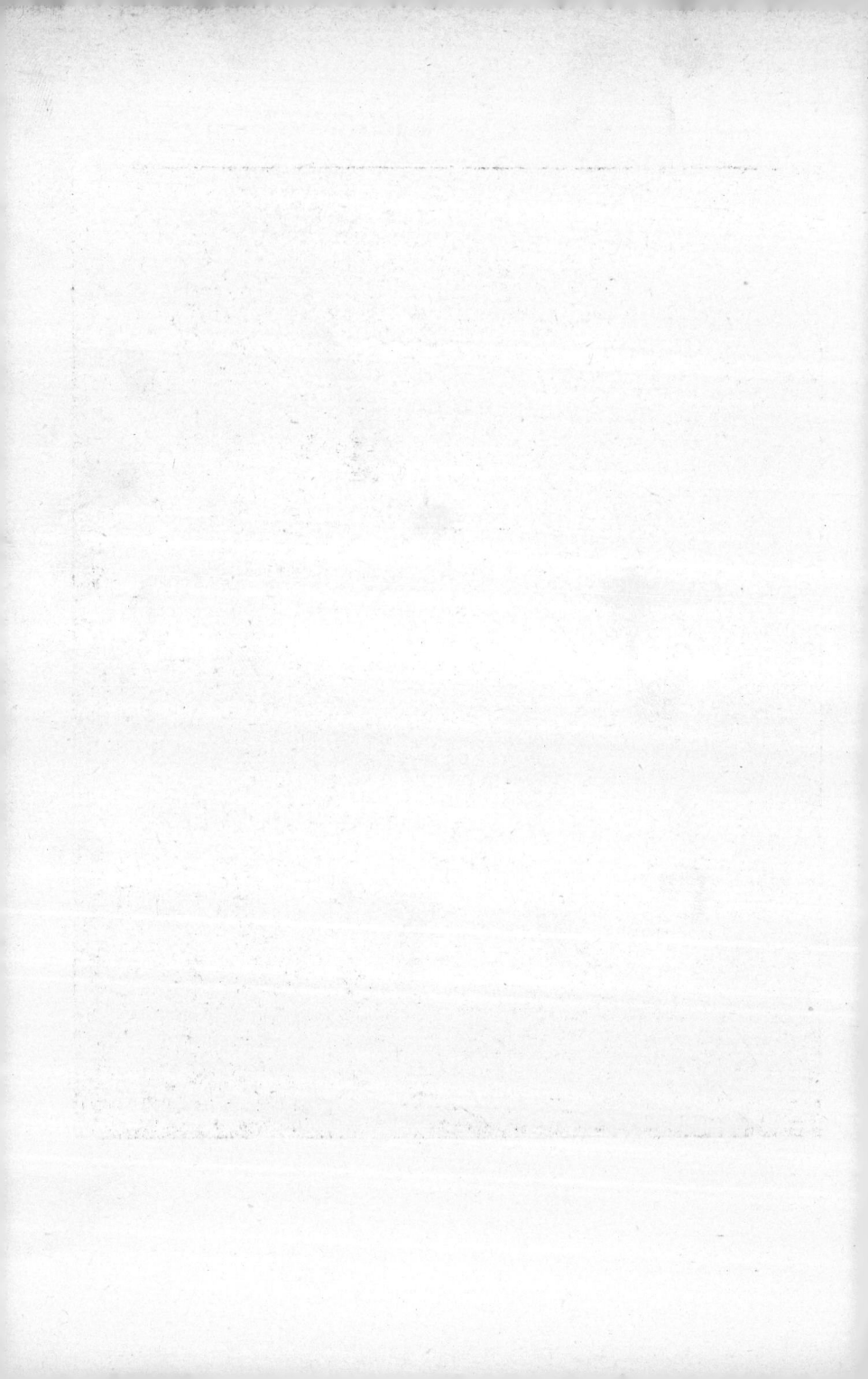

CHAPTER XV

DANTÈS, although giddy, and almost suffocated, had yet sufficient presence of mind to hold his breath; and as his right hand held his knife open, he rapidly ripped up the sack, extricated his arm, and then his body; but in spite of all his efforts to free himself from the shot, he felt it dragging him down still lower; he then bent his body, and by a desperate effort severed the cord that bound his legs at the moment he was suffocating. With a vigorous spring he rose to the surface of the sea, whilst the shot bore to its depths the sack that had so nearly become his shroud.

Dantès merely paused to breathe, and then dived again in order to avoid being seen. When he rose a second time he was fifty paces from where he had first sunk. He saw overhead a black and tempestuous sky, over which the wind was driving the fleeting vapours that occasionally suffered a twinkling star to appear: before him was the vast expanse of waters, sombre and terrible, whose waves foamed and roared as if before the approach of a storm. Behind him, blacker than the sea, blacker than the sky, rose like a phantom the giant of granite, whose projecting crags seemed like arms extended to seize their prey; and on the highest rock was a torch that lighted two figures. He fancied these two forms were looking at the sea; doubtless these strange grave-diggers had heard his cry. Dantès dived again, and remained a long time beneath the water. This manœuvre was already familiar to him, and usually attracted a crowd of spectators in the bay before the lighthouse at Marseilles when he swam there. When he reappeared the light had disappeared.

It was necessary to strike out to sea; Ratonneau and Pomègue are the nearest isles of all those that surround the Château d'If. But Ratonneau and Pomègue are inhabited, together with the islet of Daume; Tiboulen or Lemaire were the most secure. The isles of Tiboulen and Lemaire are a league from the Château d'If. Dantès, nevertheless, determined to make for them; but how

111

could he find his way in the darkness of the night. At this moment he saw before him, like a brilliant star, the lighthouse of Planier.

By leaving this light on the right he kept the isle of Tiboulen a little on the left; by turning to the left, therefore, he would find it. But as we have said, it was at least a league from the Château d'If to this island.

Fear, that relentless pursuer, clogged Dantès' efforts; he listened if any noise was audible; each time that he rose over the waves his looks scanned the horizon, and strove to penetrate the darkness; every wave seemed a boat in his pursuit, and he redoubled exertions that increased his distance from the Château, but the repetition of which weakened his strength. He swam on still, and already the terrible Château had disappeared in the darkness. He could not see it, but he *felt* its presence. An hour passed, during which Dantès, excited by the feeling of freedom, continued to cleave the waves.

"Let us see," said he, "I have swum above an hour; but as the wind is against me, that has retarded my speed; however, if I am not mistaken, I must be close to the isle of Tiboulen. But what if I were mistaken?"

A shudder passed over him. He sought to tread water in order to rest himself, but the sea was too violent, and he felt that he could not make use of this means of repose.

"Well," said he, "I will swim on until I am worn out, or the cramp seizes me, and then I shall sink;" and he struck out with the energy of despair.

Suddenly the sky seemed to him to become still darker and more dense, and compact clouds lowered towards him; at the same time he felt a violent pain in his knee, his imagination told him a ball had struck him, and that in a moment he would hear the report: but he heard nothing. Dantès put out his hand, and felt resistance; he then extended his leg and felt the land, and in an instant guessed the nature of the object he had taken for a cloud. Before him rose a mass of strangely formed rocks, that resembled nothing so much as a vast fire petrified at the moment of its most fervent combustion. It was the isle of Tiboulen.

Dantès rose, advanced a few steps, and with a fervent prayer of gratitude, stretched himself on the granite, which seemed to him softer than down. Then, in spite of the wind and rain, he fell into the deep sweet sleep of those worn out by fatigue.

At the expiration of an hour he was awakened by the roar of the thunder. An overhanging rock offered him a temporary

shelter; and scarcely had he availed himself of it, when the
tempest burst forth in all its fury. He felt the rock beneath
which he lay tremble ; the waves dashing themselves against the
granite, wetted him with their spray. In safety as he was, he felt
himself become giddy in the midst of this war of the elements, and
the dazzling brightness of the lightning. It seemed to him that
the island trembled to its base, and that it would, like a vessel
at anchor, break her moorings, and bear him off into the centre
of the storm. He then recollected that he had not eaten or drunk
for four-and-twenty hours. He extended his hands and drank
greedily of the rain-water that had lodged in a hollow of the rock.

As he rose, a flash of lightning, that seemed as if the whole of
the heavens were opened, illumined the darkness. By its light,
between the isle of Lemaire and Cape Croiselle, a quarter of a
league distant, he saw, like a spectre, a fishing-boat driven rapidly
on by the force of the winds and waves. A second after he saw
it again approaching nearer. He cried at the top of his voice to
warn the men of their danger, but they saw it themselves. Another
flash shewed him four men clinging to the shattered mast and
the rigging, while a fifth clung to the broken rudder.

The men he beheld saw him doubtless, for their cries were
carried to his ears by the wind. Above the splintered mast a
sail rent to tatters was waving ; suddenly the ropes that still held
it gave way, and it disappeared in the darkness of the night like
a vast sea-bird. At the same moment a violent crash was heard,
and cries of distress. Perched on the summit of the rock, Dantès
saw by the lightning the vessel in pieces ; and amongst the
fragments were visible the agonised features of the unhappy
sailors. Then all became dark again.

Dantès ran down the rocks at the risk of being himself dashed
to pieces ; he listened, he strove to examine, but he heard and
saw nothing,—all human cries had ceased : and the tempest alone
continued to rage. By degrees the wind abated ; vast grey clouds
rolled towards the west; and the blue firmament appeared studded
with bright stars. Soon a red streak became visible in the horizon ;
the waves whitened, a light played over them, and gilded their
foaming crests with gold. It was day.

Dantès stood silent and motionless before this vast spectacle;
for since his captivity he had forgotten it. He turned towards
the fortress, and looked both at the sea and the land.

As his eyes turned in the direction of the Château d'If, he
saw at the extremity of the isle of Pomègue, like a bird skim-

8

ming over the sea, a small bark, that the eye of a sailor alone could recognise as a Genoese tartane. She was coming out of Marseilles harbour, and was standing out to sea rapidly, her sharp prow cleaving through the waves.

In an instant Dantès' plan was formed. He swam to where the cap of one of the dead sailors hung to a point of the rock; placed it on his head, seized one of the beams floating near, and struck out so as to cross the line the vessel was taking.

"I am saved," murmured he.

And this conviction restored his strength.

He soon perceived that the vessel, having the wind right ahead, was tacking between the Château d'If and the tower of Planier.

Although almost sure as to what course she would take, yet he watched her anxiously until she tacked and stood towards him. Then he advanced; but, before they had met, the vessel again changed her direction. By a violent effort, he rose half out of the water, waving his cap, and uttering a loud shout peculiar to sailors. This time he was both seen and heard, and the tartane instantly steered towards him. He saw they were about to lower the boat. An instant after, the boat, rowed by two men, advanced rapidly towards him. Dantès abandoned the beam, which he thought now useless, and swam vigorously to meet them. But he had reckoned too much upon his strength, his arms grew stiff, his legs had lost their flexibility, and he was almost breathless. He uttered a second cry. The two sailors redoubled their efforts, and one of them cried in Italian, "Courage!"

The word reached his ear as a wave, which he no longer had the strength to surmount, passed over his head. He rose again to the surface, supporting himself by one of those desperate efforts a drowning man makes, uttered a third cry, and felt himself sink again, as if the fatal shot were again tied to his feet. He felt some one seize him by the hair; but he saw and heard nothing. He had fainted.

When he opened his eyes Dantès found himself on the deck of the tartane. His first care was to see what direction they were pursuing. They were rapidly leaving the Château d'If behind. Dantès was so exhausted, that the exclamation of joy he uttered was mistaken for a sigh. He was lying on the deck, a sailor was rubbing his limbs with a woollen cloth; another, whom he recognised as the one who had cried out "Courage!"

held a gourd full of rum to his mouth ; whilst the third, an old sailor, at once the pilot and captain, looked on with that egotistical pity men feel for a misfortune that they have escaped yesterday and which may overtake them to-morrow.

A few drops of the rum restored suspended animation, whilst the friction of his limbs restored their elasticity.

" Who are you ?" said the pilot, in bad French.

" I am," replied Dantès, in bad Italian, " a Maltese sailor. We were coming from Syracuse laden with grain. The storm of last night overtook us at Cape Morgion, and we were wrecked on these rocks."

" Where do you come from ?"

" From these rocks that I had the good luck to cling to whilst our captain and the rest of the crew were all lost. I saw your ship, and fearful of being left to perish on the desolate island, I swam off on a fragment of the vessel in order to try and gain your bark. You have saved my life, and I thank you," continued Dantès. " I was lost when one of your sailors caught hold of my hair."

" It was I," said a sailor, of a frank and manly appearance ; " and it was time, for you were sinking."

" Yes," returned Dantès, holding out his hand, " I thank you again."

" Now what are we to do with you ?" said the captain.

" Anything you please. My captain is dead ; I have barely escaped ; but I am a good sailor. Leave me at the first port you make ; I shall be sure to find employment."

" Do you know the Mediterranean ?"

" I have sailed over it since my childhood."

" You know the best harbours ?"

" There are few ports that I could not enter or leave with my eyes blinded."

" I say, captain," said the sailor, who had cried " Courage !" to Dantès, " if what he says is true, what hinders his staying with us ?"

" Where are you going to ?" asked Dantès in his turn.

" To Leghorn."

" Then why, instead of tacking so frequently, do you not sail nearer the wind ?"

" Because we should run straight on the island of Rion."

" You shall pass it by twenty fathoms."

" Take the helm, and let us see what you know."

The young man took the helm, ascertaining by a slight pressure if the vessel answered the rudder, and seeing that, without being a first-rate sailer, she yet was tolerably obedient,—

" To the braces," said he.

The four seamen, who composed the crew, obeyed, whilst the pilot looked on.

" Haul taut."

They obeyed.

" Belay."

This order was also executed, and the vessel passed, as Dantès had predicted, twenty fathoms to the right.

" You see," said Dantès quitting the helm, " I shall be of some use to you, at least, during the voyage. If you do not want me at Leghorn, you can leave me there, and I will pay you out of the first wages I get for my food and the clothes you lend me."

" Ah," said the captain, " we can agree very well if you are reasonable."

" Give me what you give the others, and all will be arranged," returned Dantès.

" That's not fair," said the seaman who had saved Dantès. " For you know more than we do."

" What is that to you, Jacopo?" returned the captain. " Every one is free to ask what he pleases."

" That's true," replied Jacopo. " I only made a remark."

" Well, you would do much better to lend him a jacket and a pair of trousers if you have them."

" No," said Jacopo; " but I have a shirt and a pair of trousers."

" That is all I want," interrupted Dantès.

Jacopo dived into the hold, and soon returned with the articles of clothing.

" Now, then, do you wish for anything else?" said the captain.

" A piece of bread and another glass of the capital rum I tasted, for I have not eaten or drunk for a long time."

He had not tasted food for forty hours.

A piece of bread was brought, and Jacopo offered him the gourd.

" Larboard your helm," cried the captain to the steersman.

Dantès glanced to the same side as he lifted the gourd to his mouth; but his hand stopped.

" Halloa! what's the matter at the Château d'If?" said the captain. A small white cloud, which had attracted Dantès' attention, crowned the summit of the bastion of the Château d'If. At the same moment the faint report of a gun was heard. The sailors looked at one another.

" A prisoner has escaped from the Château d'If, and they are firing the alarm gun," said Dantès calmly.

The captain glanced at him, but he had lifted the rum to his lips, and was drinking it with so much composure, that his suspicions, if he had any, died away.

" I have been so frightened last night," continued Dantès, smiling, " that I have almost lost my memory. I ask you what year it is ?"

" The year 1829," returned Jacopo.

It was fourteen years day for day since Dantès' arrest. He was nineteen when he entered the Château d'If ; he was thirty-three when he escaped.

A sorrowful smile passed over his face, he asked himself what had become of Mercédès, who must believe him dead. Then his eyes lighted up with hatred as he thought of the three men who had caused him so long and wretched a captivity. He renewed against Danglars, Fernand, and Villefort, the oath of implacable vengeance he had made in his dungeon.

This oath was no longer a vain menace, for the fastest sailor in the Mediterranean would have been unable to overtake the little tartane, that with every stitch of canvas set was flying before the wind to Leghorn.

Dantès had not been a day on board before he had an insight into the persons with whom he sailed. Without having been in the school of the Abbé Faria, the worthy master of La Jeune Amélie (the name of the Genoese tartane) knew a smattering of all the tongues spoken on the shores of that large lake called the Mediterranean, from the Arabic to the Provençal ; and this, whilst it spared him interpreters, persons always troublesome and frequently indiscreet, gave him great facilities of communication, either with the vessels he met at sea, with the small barks sailing along the coast, or with those persons without name, country, or apparent calling, who are always seen on the quays of seaports. We may thus suppose that Dantès was on board a smuggling lugger.

In the first instance the master had received Dantès on board with a certain degree of mistrust. He was very well known to the custom-house officers of the coast, and as there was between these worthies and himself an exchange of the most cunning stratagems, he had at first thought that Dantès might be an emissary of these illustrious executors of rights and duties, who employed this ingenious means of penetrating some of the secrets of his trade. But the skilful manner in which Dantès had manœuvred the little bark had entirely reassured him, and then when he saw the light smoke floating like a plume above the bastion of the Château d'If, and heard the distant explosion, he guessed he had on board an escaped prisoner. This made him less uneasy, it must be owned, than if the new comer had proved a custom-house officer, but this latter supposition also disappeared like the first, when he beheld the perfect tranquillity of his recruit.

Dantès had entered the Château d'If with the round, open smiling face of a young and happy man, with whom the early paths of life have been smooth.

His oval face was now lengthened, his smiling mouth had assumed the firm and marked lines which betoken resolution; his eyebrows were arched beneath a large and thoughtful wrinkle; his eyes were full of melancholy, and from their depths occasionally sparkled gloomy fires of misanthropy and hatred; his complexion, so long kept from the sun, had now that pale colour which produces, when the features are encircled with black hair, the aristocratic beauty of the men of the south; the deep learning he had acquired had besides diffused over his features the look of intellect; and he had also acquired, although previously a tall man, the vigour of a frame which has long concentrated all its force within itself.

To the elegance of a nervous and slight form had succeeded the solidity of a rounded and muscular figure. As to his voice, prayers, sobs, and imprecations, had changed it into a soft and singularly touching tone. Moreover, being perpetually in twilight or darkness, his eyes had acquired that singular faculty of distinguishing objects in the night, common to the hyena and the wolf.

Edmond smiled when he beheld himself first in a glass after this lapse of years: it was impossible that his best friend—if, indeed, he had any friend left—could recognise him: he could not recognise himself.

La Jeune Amélie had a very active crew, very obedient to their captain, who lost as little time as possible. He had scarcely been a week at Leghorn, before the hold of his vessel was filled with painted muslins, prohibited cottons, English powder, and tobacco on which the crown had forgotten to put its mark. The master was to get all this out of Leghorn free of duties, and land it on the shores of Corsica, where certain speculators undertook to forward the cargo to France.

They sailed; Edmond was again cleaving the azure sea which had been the first horizon of his youth.

The next morning going on deck, which he always did at an early hour, he leaned against the bulwarks gazing with intense earnestness at a pile of granite rocks, which the rising sun tinged with rosy light. It was the Isle of Monte-Cristo.

La Jeune Amélie left it three quarters of a league to the larboard, and kept on for Corsica.

The next morn broke off the coast of Aleria; all day they coasted, and in the evening saw the fires lighted on land; when they were extinguished, they no doubt recognised the signals for landing, for a ship's lantern was hung up at the mast-head instead of the streamer, and they neared the shore within gunshot.

Dantès remarked that at this time, too, the captain of La Jeune Amélie had, as he neared the land, mounted two small culverines, which without making much noise, can throw a ball of four to the pound a thousand paces or so.

But on this occasion the precaution was superfluous, and every thing proceeded with the utmost smoothness and politeness. Four shallops came off with very little noise alongside the bark, which, no doubt in acknowledgment of the compliment, lowered her own shallop into the sea, and the five boats worked so well, that by two o'clock in the morning all the cargo was out of La Jeune Amélie and on *terra firma.*

The same night, such a man of regularity was the patron of La Jeune Amélie, that the profits were shared out, and each man had had a hundred Tuscan livres, or about three guineas English. But the voyage was not ended. They turned the bowsprit towards Sardinia, where they intended to take in a cargo, which was to replace what had been discharged. The second operation was as successful as the first, La Jeune Amélie was in luck. This new cargo was destined for the coast of the Duchy of Lucca, and consisted almost entirely of Havannah cigars, sherry, and Malaga wines.

Two months and a half elapsed in these trips, and Edmond had become as skilful a coaster as he had been a hardy seaman; he had formed an acquaintance with all the smugglers on the coast, and learned the masonic signs by which these half pirates recognise each other. He had passed and re-passed his isle of Monte-Cristo twenty times, but not once had found an opportunity of landing there.

He then formed a resolution. This was, as soon as his engagement with the patron of La Jeune Amélie ended, he would hire a small bark on his own account (for in his several voyages he had amassed a hundred piastres), and under some pretext land at the isle of Monte-Cristo.

But in vain did he rack his imagination; fertile as it was, he could not devise any plan for reaching the wished-for isle without being accompanied.

Dantès was tossed about on these doubts and wishes, when the patron who had great confidence in him, and was very desirous of retaining him in his service, took him by the arm one evening, and led him to a tavern on the Via del'Oglio, where the leading smugglers of Leghorn used to congregate.

It was here they discussed the affairs of the coast.

This time it was a great matter that was under discussion, connected with a vessel laden with Turkey carpets, stuffs of the Levant, and cashmeres. It was requisite to find some neutral ground on which an exchange could be made, and then to try and land these goods on the coast of France. If successful the profit would be enormous, there would be a gain of fifty or sixty piastres each for the crew.

The patron of La Jeune Amélie proposed as a place of landing the isle of Monte-Cristo, which was completely deserted.

At the mention of Monte-Cristo Dantès started with joy, he rose to conceal his emotion, and took a turn round the smoky tavern, where all the languages of the known world were jumbled in a *lingua franca*. When he again joined the two persons who had been discussing this momentous question, it had been decided that they should touch at Monte-Cristo, and set out on the following night.

Thus at length, by one of those pieces of unlooked-for good fortune, which sometimes occur to those on whom misfortune has for a long time spent itself, Dantès was about to arrive at his wished-for opportunity by simple and natural means, and land in the island without incurring any suspicion. One night only separated him from his departure so ardently wished for.

At seven o'clock in the evening all was ready, and at ten minutes past seven they doubled the lighthouse just as the beacon was kindled. The sea was calm, and with a fresh breeze from the south-east they sailed beneath a bright blue sky, in which God also lighted up in turn his beacon lights, each of which is a world. Dantès told them that all hands might turn in and he would take the helm. When the Maltese (for so they called Dantès) had said this, it was sufficient, and all went to their cots contentedly. This frequently happened. When the captain awoke, the vessel was hurrying on with every sail set, and every sail full with the breeze. They were making nearly ten knots an hour. The isle of Monte-Cristo loomed large in the horizon.

Dantès resigned the bark to the master's care, and went and lay down in his hammock, but in spite of a sleepless night he could not close his eyes for a moment. Two hours afterwards he came on deck as the boat was about to double the isle of Elba. They were just abreast of Mareciana, and beyond the flat but verdant island of La Pianosa. The peak of Monte-Cristo, reddened by the burning sun, was seen against the azure sky.

As they drew near Dantès gazed most earnestly at the mass of rocks which gave out all the variety of twilight colours, from the brightest pink to the deepest blue, and from time to time his cheeks flushed, his brow became purple, and a mist passed over his eyes. Never did gamester, whose whole fortune is staked on one cast of the die, experience the anguish which he felt in his paroxysms of hope. Night came, and at ten o'clock p.m. they anchored. La Jeune Amélie was the first at the rendezvous.

In spite of his usual command over himself, Dantès could not restrain his impetuosity. He was the first who jumped on shore.

He questioned Jacopo. " Where shall we pass the night ?" he inquired.

" Why, on board the tartane," replied the sailor.

" Should we not be better in the grottoes ?"

" What grottoes ?"

" Why the grottoes—caves of the island."

" I do not know of any grottoes," replied Jacopo.

A cold damp sprang to Dantès' brow.

" What ! are there no grottoes at Monte-Cristo ?"

" None."

For a moment Dantès was speechless, then he remembered that these caves might have been filled up by some accident, or even stopped up for the sake of greater security by Cardinal Spada.

The point was then to discover the last opening. It was useless to search at night, and Dantès therefore delayed all investigation until the morning.

No one had the slightest suspicion ; and when next day, taking a fowling-piece, powder, and shot, Dantès testified a desire to go and kill some of the wild goats that were seen springing from rock to rock, his wish was construed into a love of sport or a desire for solitude. However, Jacopo insisted on following him, and Dantès did not oppose this, fearing if he did so that he might incur distrust. Scarcely, however, had he gone a quarter of a league than, having killed a kid, he begged Jacopo to take it to his comrades and request them to cook it, and when ready to let him know by firing a gun. This, and some dried fruits, and a flask of the wine of Monte Pulciano, was the bill of fare.

Dantès went forward, looking behind and round about him from time to time. Having reached the summit of a rock, he saw, a thousand feet beneath him, his companions, whom Jacopo had rejoined, who were all busy preparing the repast which Edmond's skill as a marksman had augmented with a capital dish.

He looked at them for a moment with the sad and soft smile of a man superior to his fellows.

Meanwhile, by a way between two walls of rock, following a path worn by a torrent, which, in all human probability, human foot had never before trod, Dantès approached the spot where he supposed the grottoes must have existed. Keeping along the coast, and examining the smallest object with serious attention, he thought he could trace on certain rocks marks made by the hand of man.

Time, which encrusts all physical substances with its mossy mantle, as it invests all things moral with its mantle of forgetfulness, seemed to have respected these signs, traced with a certain regularity, and probably with the design of leaving traces. Occasionally these marks disappeared beneath tufts of myrtle, which spread into large bushes laden with blossoms, or beneath parasitical lichen. It was thus requisite that Dantès should move branches on one side, or remove the mosses in order to retrace the indicating marks which were to be his guides in this labyrinth. These signs had renewed the best hopes in his mind. Why should it not have been the cardinal who had first traced them, in order that they might, in the event of a catastrophe which he could not foresee would have been so complete, serve as a guide for his nephew? This solitary place was precisely suited for a man desirous of burying a treasure. Only, might not these betraying marks have attracted other eyes than those for whom they were made? and had the dark and wondrous isle indeed faithfully guarded its precious secret?

It seemed, however, to Dantès, who was hidden from his comrades by the inequalities of the ground, that at sixty paces from the harbour the marks ceased; nor did they terminate at any grotto. A large round rock, placed solidly on its base, was the only spot to which they seemed to lead. He reflected that perhaps instead of having reached the end he might have only touched on the beginning, and he therefore turned round and retraced his steps.

During this time his comrades had prepared the repast, had got some water from a spring, spread out the fruit and bread, and cooked the kid. Just at the moment when they were taking the dainty animal from the spit, they saw Dantès, who, light and daring as a chamois, was springing from rock to rock, and they fired the signal agreed upon. The sportsman instantly changed his direction, and ran quickly towards them. But at the moment when they were all following with their eyes his agile bounds, Dantès' foot slipped, and they saw him stagger on the edge of a rock and disappear. They all rushed towards him, but Jacopo reached him first.

He found Dantès stretched bleeding and almost senseless. He had rolled down a height of twelve or fifteen feet. They poured some drops of rum down his throat. Dantès opened his eyes, complained of a great pain in his knee, a feeling of heaviness in his head, and severe pains in his loins. They wished to carry him to the shore, but when they touched him, although under Jacopo's directions, he declared, with heavy groans, that he could not bear to be moved.

"He has broken his ribs," said the commander, in a low voice. "No matter; he is an excellent fellow, and we must not leave him. We will try and carry him on board the tartane."

Dantès declared, however, that he would rather die where he was, than undergo the agony caused by the slightest movement he made.

"Well," said the captain, "let what may happen, it shall never be said that we deserted a good comrade like you.   We will not go till evening."

"No, no," said Dantès, "I was awkward, and it is just that I pay the penalty of my clumsiness.   Leave me a small supply of biscuit, a gun, powder, and balls, to kill the kids, or defend myself at need, and a pickaxe to build me something like a shed if you delay in coming back for me."

"We shall be absent at least a week," said the patron, "and then we must run out of our course to come here and take you up again."

"Why," said Dantès, "if in two or three days you hail any-fishing-boat, desire them to come here to me.   I will pay twenty-five piastres for my passage back to Leghorn.   If you do not come across one return for me."

The master shook his head.

"Listen, Captain Baldi; there's one way of settling this," said Jacopo.   "Do you go, and I will stay and take care of the wounded man."

"And give up your share of the venture," said Dantès, "to remain with me?"

"Yes," said Jacopo, "and without any hesitation."

"You are a good fellow and a kind-hearted messmate," replied Dantès, "and heaven will recompense you for your generous intentions; but I do not wish anyone to stay with me. A day or two's rest will set me up, and I hope I shall find amongst the rocks certain herbs most excellent for contusions."

It took some time to persuade them that he really meant what he said, but at length they agreed to go as arranged.

However, they did not set sail without turning about several times, and each time making signs of a cordial leave-taking, to which Edmond replied with his hand only, as if he could not move the rest of his body.

Then, when they had disappeared, he said with a smile—

"'Tis strange that it should be amongst such men that we find proofs of friendship and devotion."

He dragged himself cautiously to the top of a rock, from which he had a full view of the sea, and thence he saw the tartane complete her preparations for sailing, weigh anchor, and, balancing herself as gracefully as a water-fowl ere it takes to the wing, set sail.   At the end of an hour she was completely out of sight; at least it was impossible for the wounded man to see her any longer from the spot where he was.

Then Dantès rose more agile and light than the kid amongst the myrtles and shrubs of these wild rocks, took his gun in one hand, his pickaxe in the other, and hastened towards the rock on which the marks he had noted terminated.

"And now," he exclaimed, remembering the tale of the Arabian fisherman, which Faria had related to him—" now open sesame!"

CHAPTER XVI.

THE SECRET CAVE

THE sun had nearly reached the meridian, and his scorching rays fell full on the rocks, which seemed themselves sensible of the heat. Thousands of grasshoppers, hidden in the bushes, chirped with a monotonous and dull note; the leaves of the myrtle and olive-trees waved and rustled in the wind. At every step that Dantès took he disturbed the lizards glittering with the hues of the emerald; afar off he saw the wild goats bounding from crag to crag. In a word, the isle was inhabited, yet he felt himself alone, guided by the hand of God.

He went instantly back to the circular rock. One thing only perplexed him. How could this rock, which weighed several tons, have been lifted to this spot without the aid of many men? Suddenly an idea flashed across his mind. Instead of raising it, thought he, they have lowered it. And he sprang from the rock in order to inspect the base on which it had formerly stood.

He soon perceived that a slope had been formed; and the rock had slid along this until it stopped at the spot it now occupied. A large stone had served as a wedge; flints and pebbles had been inserted around it, so as to conceal the orifice; this species of masonry had been covered with earth, and grass and weeds had grown there; moss had clung to the stones, myrtle-bushes had taken root, and the old rock seemed fixed to the earth.

Dantès raised the earth carefully, and detected, or fancied he detected, the ingenious artifice. He attacked this wall, cemented by the hand of time, with his pickaxe. After ten minutes' labour the wall gave way, and a hole large enough to insert the arm was opened. Dantès went and cut the strongest olive-tree he could find, stripped off its branches, inserted it in the hole, and used it as a lever. But the rock was too heavy, and too firmly wedged to be moved by any one man, were he Hercules himself. Dantès reflected that he must attack this wedge.

126

But how? He cast his eyes around, and saw the horn full of powder, which his friend Jacopo had left him. He smiled; the infernal invention would serve him for this purpose. With the aid of his pickaxe Dantès dug, between the upper rock and the one that supported it, a mine similar to those formed by pioneers when they wish to spare human labour, filled it with powder, then made a match by rolling his handkerchief in salt-petre. He lighted it and retired.

The explosion was tremendous; the upper rock was lifted from its base by the terrific force of the powder; the lower one flew into pieces; thousands of insects escaped from the aperture Dantès had previously formed, and a huge snake, like the guardian demon of the treasure, rolled himself along with a sinuous motion, and disappeared.

Dantès approached the upper rock which, now without any support, leant towards the sea. The intrepid treasure-seeker walked round it, and selecting the spot from whence it appeared most easy to attack it, placed his lever in one of the crevices, and strained every nerve to move the mass.

The rock, already shaken by the explosion, tottered on its base as Dantès redoubled his efforts. He seemed like one of the ancient Titans, whose strength was far above that of mortal men. The rock yielded, rolled, bounded, and finally disappeared in the ocean.

On the spot it had occupied was visible a circular place, with an iron ring let into a square flag-stone. Dantès uttered a cry of joy and surprise; never had a first attempt been crowned with more perfect success. He would fain have continued, but his knees trembled, his heart beat so violently, and his eyes became so dim, that he was forced to pause. This feeling lasted but for a moment. Then he inserted his lever in the ring, and, exerting all his strength, the flag-stone yielded, and disclosed a kind of stair that descended until it was lost in the obscurity of a subterranean grotto. Anyone else would have rushed on with a cry of joy. Dantès turned pale, hesitated, and reflected.

Then he descended; a smile on his lips, and murmuring that last word of human philosophy, " perhaps!" But instead of the darkness, and the thick and mephitic atmosphere he had expected to find, he saw a dim and bluish light, which, as well as the air, entered, not merely by the aperture he had just formed, but by the interstices and crevices of the rock, which were visible from without, and through which he could distinguish the blue sky and the waving branches of the evergreen oaks, and the tendrils of the creepers that grew from the rocks.

After having stood a few minutes in the cavern, the atmosphere of which was rather warm than damp, Dantès' eye, habituated as it was to darkness, could pierce even to the remotest angles of the cavern which was of granite that sparkled like diamonds.

He recalled to memory the will which he knew by heart: "In the farthest angle of the second opening," were the cardinal's words. He had only found the first grotto, he had now to seek the second. Dantès commenced his search. He reflected that this second grotto must, doubtless, penetrate deeper into the isle; he examined the stones, and sounded one part of the wall where he fancied the opening existed, masked for precaution's sake. The pickaxe sounded for a moment with a dull sound that covered his forehead with large drops of perspiration. At last it seemed to him that one part of the wall gave forth a more hollow and deeper echo; he eagerly advanced, and with the quickness of perception that no one but a prisoner possesses, saw that it was there, in all probability, the opening must be.

He again struck it, and with greater force. A species of stucco fell to the ground in flakes, exposing a large white stone. The aperture of the rock had been closed with stones, then this stucco had been applied, and painted to imitate granite.

Dantès struck with the sharp end of his pickaxe, which entered some way between the interstices of the stone. It was there he must dig. But by some strange phenomenon in proportion as the proofs that Faria had not been deceived became stronger, so did his heart give way, and a feeling of discouragement steal over him. This last proof, instead of giving him fresh strength, deprived him of it; the pickaxe descended, or rather fell; he placed it on the ground, passed his hand over his brow, and remounted the stairs, alleging to himself as an excuse a desire to be assured that no one was watching him, but in reality because he felt he was ready to faint. The isle was deserted, and the sun seemed to cover it with its fiery glance; afar off a few small fishing-boats studded the bosom of the blue ocean.

Dantès had tasted nothing, but he thought not of hunger at such a moment; he hastily swallowed a few drops of rum, and again entered the cavern. The pickaxe that had seemed so heavy was now like a feather in his grasp; he seized it and again attacked the wall. After several blows he perceived that the stones were not cemented, but merely placed one upon the other, and covered with stucco; he inserted the point of his pickaxe, and using the handle as a lever, soon saw with joy the stone turn, as if on hinges, and fall at his feet. He had nothing more to do now but with the iron tooth of the pickaxe to draw the stones towards him one by one.

At last, after fresh hesitation, Dantès entered the second grotto, which was lower and more gloomy than the former; the air that could only enter by the newly formed opening had that mephitic smell Dantès was surprised not to find in the first. He waited in order to allow pure air to displace the foul atmosphere, and then entered. At the left of the opening was a dark and deep angle.

The treasure, if it existed, was buried in this corner. The time had at length arrived; two feet of earth removed, and Dantès' fate would be decided. He advanced towards the angle, and summoning all his resolution, attacked the ground with the pickaxe. At the fifth or sixth blow the pickaxe struck against an iron substance. Never did funeral knell, never did alarm-bell produce a greater effect on the hearer. Had Dantès found nothing, he could not have become more ghastly pale. He again struck his pickaxe into the earth, and encountered the same resistance, but not the same sound.

" It is a casket of wood bound with iron," thought he.

At this moment a shadow passed rapidly before the opening; Dantès seized his gun, sprang through the opening, and mounted the stair. A wild goat had passed before the mouth of the cave, and was feeding at a little distance.

This would have been a favourable occasion to secure his dinner; but Dantès feared lest the report of his gun should attract attention.

He reflected an instant, cut a branch of a resinous tree, lighted it at the fire at which the smugglers had prepared their breakfast, and descended with this torch. He wished to see all. He approached the hole he had formed, with the torch, and saw that his pickaxe had in reality struck against iron and wood. He planted his torch in the ground and resumed his labour. In an instant a space three feet long by two feet broad was cleared, and Dantès could see an oaken coffer bound with cut steel; in the midst of the lid he saw engraved on a silver plate, which was still untarnished, the arms of the Spada family, viz., a sword *pale* on an oval shield, like all the Italian armorial bearings, and

9

surmounted by a cardinal's hat; Dantès easily recognised them, Faria had so often drawn them for him. There was no longer any doubt, the treasure was there; no one would have been at such pains to conceal an empty casket.

In an instant he had cleared every obstacle away, and he saw successively the lock, placed between two padlocks, and the two handles at each end, all carved as things were carved at that epoch, when art rendered the commonest metals precious. Dantès seized the handles, and strove to lift the coffer; it was impossible. He sought to open it; lock and padlock were closed; these faithful guardians seemed unwilling to surrender their trust. Dantès inserted the sharp end of the pickaxe between the coffer and the lid, and pressing with all his force on the handle, burst open the fastenings. The hinges yielded in their turn and fell, still holding in their grasp fragments of the planks, and all was open.

A vertigo seized Edmond, he cocked his gun and laid it beside him. He then closed his eyes as children do, then he opened them, and stood motionless with amazement.

Three compartments divided the coffer. In the first, blazed piles of golden coin. In the second, bars of unpolished gold were ranged. In the third were piles of diamonds, pearls, and rubies, which, as they fell on one another, sounded like hail against glass.

After having touched, felt, and examined these treasures, Edmond rushed through the caverns like a man seized with frenzy; he leapt on a rock, from whence he could behold the sea. He was alone. Alone with these countless, these unheard-of treasures! Was he awake, or was it but a dream?

He would fain have gazed upon his gold, and yet he had not strength enough; for an instant he leaned his head in his hands as if to prevent his senses from leaving him, and then rushed madly about the rocks of Monte-Cristo, terrifying the wild goats and scaring the sea-fowls with his wild cries and gestures; at last he returned, and still unable to believe the evidence of his senses, rushed into the grotto, and found himself before this mine of gold and jewels. This time he fell on his knees, and, clasping his hands convulsively, uttered a prayer intelligible to God alone.

He then set himself to work to count his fortune. There were a thousand ingots of gold, each weighing from two to three pounds; then he piled up twenty-five thousand crowns, each worth about four pounds sterling of our money, and bearing the effigies of Alexander VI. and his predecessors; and he saw that the compartment was not half empty. And he measured ten double handsful of precious stones, many of which, mounted by the most famous workmen, were valuable for their execution. Dantès saw the light gradually disappear; and fearing to be surprised in the cavern, left it, his gun in his hand. A piece of biscuit and a small quantity of rum formed his supper, and he snatched a few hours' sleep, lying over the mouth of the cave.

This night was one of those delicious, and yet terrible ones, of which he had already passed two or three in his lifetime.

Daylight, for which Dantès had so eagerly and impatiently waited, again dawned upon the desert shores of Monte-Cristo. With the first dawn of day he resumed his researches. Again he climbed the rocky height he had ascended the previous evening, and strained his view to catch every peculiarity of the landscape; but it wore the same wild barren aspect when seen by the rays of the morning sun which it had done when surveyed by the fading glimmer of eve. Returning to the entrance of the cave, he raised the stone that covered it; and descending to the place that contained the treasure, filled his pockets with precious stones, put the box together as well and securely as he could, sprinkled fresh sand over the spot from which it had been taken, and then carefully trod down the ground to give it everywhere a similar appearance; quitting the grotto, he replaced the stone, heaping on it broken masses of rocks and rough fragments of crumbling granite, filling the interstices with earth, into which was skilfully mingled a quantity of rapidly growing plants, such as the wild myrtle, and flowering thorn; carefully watering these new plantations, he scrupulously effaced every trace of footmark, leaving the approach to the cavern as savage-looking and untrodden as he had found it. This done, he impatiently awaited the return of his companions. To wait at Monte-Cristo for the purpose of watching over the almost incalculable riches that had thus fallen into his possession satisfied not the cravings of his heart, which yearned to return to dwell among mankind, and to assume the rank, power, and influence, unbounded wealth alone can bestow.

On the sixth day the smugglers returned. From a distance Dantès recognised the cut and manner of sailing of La Jeune Amélie, and dragging himself with affected difficulty towards the landing-place, he met his companions with an assurance that, although considerably better than when they quitted him, he still suffered acutely from his late accident. He then inquired how they had fared in their trip.

To this question the smugglers replied that although successful in landing their cargo in safety, they had scarcely done so when they received intelligence that a guard-ship had just quitted the port of Toulon, and was crowding all sail towards them; this obliged them to make all the speed they could to evade the enemy; when they lamented the absence of Dantès, whose superior skill in the management of a vessel would have availed them so materially. In fact the chasing vessel had almost overtaken them, when, fortunately, night came on and enabled them to double the Cape of Corsica, and so elude all further pursuit.

Upon the whole, however, the trip had been sufficiently successful to satisfy all concerned; while the crew, and particularly Jacopo, expressed great regrets at Dantès not having been an equal sharer with themselves in the profits, amounting to no less a sum than fifty piastres each.

Edmond preserved the most admirable self-command, not suffering the faintest indication of a smile to escape him at the enumeration of all the benefits he would have reaped had he been able to quit the isle; but as La Jeune Amélie had merely come to Monte-Cristo to fetch him away, he embarked that same evening, and proceeded with the captain to Leghorn. Arrived at Leghorn, he repaired to the house of a Jew, a dealer in precious stones, to whom he disposed of four of his smallest diamonds for five thousand francs each.

Dantès half feared that such valuable jewels in the hands of a poor sailor like himself might excite suspicion; but the cunning purchaser asked no troublesome questions concerning a bargain by which he gained at least four thousand francs.

The following day Dantès presented Jacopo with an entirely new vessel, accompanying the gift by a donation of one hundred piastres, that he might provide himself with a suitable crew and other requisites for his outfit; upon conditions of his going direct to Marseilles, for the purpose of inquiring after an old man named Louis Dantès, residing in the Allées de Meillan, and also a young female called Mercédès, an inhabitant of the Catalan village.

Jacopo could scarcely believe his senses at receiving this munificent present, which Dantès hastened to account for by saying that he had merely been a sailor from whim, and a desire to spite his friends, who did not allow him as much money as he liked to spend; but that on his arrival at Leghorn, he had come into possession of a large fortune, left him by an uncle, whose sole heir he was. The superior education of Dantès gave an air of such probability to this statement, that it never once occurred to Jacopo to doubt its accuracy.

The term for which Edmond had engaged to serve on board La Jeune Amélie having expired, Dantès took leave of the captain, who at first tried all his powers of persuasion to induce him to remain one of the crew, but after having been told the history of the legacy ceased to importune him further. The succeeding morning Jacopo set sail for Marseilles, with directions from Dantès to rejoin him at the island of Monte-Cristo.

Having seen Jacopo fairly out of the harbour, Dantès proceeded to make his final adieux on board La Jeune Amélie distributing so liberal a gratuity among her crew as procured him unanimous good wishes, and expressions of cordial interest in all that concerned him ; to the captain he promised to write when he had made up his mind as to his future plans : this leave-taking over, Dantès departed for Genoa. At the moment of his arrival a small yacht was being tried in the bay ; this yacht had been built by order of an Englishman, who, having heard that the Genoese excelled all other builders along the shores of the Mediterranean in the construction of fast-sailing vessels, was desirous of possessing a specimen of their skill ; the price agreed upon between the Englishman and Genoese builder was forty thousand francs.

Dantès, struck with the beauty and capability of the little vessel, applied to its owner to transfer it to him, offering sixty thousand francs, upon condition of being allowed to take immediate possession of it ; the proposal was too advantageous to be refused ; the more so, as the person for whom the yacht was intended had gone upon a tour through Switzerland, and was not expected back in less than three weeks or a month, by which time the builder reckoned upon being able to complete another.

A bargain was therefore struck. Dantès led the owner of the yacht to the dwelling of a Jew; retired with the latter individual for a few minutes to a small back parlour, and upon their return from thence the Jew counted out to the ship-builder the sum of sixty thousand francs in bright golden money.

The delighted builder then offered his services in providing a suitable crew for the little vessel, but this Dantès declined, with many thanks ; saying he was accustomed to cruise about quite alone, and his principal pleasure consisted in managing his yacht himself ; the only thing the builder could oblige him in would be to contrive a sort of secret closet, in the cabin at his bed's head; the closet to contain three divisions, so constructed as to be concealed from all but himself. The builder cheerfully undertook the commission, and promised to have these secret places completed by the next day; Dantès furnishing the size and plan upon which he desired they should be arranged.

The following day Dantès sailed with his yacht from the port of Genoa, amid the gaze of an immense crowd drawn together by curiosity to see the rich Spanish nobleman who preferred managing his vessel himself; but their wonder was soon exchanged for admiration at the perfect skill with which Dantès handled the helm, and without quitting it, making his little vessel perform every movement he chose to direct; his bark seemed indeed all but human in her intelligence, so promptly did she obey the slightest impulse given; and Dantès required but a short trial of his beautiful craft to acknowledge that it was not without truth the Genoese had attained their high reputation in the art of ship-building.

The spectators followed the little vessel with their eyes so long as it remained visible, they then turned their conjectures upon her probable destination; some insisted she was making for Corsica, others the Isle of Elba; bets were offered to any amount that she was bound for Spain; while Africa was positively reported by many persons as her intended course, but no one thought of Monte-Cristo.

Yet, thither it was that Dantès guided his vessel, and at Monte-Cristo he arrived at the close of the second day; his bark having proved herself a first-class sailer, and had come the distance from Genoa in thirty-five hours. Dantès had carefully noted the general appearance of the shore, and instead of landing at the usual place, he dropped anchor in the little creek.

The isle was utterly deserted, nor did it seem as though human foot had trodden on it since he quitted it; his treasure was just as he had left it.

Early on the following morning he commenced the removal of his riches, and ere night-fall the whole of his immense wealth was safely deposited in the secret compartments of his hidden closet.

A week passed by. Dantès employed it in manœuvring his yacht round the island, studying it as a skilful horseman would the animal he destined for some important service, till at the end of that time he was perfectly conversant with its good and bad qualities.

Upon the eighth day of his being on the island, he discerned a small vessel crowding all sail towards Monte-Cristo. As it neared, he recognised it as the bark he had given to Jacopo ; he immediately signalled it ; his signal was returned, and in two hours afterwards the bark lay at anchor beside the yacht.

A mournful answer awaited each of Edmond's eager inquiries as to the information Jacopo had obtained.

Old Dantès was dead, and Mercédès had disappeared.

Dantès listened to these melancholy tidings with outward calmness ; but leaping lightly ashore, he signified his desire to be quite alone. In a couple of hours he returned. Two of the men from Jacopo's bark came on board the yacht to assist in navigating it, and he commanded she should be steered direct to Marseilles.

For his father's death, he was in some manner prepared ; but how to account for the mysterious disappearance of Mercédès he knew not.

Without divulging his secret, Dantès could not give sufficiently clear instructions to an agent—there were, besides, other particulars he was desirous of ascertaining, and those were of a nature he alone could investigate in a manner satisfactory to himself. His looking-glass had assured him during his stay at Leghorn that he ran no risk of recognition ; added to which, he had now the means of adopting any disguise he thought proper. One fine morning, then, his yacht, followed by the little bark, boldly entered the port of Marseilles, and anchored exactly opposite the memorable spot, from whence, on the never-to-be-forgotten night of his departure for the Château d'If, he had been put on board the vessel destined to convey him thither.

Still Dantès could not view without a shudder the approach of a gendarme, who accompanied the officers, deputed to demand his bill of health ; but with that perfect self-possession he had acquired during his acquaintance with Faria, Dantès coolly presented an English passport he had obtained from Leghorn, and with that prompt attention which all such English documents receive, he was informed there existed no obstacle to his immediate debarkation.

The first object that attracted the attention of Dantès as he landed on the Canebière, was one of the crew belonging to the Pharaon. Edmond hailed the appearance of this man, who had served under himself, as test of the safe and perfect change time had worked in his own appearance ; going straight towards him, he began questioning him on different subjects, carefully watching the man's countenance as he did so ; but not a word or look implied the sailor had the slightest idea of ever having seen him before.

Giving the man a piece of money in return for his civility, Dantès proceeded onwards ; but ere he had gone many steps, he heard him loudly calling him to stop.

"I beg your pardon, sir," said the honest fellow, in almost breathless haste ; "but I believe you made a mistake, you intended to give me a two-franc piece, and see, you gave me a double Napoleon."

"Thank you, my good friend ; I see that I made a trifling mistake as you say, but by way of rewarding your honest spirit, I give you another double Napoleon, that you may drink to my health, and be able to ask your messmates to join you."

So extreme was the surprise of the sailor, that he was unable even to say thank you.

Dantès meanwhile continued his route, each step he trod oppressed his heart with fresh emotion ; his first and most indelible recollections were there, not a tree, not a street that he passed but seemed filled with dear and cherished reminiscences. And thus he proceeded onwards till he arrived at the end of Rue de Noailles, from whence a full view of the Allées de Meillan was obtained.

The nasturtiums and other plants which his father had delighted to train before his window had all disappeared from the upper part of the house ; yet, leaning against a tree, he remained long gazing on those windows where the busy hand of the active old man might have once been daily seen training and arranging his floral treasures. Then he advanced to the door and inquired whether there were any chambers to be let in the house ; though answered in the negative, he begged so earnestly to be permitted to visit those on the fifth floor, that, in spite of the *concierge's* oft-repeated assurance of their being occupied, he succeeded in inducing the man to go up to the present possessors, and ask permission for a gentleman to be allowed to look at them. The tenants of the humble lodging, once the scene of all Dantès' early joys, consisted of a young couple who had been scarcely married a week, and the sight of a wedded happiness he was doomed never to experience drove a bitter pang through his heart. Nothing in the two small chambers forming the apartments remained as it had been in time of the elder Dantès ;

the very paper was different, while the articles of antiquated furniture had all disappeared. When he withdrew from the scene of his painful recollections, the young couple accompanied him down stairs, reiterating their hope that he would come again whenever he pleased, and assuring him their poor dwelling should ever be open to him. As Edmond passed the door of similar rooms on the fourth floor, he paused to inquire whether Caderousse, the tailor, still dwelt there; but he received for reply, that the individual in question had got into difficulties, and at the present time kept a small inn on the route from Bellegarde to Beaucaire.

Having obtained the address of the person to whom the house in the Allées de Meillan belonged, Dantès next proceeded thither, and, under the name of Lord Wilmore (the same name as that in his passport), purchased the small dwelling for the sum of 25,000 francs, at least 10,000 more than it was worth. The very same day the occupants of the apartments on the fifth floor of the house, now become the property of Dantès, were duly informed by the notary, who had arranged the necessary transfer of deeds, &c., that the new landlord gave them their choice of any of the rooms in the house without any increase of rent, upon condition of their giving instant possession of the two small chambers they at present inhabited.

CHAPTER XVII

THE AUBERGE OF PONT DU GARD

MIDWAY between the town of Beaucaire and the village of Bellegarde stood a small roadside inn, from the front of which hung, creaking and flapping in the wind, a sheet of tin, covered with a caricature resemblance of the Pont du Gard. The garden, scorched up beneath the ardent sun of a latitude of thirty degrees, permitted nothing to thrive, or scarcely live in its arid soil; a few dingy olives and stunted fig-trees struggled hard for existence, but their withered, dusty foliage abundantly proved how unequal was the conflict; between these sickly shrubs grew a scanty supply of garlic, tomatoes and onions, while lone and solitary, like a forgotten sentinel, a tall pine raised its melancholy head in one of the corners of this unattractive spot, and displayed its flexible stem and fanshaped summit, dried and cracked by the withering influence of the mistral, that scourge of Provence.

The inn-keeper himself was a man of from forty to fifty-five years of age, tall, strong and bony, a perfect specimen of the natives of those southern latitudes; he had the dark, sparkling, and deep-set eye, curved nose, and teeth white as those of a carnivorous animal; his hair, which, spite of the light touch time had as yet left on it, seemed as though it refused to assume any other colour than its own, was like his beard, which he wore under his chin, thick and curly, and but slightly mingled with a few silvery threads. His naturally murky complexion had assumed a still further shade of brown, from the habit the unfortunate man had acquired of stationing himself from early morn till latest eve at the threshold of his door, in eager hope that some traveller, either equestrian or pedestrian, might bless his eyes. This anxious man was no other than Caderousse. His wife, on the contrary, whose maiden name had been Madeleine Radelle, was pale, meagre, and sickly-looking. Born in the neighbourhood of Arles, she had shared

138

in the beauty for which its females are proverbial; but that beauty had gradually withered beneath the devastating influence of a slow fever. She never saw her husband without breaking out into bitter invectives against fate, to all of which he would calmly return an unvarying reply:—

"Cease to grieve about it, La Carconte. It is God's pleasure that you should suffer, and whether you like it or not you must bear it."

Caderousse was, as usual, at his place of observation before the door, his eyes glancing listlessly from a piece of closely-shaven grass—on which some fowls were industriously, though fruitlessly, endeavouring to turn up some grain or insect suited to their palate—to the deserted road, the two extremities of which pointed respectively north and south, when he saw a priest, dressed in black and wearing a three-cornered hat come riding along.

Having arrived before the auberge du Pont du Gard, the horse stopped.

"You are welcome, sir, most welcome!" said the astonished Caderousse, in his blandest tones. "A thousand pardons, your reverence! I really did not observe whom I had the honour to receive under my poor roof. What would you please to have, M. l'Abbé? What refreshment can I offer you? All I have is at your service."

The priest gazed on the individual addressing him with a long and searching gaze; then he said, speaking with a strong Italian accent—

"You are, I presume, M. Caderousse?"

"Your reverence is quite correct," answered the host, even more surprised at the question than he had been by the silence which had prefaced it; "I am Gaspard Caderousse, at your service."

"Gaspard Caderousse!" rejoined the priest. "Yes, that agrees both with the baptismal appellation and surname of the individual I allude to. You formerly lived, I believe, in the Allées de Meillan, on the fourth floor of a small house situated there?"

"I did."

"Where you followed the business of a tailor?"

"True, I was a tailor, till the trade fell off so as not to afford me a living. Then it was so very hot at Marseilles, that really I could bear it no longer; and it is my idea that all the respectable inhabitants will be obliged to follow my example and quit it. But, talking of heat, is there nothing I can offer you by way of refreshment?"

"Yes; let me have a bottle of your best wine, and then, with your permission, we will resume our conversation from where we left off."

"As you please, M. l'Abbé," said Caderousse.

When the priest was seated with the bottle and glass before him he asked: "Did you in the year 1814 or 1815, know anything of a young sailor named Edmond Dantés?"

"Did I? I should think I did. Poor dear Edmond! Why, Edmond Dantès and myself were intimate friends!" exclaimed Caderousse, whose countenance assumed an almost purple hue, as he caught the penetrating gaze of the abbé fixed on him, while the clear, calm eye of the questioner seemed to cover him with confusion.

"He died a more wretched, hopeless, heart-broken prisoner than the felons who pay the penalty of their crimes at the galleys of Toulon!"

A deadly paleness succeeded a deep suffusion which had before spread itself over the countenance of Caderousse, who turned away, but not so much so as to prevent the priest's observing him wiping away the tears from his eyes with a corner of a red handkerchief twisted round his head.

"You knew the poor lad, then!" sighed Caderousse.

"Nay, I was merely called to see him when on his dying bed, that I might administer to him the consolations of religion."

"And of what did he die?" asked Caderousse, in a choking voice.

"Of what think you do young and strong men die in prison, when they have scarcely numbered their thirtieth year? Edmond Dantès died in prison of sorrow and a broken heart."

Caderousse wiped away the large drops of perspiration that gathered on his brow.

"But the strangest part of the story is," resumed the abbé, "that Dantès, even in his dying moments, swore by his crucified Redeemer, that he was utterly ignorant of the cause of his imprisonment."

"And so he was!" murmured Caderousse. "How should he have been otherwise? Ah, M. l'Abbé, the poor fellow told you the truth."

" And for that reason he besought me to try and penetrate the mystery and to clear his memory."

And here the look of the abbé, becoming more and more fixed, seemed to rest with ill-concealed satisfaction on the gloomy depression which seemed rapidly spreading over the countenance of Caderousse.

" A rich Englishman," continued the abbé, "who had been his companion in misfortune, but had been released from prison during the second restoration, was possessed of a diamond of immense value ; this precious jewel he bestowed on Dantès upon himself quitting the prison, as a mark of his gratitude for the kindness and brotherly care with which Dantès had nursed him in a severe illness he underwent during his confinement. Instead of employing this diamond in attempting to bribe his gaolers, who might only have taken it and then betrayed him to the governor, Dantès carefully preserved it, that in the event of his getting out of prison he might have wherewithal to live, for the produce of such a diamond would have sufficed to make his fortune."

" Then I suppose," asked Caderousse, with eager glowing looks, "that it was a stone of immense value ?"

" You shall judge for yourself, I have it with me."

Calmly drawing forth from his pocket a small box covered with black shagreen, the abbé opened it, and displayed to the delighted eyes of Caderousse, the sparkling jewel it contained, set in a ring of admirable workmanship.

" And that diamond," cried Caderousse, almost breathless with eager admiration, " is worth 50,000 francs ?"

" It is, without the setting which is also valuable," replied the abbé, as he closed the box, and returned it to his pocket, whilst its brilliant hues seemed still to dance before the eyes of the fascinated inn-keeper.

" But how comes this diamond in your possession, M. l'Abbé?" Did Edmond make you his heir."

" No, merely his testamentary executor. When dying the unfortunate youth said to me, ' I once possessed four dear and faithful friends, besides the maiden to whom I was betrothed ; and I feel convinced they have all unfeignedly grieved over my loss. The name of one of the four friends I allude to is Caderousse.' "

The inn-keeper shivered as though he felt the dead cold hand of the betrayed Edmond grasping his own.

"'Another of the number,'" continued the abbé, without seeming to notice the emotion of Caderousse, "'is called Danglars; and the third, in spite of being my rival, entertained a very sincere affection for me. His name was Fernand; that of my betrothed was——' Stay, stay," continued the abbé, "I have forgotten what he called her."

"Mercédès!" cried Caderousse, eagerly.

"Bring me a carafe of water," said the abbé.

Caderousse quickly performed the stranger's bidding; and after pouring some into a glass, and slowly swallowing its contents, the abbé, resuming his usual placidity of manner, said as he placed his empty glass on the table—

"'Well, then,' said Dantès—for you understand I repeat his words just as he uttered them—'you will go to Marseilles for the purpose of selling this diamond: the produce of which you will divide into five equal parts, and give an equal portion to the only persons who have loved me upon earth.'"

"But why into five parts?" asked Caderousse, "you only mentioned four persons."

"Because the fifth is dead, as I hear. The fifth sharer in Edmond's bequest was his own father."

"Too true, too true!" ejaculated Caderousse, almost suffocated by the contending passions which assailed him, "The poor old man did die!"

"Of what?" asked the priest, anxiously and eagerly.

"Why, of downright starvation."

"Starvation!" exclaimed the abbé, springing from his seat.

"What I have said, I have said," answered Caderousse.

"It appears then, that the miserable old man you were telling me of was forsaken by every one. Surely had not such been the case, he would not have perished by so dreadful a death as you described."

"Why, he was not altogether forsaken," continued Caderousse; "for Mercédès the Catalan, and M. Morrel were very kind to him; but somehow the poor old man had contracted a profound hatred of Fernand—the very person," added Caderousse, with a bitter smile, "that you named just now as being one of Dantès' faithful and attached friends."

"And was he not so?" asked the Abbé.

"Can a man be faithful to another whose wife he covets and desires for himself? But Dantès was so honourable and true in his own nature, that he believed every body's professions of friendship. Poor Edmond! he was cruelly deceived; but it was a happy thing he never knew it, or he might have found it more difficult, when on his death-bed, to pardon his enemies."

"Do you then know in what manner Fernand injured Dantès!" inquired the abbé of Caderousse.

"Do I. No one better."

"Speak out, then; say what it was!"

So saying the abbé again drew the small box from his pocket, opened it, and contrived to hold it in such a light that a bright flash of brilliant hues passed before the dazzled gaze of Caderousse.

"Wife, wife!" cried he, in a voice almost hoarse with eager emotion, "come hither and behold this rich diamond!"

"Diamond!" exclaimed La Carconte, rising and descending to the chamber with a tolerably firm step, "what diamond are you talking about?"

"Why, did you not hear all we said?" inquired Caderousse. "It is a beautiful diamond left by poor Edmond Dantès, to be sold and the money divided between his father, Mercédès, his betrothed bride, Fernand, Danglars, and myself. The jewel is worth, at least, 50,000 francs."

"Oh, what a splendid diamond!" cried the astonished woman.

"The fifth part of the produce of this stone belongs to us, then, does it not?" asked Caderousse still devouring the glittering gem with his eyes.

"It does," replied the abbé; "with the addition of an equal division of that part intended for the elder Dantès, which I conceive myself at liberty to share equally among the four surviving persons."

"And wherefore among us four?" inquired Caderousse.

"As being the friends Edmond esteemed most faithful and devoted to him."

"I don't call those friends who betray and ruin you," murmured the wife, in her turn, in a low, muttering voice.

So saying, she once more climbed the staircase leading to her chamber, her frame shuddering with aguish chills and her teeth rattling in her head, in spite of the intense heat of the weather. Arrived at the top stair, she turned round, and called out in a warning tone to her husband—

"Gaspard, consider well what you are about to do!"

"I have decided to tell you all I know," said Caderousse to

the abbé, without heeding her. "First, sir, you must make me a promise that if you ever make use of the details I am about to give you, that you will never let any one know that it was I who supplied them, for the persons of whom I am about to talk are rich and powerful, and if they only laid the tips of their fingers on me, I should break to pieces like glass."

"Make yourself easy, my friend," replied the abbé; "I am a priest, and confessions die in my breast; recollect our only desire is to carry out in a fitting manner the last wishes of our friend. Speak, then, without reserve as without hatred; tell the truth, the whole truth; I do not know, never may know, the persons of whom you are about to speak; besides I am an Italian and not a Frenchman, and belong to God, and not to man, and I retire to my monastery, which I have only quitted to fulfil the last wishes of a dying man."

This last assurance seemed to give Caderousse courage.

"Well, then, under these circumstances," said Caderousse, "I will; indeed I ought to undeceive you as to the friendship which poor Edmond believed so sincere and unquestionable."

"Begin with his father, if you please," said the abbé: "Edmond talked to me a great deal about the old man, for whom he had the deepest love."

"The history is a sad one, sir," said Caderousse, shaking his head. "From day to day the old man lived on alone when his boy was lost to him, and more and more solitary. M. Morrel and Mercédès came to see him. At length, the poor old fellow reached the end of all he had, he owed three quarters' rent, and they threatened to turn him out, he begged for another week, which was granted to him. I know this, because the landlord came into my apartment when he left his. For the three first days I heard him walking about as usual, but on the fourth I heard him no longer. I then resolved to go up to him at all risks. The door was closed, but I looked through the key-hole, and saw him so pale and haggard, that believing him very ill I went and told M. Morrel, and then ran on to Mercédès. They both came immediately. M. Morrel bringing a doctor, and the doctor said it was an affection of the stomach, and ordered him a limited diet. I was there too, and I never shall forget the old man's smile at this prescription. From that time he opened his door he had an excuse for not eating any more as the doctor had put him on a diet."

The abbé uttered a kind of groan.

" Mercédès came again, and she found him so altered that she was even more anxious than before to have him taken to her own abode. This was M. Morrel's wish also, who would fain have conveyed the old man against his consent; but the old man resisted, and cried so, that they were actually frightened. Mercédès remained, therefore, by his bed-side, and M. Morrel went away, making a sign to the Catalane that he had left his purse on the chimney-piece. But availing himself of the doctor's order, the old man would not take any sustenance ; at length (after nine days' despair and fasting), he died, cursing those who had caused his misery, and saying to Mercédès—

" ' If you ever see my Edmond again, tell him I die blessing him.' "

The abbé rose from his chair, made two turns round the chamber, and pressed his trembling hand against his parched throat.

" And you believed he died——"

" Of hunger, sir, of hunger," said Caderousse ; " I am as certain of it as that we two are Christians."

The abbé with a shaking hand seized a glass of water that was standing by him half full, swallowed it at one gulp, and then resumed his seat with red eyes and pale cheeks.

" Tell me, now," he cried, " who are these men who have killed the son with despair, and the father with famine !"

" Two men jealous of him, sir, one from love and the other ambition—Fernand and Danglars. They denounced Edmond as a Bonapartist agent ; one wrote a letter, and the other put it in the post. They wrote it at La Réserve, the day before the festival of the betrothal."

" 'Twas so then—'twas so then," murmured the abbé, " oh ! Faria ! Faria ! how well did you judge men and things !"

" It was Danglars who wrote the denunciation with his left hand, that his writing might not be recognised, and Fernand who put it in the post."

" But," exclaimed the abbé, suddenly, " you were there yourself."

" I !" said Caderousse, astonished, " who told you I was there ?"

The abbé saw he had overshot the mark, and he added quickly—

" No one ; but in order to have known every thing so well, you must have been an eye-witness."

10

"True! true!" said Caderousse in a choking voice, "I was there."

"And did you not remonstrate against such infamy ?" asked the abbé, " if not you were an accomplice."

" Sir," replied Caderousse, " they had made me drink to such an excess that I nearly lost all perception. I had only an indistinct understanding of what was passing around me ; I said all that a man in such a state could say ; but they both assured me that it was a jest they were carrying on, and perfectly harmless."

"Next day,—next day, sir, you must have seen plain enough what they had been doing, yet you said nothing, though you were present when Dantès was arrested."

" Yes, sir, I was there, and very anxious to speak ; but Danglars restrained me.

" ' If he should really be guilty,' said he, ' and did really put into the isle of Elba ; if he is really charged with a letter for the Bonapartist committee at Paris, and if they find this letter upon him, those who have supported him will pass for his accomplices.'

"I confess I had my fears in the state in which politics then were, and I held my tongue ; it was cowardly I confess, but it was not criminal. My remorse preys on me night and day. I often ask pardon of God, I swear to you, because this action, the only one with which I have seriously to reproach myself with in all my life, is no doubt the cause of my abject condition."

"You have two or three times mentioned a M. Morrel," said the abbé after a silence, " who was he ?"

"The owner of the Pharaon, and patron of Dantès, he was an honest man, full of courage and real regard. Twenty times he interceded for Edmond ; when the emperor returned, he wrote, implored, threatened, and so energetically, that on the second restoration he was persecuted as a Bonapartist. Ten times, as I told you, he came to see Dantès' father, and offered to receive him in his own house ; and the night or two before his death, as I have already said, he left his purse on the mantel-piece, with which they paid the old man's debts and buried him decently, and then Edmond's father died as he had lived, without doing harm to any one. I have the purse still by me, a large one made of red silk."

" And," asked the abbé, " is M. Morrel still alive ?"

" Yes," replied Caderousse, " but he is reduced almost to the last extremity,—nay, he is almost at the point of dishonour. He has lost five ships in two years, has suffered by the bankruptcy of three large houses, and his only hope now is in that very Pharaon which poor Dantès commanded, which is expected from the Indies with a cargo of cochineal and indigo. If this ship founders like the others, he is a ruined man."

"What has become of Danglars, the instigator, and therefore the most guilty?"

"What has become of him? why he left Marseilles, and was taken on the recommendation of M. Morrel, who did not know his crime, as cashier into a Spanish bank. During the war with Spain, he was employed in the commissariat of the French army, and made a fortune; then with that money he speculated in the funds, and trebled or quadrupled his capital; and, having first married his banker's daughter, who left him a widower, he has married a second time, a widow, a Madame de Nargonne, daughter of M. de Servieux, the king's chamberlain, who is in high favour at court. He is a millionaire, and they have made him a count, and now he is Le Compte Danglars, with a house in the Rue de Mont Blanc, with ten horses in his stables, six footmen in his ante-chamber, and I know not how many hundreds of thousands in his strong box."

"And Fernand?"

"Some days before the return of the emperor Fernand was drawn in the conscription. The Bourbons left him quietly enough at the Catalans, but Napoleon returned, an extraordinary muster was determined on, and Fernand was compelled to join. I went, too, but as I was older than Fernand, and had just married my poor wife, I was only sent to the coast. Fernand was enrolled in the active troop, went to the frontier with his regiment, and was at the battle of Ligny. The night after that battle he was sentry at the door of a general, who carried on a secret correspondence with the enemy. That same night the general was to go over to the English. He proposed to Fernand to accompany him, Fernand agreed to do so, deserted his post and followed the general.

"That which would have brought Fernand to a court-martial, if Napoleon remained on the throne, served for his recommendation to the Bourbons. He returned to France with the epaulette of sub-lieutenant, and as the protection of the general, who is in the highest favour, was accorded to him, he was a captain in 1823, during the Spanish war, that is to say, at the time when

Danglars made his early speculations. Fernand was a Spaniard, and being sent to Spain to ascertain the feeling of his fellow-countrymen, found Danglars there, became on very intimate terms with him, procured his general support from the royalists of the capital and the provinces, received promises and made pledges on his own part, guided his regiment by paths known to himself alone in gorges of the mountains kept by the royalists, and in fact, rendered such services in this brief campaign, that after the taking of Trocadero he was made colonel, and received the title of count, and the cross of an officer of the Legion of Honour.

" Yes, but listen, this was not all. The war with Spain being ended, Fernand's career was checked by the long peace which seemed likely to endure throughout Europe. Greece only had risen against Turkey, and had begun her war of independence ; all eyes were turned towards Athens, it was the fashion to pity and support the Greeks. The French government, without protecting them openly, as you know, tolerated partial migrations. Fernand sought and obtained leave to go and serve in Greece, still having his name kept in the ranks of the army. Some time after, it was stated that the Comte de Morcerf, this was the name Fernand bore, had entered the service of Ali Pacha, with the rank of instructor-general. Ali Pacha was killed as you know, but before he died he recompensed the service of Fernand by leaving him a considerable sum, with which he returned to France, when his rank of lieutenant-general was confirmed."

" So that now——" inquired the abbé.

" So that now," continued Caderousse, " he possesses a magnificent mansion, No. 27 Rue du Helder, Paris."

The abbé opened his mouth, remained for a moment like a man who hesitates, then making an effort over himself, he said,—

" And Mercédès, they tell me that she has disappeared ?"

" Mercédès was at first in the deepest despair at the blow which deprived her of Edmond. I have told you of her attempts to propitiate M. de Villefort, her devotion to the father of Dantès. In the midst of her despair a fresh trouble overtook her, this was the departure of Fernand, of Fernand whose crime she did not know, and whom she regarded as her brother. One evening, she heard a step she knew, turned round anxiously, the door opened, and Fernand, dressed in the uniform of a sub-lieutenant, stood before her. She seized Fernand's hands with a transport, which he took for love, but which was only joy at being no longer alone in the world, and seeing at last a friend after long hours of solitary sorrow. And then, it must be confessed, Fernand had never been hated, he was only not precisely loved. Another possessed all Mercédès' heart, that other was absent, had disappeared, perhaps was dead. Fernand was now a lieutenant. He reminded Mercédès that he loved her. She begged for six months more to expect and bewail Edmond."

"So that," said the abbé, with a bitter smile, " that makes eighteen months in all, what more could the most devoted lover desire ?"

" Six months afterwards," continued Caderousse, " the marriage took place in the church of Accoules."

" Did you ever see Mercédès again ?" inquired the priest.

" Yes, during the war of Spain at Perpignan, where Fernand had left her : she was attending to the education of her son."

The abbé started.

" Her son ?" said he.

" Yes," replied Caderousse, " little Albert,"

" But, then, to be able to instruct her child," continued the abbé, "she must have received an education herself. I understood from Edmond that she was the daughter of a simple fisherman, beautiful, but uneducated."

"Oh!" replied Caderousse, "did he know so little of his lovely betrothed? Mercédès might have been a queen, sir, if the crown were to be placed on the heads of the loveliest and most intelligent. Fernand's fortune already became greater, and she became greater with his growing fortune. She learned drawing, music, everything. Besides, I believe, between ourselves, she did this in order to distract her mind, that she might forget, and she only filled her head thus in order to alleviate the weight on her heart. But now everything must be told," continued Caderousse ; "no doubt, fortune and honours have comforted her. She is rich, a countess, and yet——"

Caderousse paused.

" Yet what ?" asked the abbé.

" Yet, I am sure she is not happy," said Caderousse.

" And M. de Villefort ?" asked the abbé.

" Oh ! he was never a friend of mine, I did not know him, and I had nothing to ask of him."

" Do you not know what became of him, and the share he had in Edmond's misfortunes ?"

" No. I only know that some time after having arrested

him, he married Mademoiselle de Saint-Méran, and soon after left Marseilles; no doubt he has been as lucky as the rest, no doubt he is as rich as Danglars, as high in station as Fernand. I only, as you see, have remained poor, wretched, and forgotten!"

"You are mistaken, my friend," replied the abbé; "God may seem sometimes to forget for a while, whilst his justice reposes, but there always comes a moment when He remembers—and behold! a proof."

As he spoke, the abbé took the diamond from his pocket, and giving it to Caderousse, said,—

"Here my friend, take this diamond, it is yours."

"What! for me only?" cried Caderousse; "ah! sir, do not jest with me!"

"This diamond was to have been shared amongst his friends. Edmond had one friend only, and thus it cannot be divided. Take the diamond then, and sell it: it is worth fifty thousand francs (2,000l.), and I repeat my wish that this sum may suffice to release you from your wretchedness."

"Oh, sir," said Caderousse, putting out one hand timidly, and with the other wiping away the perspiration which bedewed his brow,—"oh, sir, do not make a jest of the happiness or despair of a man!"

"I know what happiness and what despair are, and I never make a jest of such feelings. Take it then, but in exchange——"

Caderousse, who touched the diamond, withdrew his hand.

The abbé smiled.

"In exchange," he continued, "give me the red silk purse that M. Morrel left on old Dantès' chimney-piece, which you tell me is still in your hands."

Caderousse, more and more astonished, went towards a large oaken cupboard, opened it, and gave the abbé a long purse of faded red silk, round which were two copper runners that had once been gilt. The abbé took it, and in return gave Caderousse the diamond.

The abbé with difficulty got away from the enthusiastic thanks of Caderousse, opened the door himself, got out and mounted his horse, once more saluted the innkeeper, who kept uttering his loud farewells, and then returned by the road he had travelled in coming. When Caderousse turned round, he saw behind him La Carconte paler and trembling more than ever.

"Fifty thousand francs!" muttered La Carconte, "it is a large sum of money, but it is not a fortune."

CHAPTER XVIII

THE PRISON REGISTER

THE day after, a man of about thirty or two-and-thirty, dressed in a bright blue frock-coat, nankeen trousers, and a white waistcoat, having the appearance and accent of an Englishman, presented himself before the mayor of Marseilles.

"Sir," said he, "I am chief clerk of the house of Thomson and French of Rome. We are, and have been these ten years, connected with the house of Morrel and Son of Marseilles. We have a hundred thousand francs (4,000*l.*) or thereabouts engaged in speculation with them, and we are a little uneasy at reports that have reached us that the firm is on the eve of ruin. I have come, therefore, express from Rome to ask you for information as to this house."

"Sir," replied the mayor, "I know very well that during the last four or five years misfortune seems to pursue M. Morrel. He has lost four or five vessels and suffered by three or four bankruptcies; but it is not for me, although I am a creditor myself to the amount of ten thousand francs (400*l.*), to give any information as to the state of his finances. Ask of me, as mayor, what is my opinion of M. Morrel, I shall say he is a man honourable to the last degree, and who has up to this time fulfilled every engagement with scrupulous punctuality. This is all I can say, sir; if you wish to learn more, address yourself to M. de Boville, the Inspector of Prisons, No. 15, Rue de Nouailles; he has, I believe, two hundred thousand francs placed in the hands of Morrel, and if there be any grounds for apprehension, as this is a greater amount than mine, you will most probably find him better informed than myself."

The Englishman seemed to appreciate this extreme delicacy, made his bow, and went away, walking with that step peculiar to the sons of Great Britain, towards the street mentioned. M. de Boville was in his private room, and the Englishman, on perceiving him, made a gesture of surprise, which seemed to indicate that it was not the first time he had been in his presence.   As to M. de Boville he was in such a state of despair that it was evident all the faculties of his mind, absorbed in the thought which occupied him at the moment, did not allow either his memory or his imagination to stray to the past.   The Englishman, with the coolness of his nation, addressed him in terms nearly similar to those with which he had accosted the mayor of Marseilles.

"Oh, sir," exclaimed M. de Boville, " your fears are unfortunately but too well founded, and you see before you a man in despair.   I had two hundred thousand francs placed in the hand of Morrel and Son ; these two hundred thousand francs were the dowry of my daughter, who is to be married in a fortnight, and these two hundred thousand francs were payable, half on the 15th of this month, and the other half on the 15th of next month.   I had informed M. Morrel of my desire to have these payments punctually, and he has been here within the last half-hour to tell me that if his ship the Pharaon does not come into port on the 15th he would be wholly unable to make this payment."

" But," said the Englishman, " this looks very much like a suspension of payments !"

" Say, sir, that it resembles a bankruptcy !" exclaimed M. de Boville, despairingly.

The Englishman appeared to reflect a moment, and then said—

" Thus, then, sir, this credit inspires you with considerable apprehensions !"

" To tell you the truth, I consider it lost."

" Well, then, I will buy it of you."

" But at a tremendous discount, of course ?"

" No ; for two hundred thousand francs.   Our house," added the Englishman, with a laugh, " does not do things in that way."

" And you will pay——"

" Ready money."

And the Englishman drew from his pocket a bundle of banknotes, which might have been twice the sum M. de Boville feared to lose.   A ray of joy passed across M. de Boville's countenance, yet he made an effort over himself, and said—

" Sir, I ought to tell you that in all probability you will not get six per cent of this sum."

" That's no affair of mine," replied the Englishman, " that is the affair of the house of Thomson and French, in whose name I act. They have, perhaps, some motive to serve in hastening the ruin of a rival firm. But all I know, sir, is, that I am ready to hand you over this sum in exchange for your assignment of the debt. I only ask a brokerage."

"Of course, that is perfectly just," cried M. de Boville. "The commission is usually one and a half ; will you have two— three—five per cent, or even more ? Say !"

"Sir," replied the Englishman, laughing, "I am like my house, and do not do such things—no, the commission I ask is quite different."

"Name it, sir, I beg."

"You are the inspector of prisons, and you keep the registers of entries and departures ?"

"I do."

"To these registers there are added notes relative to the prisoners ?"

"There are special reports on every prisoner."

"Well, sir, I was educated at Rome by a poor devil of an abbé, called Faria, who disappeared suddenly. I have since learned that he was confined in the Château d'If, and I should like to learn some particulars of his death."

"Oh, I recollect him perfectly," cried M. de Boville, "he was crazy, but he is dead, five or six months ago, last February."

"You have a good memory, sir, to recollect dates so well !"

"I recollect this, because the poor devil's death was accompanied by a singular circumstance."

"May I ask what that was ?" said the Englishman, with an expression of curiosity.

"Oh dear, yes, sir; the abbé's dungeon was forty or fifty feet distant from that of an old agent of Bonaparte—one of those who had the most contributed to the return of the usurper in 1815, a very resolute and very dangerous man. I myself had occasion to see him in 1816 or 1817, and we could only go into his dungeon with a file of soldiers : that man made a deep impression on me ; I shall never forget his countenance !"

"And you say, sir, that the two dungeons——"

"Were separated by a distance of fifty feet ; but it appears that this Edmond Dantès had procured tools, or made them, for they found a passage by which the prisoners communicated."

"But the abbé died ?"

"Dantès then saw a means of accelerating his escape. He, no doubt, thought that prisoners who died in the Château d'If were interred in a burial-ground as usual, and he conveyed the dead man into his own cell, assumed his place in the sack in which they had sewn him up, and awaited the moment of interment."

"It was a bold step, and one that indicated some courage," remarked the Englishman.

" As I have already told you, sir, he was a very dangerous man ; and fortunately, by his own act disembarrassed the government of the fears it had on his account, for the Château d'If has no cemetery, and they simply throw the dead into the sea after having fastened a thirty-six pound shot to their feet."

" Really !" exclaimed the Englishman.

" Yes, sir," continued the inspector of prisons. " You may imagine the amazement of the fugitive when he found himself flung head-long upon the rocks! I should like to have seen his face at this moment."

" That would have been difficult."

" No matter," replied De Boville, in supreme good humour at the certainty of recovering his two hundred thousand francs—" no matter, I can fancy it."

And he shouted with laughter.

"So can I," said the Englishman, and he laughed too ; but he laughed as the English do, at the end of his teeth.

After which they both entered M. de Boville's study.

All was here arranged in perfect order ; each register had its number, each file of paper its place. The inspector begged the Englishman to seat himself in an arm-chair, and placed before him the register and documents relative to the Château d'If, giving him all the time he desired to examine it, whilst he seated himself in a corner, and began to read his newspaper.

The Englishman easily found the entries relative to the Abbé Faria ; but it seemed that the history which the inspector had related interested him greatly, for, after having perused the first documents he turned over the leaves until he reached the deposition respecting Edmond Dantès. There he found everything arranged in due order,—the denunciation, examination, Morrel's petition, M. de Villefort's marginal notes. He folded up the denunciation quietly, and put it in his pocket ; read the examination, and saw that the name of Noirtier was not mentioned in it ; perused, too, the application, dated 10th April, 1815, in which Morrel, by the deputy-procureur's advice, exaggerated with the best intentions (for Napoleon was then on the throne) the services Dantès had rendered to the imperial cause,—services which Villefort's certificates rendered indispensable. Then he saw through all. This petition to Napoleon, kept back by Villefort, had become, under the second restoration, a terrible weapon against him in the hands of the procureur du roi. He was no longer astonished when he searched on to find in the register this note placed in a bracket against his name :—

EDMOND DANTÈS, { Violent Bonapartist; took an active part in the return from Elba. The greatest watchfulness and care to be exercised.

Beneath these lines was written in another hand,— " Nothing to be done."

He compared the writing in the bracket with the writing of the certificate placed beneath Morrel's petition, and discovered that they were the same—that is to say, were in Villefort's hand-writing.

As to the note which accompanied this, the Englishman understood that it might have been added by some inspector, who had taken a momentary interest in Dantès' situation, but who had found it impossible to give any effect to the interest he experienced.

As we have said, the inspector, from discretion, and that he might not disturb the Abbé Faria's pupil in his researches, had seated himself in a corner, and was reading " Le Drapeau Blanc."

He did not see the Englishman fold up and place in his pocket the denunciation written by Danglars under the arbour of La Réserve, and which had the post-mark of Marseilles, 2nd March, delivery 6 o'clock p.m.

Any one who had quitted Marseilles a few years previously well acquainted with the interior of Morrel's house, and had returned at this date, would have found a great change.

Instead of that air of life, of comfort, and of happiness that exhales from a flourishing and prosperous house,—instead of the merry faces seen at the windows, of the busy clerks hurrying to and fro in the long corridors,—instead of the court filled with bales of goods, re-echoing the cries and the jokes of the porters, there was an air of sadness and gloom. In the deserted corridor and the empty office, out of all the numerous clerks that used to fill the office, but two remained. One was a young man of three or four and twenty, who was in love with M. Morrel's daughter, and had remained with him, spite of the efforts of his friends to induce him to withdraw; the other was an old one-eyed cashier, named Coclès, a nickname given him by the young men who used to inhabit this vast beehive, now almost deserted, a name which had completely replaced his real one.

Coclès remained in M. Morrel's service, and a most singular change had taken place in his situation, he had at the same time risen to the rank of cashier and sunk to the rank of servant. He was, however, the same Coclès, good, patient, devoted, but inflexible on the subject of arithmetic, the only point on which he would have stood firm against the world, even against M. Morrel, and strong in the multiplication-table which he had at his fingers' ends, no matter what scheme or what trap was laid to catch him. In the midst of the distress of the house Coclès was the only one unmoved. Everything was a question of arithmetic to Coclès, and during twenty years he had always seen all payments made with such exactitude, that it seemed as impossible to him that the house should stop payment as it would to a miller that the river that had so long turned his mill should cease to flow.

Nothing had as yet occurred to shake Coclès' belief; the last month's payment had been made with the most scrupulous exactitude; Coclès had detected an error of fourteen sous to the prejudice of Morrel, and the same evening he had brought them to M. Morrel, who, with a melancholy smile, threw them into an almost empty drawer, saying,—

"Thanks, Coclès, you are the pearl of cashiers."

Coclès retired perfectly happy, for this eulogism from M. Morrel, himself the pearl of the honest men of Marseilles, flattered him more than a present of fifty pounds. But since the end of the month M. Morrel had passed many an anxious hour. In order to meet the end of the month he had collected all his resources, and, fearing lest the report of his distress should get bruited abroad at Marseilles when he was known to be reduced to such an extremity, he went to the fair of Beaucaire to sell his wife and daughter's jewels and a portion of his plate. By this means the end of the month was passed, but his resources were now exhausted. Credit, owing to the reports afloat, was no longer to be had; and to meet the 4,000l. due on the 15th

of the present month to M. de Boville, and the 4,000*l.* due to
him on the 15th of the next month, M. Morrel had, in reality,
no hope but the return of the Pharaon, whose departure he had
learnt from a vessel which had weighed anchor at the same
time, and which had already arrived in harbour.

But this vessel which, like the Pharaon, came from Calcutta,
had arrived a fortnight, whilst no intelligence had been received
of the Pharaon.

Such was the state of things when, the day after his interview
with M. de Boville, the confidential clerk of the house of
Thomson and French, of Rome, presented himself at M. Morrel's.
Emmanuel received him. The young man, wishing to spare his
employer the pain of this interview, questioned the newcomer;
but the stranger declared he had nothing to say to M. Emmanuel,
and that his business was with M. Morrel in person.

Emmanuel sighed, and summoned Coclès. Coclès appeared,
and the young man bade him conduct the stranger to M
Morrel's apartment. Coclès went first, and the stranger followed
him. On the staircase they met a beautiful girl, of sixteen or
seventeen, who looked with anxiety at the stranger.

"M. Morrel is in his room, is he not, Mademoiselle Julie?"
said the cashier.

"Yes; I think so, at least," said the young girl, hesitatingly.
"Go and see, Coclès, and if my father is there, announce this
gentleman."

"It will be useless to announce me, Mademoiselle," returned
the Englishman. "M. Morrel does not know my name; this
worthy gentleman has only to announce the confidential clerk
of the house of Thomson and French, of Rome, with whom your
father does business."

The young girl turned pale, and continued to descend, whilst
the stranger and Coclès mounted the staircase. She entered
the office where Emmanuel was, whilst Coclès, by the aid of
a key he possessed, opened a door in the corner of a landing-
place on the second staircase, conducted the stranger into an
ante-chamber, opened a second door, which he closed behind
him, and after having left the clerk of the house of Thomson
and French alone, returned and signed to him that he could enter.

The Englishman entered, and found Morrel seated at a table,
turning over the formidable columns of his ledger, which contained the list of his liabilities. At the sight of the stranger
M. Morrel closed the ledger, rose, and offered a seat to the

stranger, and when he had seen him seated resumed his own chair.

Fourteen years had changed the worthy merchant, who, in his thirty-sixth year at the opening of this history, was now in his fiftieth ; his hair had turned white, time and sorrow had ploughed deep furrows on his brow, and his look, once so firm and penetrating, was now irresolute and wandering, as if he feared being forced to fix his attention on an idea or a man. The Englishman looked at him with an air of curiosity, evidently mingled with interest.

" Monsieur," said Morrel, whose uneasiness was increased by this examination, " you wish to speak to me."

" Yes, monsieur ; you are aware from whom I come ?"

" The house of Thomson and French ; at least, so my cashier tells me."

" He has told you rightly. The house of Thomson and French had 3 or 400,000 francs (12 to 16,000*l.*) to pay this month in France, and knowing your strict punctuality, have collected all the bills bearing your signature and charged me as they became due to present them and to employ the money otherwise."

Morrel sighed deeply and passed his hand over his forehead which was covered with perspiration.

" So then, sir," said Morrel, " you hold bills of mine ?"

" Yes, and for a considerable sum."

" What is the amount ?" asked Morrel, with a voice he strove to render firm.

" Here is," said the Englishman, taking a quantity of papers from his pocket, " an assignment of 200,000 francs to our house by M. de Boville, the inspector of prisons, to whom they are due. You acknowledge, of course, you owe this sum to him ?"

" Yes, he placed the money in my hands at four and half per cent nearly five years ago."

" When are you to pay ?"

" Half the 15th of this month, half the 15th of next."

" Just so ; and now here are 32,500 francs payable shortly, they are all signed by you and assigned to our house by the holders."

" I recognise them," said Morrel, whose face was suffused as he thought that for the first time in his life he would be unable to honour his own signature. " Is this all ?"

" No, I have for the end of the month these bills which have

been assigned to us by the house of Pascal and the house of
Wild and Turner of Marseilles amounting to nearly 55,000 francs
(22,000*l*.) ; in all, 287,500 francs (11,500*l*.)."

It is impossible to describe what Morrel suffered during this
enumeration.

"Two hundred and eighty-seven thousand five hundred francs,"
repeated he.

" Yes, sir," replied the Englishman.

" I will not," continued he, after a moment's silence, " conceal
from you, that whilst your probity and exactitude up to this
moment are universally acknowledged, yet the report is current
in Marseilles that you are not able to meet your engagements."

At this almost brutal speech Morrel turned deathly pale.

" Sir," said he, " up to this time, and it is now more than
four-and-twenty years since I received the direction of this house
from my father, who had himself conducted it for five-and-thirty
years, never has anything bearing the signature of Morrel and
Son been dishonoured."

" I know that," replied the Englishman.   " But as a man of
honour should answer another, tell me fairly, shall you pay these
with the same punctuality ?"

Morrel shuddered, and looked at the man, who spoke with
more assurance than he had hitherto shewn.

" To questions frankly put," said he, " a straightforward
answer should be given.   Yes, I shall pay, if, as I hope, my
vessel arrives safely ; for its arrival will again procure me the
credit which the numerous accidents, of which I have been the
victim, have deprived me ; but if the Pharaon should be lost,
and this last resource be gone——"

The poor man's eyes filled with tears.

" Well," said the other, " if this last resource fail you ?"

" Well," returned Morrel, " it is a cruel thing to be forced to
say, but, already used to misfortune, I must habituate myself to
shame.   I fear I shall be forced to suspend my payments."

" Have you no friends who could assist you ?"

Morrel smiled mournfully.

" In business, sir," said he, " one has no friends, only correspondents."

" It is true," murmured the Englishman ; " then you have
but one hope."

" But one."

" The last ?"

" The last."

" So that if this fail——"

" I am ruined,—completely ruined !"

At this instant the door opened, and the young girl, her eyes bathed with tears, appeared. Morrel rose tremblingly, supporting himself by the arm of the chair. He would have spoken, but his voice failed him.

" Oh, father !" said she, clasping her hands, " forgive your child for being the messenger of ill."

Morrel again changed colour. Julie threw herself into his arms.

" Oh, father, father !" murmured she, " courage !"

" The Pharaon has then perished ?" said Morrel, in a hoarse voice.

The young girl did not speak; but she made an affirmative sign with her head as she lay on her father's breast.

" And the crew ?" asked Morrel.

" Saved," said the girl ; " saved by the crew of the vessel that has just entered the harbour."

Morrel raised his two hands to heaven.

" Thanks, my God," said he, " at least you strike but me alone."

Scarcely had he uttered these words when Madame Morrel entered weeping bitterly, Emmanuel followed her, and in the antechamber were visible the rough faces of seven or eight half-naked sailors.

At the sight of these men the Englishman started and advanced a step ; then restrained himself, and retired into the farthest and most obscure corner of the apartment.

Madame Morrel sat down by her husband and took one of his hands in hers, Julie still lay with her head on his shoulder, Emmanuel stood in the centre of the chamber, and seemed to form the link between Morrel's family and the sailors at the door.

" How did this happen ?" said Morrel.

" Draw nearer, Penelon," said the young man, " and relate all."

An old seaman, bronzed by the tropical sun, advanced twirling the remains of a hat between his hands.

" You see, M. Morrel," said the old seaman, " we were somewhere between Cape Blanc and Cape Mogador, when we were struck by a gale, and after twelve hours we sprang a leak.

" We soon launched the boat, and all eight of us got into it. The captain descended the last, or, rather, he did not descend, he would not quit the vessel, so I took him round the waist, and threw him into the boat, and then I jumped after him. It was time, for just as I jumped, the deck burst with a noise like the broadside of a man-of-war. Ten minutes after she pitched forward, then the other way, span round and round, and then good-bye to the Pharaon. As for us, we were three days without anything to eat or drink, so that we began to think of drawing lots who should feed the rest, when we saw La Gironde ; we made signals of distress, she perceived us, made for us, and took us all on board. The Captain, however, was too ill to come on, so he was landed at Palma. There now, M. Morrel, that's the whole truth on the honour of a sailor ; is not it true, you fellows there ?"

A general murmur of approbation shewed that the narrator had faithfully detailed their misfortunes and sufferings.

" Well, well," said Morrel, " I know there was no one in fault but destiny. It was the will of God that this should happen, blessed be His name. What wages are due to you ?"

" Oh, don't let us talk of that, M. Morrel."

" On the contrary, let us speak of it."

" Well, then, three months," said Penelon.

" Coclès ! pay 200 francs to each of these good fellows," said Morrel. " At another time," added he, " I should have said, Give them, besides, 200 francs over as a present ; but times are changed, and the little money that remains to me is not my own.

" Now," said the owner, to his wife and daughter, " leave me, I wish to speak to this gentleman."

And he glanced towards the clerk of Thomson and French, who had remained motionless in the corner during this scene, in which he had taken no part. The two females looked at this person, whose presence they had entirely forgotten and retired ; but as she left the apartment, Julie gave the stranger a suppli-cating glance, to which he replied by a smile, that an indifferent spectator would have been surprised to see on his stern features.

The two men were left alone.

" Well, sir," said Morrel, sinking into a chair, " you have heard all, and I have nothing further to tell you."

" I see," returned the Englishman, " that a fresh and un-merited misfortune has overwhelmed you, and this only increases my desire to serve you ; how long a delay do you wish for ?"

Morrel reflected.

" Two months," said he.

" I will give you three," replied the stranger.

" But," asked Morrel, " will the house of Thomson and French consent ?"

" Oh! I take everything on myself. To-day is the 5th of June."

" Yes."

" Well, renew these bills up to the 5th of September, and on the 5th of September at eleven o'clock " (the hand of the clock pointed to eleven), " I shall come to receive the money."

" I shall expect you," returned Morrel, " and I will pay you, or I shall be dead."

These last words were uttered in so low a tone that the stranger could not hear them. The bills were renewed, the old ones destroyed, and the poor ship-owner found himself with three months before him to collect his resources. The English-man received his thanks with the phlegm peculiar to his nation, and Morrel overwhelming him with grateful blessings conducted him to the staircase.

The stranger met Julie on the stairs; she affected to be descending, but, in reality, she was waiting for him.

" Oh, sir——" said she, clasping her hands.

" Mademoiselle," said the stranger, " one day you will receive a letter, signed ' Sinbad the Sailor'; do exactly what the letter bids you, however strange it may appear."

" Yes, sir," returned Julie.

" Do you promise ?"

" I swear to you I will."

" It is well. Adieu, mademoiselle!—remain as pure and vir-tuous as you are at present, and I have great hopes that Heaven will reward you by giving you Emmanuel for a husband."

Julie uttered a faint cry, blushed like a rose, and leaned against the baluster.

The stranger waved his hand, and continued to descend. In the court he found Penelon ; who, with a rouleau of a hundred francs in either hand, seemed unable to make up his mind to retain them.

" Come with me, my friend," said the Englishman, " I wish to speak to you."

CHAPTER XIX

THE delay afforded by the agent of the house of Thomson and French at the moment when Morrel expected it least, appeared to the poor ship-owner one of those returns of good fortune, which announce to a man that fate is at length weary of wasting her spite upon him. The same day he related to his wife, to Emmanuel, and his daughter, what had occurred to him, and a ray of hope, if not tranquillity, returned to the family. Unfortunately, however, Morrel had not only engagements with the house of Thomson and French, who had shown themselves so considerate towards him ; and, as he had said, in business he had correspondents and not friends. When he reflected deeply, he could by no means account for this generous conduct on the part of Thomson and French towards him, and could only attribute it to the selfish reflection of the firm : "We had better support a man who owes us nearly 300,000 francs, and have that 300,000 francs at the end of three months than hasten his ruin, and have six or eight per cent of capital."

Unfortunately, whether from hate or blindness, all Morrel's correspondents did not reflect similarly, and some made even a contrary reflection. The bills signed by Morrel were thus presented at his office with scrupulous exactitude, and, thanks to the delay granted by the Englishman, were paid by Coclès with equal punctuality. Coclès thus remained in his accustomed tranquillity.

The opinion of all the commercial men, was that after the reverses which had successively weighed down Morrel, it was impossible for him to stand. Great, therefore, was the astonishment, when they saw the end of the month come, and that he fulfilled all his engagements with his usual punctuality. Still confidence was not restored to all minds, and the general voice postponed only until the end of the month the complete ruin

163

of the unfortunate ship-owner. The month passed amidst unheard-of efforts on the part of Morrel, to get in all his resources. Formerly his paper at any date was taken with confidence and was even in request. Morrel now tried to negotiate bills at ninety days only, and found all the banks closed. Fortunately, he had some money coming in on which he could rely, and as it reached him he found himself in a condition to meet his engagements when the end of July came.

The agent of Thomson and French had not been again seen at Marseilles : the day after, or two days after his visit to Morrel, he had disappeared, and as in that city he had had no intercourse but with the mayor, the inspector of prisons, and M. Morrel, his appearance left no other trace than the different remembrances of him which these three persons retained. As to the sailors of the Pharaon, it seemed that they must have found some engagement, for they had disappeared also.

Captain Gaumard, recovered from his illness, had returned from Palma. He hesitated to present himself at Morrel's, but the owner hearing of his arrival, went to him. The worthy ship-owner knew from Penelon's recital, of the captain's brave conduct during the storm, and tried to console him. He brought him also the amount of his wages, which Captain Gaumard had not dared to apply for. As he descended the staircase, Morrel met Penelon who was going up. Penelon had, it would seem, made good use of his money, for he was newly clad ; when he saw his employer, the worthy tar seemed much embarrassed, drew on one side into the corner of the landing-place, passed his quid from one cheek to the other, stared stupidly with his great eyes, and only acknowledged the squeeze of the hand which Morrel as usual gave him by a slight pressure in return. Morrel attributed Penelon's embarrassment to the elegance of his attire, it was evident the good fellow had not gone to such an expense on his own account ; he was no doubt engaged on board some other vessel, and thus his bashfulness arose from the fact of his not having, if we may so express ourselves, worn mourning for the Pharaon longer. Perhaps, he had come to tell Captain Gaumard of his good luck, and to offer him employment from his new master.

"Worthy fellow," said Morrel, as he went away, " may your new master love you as I loved you, and be more fortunate than I have been !"

August rolled by in unceasing efforts on the part of Morrel

to renew his credit or revive the old. On the 20th of August it was known at Marseilles, that his name was in the "black book," and that it was said that, at the end of the month, the docket was to be struck and Morrel had gone away before, that he might not be present at this cruel act ; but had left his chief clerk Emmanuel, and his cashier Coclès to meet it. But contrary to all expectation, when the 31st of August came the house opened as usual, and Coclès appeared behind the grating of the counter, examined all bills presented with the same scrutiny, and, from first to last, paid all with the same precision. There came in, moreover, two repayments which M. Morrel had anticipated, and which Coclès paid as punctually as those bills which the ship-owner had accepted. All this was incomprehensible, and then with the tenacity peculiar to prophets of bad news, the failure was put off until the end of September.

M. Morrel, meantime, had gone to Paris. He had thought of Danglars, who was now immensely rich, and had lain under great obligations to him in former days. It was said at this moment that Danglars was worth from 200,000*l.* to 300,000*l.*, and had unlimited credit. Danglars then, without taking a crown from his pocket, could save Morrel ; he had but to pass his word for a loan. Morrel had long thought of this resource, but pride withheld him, and he had delayed as long as possible. His instinct had been right, for he returned home borne down by all the humiliation of a refusal. Yet on his arrival he did not utter a complaint nor say one harsh word, he embraced his weeping wife and daughter, pressed Emmanuel's hand with friendly warmth, and then going to his private room on the second floor, had sent for Coclès.

"Then," said the two women to Emmanuel, "we are indeed ruined."

It was agreed in a brief council held amongst them, that Julie should write to her brother, who was in garrison at Nismes, to come to them as speedily as possible.

The two next days passed almost heavily.

On the second, the young girl had just left her father by his own request, when, on the first step of the staircase, she found a man holding a letter in his hand.

"Are you not Mademoiselle Julie Morrel?" inquired the man with a strong Italian accent.

"Yes," replied Julie, with hesitation.

"Read this letter," he said, handing it to her.   "It concerns the best interests of your father."

She hastily took the letter from him.   She opened it quickly and read—

"Go this moment to the Allées de Meillan, enter the house No. 15, ask the porter for the key of the room on the fifth floor, enter the apartment, take from the corner of the mantel-piece a purse netted in red silk, and give it to your father.   It is important that he should receive it before eleven o'clock.   You promised to obey me implicitly.   Remember your oath.

"SINBAD THE SAILOR."

She uttered a joyful cry, raised her eyes, looked round to question the messenger, but he had disappeared.   Then she saw there was a postscript.   She read—

"It is important that you should fulfil this mission in person and alone, if you go accompanied by any other person, or should any one else present themselves, the porter will reply that he does not know anything about it."

Julie hastened down and told Emmanuel what had occurred on the day when the agent of the house of Thomson and French had come to her father's, related the scene on the staircase, repeated the promise she had made, and showed him the letter.

"You must go, then, mademoiselle," said Emmanuel, "but you shall be alone.   I will await you at the corner of the Rue du Musée, and if you are so long absent as to make me uneasy, I will hasten to rejoin you."

"But what danger threatens us, then, Emmanuel?" she asked.

Emmanuel hesitated a moment.

"Listen," he said, "to-day is the 5th of September—is it not? and at eleven o'clock, your father has nearly 300,000 francs to pay.   Well, we have not 15,000 francs in the house, and if before eleven o'clock your father has not found some one who will come to his aid, he will be compelled at twelve o'clock to declare himself a bankrupt."

"Oh, come, then, come!" cried she, hastening away with the young man.

Morrel was alone in his cabinet.   He heard the door of the staircase creak on its hinges.   The clock gave its warning to strike eleven.   The door of his cabinet opened—Morrel did not turn round, he expected these words of Coclès—

" The agent of Thomson and French."

He had resolved to put an end to his life sooner than face dishonour. He placed the muzzle of the pistol between his teeth. Suddenly he heard a cry,—it was his daughter's voice. He turned and saw Julie, the pistol fell from his hands.

" My father !" cried the young girl, out of breath and half dead with joy. " Saved !—you are saved !" And she threw herself into his arms, holding in her extended hand a red netted silk purse.

Morrel took the purse, and started as he did so, for a vague remembrance reminded him that it once belonged to himself, at one end was the bill for the 287,500 francs *receipted*, at the other was a diamond as large as a hazel nut, with these words on a small slip of parchment :—

" JULIE'S DOWRY."

Morrel passed his hand over his brow ; it seemed to him a dream. At this moment the clock struck eleven. The sound vibrated as if each stroke of the hammer struck on Morrel's heart.

" Explain, my child," he said ; " explain where did you find this purse ?"

" In a house in the Allées de Meillan, No. 15, on the corner of a mantel-piece, in a small room on the fifth floor."

And she handed to her father the letter she had received in the morning.

" Monsieur Morrel !" exclaimed a voice on the stairs. " Monsieur Morrel !" And Emmanuel entered, his countenance full of animation and joy.

" The Pharaon !" he cried ; " the Pharaon ! The Pharaon, sir—they signal the Pharaon ! The Pharaon is entering the harbour !"

Morrel fell back in his chair, his strength was failing him ; his understanding weakened by such events refused to comprehend such incredible, unheard-of, fabulous facts.

At that moment his son arrived from Paris, and before greeting him cried out in his astonishment : " Father, how could you say the Pharaon was lost ? The watch-tower has signalled her, and they say she is now coming into port."

" My dear friends !" said Morrel, " if this were so, it must be a miracle of Heaven ! Impossible ! impossible !"

But what was real and not less incredible was the purse he held in his hand ; the acceptance receipted—the splendid diamond.

" Ah! sir," exclaimed Coclès, " what can it mean ?—the Pharaon ?"

" Come, my dear," said Morrel, rising from his seat, " let us go and see, and Heaven have pity upon us if it be false intelligence."

They all went out, and on the stairs met Madame Morrel, who had been afraid to go up into the cabinet. In an instant they were at the Cannebière. There was a crowd on the pier. All the crowd gave way before Morrel.

" The Pharaon ! the Pharaon !" said every voice.

And, wonderful to say, in front of the tower of Saint-Jean, was a ship bearing on her stern these words printed in white letters, " The Pharaon, Morrel and Son, of Marseilles." It was a new ship but one which precisely resembled the other Pharaon, and carried a similar cargo of cochineal and indigo. It cast anchor, brailed all sails, and on the deck was Captain Gaumard giving orders, and Maître Penelon making signals to M. Morrel.

To doubt any longer was impossible ; there was the evidence of the senses and ten thousand persons, who came to corroborate the testimony.

As Morrel and his son embraced on the pier-head, a man with his face half covered by a black beard, who, concealed behind the sentry-box, watched the scene with delight, uttered these words in a low tone, " Be happy, noble heart, be blessed for all the good thou hast done and wilt do hereafter, and let my gratitude rest in the shade with your kindness."

And with a smile in which joy and happiness were revealed, he left his hiding-place, and without being observed descended one of those flights of steps which serve for debarkation, and hailing three times, shouted, " Jacopo ! Jacopo ! Jacopo !"

Then a shallop came to shore, took him on board, and conveyed him to a yacht splendidly fitted up, on the deck of which he sprang with the activity of a sailor ; thence he once again looked towards Morrel, who weeping with joy was shaking hands most cordially with all the crowd around him, and thanking the unknown benefactor whom he seemed to be seeking in the skies.

CHAPTER XX

TOWARDS the commencement of the year 1838, two young men belonging to the first society of Paris, the Viscount Albert de Morcerf and the Baron Franz d'Epinay, were at Florence. They had agreed to see the carnival at Rome that year, and that Franz, who for the last three or four years had lived in Italy, should act as *cicerone* to Albert.

As it is no inconsiderable affair to spend the carnival at Rome, especially when you have no great desire to sleep on the Place du Peuple, or the Campo Vaccino, they wrote to Maître Pastrini, the proprietor of the Hôtel de Londres, Place d'Espagne, to reserve comfortable apartments for them. Maître Pastrini replied that he had only two rooms and a cabinet *al-secondo piano*, which he offered at the low charge of a louis per diem. They accepted his offer ; but wishing to make the best use of the time that was left Albert started for Naples. As for Franz he remained at Florence. After having passed several days here, when he had walked in the Eden called the Casines, and had passed two or three evenings at the houses of the nobles of Florence, he took a fancy into his head, after having already visited Corsica, the cradle of Bonaparte, to visit Elba, the halting-place of Napoleon.

One evening he loosened a bark from the iron ring that secured it to the port of Leghorn, laid himself down, wrapped in his cloak, at the bottom, and said to the crew,—

" To the isle of Elba."

The bark shot out of the harbour like a bird, and the next morning Franz disembarked at Porto-Ferrajo. He traversed the island, after having followed the traces which the footsteps of the giant have left, and re-embarked for Marciana. Two hours after he again landed at Pianosa, where he was assured red partridges abounded. The sport was bad ; Franz only succeeded in killing a few partridges, and, like every unsuccessful sportsman, he returned to the boat very much out of temper.

169

" Ah, if your excellency chose," said the captain, whose name was Gaetano, " you might have capital sport."

" Where ?"

" Do you see that island ?" continued the captain, pointing to a conical pile that 'rose from out the azure main.'

" Well ; what is this island ?"

" The island of Monte-Cristo."

" But I have no permission to shoot over this island."

" Your excellency does not require permission, there is rarely anyone there."

To the island accordingly they went, arriving there as night was falling. They saw from some distance the light of a fire on the shore, and turning an angle of the rock, they saw the fire round which five or six persons were seated.

The blaze illumined the sea for a hundred paces round. Gaetano skirted the light, carefully keeping the bark out of its rays, then, when they were opposite the fire, he entered into the centre of the circle, singing a fishing song, of which his companions sang the chorus.

At the first words of the song, the men seated round the fire rose and approached the landing-place, their eyes fixed on the bark. They soon appeared satisfied, and returned (with the exception of one who remained at the shore) to their fire, at which a whole goat was roasting.

When the bark was within twenty paces of the shore the man on the beach made with his carbine the movement of a sentinel who sees a patrol, and cried, " Who goes there ?" in Sardinian. Franz coolly cocked both barrels. Gaetano exchanged a few words with this man, which the traveller did not understand, but which evidently concerned him.

" Will your excellency give your name or remain incognito ?" asked the captain.

" My name must rest unknown—merely say I am a Frenchman travelling for pleasure."

As soon as Gaetano had transmitted this answer, the sentinel gave an order to one of the men seated round the fire, who rose and disappeared among the rocks. Not a word was spoken, every one seemed occupied, Franz with his disembarkment, the sailors with their sails, the smugglers with their goat; but in the midst of all this carelessness it was evident that they mutually observed each other.

One of the men had disappeared on first sighting them, he now returned and spoke to Gaetano, who translated to Franz.

" The chief of the island is here, it appears, and invites you to sup with him."

" But you told me there was no one here," objected the young man.

" I have heard of this chief, but did not know he ever stayed here. He makes one condition.'

" The devil !—and what is this condition ?"

" That you are blindfolded, and do not take off the bandage until he himself bids you."

Franz looked at Gaetano to see, if possible, what he thought of this proposal.

" Ah !" replied he, guessing Franz's thought, " I do not know if what they say is true——"

He stopped to look if any one was near.

" What do they say ?"

" That this chief inhabits a cavern to which the Pitti Palace is nothing."

" What nonsense !" said Franz, reseating himself.

" It is no nonsense, it is quite true.   Cama, the pilot of the Saint Ferdinand, went in once, and he came back amazed, vowing that such treasures were only to be heard of in fairy tales."

" Do you know," observed Franz, " that with such stories you would make me enter the enchanted cavern of Ali Baba ?"

Franz reflected a few moments, felt that a man so rich could not have any intention of plundering him of what little he had, and seeing only the prospect of a good supper, he accepted. Gaetano departed with the reply.

Franz turned to one of the men.   " What does this chief call himself ?" he asked.

" Sinbad the Sailor."

" Where will he receive me ?"

" No doubt in the subterranean palace Gaetano told you of."

" Have you never had the curiosity, when you have landed and found this island deserted, to seek for this enchanted palace ?"

" Oh, yes, more than once, but always in vain ; we examined the island all over, but we never could find the slightest trace of any opening ; they say that the door is not opened by a key, but a magical word."

" Decidedly," muttered Franz, " this is an adventure of the Arabian Nights."

" His excellency waits for you," said a voice, which he recognised as that of the sentinel.

He was accompanied by two of the yacht's crew. Franz drew
his handkerchief from his pocket and presented it to them an
who had spoken to him.   Without uttering a word they
bandaged his eyes with a care that showed their apprehensions
of his committing some indiscretion.   Afterwards he was made
to promise he would not make the least attempt to raise the
bandage. He promised. Then his two guides took his arms,
and he advanced guided by them, and preceded by the sentinel.
After advancing about thirty paces he smelt the appetising
odour of the kid that was roasting, and knew thus that he was
passing the bivouac ; they then led him on about fifty paces
farther, evidently advancing towards the shore, where they
would not allow Gaetano to penetrate—a refusal he could now
comprehend. Presently, by a change in the atmosphere, he
gathered that they were entering a cave ; after going on
for a few seconds more he heard a crackling, and it seemed to
him as though the atmosphere again changed, and became
balmy and perfumed. At length his feet touched a thick and
soft carpet, and his guides let go their hold of him. There
was a moment's silence, and then a voice, in excellent French,
although with a foreign accent, said—

" Welcome, sir.   I beg you will remove your bandage."

It may be supposed Franz did not wait for a repetition
of this permission, but took off the handkerchief, and found
himself in the presence of a man from thirty-eight to forty
years of age, dressed in a Tunisian costume, that is to say, a red
cap with a long blue silk tassel, a vest of black cloth embroidered
with gold, pantaloons of deep red, large and full gaiters of the
same colour, embroidered with gold, like the vest, and yellow
slippers; he had a splendid cachemire round his waist, and a
small sharp and crooked dagger was passed through his girdle.
Although of a paleness that was almost livid, this man had a
remarkably handsome face ; his eyes were penetrating and sparkling ; a nose, quite straight and projecting direct from the brow,
showed the Greek type in all its purity, whilst his teeth, as
white as pearls, were set off to admiration by the black moustache
that encircled them.

This pallor was so peculiar that it seemed as though it were
that which would be exhibited by a man who had been inclosed
for a long time in a tomb, and who was unable to resume the
healthy glow and hue of the living. He was not particularly
tall, but extremely well made, and, like the men of the south

had small hands and feet. But what astonished Franz, who had treated Gaetano's description as a fable, was the splendour of the apartment in which he found himself. The entire chamber was lined with crimson brocade, worked with flowers of gold. In a recess was a kind of divan, surmounted with a stand of Arabian swords in silver scabbards, and the handles resplendent with gems; from the ceiling hung a lamp of Venice glass, of beautiful shape and colour, whilst the feet rested on a Turkey carpet, in which they sank to the instep; tapestry hung before the door by which Franz had entered, and also in front of another door, leading into a second apartment, which seemed to be brilliantly lighted up. The host gave Franz time for his surprise, and, moreover, rendered him look for look, not even taking his eyes off him.

"Sir," he said, after some pause, "a thousand excuses for the precaution taken in your introduction hither; but as, during the greater portion of the year, this island is deserted, if the secret of this abode were discovered I should, doubtless, find on my return my temporary residence in a great state of disorder, which would be exceedingly annoying, not for the loss it occasioned me, but because I should not have the certainty I now possess of separating myself from all the rest of mankind at pleasure. Let me now endeavour to make you forget this temporary unpleasantness, and offer you what no doubt you did not expect to find here, that is to say, a tolerable supper and pretty comfortable beds."

"*Ma foi!* my dear sir," replied Franz, "make no apologies. I have always observed that they bandage people's eyes who penetrate enchanted palaces, for instance, those of Raoul in the *Huguenots*, and really I have nothing to complain of, for what I see is a sequel to the wonders of the Arabian Nights."

At this moment the tapestry moved aside, and a Nubian, black as ebony, and dressed in a plain white tunic, made a sign to his master that all was prepared in the dining-room.

"Now," said the unknown to Franz, " to put you at your ease, I tell you that I am generally called 'Sinbad the Sailor.'"

"And I," replied Franz, "will tell you, as I only require his wonderful lamp to make me precisely like Aladdin, that I see no reason why at this moment I should not be called Aladdin. That will keep us from going away from the East, whither I am tempted to think I have been conveyed by some good genius."

"Well, then, Signor Aladdin," replied the singular host,

"you heard our repast announced, will you now take the trouble to enter the dining-room, your humble servant going first to shew you the way?"

At these words, moving aside the tapestry, Sinbad preceded his guest. Franz proceeded from one enchantment to another; the table was splendidly covered, and, once convinced of this important point, he cast his eyes around him. The dining-room was scarcely less striking than the boudoir he had just left; it was entirely of marble, with antique bas-reliefs of priceless value; and at the four corners of this apartment, which was oblong, were four magnificent statues, having baskets on their heads. These baskets contained four pyramids of most splendid fruit; there were the pine-apples of Sicily, pomegranates of Malaga, oranges from the Balearic Isles, peaches from France, and dates from Tunis.

The supper consisted of a roast pheasant, garnished with Corsican blackbirds; a boar's ham *à la gelée*, a quarter of a kid *à la tartare*, a glorious turbot, and a gigantic lobster. Between these large dishes were smaller ones, containing various dainties. The dishes were of silver, and the plates of Japanese china.

Franz rubbed his eyes in order to assure himself that this was not a dream. Ali alone was present to wait at table, and acquitted himself so admirably, that the guest complimented his host thereupon.

"Yes," replied he, whilst he did the honours of the supper with much ease and grace,—"yes, he is a poor devil who is much devoted to me, and does all he can to prove it. He remembers I saved his life, and as he has a regard for his head he feels some gratitude towards me for having kept it on his shoulders."

Ali approached his master, took his hand and kissed it.

"Like the celebrated sailor whose name you have assumed," Franz asked after a moment, "you pass your life in travelling?"

"Yes! I made a vow at a time when I little thought I should ever be able to accomplish it," said the unknown, with a singular smile; "and I made some others also, which I hope I may fulfil in due season."

Although Sinbad pronounced these words with much calmness, his eyes darted gleams of singular ferocity.

"You have suffered a great deal, sir?" said Franz, inquiringly.

Sinbad started and looked fixedly at him, as he replied, "What makes you suppose so?"

"Everything!" answered Franz,—"your voice, your look, your pallid complexion, and even the life you lead."

" I ! I live the happiest life possible, the real life of a pacha. I am king of all creation. Ah! if you had tasted of my life, you would not desire any other, and would never return to the world unless you had some great project to accomplish there."

" Vengeance, for instance !" observed Franz.

The unknown fixed on the young man one of those looks which penetrate into the depth of the heart and thoughts.

" And why vengeance ?" he asked.

" Because," replied Franz, " you seem to me like a man who, persecuted by society, has a fearful account to settle with it."

" Ah !" responded Sinbad, laughing with his singular laugh, which displayed his white and sharp teeth. " You have not guessed rightly !"

The supper appeared to have been supplied solely for Franz, for the unknown scarcely touched one or two dishes of the splendid banquet to which his guest did ample justice. Then Ali brought on the dessert, or rather took the baskets from the hands of the statues and placed them on the table.

At length Sinbad rose. " Let us now go into the chamber beside you, which is your apartment, and Ali will bring us coffee and pipes."

They both arose, and while Sinbad gave some orders to the servant, Franz entered the adjoining apartment. It was simply yet richly furnished. It was round, and a large divan completely encircled it. Divan, walls, ceiling, floor, were all covered with magnificent skins, soft and downy as the richest carpets ; there were skins of the lions of Atlas, with their large manes, skins of Bengal tigers, with their striped hides ; skins of the panthers of the Cape spotted beautifully, like those that appeared to Dante ; skins of the bears of Siberia, the foxes of Norway, &c. ; and all these skins were strewn in profusion one on the other, so that it seemed like walking over the most mossy turf, or reclining on the most luxurious bed.

Both laid themselves down on the divan : chibouques, with jasmine tubes and amber mouth-pieces, were within reach, and all prepared so that there was no need to smoke the same pipe twice. Each of them took one, which Ali lighted, and then retired to prepare the coffee. There was a moment's silence, during which Sinbad gave himself up to thoughts that seemed to occupy him incessantly, even in the midst of his conversation, and Franz abandoned himself to that mute reverie, into which we always sink when smoking excellent tobacco. Ali brought in the coffee.

After taking it, a strange transformation happened. All the bodily fatigue of the day, all the pre-occupation of mind which the events of the evening had brought on disappeared. His body seemed to acquire an airy lightness, his perception brightened in a remarkable manner, his senses seemed to redouble their power, the horizon continued to expand until he passed into unconsciousness.

When Franz returned to himself, he stretched forth his hand and touched stone, he rose to his seat and found himself lying on his burnous in a bed of dry heather, very soft and odoriferous.

On rising to his feet, he found that he was in a grotto, went towards the opening, and through a kind of fanlight saw a blue sea and an azure sky. The air and water were shining in the beams of the morning sun, on the shore the sailors were sitting chatting and laughing, and at ten yards from them the bark was at anchor, undulating gracefully on the water.

He went gaily up to the sailors, who rose as soon as they perceived him, the Captain accosting him said,—

"The Count of Monte-Cristo has left his compliments for your excellency, and desired us to express the regret he feels at not being able to take his leave in person, but he trusts you will excuse him, as very important business calls him to Malaga."

"So then, Gaetano," said Franz, "this is all reality, there exists a man who has received me in this isle, entertained me right royally, and has departed whilst I was asleep."

"He exists certainly, as you may see if you will use your glass."

So saying, Gaetano pointed in a direction in which a small vessel was making sail towards the southern point of Corsica. Franz adjusted his telescope and directed it towards the bark.

Gaetano was not mistaken. At the stern the mysterious stranger was standing up looking towards the shore, and holding a spy-glass in his hand ; he was attired as he had been on the previous evening, and waved his pocket-handkerchief to his guest in token of adieu. Franz returned the salute by shaking his handkerchief as an exchange of signals.

After a second, a slight cloud of smoke was seen at the stern of the vessel, which rose gracefully as it expanded in the air, and then Franz heard a slight report.

"There ! do you hear ?" observed Gaetano, "he is bidding you adieu !"

The young man took his carbine and fired it in the air, but

without any idea that the noise could be heard at the distance which separated the yacht from the shore.

"What are your excellency's orders?" inquired Gaetano.

"In the first place, light me a torch."

"Ah! yes! I understand," replied the patron, "to find the entrance to the enchanted apartment. With much pleasure, your excellency, if it would amuse you, and I will get you the torch you ask for. I, too, have had the idea you have, and two or three times the same fancy has come over me; but I have always given it up. Giovanni, light a torch," he added, "and give it to his excellency."

Giovanni obeyed, Franz took the lamp, and entered the subterranean grotto followed by Gaetano. He recognized the place where he awoke by the bed of heather that was there, but it was in vain that he carried his torch all around the exterior surface of the grotto, he saw nothing. Yet he did not leave a foot of this granite wall, as impenetrable as futurity, without strict scrutiny: he did not see a fissure without introducing the blade of his hunting sword in it, nor a projecting point on which he did not lean and press in the hopes it would give way: all was vain, and he lost two hours in his attempts, which were utterly useless.

CHAPTER XXI

THE CARNIVAL AT ROME

FRANZ reached the Place de la Douane in Rome a day later. An apartment, as we have said, had been retained beforehand, and thus he had but to go to the hotel of Maître Pastrini; but this was not so easy a matter, for the streets were thronged with people, and Rome was already a prey to that low and feverish murmur which precedes all great events, and at Rome there are four great events in every year—the Carnival, the Holy Week, the Fête Dieu, and the Saint Peter. All the rest of the year the city is in a state of dull apathy, between life and death. He made his way through this mob, which was continually increasing and becoming more agitated, and at last reached the hotel. On his first inquiry, he was told, with the impertinence peculiar to hackney-coachmen who are hired and inn-keepers with their house full, that there was no room for him at the Hôtel de Londres. Then he sent his card to Maître Pastrini, and demanded Albert de Morcerf. This plan succeeded, and Maître Pastrini himself ran to him, excusing himself for having made his excellency wait, scolding the waiters, taking the candlestick in his hand from the cicerone, who was ready to pounce on the traveller, and was about to lead him to Albert, when Morcerf himself appeared.

The apartment consisted of two small rooms and a closet. The two rooms looked on to the street, a fact which Maître Pastrini commented upon as an extraordinary advantage. The remainder of the flat, he told them, was hired by a very rich gentleman, who was supposed to be a Sicilian or Maltese.

The two young men greeted each other with the nonchalance of youth and ordered a carriage at eight o'clock to visit the Colosseum by night.

Maître Pastrini instantly warned them not to go.

" It is very dangerous, to say the least," said he.

" Dangerous! and why ?"

" On account of the famous Luigi Vampa."

" Pray who may this famous Luigi Vampa be ?" inquired Albert.

" He is a bandit, compared with whom the Decesaris and the Gasparones were mere children."

" Now then, Albert," cried Franz, " here is a bandit for you at last."

" After nightfall," continued Maître Pastrini, " you are not safe fifty yards from the gate."

" On your honour, is that true ?" cried Albert.

" M. le Comte," returned Maître Pastrini, " I do not say this to you, but to your companion, who knows Rome, and knows, too, that these things are not to be laughed at."

" My dear fellow," said Albert, turning to Franz, " here is an admirable adventure; we will fill our carriage with pistols, blunderbusses, and double-barrelled guns. Luigi Vampa comes to take us, and we take him—we bring him back to Rome, and present him to His Holiness the Pope, who asks how he can repay so great a service ; then we merely ask for a carriage and a pair of horses, and we see the Carnival in the carriage, and doubtless the Roman people will crown us at the Capitol, and proclaim us, like Curtius and Horatius Cocles, the preservers of the country."

" Well, Maître Pastrini," said Franz, " tell me who is this Luigi Vampa. Is he a shepherd or a nobleman ?—young or old ?—tall or short ? Describe him, in order that, if we meet by chance, we may recognise him."

" Of the middle height—about the same stature as his excellency," returned the host, pointing to Albert.

For some reason Franz did not feel at all inclined to confide in Albert his strange adventure. Though they were together all the afternoon he did not mention it.

It was he who arranged the route they were to take that evening, and he so contrived it that during the ride to the Colosseum they passed not a single ancient ruin, so that no gradual preparation was made on the mind of his companion for the colossal proportions of the gigantic building they came to admire. This itinerary possessed another great advantage, that of leaving Franz at full liberty to indulge his deep reverie upon the subject of his mysterious host of the isle of Monte-Cristo. Seated with folded arms in a corner of the carriage, he continued to ponder over the scenes he had so lately been through.

But however the mind of the young man might be absorbed in these reflections, they were at once dispersed at the sight of the dark frowning ruins of the stupendous Colosseum, through the various openings of which the pale moonlight played and flickered like the unearthly gleam from the eyes of the wandering dead. The carriage stopped near the Meta Sudans, the door was opened, and the young men eagerly alighting, found themselves opposite a cicerone, who appeared to have sprung up from the ground, so unexpected was his appearance.

The usual guide from the hotel having followed them, they had paid two conductors ; nor is it possible, at Rome, to avoid this abundant supply of guides ; besides the ordinary cicerone who seizes upon you directly you set foot in your hotel, and never quits you while you remain in the city, there is also a special cicerone belonging to each monument—nay, almost to each part of a monument.

Scarcely, however, had the reflective Franz walked a hundred steps beneath the interior porticoes of the ruin, than, abandoning Albert to the guides who would by no means yield their prescriptive right of carrying their victims through the routine regularly laid down, he ascended a half-dilapidated staircase, and seated himself at the foot of a column, immediately opposite a large gap, which permitted him to enjoy a full and undisturbed view of the gigantic dimensions of this majestic ruin.

Franz remained for nearly a quarter of an hour hidden by the shadow, but he followed with his eyes the motions of Albert and his guides, who were holding torches in their hands, until they at last disappeared down the steps conducting to the seats reserved for the Vestal virgins. No sooner was Franz thus left totally alone, than his ear caught a sound resembling that of a stone rolling down a staircase opposite to the place where he was seated. Immediately afterwards the figure of a man emerged from the staircase into the full tide of the moon's silvery brightness.

The person whose mysterious arrival had attracted the attention of Franz stood in a kind of half light, that rendered it impossible to distinguish his features, although his dress was easily made out ; he wore a large brown mantle, one fold of which thrown over his left shoulder served likewise to mask the lower part of his countenance, while the upper part was completely hidden by his broad-brimmed hat.

Directly he appeared, a slight noise was heard outside, and almost immediately a dark shadow obstructed the flood of light, and a second man appeared.

Franz could not distinguish a word of the conversation that followed, but he could see that the second comer treated the first with a manner indicating deference. Yet, though he could not hear the words, the tone of the deep sonorous, yet well-pitched voice, that had spoken to him in the grotto of Monte-Cristo, fell on his ear, and with a start of surprise he realised that the first comer was no other than the Count of Monte-Cristo! Almost immediately after he had made this discovery, he heard Albert shouting for him, and at the sound the men, who had not seen him, disappeared as mysteriously as they had come.

In vain did Franz endeavour to forget the many perplexing thoughts which assailed him as he tried to sleep that night. Slumber refused to visit his eyelids, and his night was passed in feverish contemplation of the reason which linked Monte-Cristo to the bandits of the Colosseum, for that the second man was one of them he had no doubt.

The Carnival was to commence on the morrow; therefore Albert had engaged a box in the most conspicuous part of the theatre, and exerted himself to set off his personal attractions by the aid of the most *recherchée* and elaborate toilette.

Sitting alone, in the front of a box immediately opposite, was a woman of exquisite beauty, dressed in a Greek costume, which it was evident, from the ease and grace with which she wore it, was her national attire. Behind her, but in deep shadow, was the outline of a man, who kept in the background.

The second act of Parisina opens with the celebrated and effective duet, in which Parisina, while sleeping, betrays to Azzo the secret of her love for Ugo. The injured husband goes through all the workings of jealousy, until conviction seizes on his mind, and then, in a frenzy of his rage and indignation, he awakens his guilty wife to tell her he knows her guilt and to threaten her with his vengeance. This duet is one of the finest conceptions that has ever emanated from the fruitful pen of Donizetti. Franz now listened to it for the third time, yet its notes, so tenderly expressive and fearfully grand, as the wretched husband and wife give vent to their different griefs and passions, thrilled through his soul with an effect equal to his first emotions upon hearing it. Excited beyond his usual calm demeanour

Franz rose with the audience, and was about to join the loud enthusiastic applause that followed, when suddenly his purpose was arrested, his hands fell by his sides, and the half-uttered " bravos " expired on his lips.

The occupant of the box, in which the Greek girl sat, appeared to share the universal animation that prevailed, for he left his seat to stand up in the front, so that his countenance being fully revealed, Franz had no difficulty in recognising him as the mysterious inhabitant of Monte-Cristo, and the very same individual he had encountered the preceding evening in the ruins of the Colosseum.   All doubt of his identity was now at an end ; his singular host evidently resided at Rome.

Still more astonished was he the following day, when Maître Pastrini appeared in a mysterious manner in the rooms occupied by the two young men, and began :

" Your excellencies are aware that the Count of Monte-Cristo is living on the same floor with yourselves ?"

" Why certainly," exclaimed Albert, " I heard that yesterday."

" The Count of Monte-Cristo, knowing of the difficulties there are in procuring vehicles, has sent to offer you the loan of one of his carriages for the Carnival."

The friends looked at each other with unutterable surprise.

" Do you think," Albert continued, " that we ought to accept such an offer from a perfect stranger ?"

" What sort of person is this Count of Monte-Cristo ?" asked Franz of his host, to cover his momentary confusion.

" A very great nobleman, but whether Maltese or Sicilian I cannot exactly say ; but this I know, that he is noble as a Borghese and rich as a gold-mine."

There seemed no reason why they should not accept the Count's courtesy.   Franz naturally believed it was especially to himself that it was offered.   That afternoon they descended ; the carriage awaited them at the door, filled with sweetmeats and bouquets.   They fell into the line of carriages.

The Place del Popolo presented a spectacle of gay and noisy mirth and revelry.   A crowd of masks flowed in from all sides, escaping from the doors, descending from the windows.   From every street and every turn drove carriages filled with pierrots, harlequins, dominoes, marquises, ladies, knights, and peasants—screaming, fighting, gesticulating, whirling eggs filled with flour, confetti, nosegays—attacking, with their sarcasms and their missiles, friends and foes, companions and strangers, indiscriminately, without anyone taking offence, or doing anything else than laugh. A handful of confetti that came from a neighbouring carriage filled with people disguised as Roman peasants, covered Morcerf and his companion with dust, pricked his neck and that portion of his face uncovered by his mask like a hundred pins, plunged him into the general combat in which all the masks around him were engaged. He rose in his turn, and, seizing handfuls of confetti and sweetmeats, with which the carriage was filled, cast them with all the force and address he was master of.

The day passed unmarked by any incident, except meeting two or three times a calèche with the Roman peasants. At one of these encounters, accidentally or purposely, Albert's mask fell off. He instantly rose and cast the remainder of the bouquets into the carriage. One of the women, rising in her turn, threw a bunch of violets at him. Albert seized it, placed it in his button-hole, and the carriage went triumphantly on.

"Well," said Franz to him; "here is the commencement of an adventure."

"Laugh if you please. I really think so. So I will not abandon this bouquet."

At the second turn, a bunch of fresh violets, thrown from the carriage again, indicated to Albert that he had indeed been noticed particularly.

Albert placed the fresh bouquet in his button-hole: but he kept the faded one in his hand; and when he again met the calèche, he raised it to his lips, an action which seemed greatly to amuse not only the fair lady in the peasant disguise, but her joyous companions also.

The next morning Franz saw Albert pass and repass at the same place. He held an enormous bouquet, which he, doubtless, meant to make a bearer of an amorous epistle. This belief was changed into certainty when the bouquet (remarkable by a circle of white camelias) appeared that evening at the opera in the hand of a charming young girl dressed in rose-coloured satin.

The evening was no longer joy but delirium. Albert nothing doubted but that the fair unknown would send him some reply and he was not deceived; for the next evening Franz saw him enter, shaking triumphantly a folded paper he held by one corner.

"Read!"

This word was pronounced in a manner impossible to describe. Franz took the letter and read—

" Tuesday evening, at seven o'clock, descend from your carriage opposite the Via dei Pontefici, and follow the Roman peasant who snatches your torch from you. When you arrive at the first step of the church of San Giacomo, be sure to fasten a knot of rose-coloured ribands to the shoulder of your costume of *paillasse*, in order that you may be recognised. Until then you will not see me. Constancy and Discretion."

At length arrived the Tuesday, the last and most tumultuous day of the Carnival. That Tuesday the theatres opened at ten o'clock in the morning, as Lent begins after eight at night; all those who through want of money, time, or enthusiasm, have not been to see the Carnival before that day, mingle in the gaiety and contribute to the noise and excitement. From two o'clock till five Franz and Albert followed in the fête, exchanging handfuls of confetti with the other carriages and the pedestrians, who crowded amongst the horses' feet and the carriage-wheels without a single accident, a single dispute, or a single fight.

As the day advanced the tumult became greater. There was not on the pavement, in the carriages, at the windows, a single tongue that was silent, a single arm that did not move. It was a human storm composed of a thunder of cries, and a hail of sweetmeats, flowers, eggs, oranges, and nosegays. At three o'clock the sound of fireworks, let off on the Place del Popolo and the Palais de Vénise (heard with difficulty amid the din and confusion), announced that the races were about to begin. The races are one of the episodes peculiar to the last days of the Carnival. At the sound of the fireworks the carriages instantly broke the ranks and retired by the adjacent streets. All these evolutions are executed with an inconceivable address and marvellous rapidity, without the police interfering in the matter.

The races continued for two hours; the Rue du Cours was light as day; the features of the spectators on the third and fourth stories were visible. Every five minutes Albert took out his watch : at length it pointed to seven. The two friends were in the Via dei Pontefici. Albert sprang out, bearing his torch in his hand. Two or three masks strove to knock his torch out of his hand; but Albert, a first-rate pugilist, sent

The Carnival at Rome

them rolling in the street one after the other, and continued his course towards the church of San Giacomo. The steps were crowded with masks, who strove to snatch each other's flambeau. Franz followed Albert with his eyes, and saw him mount the first step. Instantly a mask, wearing the well-known costume of a female peasant, snatched his torch from him without his offering any resistance. Franz was too far off to hear what they said, but without doubt nothing hostile passed, for he saw Albert disappear arm-in-arm with the peasant girl.

He watched them pass through the crowd some time, but at length he lost sight of them in the Via Macello. Suddenly the bell that gives the signal for the end of Carnival sounded, and at the same instant all the torches were extinguished as if by enchantment. Franz found himself in utter darkness. No sound was audible save that of the carriages that conveyed the masks home; nothing was visible save a few lights that burnt behind the windows.

The Carnival was finished.

CHAPTER XXII

VAMPA THE BRIGAND

IN his whole life, perhaps, Franz had never before experienced so sudden an impression, so rapid a transition from gaiety to sadness, as in this moment. It seemed as though Rome, under the magic breath of some demon of the night, had suddenly changed into a vast tomb. By chance, which added yet more to the intensity of the darkness, the moon, which was on the wane, did not rise until eleven o'clock, and the streets which the young man traversed were plunged in the deepest obscurity. The distance was short: and at the end of ten minutes his carriage, or rather the count's, stopped before the Hôtel de Londres.

Dinner was waiting; but as Albert had told him that he should not return so soon, Franz sat down without him.

Maître Pastrini, who had been accustomed to see them dine together, inquired into the cause of his absence, but Franz merely replied, that Albert had received on the previous evening an invitation which he had accepted. The sudden extinction of the torches, the darkness which had replaced the light, the silence which had succeeded, and the turmoil, had left in his mind a certain depression which was not free from uneasiness. He therefore dined very silently, in spite of the officious attentions of his host, who presented himself two or three times to inquire if he wanted anything.

Franz resolved to wait for Albert as late as possible. He ordered the carriage, therefore, for eleven o'clock, desiring Maître Pastrini to inform him the moment Albert returned to the hôtel. At eleven o'clock Albert had not come back.

But a letter was brought to him which caused him great anxiety.

"MY DEAR FELLOW,—The moment you receive this, have the kindness to take from my pocket-book, which you will find in the square drawer of the secrétaire, the letter of credit:

add your own to it, if it be not sufficient. Run to Torlonia, draw from him instantly four thousand piastres, and give them to the bearer. It is urgent that I should have this money without delay.

"I do not say more, relying on you as you may rely on me.
"Your friend,
"ALBERT DE MORCERF.

"P.S. I now believe in Italian banditti."

Below these lines were written in a strange hand the following in Italian—

"*If by six in the morning the four thousand piastres are not in my hands, by seven o'clock the Viscount Albert de Morcerf will have ceased to live.*
"LUIGI VAMPA."

There was no time to lose. He hastened to open the secré-taire, and found the pocket-book in the drawer, and in it the letter of credit; there was in all six thousand piastres, but of these six thousand Albert had already expended three thousand. As to Franz he had no letter of credit as he lived at Florence, and had only come to Rome to pass seven or eight days; he had brought but a hundred louis, and of these he had not more than fifty left.

Thus seven or eight hundred piastres were wanting to them both to make up the sum that Albert required. True he might in such a case rely on the kindness of M. Torlonia.

He was, therefore, about to return to the Palazzo Bracciano without loss of time when suddenly a luminous idea crossed his mind. He remembered the Count of Monte-Cristo. He and Albert had already thanked the count by letter for his civility in the matter of the carriage; now he remembered the count's curious encounter with the brigand in the Colosseum, and he resolved to appeal to him for help. He accordingly went to Monte-Cristo's flat. He found the count was still up and agreed to see him without delay. He manifested no sign of ever having met Franz before, and Franz followed his lead, telling his story as if to a stranger. When he had heard it, the count went to his secrétaire, opened it, and pulling out a drawer filled with gold, said,—

"I am glad that you did not offend me by applying to anyone but myself; have what you will."

And he made a sign to Franz to take what he pleased.

"Is it absolutely necessary, then, to send the money to Luigi Vampa?" asked the young man, looking fixedly in his turn at the count.

"Judge yourself," replied he. "The postscript is explicit."

"If we were to go together to Luigi Vampa, I am sure he would not refuse you Albert's freedom."

The count knit his brows and remained silent an instant.

"And if I went to seek Vampa, would you accompany me?"

"If my society would not be disagreeable."

"Be it so ; it is a lovely night, and a walk without Rome will do us both good.   Where is the man who brought the letter?"

"In the street."

"I must learn where we are going. I will summon him hither."

"It is useless, he would not come up."

"To your apartments, perhaps : but he will not make any difficulty in entering mine."

The count went to the window of the apartment that looked on to the street, and whistled in a peculiar manner. The man in the mantle quitted the wall, and advanced into the centre of the street.

"*Salite!*" said the count, in the same tone in which he would have given an order to his servant. The messenger obeyed without the least hesitation, but rather with alacrity, and mounting the steps of the passage at a bound, entered the hôtel : five seconds afterwards he was at the door of the apartment.

"How did the Viscount Albert fall into Luigi's hands, Peppino?" Monte-Cristo asked the man, who seemed known to him.

"Excellency, the Frenchman's carriage passed several times the one in which was Teresa, Luigi's lover. The Frenchman threw her a bouquet, Teresa returned it ; all this with the consent of the chief, who was in the carriage."

"What!" cried Franz, "was Luigi Vampa in the carriage with the Roman peasants?"

"It was he who drove, disguised as the coachman," replied Peppino. "The Frenchman asked for a rendezvous ; Teresa gave him one ; only instead of Teresa it was Beppo who was on the steps of the church of San Giacomo."

"What!" exclaimed Franz, "the peasant girl——"

"Was a lad of fifteen," replied Peppino ; "but it was no disgrace of your friend to have been deceived. Beppo has taken in plenty to others."

" And Beppo led him outside the walls ?" said the count.

" Exactly so; where he was over-powered by five armed men, and was forced to yield; they made him get out, walk along the banks of the river, and then brought him to Teresa and Luigi, who were waiting for him in the catacombs of Saint Sebastian."

The count took out his watch.

" Half-past twelve," he said; " we might start at five o'clock and be in time, but the delay may cause your friend to pass an uneasy night; and, therefore, we had better go with all speed to extricate him from the hands of the infidels."

Franz and the count went down-stairs, accompanied by Peppino. At the door they found the carriage. Ali was on the box. Franz and the count got into the carriage. Peppino placed himself beside Ali, and they set off at a rapid pace. Ali had received his instructions, and went down the Rue du Cours, crossed the Campo Vaccino, went up the Strada San Gregorio, and reached the gates of Saint Sebastian; then the porter raised some difficulties; but the Count of Monte-Cristo produced an authority from the governor of Rome to quit or enter the city at any and all hours of the day or night; the portcullis was therefore raised, the porter had a louis for his trouble, and they went on their way. The road which the carriage now traversed was the ancient Appian Way, and bordered with tombs. From time to time, by the light of the moon which began to rise, Franz imagined that he saw something like a sentinel appear from various points of the ruin, and suddenly retreat into the darkness on a signal from Peppino.

A short time before they reached the Circus of Caracalla the carriage stopped, Peppino opened the door, and the count and Franz alighted. Peppino led them to an opening behind a clump of bushes, and in the midst of a pile of rocks by which a man could scarcely pass. He glided first into this crevice, but after advancing a few paces the passage widened. Then he paused, lighted a torch, and turned round to see if they came after him. The count first reached a kind of square space, and Franz followed him closely. The earth sloped in a gentle descent, enlarging as they proceeded, still Franz and the count were compelled to advance stooping and scarcely able to proceed two abreast. They went on a hundred and fifty paces thus, and then were stopped by " Who goes there ?"

At the same time they saw the reflection of a torch on the barrel of a carbine.

"A friend!" responded Peppino, and advancing alone towards the sentry he said a few words to him in a low tone, when he, like the rest, saluted the nocturnal visitors, making a sign that they might proceed.

Behind the sentinel was a staircase with twenty steps. Franz and the count descended these, and found themselves in a kind of cross roads, forming a burial ground. Five roads diverged like the rays of a star, and the walls, dug into niches, placed one above the other in the shape of coffins, shewed that they were at last in the catacombs. In one of the cavities, whose extent it was impossible to determine, some rays of light were visible. The count laid his hand on Franz's shoulder,—

"Peppino, extinguish the torch," he ordered.

Peppino obeyed, and Franz and the count were suddenly in utter darkness, only fifty paces in advance of them there played along the wall some reddish beams of light, more visible since Peppino had put out his torch. They advanced silently, the count guiding Franz as if he had the singular faculty of seeing in the dark. Franz himself, however, distinguished his way more plainly in proportion as he advanced towards the rays of light which served them for guides,—three arcades, of which the middle served as the door, offered themselves. These arcades opened on one side to the corridor, in which were the count and Franz, and on the other to a large square chamber, entirely surrounded by niches similar to those of which we have spoken. In the midst of this chamber were four stones, which had formerly served as an altar, as was evident from the cross which still surmounted them. A lamp, placed at the base of a pillar, lighted up with its pale and flickering flame the singular scene which presented itself to the eyes of the two visitors concealed in the shadow. A man was seated with his elbow leaning on the column, and was reading with his back turned to the arcades, through the openings of which the newcomers contemplated him. This was the chief of the band, Luigi Vampa. Around him, and in groups, according to their fancy, lying in their mantles, or with their backs against a kind of stone bench, which went all round the Columbarium, were to be seen twenty brigands or more, each having his carbine within reach. At the bottom, silent, scarcely visible, and like a shadow, was a sentinel, who was walking up and down before a kind of opening, which was only distinguishable because in that spot the darkness seemed thicker. When the count thought Franz had gazed sufficiently on this picturesque tableau, he raised his finger to his lips, to warn him to be silent, and ascending the three steps which led to the corridor of the Columbarium, entered the chamber by the centre arcade, and advanced towards Vampa, who was so intent on the book before him that he did not hear the noise of his footsteps.

" Who goes there ?" cried the sentinel, less occupied.

At this sound Vampa rose quickly, drawing at the same moment a pistol from his girdle. An instant later all the bandits were on their feet, and twenty carbines were levelled at the count.

" Well," said he, in a perfectly calm voice, " my dear Vampa, it appears to me that you receive a friend with a great deal of ceremony !"

" Ground arms !" exclaimed the chief, with an imperative sign of the hand ; then turning, he said,—" Your pardon, M. le Comte, but I was so far from expecting the honour of a visit, that I did not really recognise you."

" It seems that your memory is equally short in everything, Vampa," said the count, "and that not only do you forget people's faces, but also the conditions you make with them."

" What conditions have I forgotten, M. le Comte ?" inquired the bandit.

" Was it not agreed," asked the count, " that not only my person, but also that of my friends, should be respected by you ?"

" And how have I broken that treaty, your excellency ?"

" You have this evening carried off and conveyed hither the Viscount Albert de Morcerf. Well," continued the count, in a tone that made Franz shudder, " this young gentleman is one of *my friends*,—this young gentleman lodges in the same hôtel as myself,—this young gentleman has been up and down the Corso for eight hours in my private carriage, and yet I repeat to you, you have carried him off, and conveyed him hither, and," added the count, taking the letter from his pocket, "you have set a ransom on him as if he were an indifferent person."

" Why did you not tell me all this, you ?" inquired the brigand chief, turning towards his men, who all retreated before his look. " Why have you exposed me thus to fail in my word towards a gentleman like the count who has all our lives in his hands ? By heavens ! if I thought one of you knew that the young gentleman was the friend of his excellency, I would blow his brains out with my own hand ! What is the prisoner doing ?" he added, turning to the sentinel.

"*Ma foi!* captain," replied the man, "I do not know, for the last hour I have not heard him stir."

"Come in, your excellency," said Vampa.

The count and Franz ascended seven or eight steps after the chief, who drew back a bolt, and opened a door. Then by the gleam of a lamp, similar to that which lighted the Columbarium, Albert was seen wrapped up in a cloak which one of the bandits had lent him, lying in a corner in profound slumber.

"Come!" said the count, smiling with his own peculiar smile, "not so bad for a man who is to be shot at seven o'clock to-morrow morning!"

Vampa looked at Albert with a kind of admiration; he was not insensible to such a proof of courage.

Then, going forward, he touched him on the shoulder, saying,—

"Will your excellency please to awaken?"

Albert stretched out his arms, rubbed his eyelids, and opened his eyes.

"Ah! ah!" said he, "is it you captain? You should have allowed me to sleep. I had such a delightful dream."

Then he drew from his pocket his watch.

"Half-past one only," said he. "Why the devil do you rouse me at this hour?"

"To tell you that you are free, your excellency."

Albert looked round, and perceived Franz.

"What!" said he, "is it you, my dear Franz, whose devotion and friendship are thus displayed?"

"No, not I," replied Franz, "but our neighbour, the Count of Monte-Cristo."

"Ah! ah! M. le Comte," said Albert, gaily, arranging his cravat and wristbands, "you are really most kind, and I hope you will consider me as eternally obliged, in the first place for the carriage, and in the next for this!" and he put out his hand to the count, who shuddered as he gave his own.

Followed by many apologies from the bandit, they went out to the carriage and lost no time in getting home.

The following morning Albert's first wish was to visit the count; true, he had warmly and energetically thanked him the previous evening, but services such as he had rendered could never be too often acknowledged.

Franz, who seemed attracted by some invisible influence towards the count, made no objection to Albert's request, but at once accompanied him to the desired spot, and, after a short delay, the count joined them in the saloon.

"M. le Comte," said Albert, advancing to meet him, "permit me to repeat the poor thanks I offered last night, and to assure you that the remembrance of all I owe you will never be effaced from my memory ; believe me, while I have life I shall never cease to dwell with grateful recollection on the prompt and important service you rendered me ; as also to remember that to you I am indebted even for my life."

"My very good friend and excellent neighbour," replied the count with a smile, "you really exaggerate my trifling exertions. You owe me nothing but some trifle of 20,000 francs which you have been saved out of your travelling expenses, so that there is not much of a score between us ; but you must really permit me to congratulate you on the ease and unconcern with which you resigned yourself to your fate, and the perfect indifference you manifested as to the turn events might take."

"Upon my word," said Albert, "I deserve no credit for what I could not help, namely, a determination to take everything as I found it ; and to let those bandits see, that although men get into troublesome scrapes all over the world, the French can smile even in the face of grim Death himself. All that, however, has nothing to do with my obligation to you, and I now come to ask you, whether, in my own person, my family, or connexions, I can, in any way, serve you ? My father, the Comte de Morcerf, although of Spanish origin, possesses considerable influence, both at the court of France and Madrid, and I unhesitatingly place the best services of myself, and all to whom my life is dear, at your disposal."

"M. de Morcerf," replied the count, "your offer, far from surprising me, is precisely what I expected from you, and I accept it in the same spirit of hearty sincerity with which it is made ; —nay, I will go still further, and say that I had previously made up my mind to ask a great favour at your hands."

"Oh, pray name it."

"I am wholly a stranger to Paris—it is a city I have never yet seen, and I wish to visit it, but I know no-one there."

"My dear count," exclaimed Albert, "command me and mine to any extent you please."

"Then it is a settled affair," said the count ; "and I give you my solemn assurance, that I only waited an opportunity like the present to realise schemes I have long meditated."

13

"I shall be only too happy to receive you as my guest."

"Shall we make a positive appointment for a particular day and hour?" inquired the count; "only let me warn you that I am proverbial for my punctilious exactitude in keeping my engagements."

"The very thing!" exclaimed Albert.

"So be it, then," replied the count, and extending his hand towards an almanack, he said, "to-day is the 21st of February," and drawing out his watch, added, "it is exactly half-past ten o'clock. Now promise me to remember this, and expect me the 21st of May at the same hour in the forenoon."

"Capital!" exclaimed Albert; "and you shall find everything and everybody ready to receive you. I take upon myself to promise that your breakfast shall be smoking hot awaiting your arrival."

"Where do you live?"

"No. 27, Rue du Helder!"

"Have you bachelor's apartments there? I hope my coming will not put you to any inconvenience."

"I reside in my father's house, but occupy a pavilion at the farther side of the court-yard, entirely separated from the main building."

"Quite sufficient," replied the count, as taking out his tablets he wrote down, "No. 27, Rue du Helder, 21st May, half-past ten in the morning." "Now then," he added, "make yourself perfectly easy, the hand of your clock will not be more accurate in marking the time than myself."

Before the friends parted, Albert de Morcerf to return to Paris, and Franz d'Epinay to pass a fortnight at Venice, Franz felt that he must make known to Albert the strange story of the island, especially now that the count was to be his guest.

Albert was immensely interested. "Why did you not tell me all this before?" he cried, and asked innumerable questions.

When he had learnt all he could of the affair, he was more delighted than ever that he was to renew his acquaintance with so strange a man. And as he said adieu to Franz, he drew from his pocket with a flourish the card of Monte-Cristo, on which he had written:

"27, Rue du Helder, on the 21st May, half-past ten a.m."

CHAPTER XXIII

In the house in the Rue du Helder, where Albert de Morcerf had invited the Count of Monte-Cristo, everything was being prepared on the morning of the 21st of May to fulfil the engagement.

Albert inhabited a suite of rooms at the corner of a large court, directly opposite another building, in which were the servants' apartments. Two windows only of the pavilion faced the street; three other windows looked into the court, and two at the back into the garden. Between the court and the garden, built in the heavy style of the imperial architecture, was the large and fashionable dwelling of the Count and Countess de Morcerf. A high wall surrounded the whole of the mansion, surmounted at intervals by vases filled with flowers, and broken in the centre by a large gate of gilt iron, which served as the carriage entrance. A small door, close to the lodge of the concierge, gave ingress and egress to those who were on foot.

Before ten o'clock a carriage stopped at the door, and the servant announced M. Lucien Debray. A tall young man, with light hair, clear grey eyes, and thin and compressed lips, dressed in a blue coat with buttons of gold, beautifully carved, a white neckcloth, and wearing a tortoiseshell eye-glass suspended by a silken thread, entered, with a half-official air, without smiling or speaking.

"Good morning, Lucien! good morning!" said Albert; "your punctuality really alarms me. What do I say? punctuality! You whom I expected last, you arrive at five minutes to ten, when the time fixed was half-past! Have ministers resigned?"

"No, my dear fellow," returned the young man, seating himself on the divan; "reassure yourself: we are tottering always, but we never fall; and I begin to believe that we shall pass into a state of immobility, and then the affairs of the Peninsular will completely consolidate us."

" M. Beauchamp," announced the servant.

" Enter, enter," said Albert, rising and advancing to meet the young man.

" Here is Debray, who detests you without reading you, so he says."

" He is quite right," returned Beauchamp, " for I criticise him without knowing what he does. Good-day, Commander!"

" Ah! you know that already," said the private secretary, smiling and shaking hands with him.

" *Pardieu!*"

" And what do they say of it in the world ?"

" In which world? we have so many worlds in the year of grace 1838."

" In the entire political world, of which you are one of the leaders."

" They say that it is quite fair, and that you sow so much red, that you must reap a little blue."

" Come, come! that is not bad!" said Lucien. " Why do you not join our party, my dear Beauchamp? with your talents you would make your fortune in three or four years."

" I only await one thing before following your advice, that is, a minister who will hold office for six months. My dear Albert, one word, for I must get poor Lucien a respite. Do we breakfast or dine? I must go to the Chamber, I shall have to hear M. Danglars make a speech at the Chamber of Deputies, for our life is not an idle one."

" You only breakfast : I await two persons, and the instant they arrive we shall sit down to table. Meantime, my dear friend," said Albert to Beauchamp, " you are most desperately out of humour this morning. Recollect that Parisian gossip has spoken of a marriage between myself and Mlle. Eugénie Danglars; I cannot, in conscience, therefore, let you run down the speeches of a man who will one day say to me, ' M. le Vicomte, you know I give my daughter eighty thousand pounds.' "

" Ah, this marriage will never take place," said Beauchamp. "The king has made him a baron and can make him a peer, but he cannot make him a gentleman ; and the Count de Morcerf is too aristocratic to consent, for the paltry sum of eighty thousand pounds, to a *mésalliance*. The Viscount de Morcerf can only wed a marchioness."

" But eighty thousand pounds is a nice little sum," replied Morcerf.

" It is the social capital of a theatre on the boulevard, or a railroad from Jardin des Plantes to la Râpée."

" Never mind what he says, Morcerf," said Debray, " do you marry her. You marry a money bag, it is true ; well, but what does that matter ?"

" M. de Château-Renaud ! M. Maximilian Morrel !" said the servant, announcing two fresh guests.

" Now, then, to breakfast," said Beauchamp ; " for if I remember, you told me you only expected two persons, Albert."

" Morrel !" muttered Albert, " Morrel ! who is he ?"

But before he had finished, M. de Château-Renaud, a handsome young man of thirty, gentleman all over, that is, with the figure of a Guiche and the wit of a Mortemart, took Albert's hand.

" My dear Albert," said he, " let me introduce to you M. Maximilian Morrel, captain of Spahis, my friend."

And he stepped on one side, exhibiting the large and open brow, the piercing eyes and black moustache of the fine and noble young man, whom our readers have already heard of at Marseilles under circumstances sufficiently dramatic not to be forgotten. A rich uniform, half French, half Oriental, set off his broad chest, decorated with the order of the Legion of Honour.

The young officer bowed with easy and elegant politeness.

" There is still another guest," said Albert. " His name is the Count of Monte-Cristo."

" There is not a Count of Monte-Cristo," said Debray.

" I do not think so," added Château-Renaud, with the air of a man who knows the whole of the European nobility perfectly.

" Does any one know anything of a Count of Monte-Cristo ?"

" He comes possibly from the Holy Land, and one of his ancestors possessed Calvary as the Mortemarts did the Dead Sea."

" I think I can assist your researches," said Maximilian. " Monte-Cristo is a little island I have often heard spoken of by the old sailors my father employed. A grain of sand in the centre of the Mediterranean, an atom in the infinite."

" My Count of Monte-Cristo is a mystery. He has even a name taken from the ' Arabian Nights,' since he calls himself Sinbad the Sailor, and has a cave filled with gold."

" And you have seen this cavern, Morcerf ?" asked Beauchamp.

" No ! but Franz has : for Heaven's sake not a word of this before him. Franz went in with his eyes blindfolded."

"No Count of Monte-Cristo!" added Debray. "There is half-past ten striking, Albert!"

"Confess you have dreamed this, and let us sit down to breakfast," continued Beauchamp.

But the sound of the clock had not died away when Germain announced—

"His Excellency the Count of Monte-Cristo."

The involuntary start every one gave proved how much Morcerf's words had impressed them, and Albert could not prevent himself from feeling a sudden emotion. He had not heard a carriage stop in the street, or steps in the antechamber; the door had opened noiselessly.

The count appeared, dressed with the greatest simplicity, but the most fastidious dandy could have found nothing to cavil at in his toilette, for every article of dress, hat, coat, gloves, and boots, were from the first makers. He seemed scarcely five-and-thirty.

The Count advanced smiling into the centre of the room and approached Albert, who hastened towards him holding out his hand.

"Punctuality," said Monte-Cristo, "is the politeness of kings —according to one of your sovereigns, I think; but it is not the same with travellers. However, I hope you will excuse the two or three seconds I am behindhand; five hundred leagues are not to be accomplished without some trouble, and especially in France, where it seems it is forbidden to beat the postilions."

"M. le Comte," replied Albert, "I was announcing your visit to some of my friends, whom I had invited in consequence of the promise you did me the honour to make, and whom I now present to you. They are M. le Comte de Château-Renaud, whose nobility goes back to twelve peers, and whose ancestors had a place at the Round Table: M. Lucien Debray, private secretary to the Ministre de l'Intérieur; M. Beauchamp, an editor of a paper, and the terror of the French government, of whom, in spite of his celebrity, you have not heard in Italy, since his paper is prohibited there; and M. Maximilian Morrel, captain of Spahis."

At this name the count, who had hitherto saluted every one with courtesy, but at the same time with coldness and formality, stepped a pace forward, and a slight tinge of red coloured his pale cheeks.

"You wear the uniform of the new French conquerors, monsieur," said he. "It is a handsome uniform."

No one knew what caused the count's voice to vibrate so deeply, and what made his eye flash.

"Gentlemen," said Albert, "Germain informs me breakfast is ready. My dear count, allow me to show you the way."

They passed silently into the breakfast-room ; every one took his place.

"Gentlemen," said the count, seating himself, "permit me to make a confession. I am a stranger, and a stranger to such a degree, that this is the first time I have ever been in Paris. The French way of living is utterly unknown to me, and up to the present time I have followed the Eastern customs, which are entirely different from the Parisian. I beg you therefore to excuse me if you find anything in me too Turkish, too Italian, or too Arabian. Now, then, let us breakfast."

"With what an air he says all this!" muttered Beauchamp ; "decidedly he is a great man."

"A great man in his country," added Debray.

"A great man in every country, M. Debray," said Château-Renaud.

The count was, it may be remembered, a most temperate guest. Albert remarked this, expressing his fears lest, at the outset, the Parisian mode of life should displease the traveller in the most essential point.

The conversation was for a time general, then the count turning to Albert said: "I recollect that at Rome you said something of a projected marriage. May I congratulate you?"

"The affair is still in projection."

"And he who says ' in projection,' means already decided," said Debray.

"No," replied Morcerf, " my father is most anxious about it ; and I hope, ere long, to introduce you, if not to my wife, at least to my intended—Mademoiselle Eugénie Danglars."

"Eugénie Danglars!" said Monte-Cristo ; "tell me, is not her father M. le Baron Danglars?"

"Yes," returned Morcerf ; " a baron of a new creation."

"What matter," said Monte-Cristo, " if he has rendered the state services which merit this distinction?"

"Enormous ones," answered Beauchamp. "Although in reality a liberal, he negotiated a loan of six millions (240,000l.) for Charles X., who made him a baron and chevalier de la Légion d'Honneur ; so that he wears the riband, not as you would think, in his waistcoat-pocket, but at his button-hole."

"Ah," interrupted Morcerf, laughing, "Beauchamp, Beauchamp, keep that for the 'Charivari,' but spare my future father-in-law before me." Then turning to Monte-Cristo, "You just now pronounced his name as if you knew the baron?"

"I do not know him," returned Monte-Cristo; "but I shall probably soon make his acquaintance, for I have a credit opened with him by the house of Richard and Blount of London, Arstein and Eskeles of Vienna, and Thomson and French of Rome."

As he pronounced the two last names, the count glanced at Maximilian Morrel.

If the stranger expected to produce an effect on Morrel, he was not mistaken—Maximilian started as if he had been electrified.

"Thomson and French!" said he; "do you know this house, monsieur?"

"They are my bankers in the capital of the Christian world," returned the count quietly. "Can my influence with them be of any service to you?"

"Oh, M. le Comte, you could assist me, perhaps, in researches which have been, up to the present, fruitless. This house, in past years, did ours a great service, and has, I know not for what reason, always denied having rendered us this service."

"I shall be at your orders," said Monte-Cristo, inclining himself.

"I wonder," said Morcerf presently to the count, "if you have made any arrangement where to lodge in Paris? If not, I shall be proud to offer you hospitality."

"I will venture to offer the count a suite of apartments in a charming hôtel," said Morrel shyly, "in the Pompadour style, that my sister has inhabited for a year, in the Rue Meslay. I live there during my leave of absence," he continued; "and I shall be, together with my brother-in-law, Emmanuel Herbaut, at the disposition of M. le Comte, whenever he thinks fit to honour us."

"Thanks, monsieur," said Monte-Cristo, "I shall content myself with being presented to your sister and her husband, if you will do me the honour to introduce me; but I cannot accept either of these kind offers, since my habitation is already prepared."

"What!" cried Morcerf, "you are, then, going to an hôtel— that will be very dull for you."

"Was I so badly lodged at Rome?" said Monte-Cristo, smiling.

" Why, at Rome you spent fifty thousand piastres in furnishing your apartments, but I presume that you are not disposed to spend a similar sum every day."

"It is not that which deterred me," replied Monte-Cristo; " but as I determined to have a house to myself I sent on my valet de-chambre, and he ought by this time, to have bought the house and furnished it."

" But you have, then, a valet-de-chambre who knows Paris ?" said Beauchamp.

" It is the first time he has ever been in Paris. He is black, and cannot speak," returned Monte-Cristo.

"It is Ali !" cried Albert, in the midst of the general surprise.

" Yes, Ali himself, my Nubian mute, whom you saw, I think, at Rome."

" Certainly," said Morcerf; " I recollect him perfectly. But how could you charge a Nubian to purchase a house, and to furnish it ? he will do every thing wrong."

" Undeceive yourself," replied Monte-Cristo; "I am quite sure that, on the contrary, he will choose every thing as I wish. He knows my tastes, my caprices, my wants ; he has been here a week, with the instinct of a hound hunting by himself; he will organise every thing for me. He knew I should arrive to-day at ten o'clock ; since nine he awaited me at the Barrière de Fontainebleau. He gave me this paper ; it contains the number of my new abode ; read it yourself," and Monte-Cristo passed a paper to Albert.

" Ah, that is really original," said Beauchamp, to whom Albert passed the paper.

" And very princely," added Château-Renaud.

" Do you not know your house ?" asked Debray.

" No," said Monte-Cristo ; " I told you I did not wish to be behind my time ; I dressed myself in the carriage, and descended at the vicomte's door."

The young men looked at each other: they did not know if it was a comedy Monte-Cristo was playing : but every word he uttered had such an air of simplicity, that it was impossible to suppose what he said was false : besides why should he tell a falsehood ?

" We must content ourselves, then," said Beauchamp, " with rendering M. le Comte all the little services in our power. I, in my quality of journalist, open all the theatres to him."

"Thanks, monsieur," returned Monte-Cristo; "my steward has orders to take a box at each theatre."

"Is your steward also a Nubian?" asked Debray.

"No, he is a countryman of yours, if a Corsican is a countryman of any one's. But you know him, M. de Morcerf."

"Is it that excellent M. Bertuccio, who understands hiring windows so well?"

"Yes, you saw him the day I had the honour of receiving you in Italy; he has been a soldier, a smuggler—in fact every thing. I would not be quite sure that he has not been mixed up with the police for some trifle,—a stab with a knife, for instance."

"And you have chosen this honest citizen for your steward?" said Debray. "Of how much does he rob you every year?"

"On my word," replied the count, "not more than another. He answers my purpose, for he knows no impossibility, and so I keep him."

"My dear Albert," said Debray, rising; "it is half-past two," and as his host accompanied him to the door, he added, "Your guest is charming; but you leave the best company to go into the worst sometimes. I must return to the minister's. I will tell him of the count, and we shall soon know who he is."

"Take care," returned Albert; "no one has been able to accomplish that."

"Bravo!" said Beauchamp, who had followed them out, to Albert; "I do not go to the Chamber, but I have something better to offer my readers than a speech of M. Danglars."

"For Heaven's sake, Beauchamp!" returned Morcerf, "do not deprive me of the merit of introducing him everywhere. Is he not peculiar?"

"He is more than that," replied Château-Renaud; "he is one of the most extraordinary men I ever saw in my life."

Maximilian Morrel left the room with the Baron de Château-Renaud a few minutes later.

When Albert found himself alone with Monte-Cristo, "M. le Comte," said he, "allow me to commence my ciceroneship by shewing you a specimen of a bachelor's apartment. You, who are accustomed to the palaces of Italy, can amuse yourself by calculating in how many square feet a young man who is not the worst lodged in Paris can live. As we pass from one room to another I will open the windows to let you breathe."

From the salon they passed into the bed-chamber; it was a

model of taste and simple elegance. A single portrait, signed Leopold Robert, shone in its carved and gilded frame.

This portrait attracted the Count of Monte-Cristo's attention, for he made three rapid steps in the chamber, and stopped suddenly before it. It was the portrait of a young woman of five or six-and-twenty, with a dark complexion, and light and lustrous eyes veiled beneath their long lashes. She wore the picturesque costume of the Catalan fisherwomen, a red and black bodice and the golden pins in her hair. She was looking at the sea, and her shadow was defined on the blue ocean and sky.

The light was so faint in the room, that Albert did not perceive the count's pallor, or the nervous heaving of his chest and shoulders. Silence prevailed for an instant, during which Monte-Cristo gazed intently on the picture.

" You have there a most charming picture, viscount," he said at last, in a perfectly calm tone.

" Ah !" returned Albert, " you do not know my mother; she it is whom you see here : she had her portrait painted thus six or eight years ago. This costume is a fancy one, it appears, and the resemblance is so great that I think I still see my mother the same as she was in 1830. She had this portrait painted during my father's absence. She doubtless intended giving him an agreeable surprise, but strange to say, this portrait seemed to displease him, and he could not overcome his dislike to it."

Monte-Cristo was still engaged in examining the portrait, when a door opened, and he found himself opposite to the Count de Morcerf himself. He was a man of forty to forty-five years, but he seemed at least fifty, and his black moustache and eyebrows contrasted strangely with his almost white hair, which was cut short in the military fashion. He was dressed in plain clothes, and wore at his button-hole the ribands of the different orders to which he belonged. Monte-Cristo saw him advance towards him without making a single step. It seemed as if his feet were rooted to the ground and his eyes on the Count de Morcerf.

" Father," said the young man, " I have the honour of presenting to you M. le Comte de Monte-Cristo, the generous friend whom I had the good fortune to meet in the critical juncture of which I have told you."

" You are most welcome, monsieur," said the Count de Morcerf, saluting Monte-Cristo with a smile. "And monsieur has rendered our house, in preserving its only heir, a service which ensures him our eternal gratitude."

As he said these words, the Count de Morcerf pointed to a chair, whilst he seated himself in another opposite the window.

Monte-Cristo, whilst he took the seat Morcerf offered him, placed himself in such a manner as to remain concealed in the shadow of the large velvet curtains, and read on the care-worn and livid features of the count a whole history of secret griefs written in each wrinkle time had planted there.

"My wife," said Morcerf, "was at her toilette when she was informed of the visit she was about to receive. She will, however, be in the salon in ten minutes."

Monte-Cristo acknowledged the courtesy with a bow.

"It is a great honour for me," returned Monte-Cristo, "to be thus on the first day of my arrival in Paris brought in contact with a man whose merit equals his reputation, and to whom Fortune has for once been equitable; but has she not still on the plains of Mitidja or in the mountains of Atlas a marshal's staff to offer you?"

"Oh," replied Morcerf, reddening slightly, "I have left the service, monsieur. Made a peer at the Restoration, I served through the first campaign under the orders of Marshal Bourmont. I could, therefore, expect a higher rank, and who knows what might have happened had the elder branch remained on the throne? but the Revolution of July was, it seems, sufficiently glorious to allow itself to be ungrateful : and that was so for all services that did not date from the imperial period. I tendered my resignation, for when you have gained your epaulettes on the battle-field, you do not know how to manœuvre on the slippery ground of the salons. I have hung up my sword and cast myself into politics. I have devoted myself to industry; I study the useful arts. During the twenty years I served, I often wished to do so, but I had not the time."

"These are the ideas that render your nation superior to any other," returned Monte-Cristo.

"Ah! here is my mother!" cried Albert.

Monte-Cristo turned round hastily, and saw Madame de Morcerf at the entrance of the salon, at the door opposite to that by which her husband had entered, pale and motionless; when Monte-Cristo turned round, she let fall her arm, which for some unknown reason had been resting on the gilded door-post. She

"AH! HERE IS MY MOTHER!" CRIED ALBERT.
Page 204.

had been there some moments, and had overheard the last words of the visitor.

The latter rose and bowed to the countess, who inclined herself without speaking.

"Good heavens, madame!" said the count, "are you unwell, or is it the heat of the room that affects you?"

"Are you ill, mother?" cried Albert, springing towards her.

She thanked them both with a smile.

"No," returned she, "but I feel some emotion on seeing, for the first time, the man, without whose intervention we should have been in tears and desolation. Monsieur," she continued, advancing with the majesty of a queen, "I owe to you the life of my son, and for this I bless you. Now I thank you for the pleasure you give me in thus affording me the opportunity of thanking you as I have blessed you, from the bottom of my heart."

The count bowed again, but lower than before; he was even paler than Mercédès.

"Madame," said he, "M. le Comte and yourself recompense too generously a simple action. To save a man, to spare a father's feelings or a mother's sensibility, is not to do a good action, but a simple deed of humanity."

At these words, uttered with the most exquisite sweetness and politeness, Madame de Morcerf replied,—

"It is very fortunate for my son, monsieur, that he found such a friend, and I thank God that things are thus."

And Mercédès raised her fine eyes to heaven, with so fervent an expression of gratitude that the count fancied he saw tears in them.

M. de Morcerf approached her.

"Madame," said he, "I must make my excuses to M. le Comte for quitting him, and I pray you to do so also. The sitting commences at two, it is now three, and I am to speak."

"Go, then, and monsieur and I will strive our best to forget your absence!" replied the countess, with the same tone of deep feeling. "M. le Comte," continued she, turning to Monte-Cristo, "will you do us the honour of passing the rest of the day with us?"

"Believe me, madame, I feel most grateful for your kindness, but I got out of my travelling carriage at your door this morning, and I am ignorant how I am installed in Paris, which I scarcely know; this is but a trifling inquietude, I know, but one that may be appreciated."

" We shall have this pleasure another time !" said the countess; " you promise that ?"

Monte-Cristo inclined himself, without answering, but the gesture might pass for assent.

"I will not detain you monsieur," continued the countess.

When Albert returned to his mother, after seeing his guest to the door, he found her in the boudoir, reclining in a large velvet arm-chair; the whole room so obscure that only the shining spangle, fastened here and there to the drapery, and the angles of the gilded frames of the pictures, gave a kind of light to the room. Albert could not see his mother's face, which was lost in a thin veil she had put on her head which descended around her features like a cloud of vapour, but it seemed to him as though her voice had altered. He could distinguish amidst the perfumes of the roses and heliotropes in the flower-stands the sharp and fragrant odour of volatile salts, and he remarked in one of the chased cups on the mantel-piece the countess's smelling-bottle, taken from its shagreen case, and exclaimed in a tone of uneasiness, as he entered—

"My dear mother, are you faint ?"

"No, no, Albert ! but you know these roses, tuberoses, and orange flowers, throw out at first, before one is used to them, such violent perfumes."

"Then," said Albert, putting his hand to the bell, "they must be taken into the antechamber. You are really upset, and just now were so pale as you came into the room——"

"Was I pale, Albert ?"

"Yes; a paleness that suits you admirably, mother; but which did not the less alarm my father and myself !"

"Did your father speak of it ?" inquired Mercédès, eagerly.

"No, but he noticed it, I know."

A servant entered, summoned by Albert's ringing.

"Take these flowers into the anteroom or dressing-room," he ordered.

The footman obeyed his orders.

A long pause ensued, which lasted until all the flowers were removed.

"What is this name of Monte-Cristo ?" inquired the countess, when the servant had taken away the last vase of flowers; " is it a family name, or the name of the estate, or a simple title ?"

" I believe, mother, it is merely a simple title. The count purchased an island in the Tuscan Archipelago. You know the same thing was done for Saint Stephen of Florence, Saint George, Constantinian of Parma, and even for the Order of Malta. Except this, he has no pretension to nobility, and calls himself a chance count, although the general opinion at Rome is, that the count is a man of very high distinction."

" His manners are admirable !" said the countess : " at least, as far as I could judge in the few moments he remained here."

" They are perfect, mother—so perfect that they surpass by far all I have known in the leading aristocracy of the three proudest nations of Europe—the English aristocracy, Spanish aristocracy, and French aristocracy."

The countess paused a moment : then after a slight hesitation, she resumed,—

" You have seen, my dear Albert—I ask the question as a mother—you have seen M. de Monte-Cristo in his house ; you are quick-sighted, have much knowledge of the world, more tact than is usual at your age ; do you think the count is really what he appears to be ?"

" Ah ! what he is ; that is quite another thing. I have heard so many remarkable things of him, that if you would have me really say what I think, I shall reply that I really do look upon him as one of Byron's heroes, whom Misery has marked with a fatal brand ;—some Manfred, some Lara, some Werner, one of those wrecks, as it were, of some ancient family, who disinherited of their patrimony, achieved one by the force of their adventurous genius which has placed them above the laws of society."

" You say——"

" I believe that Monte-Cristo is an island in the midst of the Mediterranean, without inhabitants or garrison, the resort of smugglers of all nations, and pirates of every flag. Who knows whether or not these industrious worthies do not pay to their feudal lord some dues for his protection ?"

" That is possible," said the countess, reflecting.

" Never mind," continued the young man, " smuggler or not, you must agree, mother dear, as you have seen him, that the Count of Monte-Cristo is a remarkable man, who will have the greatest success in the salons of Paris. Why, this very morning, at my abode, he made his *entrée* amongst us by striking every man of us with amazement, not even excepting Château-Renaud."

"And what do you suppose is the count's age?" inquired Mercédès, evidently attaching great importance to this question.

"Thirty-five or thirty-six, mother."

"So young! it is impossible," said Mercédès, replying at the same time to what Albert said as well as to her own private reflection.

"It is the truth, however. Three or four times he has said to me, and certainly without the slightest premeditation, at such a period I was five years old, at another ten years old, at another twelve, and I, induced by curiosity, which kept me alive to these details, have compared the dates, and never found him inaccurate. The age of this singular man, who is of no age, is then, I am certain, thirty-five. Besides, mother, remark how vivid his eye, how raven-black his hair, and his brow, though so pale, is free from wrinkles,—he is not only vigorous, but also young."

The countess bent her head as if beneath a heavy wave of bitter thoughts.

"And has this man displayed friendship for you, Albert?" she asked with a nervous shudder.

"I am inclined to think so."

"And—do—you—like—him?"

"Why, he pleases me in spite of Franz d'Epinay, who tries to convince me that he is a being returned from the other world."

The countess shuddered.

"Albert," she said, in a voice which was altered by emotion, "I have always put you on your guard against new acquaintances. Now you are a man, and are able to give me advice; yet, I repeat to you, be prudent."

"Why, my dear mother, it is necessary, in order to make your advice turn to account, that I should know beforehand what I have to distrust. The count never plays, he only drinks pure water tinged with a little sherry, and is so rich that he cannot, without intending to laugh at me, try to borrow money. What, then, have I to fear from him?"

"You are right," said the countess, "and my fears are weakness, especially when directed against a man who has saved your life. How did your father receive him, Albert? It is necessary that we should be more than complaisant to the count. M. de Morcerf is sometimes occupied; his business makes him reflective; and he might, without intending it——"

"Nothing could be in better taste than my father's reception of him," said Albert; "nay, more, he seemed greatly flattered

at two or three compliments which the count very skilfully and
agreeably paid him with as much ease as if he had known him
these thirty years. Each of these little tickling arrows must
have pleased my father," he added. "And thus they parted
the best possible friends."

The countess made no reply. She fell into so deep a reverie
that her eyes gradually closed. The young man standing up
before her, gazed upon her with that filial affection which is
more tender and endearing with children whose mothers are still
young and handsome. Then, after seeing her eyes closed, and
hearing her breathe gently, he believed she had dropped asleep,
and left the apartment on tiptoe, closing the door after him with
the utmost precaution.

During this time the count had arrived at his house; it had
taken him six minutes to perform the distance.

The house Ali had chosen, which was to serve as a town
residence for Monte-Cristo, was situated on the right hand
of the Champs Elysées. A thick clump of trees and shrubs
rose in the centre, and masked a portion of the front; around
this shrubbery two alleys, like two arms, extended right and
left, and formed a carriage-drive from the iron gates to a
double portico, on every step of which stood a porcelain vase,
filled with flowers. This house, isolated from the rest, had,
besides the main entrance, another in the Rue Ponthieu. Even
before the coachman had hailed the concierge the massy gates
rolled on their hinges;—they had seen the count coming, and at
Paris, as everywhere else, he was served with the rapidity of
lightning. The coachman entered, and descending the half-
circle without slackening his speed, the gates were closed ere the
wheels had ceased to sound on the gravel. The carriage stopped
at the left side of the portico, two men presented themselves
at the carriage-window, one was Ali, who, smiling with an
expression of the most sincere joy, seemed amply repaid by
a mere look from Monte-Cristo. The other bowed respectfully,
and offered his arm to assist the count in descending.

"Thanks, Monsieur Bertuccio," said the count, springing
lightly up the three steps of the portico ; "and the notary ?"

"He is in the small salon, excellency," returned Bertuccio.

"And the cards I ordered to have engraved as soon as you
knew the number of the house ?"

"M. le Comte, it is done already. I have been myself to the
14

best engraver of the Palais Royal, who did the plate in my
presence.   The first card struck off was taken, according to your
orders, to M. le Baron Danglars, Rue de la Chaussée d'Antin,
No. 7 ; the others are on the mantelpiece of your excellency's
bedroom."

"Good ; what o'clock is it ?"

"Four o'clock."

Monte-Cristo gave his hat, cane, and gloves to the French
footman, who had called his carriage at the Count de Morcerf's,
and then he passed into the small salon, preceded by Bertuccio,
who showed him the way.

"These are but indifferent marbles in this antechamber," said
Monte-Cristo.   "I trust all this will soon be taken away."

Bertuccio bowed.   As the steward had said, the notary
awaited him in the small salon.   He was a simple looking
lawyer's clerk, elevated to the extraordinary dignity of a
provincial scrivener.

"You are the notary empowered to sell the country-house
that I wish to purchase, monsieur ?" asked Monte-Cristo.

"Yes, M. le Comte," returned the notary.   "The house you
purchase is situated at Auteuil."

"And where is Auteuil ?" asked the count.

"Close here, monsieur," replied the notary, "a little beyond
Passy ; a charming situation in the heart of Bois de Boulogne."

"So near as that ?" said the count ; "but that is not in the
country.   I read the advertisement in one of the papers, and
was tempted by the false title, 'a country-house.'   However,
no matter.   Bertuccio, give 55,000 francs to monsieur."

The steward left the room, and returned with a bundle of
bank-notes, which the notary counted like a man who never
gives a receipt for money until after legal examination.

"And now," demanded the count, "are all the forms complied
with ?"

"All, M. le Comte."

"Have you the keys ?"

"They are in the hands of the concierge, who takes care of
the house ; but here is the order I have given him to instal
Monsieur le Comte in his new possession."

"Very well ;" and Monte-Cristo made a sign with his hand to
the notary, which said, "I have no further need of you ; you
may go."

CHAPTER XXIV

UNLIMITED CREDIT

About two o'clock the following day a landau, drawn by a pair of magnificent English horses, stopped at the door of Monte-Cristo, and a person dressed in a blue coat, with buttons of a similar colour, a white waistcoat, over which was displayed a massive gold chain, brown trousers, and a quantity of black hair, descending so low over his eyebrows as to leave it doubtful whether it were not artificial, directed his groom to inquire at the porter's lodge whether the Count of Monte-Cristo resided there, and if he were within.

"His excellency does not receive visitors to-day," said the servant in answer to the question.

"Then take my master's card. You'll see who master is— M. le Baron Danglars! Be sure to give the card to the count, and say that, although in haste to attend the Chamber, my master came out of his way to have the honour of calling upon him."

"I never speak to his excellency," replied the concierge ; " the valet-de-chambre will carry your message."

The groom returned to the carriage.

"Well ?" asked Danglars.

The man, somewhat crest-fallen by the rebuke he had received, detailed to his master all that had passed between himself and the concierge.

"Bless me !" murmured M. le Baron Danglars ; " this must surely be a prince instead of a count by their styling him ' excellency,' and only venturing to address him by the medium of his valet-de-chambre. However, it does not signify ; he has a letter of credit on me, so I must see him when he requires his money."

Then, throwing himself back in his carriage, Danglars called out to his coachman, in a voice that might be heard across the road—

"To the Chambre des Députés."

Monte-Cristo had, however, surveyed his visitor from behind the blinds. As he drove away he summoned Bertuccio.

"How comes it," said Monte-Cristo with a frown, "that, when I desired you to purchase for me the finest pair of horses to be found in Paris, you permitted so splendid a couple as those which have just been here to be in the possession of any one but myself?"

"M. le Comte is not, perhaps, aware that M. Danglars gave 16,000 francs for his horses?" answered Bertuccio.

"Very well! then offer him double that sum; a banker never loses an opportunity of doubling his capital."

Bertuccio bowed, and was about to retire; but when he reached the door, he paused, and then said,—

"At what o'clock does your excellency wish the carriage and horses ready?"

"At five o'clock," replied the count.

As the hand of the clock pointed to five, the count struck thrice upon his gong. When Ali was wanted one stroke was given, two summoned Baptistin, and three Bertuccio.

The steward entered.

"My horses!" said Monte-Cristo.

"They are at the door."

The count descended to the door of his mansion, and beheld his carriage drawn by the very pair of horses he had so much admired in the morning as the property of Danglars. As he passed them he said,—

"They are extremely handsome certainly," with an approving smile, and descending the terrace steps, he sprang into his carriage, which drawn by the beautiful animals so expensively purchased, was whirled along with incredible swiftness, and stopped only before the hôtel of the banker.

Danglars was engaged at that moment presiding over a railroad committee. But the meeting was nearly concluded when the name of his visitor was announced. As the count's title sounded on his ear he rose, and addressing his colleagues, many of whom were members of either Chamber, he said,—

"Gentlemen, I must pray you to excuse my quitting you thus; but a most ridiculous circumstance has occurred, which is this, —Thomson and French, the bankers at Rome, have sent to me a certain individual calling himself the Count of Monte-Cristo, who is desirous of opening an account with me to any amount he pleases. I confess this is the drollest thing I have ever met with in the course of my extensive foreign transactions, and you may readily suppose it has greatly roused my curiosity; indeed so much did I long to see the bearer of so unprecedented an order for an unlimited credit, that I took the trouble this morning to call on the pretended count, for his title is a mere fiction—of that I am persuaded. We all know counts nowadays are not famous for their riches. But would you believe, upon arriving at the residence of the *soi-disant* Count of Monte-Cristo, I was very coolly informed, 'He did not receive visitors that day!' Upon my word such airs are ridiculous, and befitting only some great millionaire or a capricious beauty. I made inquiries and found that the house where the said count resides in the Champs Elysées is his own property, and certainly it was very decently kept up and arranged as far as I could judge from the gardens and exterior of the place. But," pursued Danglars, with one of his sinister smiles, "an order for unlimited credit calls for something like caution on the part of the banker on whom that order is given. These facts stated, I will freely confess I am very anxious to see the individual just now announced. I suspect a hoax is intended, but the good folks who thought fit to play it off on me knew but little whom they had to deal with. Well! well! we shall see. 'They laugh best who laugh last!'"

Having delivered himself of this pompous address, uttered with a degree of energy that left him almost out of breath, he bowed to the assembled party and withdrew to his drawing-room, whose sumptuous fittings-up of white and gold had caused a great and admiring sensation in the Chaussée d'Antin.

It was to this apartment he had desired his guest to be shown, fully reckoning upon the overwhelming effect so dazzling a *coup-d'œil* would produce.

He found the count standing before some copies of Albano and Fattore that had been passed off to the banker as originals; but which, copies of the paintings of those great masters as they were, seemed to feel their degradation in being brought into juxtaposition with the gaudy gilding that covered the ceiling.

The count turned round as he heard Danglars enter the room.

With a slight inclination of the head, Danglars signed to the count to be seated, pointing significantly to a gilded arm-chair, covered with white satin embroidered with gold.

The count obeyed.

"I have the honour, I presume, of addressing M. de Monte-Cristo?"

The count bowed.

"And I of speaking to Baron Danglars, Chevalier de la Légion d'Honneur, and Member of the Chamber of Deputies?"

With an air of extreme gravity Monte-Cristo slowly enumerated the various titles engraved on the card left at his hôtel by the baron.

Danglars felt all the irony contained in the address of his visitor. For a minute or two he compressed his lips as though seeking to conquer his rage ere he trusted himself to speak. Then turning to his visitor he said,—

"You will, I trust, excuse my not having called you by your title when I first addressed you, but you are aware we are living under a popular form of government, and that I am, myself, a representative of the liberties of the people."

"So much so," replied Monte-Cristo, "that while preserving the habit of styling yourself baron, you have deemed it advisable to lay aside that of calling others by their titles."

"Upon my word," said Danglars, with affected carelessness, "I attach no sort of value to such empty distinctions, but the fact is, I was made Baron, and also Chevalier de la Légion d'Honneur, in consequence of some services I had rendered the government, but——"

"You have abdicated your titles after the example set you by Messrs. de Montmorency and Lafayette? Well; you cannot possibly choose more noble models for your conduct!"

"Why," replied Danglars, "I do not mean to say I have altogether laid aside my titles; with the servants, for instance— there I think it right to preserve my rank with all its outward forms."

"I see, by your domestics you are styled, 'My lord!' 'M. le Baron!' the journalists of the day style you 'Monsieur!' while your constituents term you 'Citizen.'"

Again Danglars bit his lips with baffled spite, he saw well enough that he was no match for Monte-Cristo in an argument of this sort, and he therefore hastened to turn to subjects more familiar to him, calculating on having all the advantages on his side.

"Permit me to inform you, M. le Comte," said he, bowing, "that I have received a letter of advice from Thomson and French of Rome."

"I am glad to hear it, M. le Baron, for I must claim the privilege of so addressing you as well as your servants; I have acquired the bad habit of calling persons by their style and title from living in a country where barons are still met with, simply because persons are never suddenly elevated to a rank which is possessed only in right of ancestry. But as regards the letter of advice, I am charmed to find it has reached you; that will spare me the troublesome and disagreeable task of coming to you for money myself. You have received a regular letter of advice, therefore my cheques will be duly honoured, and we shall neither of us have to go out of our way in the transaction."

"There is one slight difficulty," said Danglars; "and that consists in my not precisely comprehending the letter itself!"

"Indeed?"

"And for that reason I did myself the honour of calling upon you, in order to beg you would explain some part of it to me."

"With much pleasure! Pray, now I am here, let me know what it was that baffled your powers of comprehension?"

"Why," said Danglars, "in the letter—I believe I have it about me"—(here he felt in his breast-pocket)—"yes, here it is! Well, this letter gives M. le Comte de Monte-Cristo unlimited credit on our house."

"And what is there that requires explaining in that simple fact, may I ask, M. le Baron?"

"Merely the term *unlimited*, nothing else, certainly."

"Is not that word known in France? Perhaps, indeed, it does not belong to the language; for the persons from whom you received your letter of advice are a species of Anglo-Germans, and very probably do not write very choice or accurate French."

"Oh, as for the composition of the letter, there is not the smallest error in it, but as regards the competency of the document, I certainly have doubts."

"Is it possible?" asked the count, assuming an air and tone of the utmost simplicity and candour. "Is it possible that Thomson and French are not looked upon as safe and solvent bankers? Pray tell me what you think, M. le Baron, for I feel uneasy, I can assure you, having some considerable property in their hands."

"Thomson and French are bankers of the highest repute," replied Danglars, with an almost mocking smile; "and it was not of their solvency or capability, I spoke, but of the word *un-*

limited, which in financial affairs is so extremely vague a term,—that—that——"

"In fact," said Monte-Cristo, "that its sense is also without limitation."

"Precisely what I was about to say," cried Danglars. "Now what is vague is doubtful; and, says the wise man, ' where there is doubt there is danger !' "

"Meaning to say," rejoined Monte-Cristo, "that however Thomson and French may be inclined to commit acts of imprudence and folly, M. le Baron Danglars is not disposed to follow their example."

"How so, M. le Comte ?"

"Simply thus; the banking-house of Thomson and Co. set no bounds to their engagements, while that of M. Danglars has its limits; truly he is wise as the sage whose prudent apophthegm he quoted but just now."

"Monsieur !" replied the banker, drawing himself up with a haughty air; "the amount of my capital, or the extent and solvency of my engagements, have never yet been questioned."

"It seems, then, reserved for me," said Monte-Cristo, coldly, "to be the first to do so."

"And by what right, sir ?"

"By right of the objections you have raised, and the explanations you have demanded, which certainly imply considerable distrust on your part, either of yourself or me,—the former, most probably."

Again did Danglars, by a forcible effort, restrain himself from betraying the vindictive passions which possessed his mind at this second defeat by an adversary who calmly fought him with his own weapons : his forced politeness sat awkwardly upon him, while his splenetic rage, although essaying to veil itself under a playful, jesting manner, approached at times almost to impertinence. Monte-Cristo, on the contrary, preserved a graceful suavity of demeanour, aided by a certain degree of simplicity he could assume at pleasure, and thus, calm and wholly at his ease, possessed an infinite advantage over his irascible companion.

"Well, sir," resumed Danglars, after a brief silence, "I will endeavour to make myself understood, by requesting you to inform me for what sum you propose to draw upon me ?"

"Why, truly," replied Monte-Cristo, determined not to lose an inch of the ground he had gained, "my reason for desiring an 'unlimited' credit was precisely because I did not know what money I might expend."

The banker now thought it his turn to show off, and make a display of wealth and consequence; flinging himself back therefore in his arm-chair, he said, with an arrogant and purse-proud air,—

"Let me beg of you not to hesitate in naming your wishes: you will then be convinced that the resources of the house of Danglars, however limited, are still equal to meeting the largest demands; and were you even to require a million——"

"I beg your pardon!" interposed Monte-Cristo.

"I observed," replied Danglars, with a patronising and pompous air, "that should you be hard pressed, the concern of which I am the head would not scruple to accommodate you to the amount of a million."

"A million?" retorted the count; "and what use can you possibly suppose so pitiful a sum would be to me? My dear sir, if a trifle like that could suffice me, I should never have given myself the trouble of opening an account for so contemptible an amount. A million! Excuse my smiling when you speak of a sum I am in the habit of carrying in my pocket-book or dressing-case."

And with these words Monte-Cristo took from his pocket a small case containing his visiting cards, and drew forth two orders on the treasury for 500,000 francs each, payable at sight to the bearer.

A man like Danglars was wholly inaccessible to any gentler method of correction; his upstart arrogance, his ostentatious vulgarity, were only assailable by blows dealt with the force and vigour of the present *coup*; its effect on the banker was perfectly stunning; and as though scarcely venturing to credit his senses, he continued gazing from the paper to the count with a confused and mystified air.

"Come, come," said Monte-Cristo, "confess honestly, that you have not perfect confidence in the responsibility of the house of Thomson and French: there is nothing very strange in your exercising what seems to you a necessary caution; however, foreseeing that such might be the case, I determined, spite of my ignorance in such matters, to be provided with the means of banishing all scruples from your mind, and at the same time leaving you quite at liberty to act as you pleased in the affair. See, here are two similar letters to that you have yourself received;

the one from the house of Arstein and Eskeles of Vienna to Baron de Rothschild, the other drawn from Baring of London to M. Laffitte.   Now, sir, you have but to say the word, and I will spare you all uneasiness and alarm on the subject, by presenting my letter of credit at one or other of the establishments I have named."

The blow had struck home, and Danglars was entirely vanquished; with a trembling hand he took the two letters from Vienna and London from the count, who held them carelessly between his finger and thumb, as though to him they were mere every-day matters to which he attached but very little interest.   Having carefully perused the documents in question, the banker proceeded to ascertain the genuineness of the signatures, and this he did with a scrutiny so severe as might have appeared insulting to the count, had it not suited his present purpose to mislead the banker in every respect.

" Well, sir," said Danglars, rising, after he had well convinced himself of the authenticity of the documents he held, and bowing, as though in adoration of a man, the thrice happy possessor of as many orders for unlimited credit on the three principal banks of Paris, " you have there signatures worth untold wealth, and I will certainly oblige you ; but though your conversation and vouchers put an end to all mistrust in the affair, you must pardon me, M. le Comte, for confessing the most extreme astonishment.

" Nay, nay," answered Monte-Cristo, with the easiest and most gentlemanly air imaginable, " 'tis not for such trifling sums as these to startle or astonish the banking-house of M. le Baron Danglars.   Then, as all is settled as to forms between us, I will thank you to send a supply of money to me to-morrow."

" By all means, M. le Comte !   What sum do you want ?"

" Why," replied Monte-Cristo, " since we mutually understand each other,—for such I presume is the case ?"

Danglars bowed assentingly.

" You are quite sure that not a lurking doubt or suspicion lingers in your mind ?"

" Oh, M. le Comte !" exclaimed Danglars; " I never for an instant entertained such a feeling towards you."

" No, no ! you merely wished to be convinced you ran no risk, nothing more; but now that we have come to so clear an understanding, and that all distrust and suspicion are laid at rest, we may as well fix a sum as the probable expenditure of the first year :—suppose we say six millions to——"

"Six millions!" gasped out Danglars,—"certainly, whatever you please."

"Then, if I should require more," continued Monte-Cristo, in a careless and indifferent manner, "why, of course, I should draw upon you; but my present intention is not to remain in France more than a year, and during that period I scarcely think I shall exceed the sum I mentioned. However, we shall see."

"The money you desire shall be at your house by ten o'clock to-morrow morning, M. le Comte," replied Danglars. "How would you like to have it? in gold, silver, or notes?"

"Half in gold, and the other half in bank-notes, if you please," said the count, rising from his seat.

"I must confess to you, M. le Comte," said Danglars, "that I have hitherto imagined myself acquainted with the degree of fortune possessed by all the rich individuals of Europe, and still wealth such as yours has been wholly unknown to me. May I presume to ask whether you have long possessed it?"

"It has been in the family a very long while," returned Monte-Cristo, "a sort of treasure expressly forbidden to be touched for a certain period of years, during which the accumulated interest has doubled the capital. The period appointed by the testator for the disposal of these riches occurred only a short time ago; and they have only been employed by me within the last few years. Your ignorance on the subject, therefore, is easily accounted for. However, you will be better informed as to me and my possessions ere long."

And the count, while pronouncing these latter words, accompanied them with one of those ghastly smiles that used to strike terror into those who saw them.

"With your tastes and means of gratifying them," continued Danglars, "you will exhibit a splendour that must effectually put us poor miserable millionaires quite in the background. If I mistake not you are an admirer of paintings, at least I judged so from the attention you appeared to be bestowing on mine when I entered the room. If you will permit me I shall be happy to show you my picture-gallery, composed entirely of works by the ancient masters—warranted as such. Not a modern picture among them. I cannot endure the modern school of painting."

"You are perfectly right in objecting to them, for this one great fault—that they have not yet had time to become old."

"Or will you allow me to shew you several fine statues by

Thorwaldsen, Bartoloni, and Canova—all foreign artists? for, as you may perceive, I think but very indifferently of our French sculptors."

"You have a right to be unjust to your own countrymen, if such is your pleasure."

"But perhaps you will prefer putting off your inspection of my poor pictures, etc., until another opportunity, when we shall be better known to each other. For the present I will confine myself (if perfectly agreeable to you) to introducing you to Madame la Baronne Danglars—excuse my impatience, M. le Comte, but a person of your wealth and influence cannot receive too much attention."

Monte-Cristo bowed in sign that he accepted the proffered honour, and the financier immediately rang a small bell which was answered by a servant in a showy livery.

"Is Madame la Baronne at home?" inquired Danglars.

"Yes, M. le Baron," answered the man.

"And alone?"

"No, M. le Baron, madame has visitors."

"Have you any objection to meet any persons, who may be with madame, or do you desire to preserve a strict incognito?"

"No, indeed," replied Monte-Cristo, with a smile, "I do not arrogate to myself the right of so doing."

"And who is with madame? M. Debray?" inquired Danglars, with an air of indulgence and good nature that made Monte-Cristo smile, acquainted as he already was with the secrets of the banker's domestic life.

"Yes, M. le Baron," replied the servant, "M. Debray is with madame."

Danglars nodded his head, then turning to Monte-Cristo said, "M. Lucien Debray is an old friend of ours, and private secretary to the Ministre de l'Intérieur. As for my wife, I must tell you, she lowered herself by marrying me, for she belongs to one of the most ancient families in France. Her maiden name was De Servières, and her first husband was M. le Colonel Marquis de Nargonne."

"I have not the honour of knowing Madame Danglars, but I have already met M. Lucien Debray."

"Ah! indeed!" said Danglars, "and where was that?"

"At the house of M. de Morcerf."

"Oh! what! you are acquainted with the young viscount, are you?"

"We were together a good deal during the Carnival at Rome."

"True, true!" cried Danglars: "let me see—have I not heard of some strange adventure with bandits or thieves hid in ruins, and of his having had a miraculous escape?—I forget how, but I know he used to amuse my wife and daughter by telling them about it after his return from Italy."

"Madame la Baronne is waiting to receive you, gentlemen," said the servant, who had gone to inquire the pleasure of his mistress.

"With your permission," said Danglars, bowing, "I will precede you to show you the way."

"By all means," replied Monte-Cristo; "I follow you."

CHAPTER XXV

THE DAPPLED GREYS

As Danglars entered he found Madame la Baronne (who, although past the first bloom of youth, was still strikingly handsome) seated at the piano, a most elaborate piece of cabinet and inlaid work, while Lucien Debray, standing before a small work-table, was turning over the pages of an album Lucien had found time, preparatory to the count's arrival, to relate many particulars respecting him to Madame Danglars.

"Baroness," said Danglars, "give me leave to present to you the Count of Monte-Cristo, who has been most warmly recommended to me by my correspondents at Rome. I need but mention one fact to make all the ladies in Paris court his notice, and that is, that the noble individual before you has come to take up his abode in our fine capital for one year, during which brief period he proposes to spend six millions of money,—think of that! It sounds very much like an announcement of balls, fêtes, dinners, and picnic parties, in all of which I trust M. le Comte will remember us as he may depend upon it we shall him, in all the entertainments we may give, be they great or small."

Spite of the gross flattery and coarseness of this address, Madame Danglars could not forbear gazing with considerable interest on a man capable of expending six millions in twelve months, who had selected Paris for the scene of his princely extravagance.

"And when did you arrive here?" inquired she.

"Yesterday morning, madame."

"Coming as usual, I presume, from the extreme ends of the globe? Pardon me—at least, such I have heard is your custom."

"Nay, madame! This time I have merely proceeded from Cadiz hither."

"You have selected a most unfavourable moment for your first visit to our city. Paris is a horrible place in summer!"

At this instant the favourite attendant of Madame Danglars entered the boudoir; approaching her mistress, she spoke some words in an undertone. Madame Danglars turned very pale, then exclaimed to her husband—

" Is this true ?"

" Is what true, madam ?" inquired Danglars, visibly agitated.

" That when my coachman was about to prepare my carriage, he discovered that the horses had been removed from the stables without his knowledge. I desire to know what is the meaning of this ?"

" Madame," replied Danglars, " the horses were not sufficiently quiet for you; they were scarcely four years old, and they made me extremely uneasy on your account."

"Nonsense !" retorted the baroness; "you could not have entertained any alarm on the subject, because you are perfectly well aware that I have recently engaged a coachman who is said to be the best in Paris. But, perhaps, you have disposed of the coachman as well as the horses ?"

" My dear love ! pray, do not say any more about them, and I promise you another pair exactly like them in appearance, only more quiet and steady."

The baroness shrugged up her shoulders with an air of ineffable contempt, while her husband, affecting not to observe it, turned towards Monte-Cristo and said—

" Upon my word, M. le Comte, I am quite sorry I was not sooner aware of your establishing yourself in Paris."

" And wherefore ?" asked the count.

" Because I should have liked to have made you the offer of these horses. I have almost given them away, as it is ; but, as I before said, I was anxious to get rid of them upon any terms. They were only fit for a young man ; not at all calculated for a person at my time of life."

"I am much obliged by your kind intentions towards me," said Monte-Cristo ; " but this morning I purchased a very excellent pair of carriage-horses, and I do not think they were dear. There they are! Come M. Debray, you are a connoisseur, I believe, let me have your opinion upon them."

As Debray walked towards the window, Danglars approached his wife.

" I could not tell you before others," said he in a low tone, " the reason of my parting with the horses ; but a most enormous price was offered me this morning for them. Some madman or fool, bent upon ruining himself as fast as he can, actually sent his steward to me to purchase them at any cost; and the fact is, I have gained 16,000 francs by the sale of them. Come, don't look so angry, and you shall have 4,000 francs of the money to do what you like with, and Eugénie shall have 2,000. There! what do you think now of the affair? Wasn't I right to part with the horses?"

Madame Danglars surveyed her husband with a look of withering contempt.

"I cannot be mistaken; there are your horses!" suddenly exclaimed Debray. "The very animals we were speaking of harnessed to the count's carriage!"

"My dear, beautiful dappled greys?" demanded the baroness, springing to the window. "'Tis indeed they!" said she.

Danglars looked absolutely stultified.

"How very singular!" cried Monte-Cristo, with well-feigned astonishment.

Madame Danglars whispered a few words in the ear of Debray, who approached Monte-Cristo, saying, "The baroness wishes to know what you paid her husband for the horses."

"I scarcely know," replied the count; "it was a little surprise prepared for me by my steward; he knew how desirous I was of meeting with precisely such a pair of horses,—and—so he bought them. I think, if I remember rightly, he hinted that he had given somewhere about 30,000 francs."

Debray conveyed the count's reply to the baroness.

Poor Danglars looked so crest-fallen and discomfited that Monte-Cristo assumed a pitying air towards him.

He took his leave ceremoniously. Two hours afterwards, Madame Danglars received a most flattering epistle from the count, in which he entreated her to receive back her favourite "dappled greys;" protesting that he could not endure the idea of making his *début* in the Parisian world of fashion with the knowledge that his splendid equipage had been obtained at the price of a lovely woman's regrets. The horses were sent back, wearing the same harness they had done in the morning; the only difference consisted in the rosettes worn on the heads of the animals being adorned with a large diamond placed in the centre of each, by order of the count.

To Danglars Monte-Cristo also wrote, requesting him to excuse the whimsical gift of a capricious millionaire, and to beg of Madame la Baronne to pardon the Eastern fashion adopted in the return of the horses.

CHAPTER XXVI

HAYDÉE

IT was the hour of noon, and Monte-Cristo had set apart one hour to be passed in the apartments of Haydée, the young Greek whom Albert and Franz had seen with him in his box at the opera in Rome.

Haydée had a suite of rooms entirely to herself. Her boudoir was circular, and lighted only from the top, which consisted of pale pink glass. The young girl was reclining upon soft downy cushions, covered with blue satin spotted with silver; her head, supported by one of her exquisitely moulded arms, rested on the divan, while she adjusted to her lips the coral tube of a rich nargilleh, whose flexible pipe, placed amid the coolest and most fragrant essences, permitted not the perfumed vapour to ascend until fully impregnated with the rich odours of the most delicious flowers. Her attitude, though perfectly natural for an Eastern woman, would have been deemed too full of coquettish straining after effect in a European. Her dress, which was that of the women of Epirus, consisted of a pair of white satin trousers, embroidered with pink roses, displaying feet so exquisitely formed and so delicately fair, that they might well have been taken for Parian marble, had not the eye been undeceived by their constantly shifting in and out of the fairy-like slippers in which they were encased; these tiny coverings were beautifully ornamented with gold and pearls, and turned up at the point; she had on a blue and white striped vest, with long open sleeves, trimmed with silver loops and buttons of pearls. She also wore a species of bodice, which, closing only from the centre to the waist, exhibited the whole of the ivory throat and upper part of the bosom; three magnificent diamond clasps fastened it. Her waist was entirely concealed by one of those many-coloured scarfs, whose brilliant hues and rich silken fringe have rendered them so precious in the eyes of Parisian belles. A small cap of gold, embroidered with pearls, was placed on one

side of her head; while, on the other a natural rose, of that
dark crimson almost inclining to purple, mingled its glowing
colours with the luxuriant masses of her hair, which, for jetty
lustre, outrivalled the raven's wing.

As Monte-Cristo approached, having sent beforehand to
announce his presence, she leaned upon the elbow of the arm
that held the nargilleh, and, extending to him her other hand,
said with a smile of captivating sweetness, in the sonorous
language spoken by the inhabitants of Athens and Sparta,
"Why demand permission ere you enter? Are you no longer
my master; or have I ceased to be your slave?"

Monte-Cristo returned her smile. "Haydée," said he, "you
well know."

"Why do you address me so coldly—so distantly?" asked the
fair Greek. "Have I by any means displeased you? Oh, if so,
punish me as you will; but do not—do not speak to me in tones
and manner so formal and constrained!"

"Listen to me, Haydée," replied the count. "I was about
to remind you of something you know well; namely, that we
are now in France, and that you are consequently free!"

"Free!" repeated the fair girl. "Of what use would freedom
be to me?"

"It would enable you to quit me!"

"Quit you! Wherefore should I do so?"

"That is not for me to say; but we are now about to mix in
society—to visit and be visited."

"I desire to see no one but yourself."

"Nay, but hear me, Haydée. You cannot remain in seclusion
in the midst of this gay capital; and should you see one whom
you could prefer, think not I would be so selfish or unjust as
to——"

"No, no!" answered Haydée, with energetic warmth, "that
can never be. No man could appear charming in my eyes but
yourself. None save yourself and my father have ever possessed
my affection; nor will it be bestowed upon any other."

"My poor child!" replied Monte-Cristo, "that is merely because
your father and myself are the only men with whom you have
ever conversed."

"And what care I for all others in the world? My father
called me his joy—you style me your love,—and both of you
bestowed on me the endearing appellation of your child!"

"Do you remember your father, Haydée?"

The young Greek smiled. " He is here, and here," said she, touching her eyes and her heart.

" And where am I?" inquired Monte-Cristo, laughingly.

" You?" cried she with tones of thrilling tenderness, " you are every where."

Monte-Cristo took the delicate hand of the young girl in his, and was about to raise it to his lips, when she hastily withdrew it, and presented her cheek instead.

" You now understand, Haydée," said the count, "that from this moment you are absolutely free; that here you excercise unlimited sway, and are at liberty to lay aside or continue the costume of your country, as it may suit your inclination. Within this mansion you are absolute mistress of your actions, and may go abroad or remain in your apartments, as may seem most agreeable to you. A carriage waits your orders, and Ali and Myrta will accompany you whithersoever you desire to go. There is but one favour I would entreat of you."

" Oh, speak !"

" Preserve most carefully the secret of your birth. Make no allusion to the past; nor upon any occasion be induced to pronounce the names of your illustrious father or ill-fated mother !"

" I have already told my lord, it is not my intention to hold converse with any one save himself."

The count, with a look of indescribable tenderness, extended his hand to the animated speaker, who carried it reverentially and affectionately to her lips. Monte-Cristo, thus soothed and calmed into a befitting state of mind to pay his intended visit to the Morrels, departed, murmuring as he went these lines of Pindar, " Youth is a flower, of which love is the fruit ; happy is he, who after having watched its silent growth, is permitted to gather and call it his own."

The carriage was prepared according to orders, and stepping lightly into it, the count drove off at his usual rapid pace.

In a very few minutes the count reached No. 7 in the Rue Meslay. The house was of white stone, and in a small court before it, were two beds full of beautiful flowers. In the concierge that opened the gate the count recognised Coclés ; but as he had but one eye, and that eye had considerably weakened in the course of nine years, Coclés did not recognise the count any more easily than those with two perfect eyes had done.

The carriages that drove up to the door were compelled to

turn, to avoid a fountain that played in a basin of rockwork, in which sported gold and silver fishes, an ornament that had excited the jealousy of the whole quarter, and had gained for the house the appellation of " *le Petit Versailles.*"

Coclés opened the gate, and Baptistin, springing from the box, inquired whether Monsieur and Madame Herbault and Monsieur Maximilian Morrel would see M. le Comte de Monte-Cristo.

" M. le Comte de Monte-Cristo ?" cried Morrel, throwing away his cigar and hastening to the carriage, " I should think we would see him. Ah, a thousand thanks, M. le Comte, for not having forgotten your promise."

And the young officer shook the count's hand so warmly that the latter could not be mistaken as to the sincerity of his joy; he saw that he had been expected with impatience, and was received with pleasure.

" Come, come !" said Maximilian ; " I will serve as your guide; such a man as you are ought not to be introduced by a servant. My sister is in the garden, plucking the dead roses ; my brother reading his two papers, *la Presse* and *les Débats*, within five steps of her, for wherever you see Madame Herbault, you have only to look within a circle of four yards and you will find M. Emmanuel, and ' reciprocally,' as they say at the École Polytechnique."

At the sound of their steps, a young woman dressed in a silk robe de chambre, and busily engaged in plucking the dead leaves off a splendid rose-tree, raised her head.

This was Julie, who had become, as the clerk of the house of Thomson and French had predicted, Madame Emmanuel Herbault.

She uttered a cry of surprise at the sight of a stranger, and Maximilian began to laugh.

" Don't disturb yourself, Julie," said he. " M. le Comte has only been two or three days in Paris, but he already knows what a woman of fashion of the Marais is, and if he does not, you will show him."

" Ah monsieur !" returned Julie ; " it is treason in my brother to bring you thus, but he never has any regard for his poor sister. Penelon ! Penelon !"

An old man who was digging busily at one of the beds of roses stuck his spade in the earth and approached cap in hand, striving to conceal a quid of tobacco he had just thrust into his cheek. A few locks of grey, mingled with his hair which was still thick and matted, whilst his bronzed features and determined glance announced the old sailor who had braved the heat of the equator and the storms of the tropics.

"Penelon," said Julie, "go and inform M. Emmanuel of this gentleman's visit, and Maximilian will conduct him to the drawing-room."

Emmanuel lost no time in complying with the summons and soon joined them there. He saluted the count with the air of a man who is aware of the rank of his guest.

The count had felt, from the moment he entered the house, the influence of happiness all around him, and he remained silent and pensive, forgetting that he was expected to re-commence the conversation, which had ceased after the first salutations had been exchanged. He perceived the pause, and, by a violent effort, tearing himself from his pleasing reverie—

"Madame," said he at length, "I pray you to excuse my emotion, which must astonish you who are accustomed to the happiness I meet here; but satisfaction is so new a sight to me, that I could never be weary of looking at yourself and your husband."

"We are very happy, monsieur," replied Julie; "but we have also known unhappiness, and few have ever undergone more bitter sufferings than ourselves."

Monte-Cristo rose, and, without making any answer (for the tremulousness of his voice would have betrayed his emotion), walked up and down the apartment with a slow step.

"Our magnificence makes you smile, M. le Comte?" said Maximilian, who had followed him with his eyes.

"No, no," returned Monte-Cristo, pale as death, pressing one hand on his heart to still its throbbings, whilst with the other he pointed to a crystal cover, beneath which a silken purse lay on a black velvet cushion, "I was wondering what could be the use of this purse, which contains a paper at one end and at the other a large diamond."

"M. le Comte," replied Maximilian, with an air of gravity, "those are our most precious family treasures."

"The stone seems very brilliant," answered the count.

"Oh, my brother does not allude to its value, although it has been estimated at 100,000 francs (4,000$l.$); he means, that the articles contained in this purse are the relics of an angel who once visited us."

"This I do not comprehend; and yet I may not ask for an explanation, madam," replied Monte-Cristo, bowing. "Pardon me, I had no intention of committing an indiscretion."

"Indiscretion!—oh, you make us happy by giving us an occasion of expiating on this subject. Did we intend to conceal the noble action this purse commemorates, we should not expose it thus. Oh! would we could relate it every where, and to every one; so that the emotion of our unknown benefactor might reveal his presence."

"Ah! really," said Monte-Cristo, in a half-stifled voice.

"Monsieur," returned Maximilian, raising the glass cover and respectfully kissing the silken purse, "this has touched the hand of a man who saved my father from suicide, us from ruin, and our name from shame and disgrace—a man by whose matchless benevolence we, poor children, doomed to want and wretchedness, can at present hear everyone envying our happy lot. This letter,"—(as he spoke, Maximilian drew a letter from the purse and gave it to the count)—"this letter was written by him the day that my father had taken a desperate resolution to destroy himself; and this diamond was given by the generous unknown to my sister as her dowry."

Monte-Cristo opened the letter, and read it with an indescribable feeling of delight. It was the letter written to Julie, and signed "Sinbad the Sailor."

"Unknown, you say, is the man who rendered you this service—unknown to you?"

"Yes, we have never had the happiness of pressing his hand," continued Maximilian. "We have supplicated Heaven in vain to grant us this favour, but all the affair has had a mysterious direction we cannot comprehend; all has been guided by a hand invisible, but powerful as that of an enchanter."

"Oh," cried Julie, "I have not lost all hope of some day kissing that hand, as I now kiss the purse which he has touched. Four years ago, Penelon was at Trieste—Penelon, M. le Comte, is the old sailor you saw in the garden, and who from quartermaster has become gardener—Penelon, when he was at Trieste, saw on the quay an Englishman, who was on the point of embarking on board a yacht; and he recognised him as the person who called on my father the 5th of June, 1829, and who wrote me this letter the 5th of September. He felt quite convinced of his identity, but he did not venture to address him."

"An Englishman!" said Monte-Cristo, who grew uneasy at the attention with which Julie looked at him. "An Englishman, you say?"

" Yes," replied Maximilian, " an Englishman, who represented himself as the confidential clerk of the house of Thomson and French at Rome. It was this that made me start when you said the other day, at M. de Morcerf's, that Messrs. Thomson and French were your bankers. That happened, as I told you, in 1829. For God's sake, tell me, did you know this Englishman ?"

" But you told me also, that the house of Thomson and French have constantly denied having rendered you this service ?"

" Yes."

" Then is it not probable that this Englishman may be some-one who, grateful for a kindness your father had shown him, and which he himself had forgotten, has taken this method of requiting the obligation ?"

" Sister, sister," said Maximilian, coming to the count's aid, " Recollect what our excellent father so often told us, ' It was no Englishman that thus saved us.' "

Monte-Cristo started.

" What did your father tell you, M. Morrel ?" said he, eagerly.

" My father thought that this action had been miraculously performed—he believed that a benefactor had arisen from the grave to serve us. Oh, it was a touching superstition, monsieur, and although I did not myself believe it, I would not for the world have destroyed my father's faith in it. How often did he muse over it and pronounce the name of a dear friend—a friend lost to him for ever ; and on his death-bed, when the near approach of eternity seemed to have illumined his mind with supernatural light, this thought which had until then been but a doubt became a conviction, and his last words were, ' Maximilian, it was Edmond Dantès !' "

At these words the count's paleness which had for some time been increasing, became alarming ; he could not speak, he looked at his watch like a man who has forgotten the time ; said a few hurried words to Madame Herbault, and pressing the hands of Emmanuel and Maximilian—

" Madame," said he, " I trust you will allow me to visit you from time to time ; I value your friendship, and feel grateful to you for your welcome, for this is the first time for many years that I have thus yielded to my feelings ;" and he hastily quitted the apartment.

"This Count de Monte-Cristo is a singular man," said Emmanuel.

"Yes," answered Maximilian; "but I feel sure he has an excellent heart and that he likes us."

"His voice went to my heart," observed Julie; "and two or three times I fancied I had heard it before."

CHAPTER XXVII

TOXICOLOGY

M. DE VILLEFORT, the procureur du roi, had lost no time in calling on the count, but had, like M. Danglars, been so unfortunate as not to find him in.

The count in his turn arrived at Madame de Villefort's, for the purpose of returning the visit of the procureur du roi.

Madame de Villefort, who was alone in her drawing-room when the count was announced, desired that her idolised son Edward might be brought hither instantly; and Edward, who heard nothing and nobody talked of for two whole days but this great personage, made all possible haste to come, not from obedience to his mother, not from any feeling of gratitude to the count, but from sheer curiosity, and so that he might find an opportunity for one of those small pertnesses which made his mother say,—

"Oh that sad child! but pray excuse him, he is really *so* clever."

After the first and usual civilities, the count inquired after M. de Villefort.

"My husband dines with the chancellor," replied the lady, "he has just gone, and I'm sure, he'll be exceedingly sorry not to have had the pleasure of seeing you before he went."

Two visitors who were there when the count arrived, having gazed at him with all their eyes, retired after that reasonable delay which politeness admits and curiosity requires.

"Ah! what is your sister Valentine doing?" inquired Madame de Villefort of Edward; "tell someone to bid her come here, that I may have the honour of introducing her to the count."

"You have a daughter, then, madame?" inquired the count; "very young, I presume?"

"The daughter of M. de Villefort," replied the young wife, "by his first marriage, a fine well-grown girl."

"But melancholy," interrupted Master Edward, snatching the

feathers out of the tail of a splendid parroquet, that was screaming on its gilded perch.

Madame de Villefort merely cried,—

" Silence, Edward !"

She then added,—

" This young madcap is, however, very nearly right, and merely re-echoes what he has heard me say with pain a hundred times ; for Mademoiselle de Villefort is, in spite of all we can do to rouse her, of a melancholy disposition and taciturn habit which injure the effect of her beauty.   But what detains her ? go, Edward, and see."

" They are looking for her where she is not to be found."

" And where are they looking for her ?"

" With grandpapa Noirtier."

" And do you think she is not there ?"

" No, no, no, no, no, she is not there," replied Edward, singing his words.

" And where is she, then ? if you know, why don't you tell ?"

" She is under the great chestnut-tree," replied the spoiled brat, as he gave, in spite of his mother's cries, live flies to the parrot, who appeared to relish such ' small deer ' excessively.

Madame de Villefort stretched out her hand to ring, intending to direct her waiting-maid to the spot where she would find Valentine, when the young lady herself entered the apartment. She appeared much dejected ; and any person who considered her attentively might have observed the traces of recent tears in her eyes.

Valentine was a tall and graceful girl of nineteen years of age, with bright chestnut hair, deep blue eyes, and that languishing air so full of distinction which had characterised her own dead mother.   Her white and slender fingers, her pearly neck, her cheeks tinted with varying hues, gave her at the first view the aspect of one of these lovely Englishwomen who have been so poetically compared to a swan admiring itself.   She entered the apartment, and seeing near her step-mother the stranger of whom she had already heard so much, saluted him without any girlish awkwardness or even lowering her eyes, and with an elegance that redoubled the count's attention.   He rose to return the salutation.

" Mademoiselle de Villefort, my step-daughter," said Madame de Villefort to Monte-Cristo, leaning back on her sofa and motioning towards Valentine with her hand.

" And M. de Monte-Cristo, king of China, emperor of Cochin-China," said the young imp, looking slyly towards his sister.

Madame de Villefort at this really did turn pale, and was very nearly angry with this household plague; but the count, on the contrary, smiled and looked at the boy complacently, which caused the maternal heart to bound again with joy and enthusiasm.

The count placed his hand on his brow as if to collect his thoughts.

" Madame, I have met you and mademoiselle also, somewhere —away from here—it was—I do not know—but it appears that this recollection is connected with a lovely sky and some religious fête ; mademoiselle was holding flowers in her hand, this interest-ing boy was chasing a beautiful peacock in a garden, and you, madame, were under the trellis of some arbour. Pray come to my aid, do not these circumstances bring to your mind, some reminiscences ?"

" Perhaps M. le Comte saw us in Italy," said Valentine, timidly.

" Yes, in Italy; it was in Italy most probably," replied Monte-Cristo, " you have travelled then in Italy, mademoiselle ?"

" Yes, madame and I were there two years ago. The doctors were afraid of my lungs, and prescribed the air of Naples. We went by Bologna, Perugia, and Rome."

" Ah, yes—true, mademoiselle," exclaimed Monte-Cristo, as if this simple indication was sufficient to determine his recollections. " The day had been burning hot: you were waiting for horses, which were delayed in consequence of the festival. Mademoiselle was walking in the shade of the garden, and your son disappeared in pursuit of the bird."

" And I caught it, mamma, don't you remember ?" interposed Edward, " and I pulled three such beautiful feathers out of his tail."

" You, madame, remained under the arbour formed by the vine; do you not remember, that whilst you were seated on a stone-bench, and whilst, as I told you, Mademoiselle de Villefort and your young son were absent, you conversed for a considerable time with somebody."

" Yes, in truth, yes," answered the lady, turning very red, " I do remember conversing with an individual wrapped in a long woollen mantle ; he was a medical man, I think."

" Precisely so, madame, this man was myself, for a fortnight I had been at that hotel, during which period I had cured my valet-de-chambre of a fever, and my landlord of the jaundice, so that I really acquired a reputation as a skilful physician.   We discoursed a long time, madame, on different subjects ; of Perugino, of Raphael, of manners, customs, of the famous *aquatofana* of which they had told you, I think you said, that certain individuals in Perugia had preserved the secret."

At this moment the clock struck six.

" It is six o'clock," said Madame de Villefort, evidently agitated.   " Valentine, will you not go and see if your grandfather will have his dinner ?"

Valentine rose, and saluting the count, left the apartment without replying a single word.

" Oh, madame !" said the count, when Valentine had left the room, " was it on my account that you sent Mademoiselle de Villefort away ?"

" By no means," replied the lady, quickly ; " but this is the hour when we give to M. Noirtier the repast which supports his sad existence.   You are aware, sir, of the deplorable condition of my husband's father ?"

" Yes, madame, I have heard of it—paralysis, I think."

" Alas, yes ! there is an entire want of movement in the frame of the poor old gentleman ; the mind alone is still active in this human machine, and that is faint and flickering, like the light of a lamp about to expire.   But excuse me, sir, for talking of our domestic misfortunes ; I interrupted you at the moment when you were telling me that you were a skilful chemist."

" No, madame, I did not say so much as that," replied the count, with a smile ; " quite the contrary.   I have studied chemistry, because, having determined to live in Eastern climates, I have been desirous of following the example of King Mithridates."

" *Mithridates, rex Ponticus*," said the young scamp, as he tore some beautiful portraits out of a splendid album, " the individual who breakfasted every morning with a cup of poison *à la crême*."

" Edward, you naughty boy !" exclaimed Madame de Villefort, snatching the mutilated book from the urchin's grasp ; " you are positively past bearing ; you really disturb the conversation : go, leave us, and join your sister Valentine in dear grandpapa Noirtier's room."

" The album," said Edward sulkily.

" What do you mean ?—the album !"

" I want the album."

" How dare you tear out the drawings ?"

" Oh, it amuses me."

" Go—go directly."

" I won't go unless you give me the album," said the boy, seating himself doggedly in an arm-chair, according to his habit of never giving way.

" Take it, then, and pray disturb us no longer," said Madame de Villefort, giving the album to Edward, who then went towards the door, led by his mother.

The count followed her with his eyes.

" Let us see if she shuts the door after him," he muttered.

Madame de Villefort closed the door carefully after the child, the count appearing not to notice her ; then casting a scrutinising glance around the chamber, the young wife returned to her chair, in which she seated herself.

" Allow me to observe, madame," said the count, with that kind tone he could assume so well, " you are really very severe with that dear clever child."

" Oh, sometimes severity is quite necessary," replied Madame de Villefort, with all a mother's real firmness.

" I was about to enquire of you," she continued, " if poisons acted equally, and with the same effect, on men of all temperaments ?"

" It depends," replied Monte-Cristo, " on how one was habituated to it. Suppose, then, that this poison was brucine, and you were to take a milligramme the first day, two milligrammes the second day, and so on. Well ! at the end of ten days you would have taken a centigramme ; at the end of twenty days increasing another milligramme, you would have taken three hundred centigrammes ; that is to say, a dose which you would support without inconvenience, and which would be very dangerous for any other person who had not taken the same precautions as yourself. Well, then, at the end of a month, when drinking water from the same *carafe*, you would kill the person who had drank this water as well as yourself, without you perceiving, otherwise than from slight inconvenience, that there was any poisonous substance mingled with this water."

" Is brucine, then, so terrible a poison ?"

" Oh, no ! In the first place, let us agree that the word poison does not exist, because in medicine use is made of the most violent poisons, which become, according as they are made use of, most salutary remedies."

" What, then, is it ?"

" A skilful preparation of my friend's, the worthy Abbé Adelmonte, who taught me the use of it."

" As for me," responded Madame de Villefort, "I am so nervous, and so subject to fainting fits, I should require a Doctor Adelmonte to invent for me some means of breathing freely and tranquillising my mind in the fear I have of dying some fine day of suffocation. Here are some lozenges which I have made up on purpose, they are compounded doubly strong."

Monte-Cristo opened the tortoise-shell box, which the lady presented to him, and imbibed the odour of the pastilles with the air of an amateur who thoroughly appreciated their composition.

" They are, indeed, exquisite," he said, " but as they are necessarily submitted to the process of deglutition,—a function which it is frequently impossible for a fainting person to accomplish, I prefer my own specific."

" Undoubtedly, and so should I prefer it, but of course it is a secret, and I am not so indiscreet as to ask it of you ?"

" But I," said Monte-Cristo, rising as he spoke,—" I am gallant enough to offer it you."

" Oh, sir !"

" Only remember one thing, a small dose is a remedy, a large one is poison. One drop will restore life from a fainting fit, five or six will inevitably kill, and in a way the more terrible, inasmuch as, poured into a glass of wine, it would not in the slightest degree affect its flavour. But I say no more, madame, it is really as if I were advising you."

The clock struck half-past six, and a lady was announced, a friend of Madame de Villefort, who came to dine with her.

" If I had had the honour of seeing you for the third or fourth time, M. le Comte, instead of only for the second," said Madame de Villefort,—" if I had had the honour of being your friend, instead of only having the happiness of lying under an obligation to you, I should insist on detaining you to dinner, and not allow myself to be daunted by a first refusal."

" A thousand thanks, madame," replied Monte-Cristo, " but I have an engagement which I cannot break ; I have promised to escort to the Académie, a Greek princess of my acquaintance who has never seen your grand Opera, and who relies on me to conduct her thither."

" Adieu, then, sir ! and do not forget my recipe."

"Ah, in truth, madame, to do that, I must forget the hour's conversation I have had with you, which is indeed impossible."

Monte-Cristo bowed and left the house.

Madame de Villefort remained immersed in thought.

"He is a very strange man," she said ; "and in my opinion is himself the Adelmonte he talks about."

As to Monte-Cristo the result had surpassed his utmost expectations.

"Good !" said he, as he went away ; "this is a fruitful soil and I feel certain that the seed sown will not be cast on barren ground."

Next morning, faithful to his promise, he sent the prescription requested.

Meanwhile, Valentine, having attended to her grandfather's needs, went out into the garden at the back of the house and paced up and down behind the trees near a little iron gate. She had not been there a moment before Maximilian Morrel sprang forward, saying :—"Fear nothing, Valentine—it is I !" "I am late to-day," she said. "It is almost the dinner hour, and I have been compelled to exercise my utmost skill to get rid of the incessant watchfulness of my maid, who, no doubt, is employed to report all I do and say."

"Dearest Valentine !" said the young man, "If you come at all it is more than I dare hope. I almost fear to offend you by speaking of my love, but yet I cannot find myself in your presence without longing to pour forth my soul and to tell you how fondly I adore you."

"Listen, dearest," he continued, as she remained silent. "You told me some days ago the dreadful news that your father wished you to engage yourself to M. Franz d'Epinay, and that your father was resolved upon completing the match, and that from his will there was no appeal, as M. de Villefort was never known to change a determination once formed. I have been patient as you wished ; hoping Providence would graciously interpose in our behalf and order events in our favour. For what cared I for delays or difficulties so long as my sweet Valentine had confessed she loved me, and accepted my fervent vows of unfailing constancy ? Blessed avowal ! the very recollection of which can at all times raise me even from despair itself. To hear you repeat those enrapturing words from time to time is all I ask, and to obtain that privilege I would cheerfully endure even double my present disquietudes."

"Ah, Maximilian! that is the very thing that makes you so bold, and which renders me at once so happy and unhappy, that I frequently ask myself whether it is better for me to endure the harshness of my step-mother, and her blind preference for her own child, or to be, as I now am, insensible to any pleasure save such as I find in these our meetings, so fraught with danger to both."

"I will not admit that idea," returned the young man; "it is cruel. You have permitted me to converse with you from time to time, Valentine, but forbidden my ever following you in your walks or elsewhere, and have I not obeyed?"

"Indeed, you have, and your courage and friendship inspires me. I am so miserable, Maximilian, harassed and persecuted by step-mother, and left to the sole companionship of a paralysed and speechless old man, whose withered hand can no longer press mine, and whose eye alone converses with me, though doubtless, however chilled his frame, there still lingers in his heart the warmest tenderness for his poor grandchild. Oh, how bitter a fate is mine to serve either as a victim or an enemy to all who are stronger than myself, while my only friend and supporter is but a living corpse! Indeed, indeed, Maximilian, I am very miserable, and you are right to love me for myself alone."

"Dear Valentine!" replied the young man deeply affected. "At the mere thought of you my heart beats more quickly, my blood flows with increased rapidity through my veins, but I solemnly promise you to restrain all this ardour, this fervour and intensity of feeling, until you yourself shall require me to render them available in serving or assisting you. M. Franz is not expected to return home for a year to come, I am told; in that time many favourable and unforeseen chances may befriend us. Let us then hope for the best."

The poor girl made no reply, but her lover could plainly hear her sobs and tears.

"In the eyes of the world," said she, "I am surrounded by kindness and affection, but the reverse is the case. The general remark is, 'Oh, it cannot be expected that one of so stern a character as M. Villefort could lavish the tenderness some fathers do on their daughters! What, though she has lost her own mother at a tender age, she has had the happiness to find a second mother in Madame de Villefort.' The world, however, is mistaken; my father abandons me from utter indifference, while my step-mother detests me with a hatred so much the more terrible as it is veiled beneath a continual smile."

" Hate you, sweet Valentine!" exclaimed the young man; " how is it possible for any one to do that?"

" Alas!" replied the weeping girl; " I am obliged to own that my step-mother's aversion to me arises from a very natural source—her overweening love for her own child, my brother Edward."

" But why should it?"

" Nay, I know not; but though unwilling to introduce money matters into our present conversation, I will just say this much, that her extreme dislike to me has its origin in mercenary motives; and I much fear she envies me the fortune I already enjoy in right of my mother, and which will be more than doubled at the death of her parents, M. and Madame Méran, whose sole heiress I am. Madame de Villefort has nothing of her own, and hates me for being so richly endowed. Alas! how gladly would I exchange the half of this wealth for the happiness of at least sharing my father's love! God knows, I would prefer sacrificing the whole, so that it would obtain me a happy and affectionate home.

" I seem to myself as though living a life of bondage, yet at the same time am so conscious of my own weakness, that I fear to break the restraint in which I am held lest I fall utterly powerless and helpless. Then, too, my father is not a person whose orders may be infringed with impunity: protected as he is by his high position, and firmly established reputation for talent and unswerving integrity, no one could oppose him; he is all powerful with even his king; he would crush you at a word, and I should be ready to expire of terror at his feet. Dear Maximilian, believe me when I assure you that I dare not attempt to resist my father's commands, more on your account than my own, for though I could willingly sacrifice myself, I would not peril your safety."

" I do not see why he should so bitterly object to me," said Maximilian. " I may not be, strictly speaking, what is termed an illustrious match for you, but I am for many reasons not altogether so much beneath your alliance. The days when such distinctions were so nicely weighed and considered no longer exist in France, and the first families of the monarchy have intermarried with those of the Empire. My prospects of military preferment are most encouraging as well as certain.

16

My fortune though small is free and unfettered, and the memory of my late father respected in our country, Valentine, as that of the most upright and honourable merchant of the city ;— I say our country, because you were born not far from Marseilles."

"Name not Marseilles, I beseech you, Maximilian, that one word brings back my mother to my recollection,—my angel mother, who died too soon for myself and all who knew her; but who, after watching over her child, during the brief period allotted to her in this world, now I fondly hope, and fully believe, contemplates her with pitying tenderness from those realms of bliss, to which her pure spirit has flown. Ah, were she still living, we need fear nothing, Maximilian, for I would confide our love to her, and she would aid and protect us."

At that moment, hearing a sound from the house, she made a sign to her lover and slipped quickly back through the trees.

CHAPTER XXVIII

Monte-Cristo's pretext of an Opera engagement was feasible as there chanced to be on that very night a more than ordinary attraction at the Académie Royale. Levasseur, who had been suffering under severe illness, made his reappearance in the character of Bertram, and, as usual, the announcement of the most admired production of the favourite composer of the day had attracted an audience consisting of the very *élite* of Parisian fashion. Morcerf, like most other young men of rank and fortune, had his orchestral stall, with the certainty of always finding a seat in at least a dozen of the principal boxes occupied by persons of his acquaintance; he had moreover his right of entry into the omnibus box. Château-Renaud rented a stall beside his own, while Beauchamp, in his editorial capacity, had unlimited range all over the theatre.

It happened that on that particular night the minister's box was placed at the disposal of Lucien Debray, who offered it to the Count de Morcerf, who again, upon his mother's rejection of it, sent the offer to Danglars with an intimation that he should probably do himself the honour of joining the baroness and her daughter during the evening in the event of their accepting the box in question. The ladies received the offer with too much pleasure to dream of a refusal. To no class of persons is the presentation of a gratuitous opera-box more acceptable than to the wealthy millionaire, who still hugs economy while boasting of carrying a king's ransom in his waistcoat-pocket.

Danglars had, however, protested against showing himself in a ministerial box, declaring that his political principles, as well as his being a member of the opposition party, would not permit him so to commit himself; the baroness had, therefore, despatched a note to Lucien Debray, bidding him call for them, it being wholly impossible for her to go alone with her daughter to the Opera. There is no gainsaying the plain fact, that a very unfavourable construction would have been put upon the circumstance of two women going together to a public place, while the addition of a third, in the person of her mother's lover, enabled Mademoiselle Danglars to defy malice and ill-nature while visiting so celebrated a place of amusement.

When they arrived Albert de Morcerf from his stall turned round just in time to receive a gracious wave of the fan from Madame la Baronne ; as for Mademoiselle Eugénie, she scarcely vouchsafed to waste the glances of her large black eyes even upon the business of the stage.

"My dear fellow," said Château-Renaud, who was seated beside him, "I cannot imagine what objection you can possibly have to Mademoiselle Danglars—that is, setting aside her want of ancestry and somewhat inferior rank, which, by the way, I don't think you care very much about ; now, barring all that, I mean to say she is a deuced fine girl!"

"Handsome certainly," replied Albert, "but not to my taste, which I confess, inclines to a softer, gentler, and more feminine style than that possessed by the young lady in question."

"Bless my heart!" exclaimed Château-Renaud, who, because he had seen his thirtieth summer, fancied himself duly warranted in assuming a sort of paternal air with his more youthful friend, "you young people are never satisfied ; why, what would you have more? your parents have chosen you a bride who might serve as the living model of the 'Hunting Diana,' and yet you are not content."

"No, for that very resemblance affrights me ; I should have liked something more in the manner of the Venus of Milo or Capua; but this chase-loving Diana, continually surrounded by her nymphs, gives me a sort of alarm, lest she should some day entail on me the fate of Actæon."

And, indeed, it required but one glance of Mademoiselle Danglars to comprehend the nature, as well as justness, of Morcerf's remark : she was certainly handsome, but her beauty was of too marked and decided a character to please a fastidious taste ; her hair was raven black, but amid its natural waves might be seen rebellion against the hand that sought to band and braid it ; her eyes, of the same colour as her hair, were richly fringed and surmounted by well-arched brows, whose great defect, however, consisted in an almost habitual frown.

When the curtain fell the whole of the audience in the parterre were directing their gaze towards the box formerly possessed by the ambassador of Russia. Following the universal example, the two friends perceived that an individual of from thirty-five to forty years of age, dressed in deep black, had just entered, accompanied by a girl dressed after the Eastern style; she was young and surpassingly beautiful, while the rich magnificence of her attire drew all eyes upon her.

"By heavens!" said Albert, "it is Monte-Cristo himself with his fair Greek!"

The strangers were, indeed, no other than the count and Haydée. The sensation excited by the beauty and dazzling appearance of the latter soon communicated itself to every part of the theatre, and even ladies leaned forward from the boxes to admire the many-coloured coruscations that darted from the superb diamonds worn by the young Greek.

The second act passed during one continued buzz of voices, one deep whisper, intimating that some great and universally interesting event had occurred; all eyes, all thoughts were occupied with the young and beautiful girl, whose gorgeous apparel and splendid jewels threw an air of insignificance upon all the fair visitants of the theatre; the business of the stage was utterly neglected—all seemed to consider the contemplation of so much loveliness far more deserving of attention.

At the second interval an unmistakable sign from Madame Danglars intimated her desire to see Albert in her box, and neither the politeness nor good taste of Morcerf would permit his neglecting an invitation so unequivocally given. At the close of the act he therefore proceeded to the baroness's *loge*. Having bowed to the two ladies, he extended his hand to Debray. By the baroness he was most graciously welcomed, while Eugénie received him with her accustomed coldness.

"My dear fellow!" said Debray, "you have just come in the very nick of time to help a fellow-creature regularly beaten and at a standstill. There is madame overwhelming me with questions respecting the count; she insists upon it that I can tell her his birth, education, and parentage, where he came from and whither he is going. Being no disciple of Cagliostro, I was wholly unable to do this; so, by way of getting out of the scrape, I said, 'Ask Morcerf, he has the whole history of his beloved Monte-Cristo at his fingers' ends;' whereupon the baroness made you a sign to come hither, and now I leave the solution of her curiosity in your hands."

"Is it not almost incredible," said Madame Danglars, "that a person having at least half a million of secret service money at his command, should possess so little information upon so every-day a matter as the present?"

"Let me assure you, madame," said Lucien, "that had I really the sum you mention at my disposal, I would employ it more profitably than in troubling myself to obtain particulars respecting the Count of Monte-Cristo, whose only merit in my eyes consists in his being twice as rich as a nabob. However, I have turned the business over to Morcerf, so pray settle it with him."

"I am very sure no nabob of our time would have sent me a pair of horses worth 32,000 francs, wearing on their heads four diamonds valued at 5,000 francs each."

"He seems to have a mania for diamonds," said Morcerf, smiling; "and I verily believe that, like Potemkin, he keeps his pockets filled for the sake of strewing them along the road, as Hop-o-my-Thumb did his flint-stones."

"Perhaps he has discovered some mine," said Madame Danglars.   "I suppose you know he has an order for unlimited credit on the baron's banking establishment?"

"I was not aware of it," replied Albert, "but I can readily believe it."

"And, further, that he stated to M. Danglars his intention of only staying a year in Paris, during which time he proposed to spend six millions. He must be the Shah of Persia travelling incognito."

"Have you remarked the extreme beauty of that young girl by whom he is accompanied, M. Lucien?" inquired Eugénie.

"I really never met with a woman so ready to do justice to the charms of another as yourself;—let us see how far she merits your praises," replied Lucien, raising his lorgnette to his eye. "A most lovely creature, upon my soul!" cried he, after a long and searching scrutiny.

"Who is she, M. Morcerf," inquired Eugénie; "does any body know?"

"Allow me to state," said Albert, replying to this direct appeal, "that I can give you very tolerable information on that subject, she is a Greek."

"So I should presume by her dress; if, therefore, you know no more than that one self-evident fact, the whole of the spectators in the theatre are as well informed as yourself."

"I am extremely sorry you find me so ignorant a cicerone," replied Morcerf, "but I am reluctantly obliged to confess, I have nothing further to communicate—yes, stay, I do know one thing more, namely, that she is a musician, for one day that I chanced to be breakfasting with the count, I heard the sound of a guzla —it is impossible it could have been touched by any finger than her own."

"Then your count entertains visitors, does he?" asked Madame Danglars.

"Indeed he does, and in a most notable manner, I can assure you."

"I must try and persuade M. Danglars to invite him to a ball or dinner, or something of the sort, that he may be compelled to ask us in return."

"What!" said Debray, laughing; "do you really mean you would go to his house?"

"Why not? my husband could accompany me."

"But do you know this mysterious count is a bachelor?"

"You have ample proof to the contrary if you look opposite," said the baroness, as she laughingly pointed to the beautiful Greek.

"No, no!" exclaimed Debray; "she is not his wife, he told us himself she was his slave; do you not recollect, Morcerf, his telling us so at your breakfast?"

"Well, then," said the baroness, "if slave she be, she has all the air and manner of a princess."

"Of the Arabian Nights?"

"If you like; but tell me, my good Lucien, what is it that constitutes a princess? gold, silver, and jewels? Our Greek beauty there is one blaze of diamonds; I doubt if any queen's could equal them."

"To me she seems overloaded," observed Eugénie; "she would look far better if she wore fewer, and we should then be able to see her finely formed throat and wrists."

"See how the artist peeps out!" exclaimed Madame Danglars; "my poor Eugénie, you must conceal your passion for the fine arts."

"I admire all that is beautiful in art or nature," returned the young lady.

"What do you think of the count?" inquired Debray; "he is not much amiss, according to my ideas of good looks."

"The count?" repeated Eugénie, as though it had not

occurred to her to observe him sooner, " the count? oh,—he is so dreadfully pale."

" I quite agree with you," said Morcerf; " and it is in that very paleness that consists the secret we want to find out. The Countess G—— insists upon it he is a vampire."

" Go and bring your Count of Monte-Cristo to us," said the baroness to Albert.

" What for?" asked Eugénie.

" What for? why that we may converse with him, of course; if you have no curiosity to hear whether he expresses himself like other people, I can assure you I have. Have you really no desire to be introduced to this singular being?"

" None whatever," replied Eugénie.

" Strange girl!" murmured the baroness.

" He will very probably come of his own accord," said Morcerf; "There! do you see, madame, he recognises you, and bows."

The baroness returned the salute in the most smiling and graceful manner.

" Well," said Morcerf, " I may as well be magnanimous and tear myself away to forward your wishes; adieu; I will go and try if there are any means of speaking to him."

" Go straight to his box, that will be the simplest plan."

" But I have never been presented to the beautiful Greek."

" You say she is only a slave?"

" While you assert that she is a queen, or at least a princess— No, no! I cannot venture to enter his box; but I hope, that when he observes me leave you, he will come and take my place."

As he had predicted, just as he was passing the count's box, the door opened, and Monte-Cristo came forth. After giving some directions to Ali, who stood in the lobby, the count observed Albert, and, taking his arm, walked onwards with him.

Carefully closing the box-door, Ali placed himself before it, while a crowd of wondering spectators assembled round the unselfconscious Nubian.

" Upon my word," said Monte-Cristo, " Paris is a strange city, and the Parisians a very singular people; do pray observe that cluster of persons collected round poor Ali, really one might suppose he was the only Nubian they had ever beheld; now I will pledge myself, that a Frenchman might show himself in public, either in Tunis, Constantinople, Bagdad, or Cairo, without drawing a circle of gazers around him."

" That shows that the Eastern nations have too much good

sense to waste their time and attention on objects undeserving
of either. However, as far as Ali is concerned, I can assure you,
the interest he excites is merely from the circumstance of his
being your attendant; you who are at this moment the most
celebrated and fashionable person in Paris."

The count laughed. "Tell me," he said, "does your father
never visit the Opera? I have been looking for him, but
without success."

"He will be here to-night."

"In what part of the house?"

"In the Baroness Danglars's box, I believe."

"Is the charming young girl with her—her daughter?"

"Yes."

"Indeed! then I congratulate you."

Morcerf smiled. "We will discuss that subject at length at
some future time," said he.

The bell rang at this moment for the rising of the curtain.

"You will excuse my leaving you," said the count turning in
the direction of his box.

"What! Are you going back?"

"Pray, say to the baroness that, with her permission, I
propose doing myself the honour of paying my respects in the
course of the evening."

The third act had now commenced; and during its progress
the Count de Morcerf, according to promise, made his appearance
in the box of Madame Danglars.

The Count de Morcerf was not one of those persons whose
aspect would create either interest or curiosity in a place of
public amusement; his presence, therefore, was wholly unnoticed,
save by the occupants of the box in which he had just seated
himself.

The quick eye of Monte-Cristo, however, marked his coming;
and a slight though meaning smile passed over his lips as he
did so.

When the curtain again fell, the spectators poured into the
lobbies and salon. The count also, quitting his, proceeded at
once to the box of Madame Danglars, who could scarcely restrain
a cry of mingled pleasure and surprise.

"Welcome, M. le Comte!" exclaimed she as he entered. "I
have been most anxious to see you that I might repeat verbally
those thanks writing can so ill express."

"Surely so trifling a circumstance cannot deserve a place in your remembrance! Believe me, madame, I had entirely forgotten it!"

"But it is not so easy to forget, M. le Comte."

"May I beg of you, Madame la Baronne, to honour me with an introduction to your charming daughter?"

"Oh! you are no stranger—at least not by name," replied Madame Danglars, "and the last two or three days we have really talked of nothing else but yourself. Eugénie," she added turning towards her daughter, "M. the Comte de Monte-Cristo."

The count bowed, while Mademoiselle Danglars returned a slight inclination of the head.

"You have a charming young person with you to-night, M. le Comte," said Eugénie. "Your daughter I presume?"

"No indeed," said Monte-Cristo, astonished at the coolness and freedom of the question. "She to whom you allude is a poor unfortunate Greek left under my care."

"And what is her name?"

"Haydée," replied Monte-Cristo.

"A Greek?" murmured the Count de Morcerf.

"Yes, indeed, count," said Madame Danglars; "and tell me, did you ever see at the court of Ali Tebelen, whom you so gloriously and valiantly served, a more exquisite beauty than is displayed in the fair Greek before us?"

"Did I hear rightly, M. le Comte," said Monte-Cristo, "that you served at Janina?"

"I was inspector-general of the pasha's troops," replied Morcerf; "and I do not conceal that I owe my fortune, such as it is, to the liberality of the illustrious Albanese chief."

"Look! pray look," exclaimed Madame Danglars, suddenly.

"Where?" stammered out Morcerf.

"There, there!" said Monte-Cristo, as wrapping his arms around the count he leaned with him over the front of the box, just as Haydée, whose eyes were occupied in examining the theatre in search of the count, perceived his pale marble features close to the head of Morcerf, whom he appeared to be embracing.

This sight produced on the astonished girl an effect similar to that of the fabulous head of Medusa. She bent forward as though to assure herself of the reality of what she beheld, then uttering a faint cry, threw herself back in her seat. The sound quickly reached the ear of the watchful Ali, who instantly opened the box-door to ascertain the cause.

"Bless me!" exclaimed Eugénie, "what has happened to your ward, M. le Comte? she seems taken suddenly ill?"

"Very probably!" answered the count. "But do not be alarmed on her account! Haydée's nervous system is delicately organised, and she is peculiarly susceptible of the odours even of flowers—nay, there are some which cause her to faint if brought into her presence. However," he continued, drawing a small phial from his pocket, "I have an infallible remedy for such attacks."

So saying, he bowed to the baroness and her daughter, exchanged a parting shake of the hand with Debray and the count, and quitted the box.

Upon his return to Haydée, he found her extremely pale and much agitated. Directly she saw him she seized his hand.

"With whom was my lord conversing a few minutes since?" asked she, in a trembling voice.

"With the Count de Morcerf," answered Monte-Cristo. "He tells me he served your illustrious father, and that he owes his fortune to him!"

"Base, cowardly traitor that he is!" exclaimed Haydée, her eyes flashing with rage; "he it was who sold my beloved parent to the Turks, and the fortune he boasts of was the price of his treachery! Knowest thou not that, my dear lord?"

"Something of this I heard in Epirus," said Monte-Cristo; "but the particulars are still unknown to me. You shall relate them to me, my child. They are, no doubt, both curious and interesting."

"Yes, yes! but let us go hence, I beseech you. I feel as though it would kill me to remain longer near that dreadful man."

So saying Haydée arose, and wrapping herself in her burnouse of white cachemire embroidered with pearls and coral, she hastily quitted the box at the moment when the curtain was rising upon the fourth act.

CHAPTER XXIX

THE RISE AND FALL OF THE STOCKS

SOME days after this, Albert de Morcerf visited the Count of Monte-Cristo at his house in the Champs Elysées. Albert was accompanied by Lucien Debray.

"You are in constant communication with the Baron Danglars?" inquired the count of Albert de Morcerf when he had greeted them cordially.

"Yes, count, you know what I told you?"

"All remains the same, then, in that quarter?"

"It is more than ever a settled thing," said Lucien.

But Albert shook his head, and looked thoughtful.

"I confess," observed Monte-Cristo, "that I have some difficulty in comprehending your objection to a young lady who is both rich and beautiful."

"Oh!" said Morcerf, "this repugnance, if repugnance it may be called, is not all on my side."

"Whence can it arise then? for you told me your father desired the marriage."

"My mother's is the dissenting voice; she has a clear and penetrating judgment, and does not smile on the proposed union. I cannot account for it, but she seems to entertain some prejudice against the Danglars."

Monte-Cristo turned away; he seemed moved by this last remark.

"Ah!" said he to Debray, who had thrown himself into an easy chair at the farthest extremity of the drawing-room, and who held a pencil in his right hand and an account-book in his left, "what are you doing there? are you making a sketch after Poussin?"

"No, I am calculating—by the way, Morcerf, this indirectly concerns you—I am calculating what the house of Danglars must have gained by the last rise in Haïti stock; from 206 they have risen to 409 in three days, and the prudent banker had purchased at 206, therefore, he must have made 300,000 pounds."

" Ah," said the count, " I see that M. Danglars is accustomed to play at gaining or losing 300,000 francs in a day; he must be enormously rich ?"

" It is not he who plays," exclaimed Lucien, "it is Madame Danglars; she is indeed daring."

" But you who are a reasonable being, Lucien, and who know how little dependence is to be placed on the news, since you are at the fountain-head, surely you ought to prevent it," said Morcerf, with a smile.

" I do not understand," stammered Lucien.

" It is very clear, notwithstanding," replied the young man, " tell her some fine morning an unheard-of piece of intelligence —some telegraphic despatch, of which you alone are in possession: for instance, that Henri IV. was seen yesterday at the house of Gabrielle; that will cause the funds to rise, she will lay her plans accordingly, and she will certainly lose when Beauchamp announces the following day in his gazette, 'The report which has been circulated by some individuals, stating the king to have been seen yesterday at Gabrielle's house, is totally without foundation. We can positively assert that his majesty did not quit the Pont-Neuf.'"

Lucien half smiled.   Monte-Cristo, although apparently indifferent, had not lost one word of this conversation, and his penetrating eye had even read a hidden secret in the embarrassed manner of the secretary.   This embarrassment had completely escaped Albert, but it caused Lucien to shorten his visit; he was evidently ill at ease.

CHAPTER XXX

THE TRYSTING PLACE

THE trysting place at M. de Villefort's house, behind the gate, half screened from view by the large chestnut-trees, had again been appointed by the lovers for their meeting.

This time Maximilian was the first to arrive. He was intently watching for a shadow to appear amongst the trees, and awaiting with anxiety the sound of a light step on the gravel-walk. At length the long-desired sound was heard, and Valentine entered the garden alone.

The delay had been occasioned by a visit from Madame Danglars and Eugénie, which had been prolonged beyond the time at which Valentine was expected.

Valentine, however, walked slowly; and, instead of immediately directing her steps towards the gate, she seated herself on a bank, and, carefully casting her eyes around to convince herself that she was not watched, she presently rose and joined Maximilian.

"Good evening, Valentine," he cried.

"Good evening, Maximilian; I know I have kept you waiting, but you saw the cause of my delay."

"I saw you a few minutes earlier on the terrace with Mademoiselle Danglars," said Maximilian, "and, on my honour, without at all wishing to depreciate the beauty of Mademoiselle Danglars, I cannot understand how any man can really love her."

"She told me that she loved no one," said Valentine; "that she disliked the idea of being married; that she would infinitely prefer leading an independent and unfettered life; and that she almost wished her father might lose his fortune, so that she might become an artist like her friend, Mademoiselle Louise d'Armilly. But I did not come here to discuss Eugénie, only to send you away, for I cannot stay to-day."

"Need you run away at once, Valentine?" asked the young man.

"I'm afraid I must. Madame de Villefort has sent to request

my presence, as she had a communication to make on which a part of my fortune depended. Let them take my fortune, I am already too rich ; and, perhaps, when they have taken it, they will leave me in peace and quietness. You would love me as much if I were poor, would you not, Maximilian ?"

"Oh! I shall always love you. What should I care for either riches or poverty, if my Valentine was near me, and I felt certain that no one could deprive me of her ? But do you not fear that this communication may relate to your marriage ?

" I was going to tell you," said Maximilian, gravely, that I met M. de Morcerf the other day ; he has received a letter from Franz, announcing his immediate return."

Valentine turned pale, and leaned against the gate for support.

" Can it really be true, and is that why Madame de Villefort has sent for me ? Yet she objects to my marriage."

"What interest can Madame de Villefort have in your remaining unmarried ?"

" Did I not tell you the other day that I was rich, Maximilian —too rich? I possess nearly 50,000 livres in right of my mother ; my grandfather, and my grandmother, the Marquis and Marquise de St. Méran, will leave me as much more ; and M. Noirtier evidently intends making me his heir. My brother Edward, who inherits nothing from his mother, will therefore be poor in comparison with me. Now, if I had taken the veil, all this fortune would have descended to my father, and, in reversion, to his son."

" I wish indeed you were not," cried Maximilian, " it makes our prospect of being married much more difficult. I want to ask you something, Valentine. I have always regarded our love in the light of something sacred ; consequently, no human being, not even my sister, is aware of its existence. Will you permit me to make a confidant of a friend, and ask his advice ?"

Valentine started. " Who is he ?" she cried.

" The Count of Monte-Cristo."

" Ah !" cried Valentine, " he is too much the friend of Madame de Villefort ever to be mine."

" Ah ! Valentine, I assure you, you are mistaken."

" He dislikes me ; he has never honoured me with the smile which you extol so loudly ; he saw that I was unhappy, he understood that I could be of no use to him, and therefore paid me no regard whatever."

" Well, Valentine," said Morrel, with a sigh, " we will not

discuss the matter further; I will not make a confidant of him. But I must tell you one other thing which seems to me curious; look through this opening, and you will see the new horse which I rode here."

"Ah! what a beautiful creature!" cried Valentine; "why did you not bring it close to the gate, that I might talk to it and pat it?"

"It is, as you say, a very valuable animal," said Maximilian; "you know that my means are limited. I went to a horse-dealer's where I saw this magnificent horse, which I have named Medea; I asked the price of it, they told me it was 4,500 francs; I was therefore obliged to give it up, as you may imagine, but I own I went away with rather a heavy heart. That same evening some friends of mine visited me, M. de Château-Renaud, M. Debray, and five or six other choice spirits, whom you do not know even by name. They proposed *la bouillotte*; I never play, for I am not rich enough to afford to lose, nor sufficiently poor to desire to gain. But I was at my own house you understand, so there was nothing to be done but to send for the cards, which I did. Just as they were sitting down to table, M. de Monte-Cristo arrived. He took his seat amongst them, they played, and I won; I am almost ashamed to own that my gains amounted to 5,000 francs. We separated at midnight. I could not defer my pleasure, so I took a cabriolet and drove to the horse-dealer's. Feverish and excited, I rang at the door, the person who opened it must have taken me for a madman, for I rushed at once to the stable. Medea was standing at the rack eating her hay, I immediately put on the saddle and bridle, then putting the 4,500 francs into the hands of the astonished dealer, I proceeded to fulfil my intention of passing the night in riding in the Champs Elysées. As I rode by the count's house, I perceived a light in one of the windows, and fancied I saw the shadow of his figure moving behind the curtain. Now, Valentine, I firmly believe that he knew of my wish to possess this horse, and that he lost expressly to give me the means of procuring it."

"My dear Maximilian, you are really too fanciful; you will not love even me long. A man who accustoms himself to live in such a world of poetry and imagination must find far too little excitement in a common, every-day sort of attachment such as ours. But they are calling me.—Do you hear?"

A moment later the young man saw Valentine hurrying towards the house, as though she were almost terrified at her own sensations.

CHAPTER XXXI

AN interview very important in its bearing on the future of the young lovers had taken place that day. M. de Villefort had entered his father's room, followed by Madame de Villefort, with an air of having come on a serious occasion. After saluting the old man and speaking to Barrois, a faithful servant, who had been twenty-five years in his service, the husband and wife took their places on either side of the paralytic.

M. Noirtier was sitting in an arm-chair, which moved upon castors, in which he was wheeled into the room in the morning, and in the same way drawn out again at night. He was placed before a large glass, which reflected the whole apartment, and permitted him to see without any attempt to move, which would have been impossible, all who entered the room, and every thing which was going on around him. M. Noirtier, although almost as immovable and helpless as a corpse, looked at the new comers with a quick and intelligent expression, perceiving at once by their ceremonious courtesy, that they were come on business of an unexpected and official character. Sight and hearing were the only senses remaining, and they appeared left, like two solitary sparks, to animate the miserable body which seemed fit for nothing but the grave. Valentine, by means of her love, her patience, and her devotion, had learned to read in Noirtier's look all the varied feelings which were passing in his mind. To this dumb language, which was so unintelligible to others, she answered by throwing her whole soul into the expression of the countenance, and in this manner were the conversations sustained between the blooming girl and the helpless invalid, whose body could scarcely be called a living one, but who, nevertheless, possessed a fund of knowledge and penetration, united with a will as powerful as ever, although clogged by a body rendered utterly incapable of obeying its impulses. As to the servant, he had, as we have said, been with his master for five-and-twenty years, therefore he knew all his habits, and it was seldom that Noirtier found it necessary to ask for any thing, so prompt was he in administering to all the necessities of the invalid.   Villefort did not need the help of either Valentine or the domestic, in order to carry on with his father the strange conversation which he was about to begin. After having seated himself he sent away Barrois and began :—

"I trust you will not be displeased, sir, that Valentine has not come with us, or that I dismissed Barrois, for our conference will be one which could not with propriety be carried on in the presence of either; Madame de Villefort and I have a communication to make to you.   We are thinking of marrying Valentine. The young man we have selected possesses fortune, a high rank in society, and every personal qualification likely to render Valentine supremely happy.   The person to whom we allude is M. Franz de Quesnel, Baron d'Epinay."

When he pronounced the name of Franz, the pupil of M. Noirtier's eye began to dilate, and his eyelids trembled with the same movement as may be perceived on the lips of an individual about to speak, and he darted a lightning glance at Madame de Villefort and his son.   The procureur du roi, who knew that a political hatred had formerly existed between M. Noirtier and the elder d'Epinay, well understood the agitation and anger which the announcement had produced.

Noirtier's look was furious ; it was very evident that something desperate was passing in the old man's mind, for the cry of anger and grief rose to his throat, and not being able to find vent in utterance, appeared almost to choke him, for his face and lips turned quite purple with the struggle.

Villefort quietly opened a window, saying, "It is very warm, and the heat affects M. Noirtier."

After that he and Madame de Villefort bowed and left the room, giving orders that Valentine should be summoned to her grandfather's presence.

Valentine, with a colour still heightened by emotion, entered the room just after her parents had quitted it.   One look was sufficient to tell her that her grandfather was suffering, and that there was much on his mind which he wished to communicate to her.

"Dear grandpapa," cried she, "what has happened ?   They have vexed you, and you are angry ?"

The paralytic closed his eyes in token of assent.

"DEAR GRANDPAPA," CRIED SHE, "WHAT HAS HAPPENED?"
Page 258.

"Ah! I know," said she lowering her voice, and going close to the old man, "they have been speaking of my marriage,— have they not?"

"Yes," replied the angry look.

"What is it then?" asked the young girl.   "You do not like M. Franz?"

The eyes repeated several times, "No, no, no."

Valentine threw herself on her knees, and put her arm round her grandfather's neck, "I am vexed too, for I do not love M. Franz d'Epinay."

An expression of intense joy illumined the old man's eyes.

"Do you think you can help me, dear grandpapa?" said Valentine.

"Yes."   Noirtier raised his eyes; it was the sign agreed on between him and Valentine when he wanted anything.

"I will trust in you then, dear grandpapa, that when the time comes you will help me," cried Valentine.

CHAPTER XXXII

A CONJUGAL SCENE

MADAME DANGLARS was in her apartment some evenings later when her husband entered. Danglars took his place on the sofa, and placing himself in a dreadfully dictatorial attitude, he began playing with the dog; but the animal, not liking him, and attempting to bite him, Danglars seized him by the skin of his neck, and threw him to the other side of the room upon a couch.

" Do you know, sir," asked the baroness, " that you are improving? Generally you are only rude, but to-night you are brutal."

" It is because I am in a worse humour than usual," replied Danglars.

Hermine looked at the banker with supreme disdain. These glances frequently exasperated the pride of Danglars, but this evening he took no notice of them.

" And what have I to do with your ill-humour?" said the baroness, irritated at the impassibility of her husband; "do these things concern me? Keep your ill-humour at home in your chests, or, since you have clerks whom you pay, vent it upon them."

" Not so," replied Danglars; " your advice is wrong, so I shall not follow it."

" And pray how am I wrong?"

" You will soon know what I mean. You are wrong because you draw out 700,000 francs of my fortune in the course of an hour."

" I do not understand you, sir," said the baroness, trying to disguise the agitation of her voice and the flush of her face.

" You understand me perfectly, on the contrary," said Danglars; " but if you will persist, I will tell you that I have just lost 700,000 francs upon the Spanish loan."

" Once for all, sir," replied the baroness, sharply, " I tell you I will not hear money named; it is a style of language I never heard in the house of my parents or in that of my first husband."

"Oh! I can well believe that, for neither of them was worth a penny."

"The better reason for my not being conversant with the slang of the bank, which is here dinned into my ears from morning to night; that noise of crowns jingling, which are constantly being counted and re-counted, is odious to me. I only know one thing I dislike more, which is the sound of your voice."

"Really!" said Danglars. "Well, this surprises me, for I thought you took the liveliest interest in my affairs!"

"I should like to know how?"

"Ah, that is very easily done! Last February you were the first who told me of the Haytian funds. You had dreamt that a ship had entered the harbour at Havre, that this ship brought news that a payment we looked upon as lost was going to be made. I know how clear-sighted your dreams are; I therefore purchased immediately as many shares as I could of the Haytian debt, and I gained 400,000 francs by it, of which 100,000 have been honestly paid to you. You spent it as you pleased, that was your business. In March there was a question about a grant to a railway. Three companies presented themselves, each offering equal securities. You told me that your instinct led you to believe the grant would be given to the company called the Southern. I bought two-thirds of the shares of that company; as you had foreseen, the shares became of triple value, and I picked up a million (40,000*l.*), from which 250,000 francs were paid to you for pin-money. How have you spent this 250,000 francs?—It is no business of mine. In April you went to dine at the minister's. You heard a private conversation respecting the affairs of Spain—on the expulsion of Don Carlos. I bought some Spanish shares. The expulsion took place and I pocketed 600,000 francs the day Charles V. repassed the Bidassoa. Of these 600,000 francs you took 50,000 crowns. They were yours, you disposed of them according to your fancy, and I asked no questions; but it is not the less true that you have this year received 500,000 pounds. Three days ago you talked politics with M. Debray, and you fancied from his words that Don Carlos had returned to Spain. Well, I sold my shares, the news was spread, and I no longer sold but gave them; next day I find the news was false, and by this false report I have lost 700,000 francs."

"Well?"

"Well! since I give you a fourth of my gains, I think you

owe me a fourth of my losses: the fourth of 700,000 francs is 175,000 francs."

"What you say is absurd, and I cannot see why M. Debray's name is mixed up in this affair."

"Because if you do not possess the 175,000 francs I reclaim you must have lent them to your friends, and Debray is one of your friends."

"For shame!" exclaimed the baroness.

"Oh! let us have no gestures, no screams, no modern drama, or you will oblige me to tell you that I see Debray leave here, pocketing nearly the whole of the 500,000 livres you have handed over to him this year; while he smiles to himself, saying, that he has found that which the most skilful players have never discovered; that is a roulette, where he wins without paying, and is no loser when he loses."

"But," said Hermine, suddenly, "if all this is, as you say, caused by M. Debray, why, instead of going direct to him, do you come and tell me of it? Why, to accuse the man, do you address the woman?"

"Do I know M. Debray?—do I wish to know him?—do I wish to know that he gives advice?—do I wish to follow it?—do I speculate? No; you do all this, not I."

"Still it seems to me, that as you profit by it——"

Danglars shrugged his shoulders.

"Foolish creature!" he exclaimed; "women fancy they have talent because they have managed two or three intrigues without being the talk of Paris! I see, and always have seen, during the last sixteen years; you may, perhaps, have hidden a thought, but not a step, not an action, not a fault, has escaped me, while you flattered yourself you had deceived me. What has been the result? That, thanks to my pretended ignorance, there are none of your friends, who have not trembled before me. There is not one who has not treated me as the master of the house, the only title I desire with respect to you; there is not one, in fact, who would have dared to speak of me as I have spoken of them this day. I will allow you to make me hateful, but I will prevent your rendering me ridiculous, and, above all, I forbid you to ruin me."

"What do you mean?"

"M. Debray has made me lose 700,000 francs; let him bear his share of the loss, and we will go on as before; if not, let him become bankrupt for the 250,000 livres, and do as all bankrupts do—disappear. He is a charming fellow, I allow, when his news is correct, but when it is not, there are fifty others in the world who would do better than him."

Madame Danglars was rooted to the spot, she made a violent effort to reply to this last attack, but she fell upon a chair. Danglars did not even look at her, though she tried all she could to faint. He shut the bedroom-door after him, without adding another word, and returned to his apartments; and when Madame Danglars recovered from her half-fainting condition, she could almost believe she had had a disagreeable dream.

The day following this scene, on leaving the Chamber, Danglars, who had shown violent marks of agitation during the sitting, and been more bitter than ever against the ministry, re-entered his carriage, and told the coachman to drive to the Avenue des Champs-Elysées, No. 30.

Monte-Cristo was at home, only he was engaged with some one, and begged Danglars to wait for a moment in the drawing-room. While the banker was waiting, the door opened, and a man dressed as an abbé entered, who, doubtless, more familiar with the house than he was, instead of waiting, merely bowed, and, passing on to the further apartments, disappeared. A minute after, the door by which the priest had entered reopened, and Monte-Cristo appeared.

" Pardon me," said he, " my dear baron, but one of my friends, the Abbé Busoni, whom you, perhaps, saw pass by, has just arrived in Paris ; not having seen him for a long time, I could not make up my mind to leave him sooner, so I hope this will be sufficient reason for my having made you wait."

" Nay," said Danglars, " it is my fault ; I have chosen my visit at a wrong time, and will retire."

" Not at all ; on the contrary, be seated : but what is the matter with you ? You look careworn : really you alarm me ; for a capitalist to be sad, like the appearance of a comet, presages some misfortune to the world."

" I have been in ill-luck for several days," said Danglars, " and I have heard nothing but bad news."

" Ah ! indeed !" said Monte-Cristo. " Have you had another fall at the Bourse ?"

" No ! I am safe for a few days at least ; I am only annoyed about a bankrupt of Trieste."

" Really ? Does it happen to be Jacopo Manfredi ?"

" Exactly so : imagine a man who has transacted business with me for I do not know how long, to the amount of eight or nine hundred thousand francs during the year.   Never a mistake or delay,—a fellow who paid like a prince.   Well! I was a million in advance with him, and now my fine Jacopo Manfredi suspends payment!"

" Really ? "

" It is an unheard-of fatality.   I draw upon him for 600,000 francs, my bills are returned unpaid, and more than that, I hold bills of exchange signed by him to the value of 400,000 francs, payable at his correspondent's in Paris at the end of this month. To-day is the 30th.   I present them ; but my correspondent has disappeared.   This, with my Spanish affairs, made a pretty end to the month."

" Then you really lost by that affair in Spain ?"

" Yes ; only 700,000 francs out of my cash-box, nothing more !"

" Why, how could you make such a mistake—such an old hand ?"

" Oh, it is all my wife's fault.   She dreamed Don Carlos had returned to Spain ; she believes in dreams.   It is magnetism, she says ; and when she dreams a thing, it is sure to happen, she assures me.   On this conviction, I allow her to speculate ; she has her bank and her stock-broker ; she speculated and lost.   It is true, she speculates with her own money, not mine ; nevertheless, you can understand that when 700,000 francs leave the wife's pocket, the husband always finds it out.   But do you mean to say you have not heard of this ?   Why the thing has made a tremendous noise."

" Yes, I heard it spoken of, but I did not know the details ; and then no one can be more ignorant than I am of the affairs in the Bourse."

" Then you do not speculate ?"

" I ?—How could I speculate when I already have so much trouble in regulating my income ?   I should be obliged, besides my steward, to keep a clerk and a boy.—But touching these Spanish affairs, I think the baroness did not dream the whole of this entrance of Don Carlos.   The newspapers said something about it, did they not ?"

" Then you believe the newspapers ?"

" So that," said Monte-Cristo, without replying directly, " you have lost nearly 1,700,000 francs this month."

" Not nearly, indeed ; that is exactly my loss."

" *Diable !*" said Monte-Cristo, compassionately, " it is a hard blow for a third-rate fortune."

" Third-rate !" said Danglars, rather humbled, " what do you mean by that ?"

" I mean," said Monte-Cristo, " I make three assortments in fortunes—first-rate, second-rate, and third-rate fortunes. I call those first-rate which are composed of treasures one possesses under one's hand, such as mines, lands, and funded property, in such states as France, Austria, and England, providing these treasures and property form a total of about a hundred millions ; I call those second-rate fortunes, gained by manufacturing enterprises, joint-stock companies, viceroyalties, and principalities, not drawing more than 1,500,000 francs, the whole forming a capital of about fifty millions ; finally, I call those third-rate fortunes, composed of a fluctuating capital, dependent upon the will of others, or upon chances which a bankruptcy involves or false news shakes ; such as banks, speculations of the day, in fact, all operations under the influence of greater or less mischances, the whole bringing in a real or fictitious capital of about fifteen millions. I think this is about your position, is it not ?"

" Confound it ! yes !" replied Danglars.

" The result, then, of six more such months as this would be to reduce the third-rate house to despair."

" Oh !" said Danglars, becoming very pale, " how you are running on ?"

" Let us imagine seven such months," continued Monte-Cristo, in the same tone. " Tell me, have you ever thought that seven times 1,700,000 francs, make nearly twelve millions ? No, you have not ;—well, you are right, for if you indulged in such reflections, you would never risk your principal, which is to the speculator what the skin is to civilised man. We have our clothes, some more splendid than others,—this is our credit ; but when a man dies he has only his skin ; in the same way, on retiring from business, you have nothing but your real principal of about five or six millions, at the most ; for third-rate fortunes are never more than the fourth of what they appear to be. Well, out of the five or six millions, which form your real capital, you have just lost nearly two millions, which must, of course, in the same degree diminish your credit and fictitious fortune ; to follow out my simile, your skin has been opened by bleeding, which, repeated three or four times, will cause death—so pay attention to it, M. Danglars. Do you want money? Do you wish me to lend you some?"

"What a bad calculator you are!" exclaimed Danglars, calling to his assistance all his philosophy and dissimulation. "I have made money at the same time by speculations which have succeeded. I have made up for the loss of blood by nutrition. I lost a battle in Spain, I have been defeated in Trieste, but my naval army in India will have taken some galleons, and my Mexican pioneers will have discovered some mine."

"You are thinking of marrying Mademoiselle Danglars to Albert de Morcerf, I believe?"

"Albert!" repeated Danglars, shrugging his shoulders, "ah, yes! he cares very little about it, I think." Then he grew more angry. "His behaviour has been positively insulting," he declared.

"Mademoiselle Danglars' fortune will be great no doubt, especially if the newspapers should not make any more mistakes," suggested Monte-Cristo.

"Listen, my dear count, M. de Morcerf has been my friend, or rather my acquaintance, during the last thirty years. You know I have made the most of my arms, though I never forget my origin."

"A proof of great humility or great pride," said Monte-Cristo.

"Well, when I was a clerk Morcerf was a mere fisherman."

"And then he was called——"

"Fernand."

"Only Fernand?"

"Fernand Mondego."

"You are sure?"

"*Pardieu!* I have bought enough fish of him to know his name!"

"Then, why did you think of giving your daughter to him?"

"It was an act of great condescension on my part, and now I begin to feel I made a mistake. This young upstart, Albert, should be humbled. It is true his father and I are both *parvenus*, and about equal in worth, but certain things have been mentioned of him that were never said of me."

"Ah, yes! what you tell me recalls to mind something about the name of Fernand Mondego. I have heard that name in Greece."

"In conjunction with the affairs of Ali Pacha?"

"Exactly so."

"This is the mystery," said Danglars; "I acknowledge I would give any thing to find it out, then perhaps I could lower the crest of that young coxscomb who disdains my daughter."

"It would be very easy if you much wished it. Probably, you have some correspondent in Greece?"

"I should think so!"

"At Janina?"

"Everywhere."

"Well, write to your correspondent in Janina, and ask him what part was played by a Frenchman named Fernand Mondego in the catastrophe of Ali Tebelen."

"You are right!" exclaimed Danglars, rising quickly; "I will write to-day."

"And if you should hear of any thing very scandalous——"

"I will communicate it to you."

"You will oblige me."

Danglars rushed out of the room, and made one leap into his *coupé*.

CHAPTER XXXIII

THE BALL

THE de Morcerfs had arranged to give a summer ball, and the Saturday upon which it was to take place was one of the warmest days of July. It was ten o'clock at night; the large trees in the garden of the count's hotel threw up their branches towards the azure canopy of heaven, studded with golden stars, where the last mists of a storm, which had threatened all day, yet glided.

From the apartments on the ground floor might be heard the sound of music, with the whirl of the waltz and galop, while brilliant streams of light shone through the openings of the Venetian blinds.

At this moment the garden was only occupied by about ten servants, who had just received orders from their mistress to prepare the supper, the serenity of the weather continuing to increase. Until now it had been undecided whether the supper should take place in the dining-room, or under a long tent erected on the lawn; but the beautiful blue sky, covered with stars, had determined the case in favour of the lawn. The gardens were illuminated with coloured lanterns, according to the Italian custom, and the supper-table was loaded with wax-lights and flowers.

At the time the Countess de Morcerf returned to the rooms, after giving her orders, many guests were arriving, more attracted by the charming hospitality of the countess than by the distinguished position of the count; for, owing to the good taste of Mercédès, one was sure of finding some arrangements at her fête worthy of relating, or even copying in case of need.

Madame Danglars appeared, not only beautiful in person, but radiant with splendour; she entered by one door at the same time that Mercédès appeared at the other. The countess took Albert to meet Madame Danglars. He offered his arm to conduct her to a seat, and as he did so he looked around him.

"You are looking for my daughter?" said the baroness, smiling.

"I confess it," replied Albert; "could you have been so cruel as not to bring her?"

"Calm yourself; she has met Mademoiselle de Villefort; see, they are following us, both in white dresses, one with a bouquet of camelias, the other with one of myosotis."

At that moment the Count of Monte-Cristo entered. There was something in the count which attracted universal attention wherever he appeared; it was not his perfectly-cut clothes that attracted attention; it was his pale complexion, his waving black hair, the expression so calm and serene, the eye so dark and melancholy, the mouth chiselled with such marvellous delicacy, which fixed all eyes upon him.

Many men might have been handsomer; but certainly there could be none whose appearance was more significant, if the expression may be used. Everything about the count seemed to have its meaning; for the constant habit of thought had given an ease and vigour to the expression of his face, and even to the most trifling gesture, scarcely to be understood. Yet the Parisian world is so strange that even this might not have won attention had there not been a mysterious story gilded by an immense fortune.

Meanwhile he advanced through the crowd of curious glances and exchange of salutations towards Madame de Morcerf, who, standing before a mantelpiece, decorated with flowers, had seen his entrance in a looking-glass placed opposite the door, and was prepared to receive him. She turned towards him with a serene smile just at the moment he was bowing to her. No doubt she fancied the count would speak to her, while on his side the count thought she was about to address him; but both remained silent; and after a mere bow Monte-Cristo directed his steps to Albert, who received him cordially.

"Have you seen my mother?" asked Albert.

"I have just had the pleasure," replied the count, "but I have not seen your father."

"See, he is down there, talking politics with that little group of great geniuses."

"Indeed!" said Monte-Cristo; "and so those gentlemen down there are men of great talent. And for what kind of talent are they celebrated? You know there are different sorts."

"That tall, harsh-looking man is very learned; he discovered in the neighbourhood of Rome a kind of lizard with a vertebre more than usual, and he immediately laid his discovery before the Institute. The thing was discussed for a long time, but finally decided in his favour. I can assure you the vertebre made a great noise in the learned world; and the gentleman, who was only a knight of the Legion of Honour, was made an officer."

"Come!" said Monte-Cristo, "this cross seems to me to be wisely awarded. I suppose, had he found an additional vertebre, they would have made him a commander."

Just then the count felt his arm pressed; he turned round, it was Danglars.

"Ah! is it you, baron?" said he.

"Why do you call me baron?" said Danglars; "you know that I care nothing for my title. I am not like you, viscount, you like your title, do you not?"

"Certainly," replied Albert, "seeing that without my title I should be nothing, while you, sacrificing the baron, would still remain the millionaire."

"Which seems to me the finest title of all," replied Danglars.

"Unfortunately," said Monte-Cristo, "one's title to a millionaire does not last for life, like that of baron, peer of France, or Academician; for example, the millionaires, Frank and Poulman, of Frankfort, have just become bankrupts."

"Indeed!" said Danglars, becoming pale.

"Yes, I received the news this evening by a courier; I had about a million in their hands, but, warned in time, I withdrew it a month ago."

"Ah!" exclaimed Danglars, "they have drawn on me for 200,000 francs."

"Well, you can guard against it; their signature is worth five per cent."

"Yes; but it is too late," said Danglars, "I have honoured their bills."

"Good!" said Monte-Cristo, "here are 200,000 francs gone after——'

"Hush! Do not mention these things," said Danglars; then approaching Monte-Cristo, he added, "especially before young Morcerf;" after which he smiled, and turned towards the young man in question.

Monte-Cristo was for an instant alone. Meanwhile the heat became excessive. The footmen were hastening through the rooms with trays loaded with ices. Monte-Cristo wiped the perspiration from his forehead, but drew back when the ices were presented to him; he took no refreshment. Madame de Morcerf did not lose sight of him. She saw that he took nothing, and even noticed the movement with which he withdrew from the offer.

"Albert," she asked her son as he came up to her, "did you notice that—that the count will never accept an invitation to dine with us?"

"Yes! but then he breakfasted with me—indeed, he made his first appearance in the world on that occasion."

"But your house is not ours," murmured Mercédès, "and since he has been here I have watched him, and he has taken nothing yet."

"The count is very temperate."

Mercédès smiled sadly.

"Approach him," said she, "and the next waiter that passes insist upon his taking something."

"But why, mother?"

"Oblige me, Albert," said Mercédès.

Albert kissed his mother's hand, and drew near to the count. Another salver passed loaded like the preceding ones; she saw Albert attempt to persuade the count, but he obstinately refused. Albert rejoined his mother; she was very pale.

"Well," said she, "you see he refuses?"

"Yes; but why need this annoy you?"

"You know, Albert, women are singular creatures. I should like to have seen the count take something in my house, if only a morsel of pomegranate. Perhaps he cannot reconcile himself to the French style of living, and might prefer something else."

"Oh, no! I have seen him eat of everything in Italy; no doubt he does not feel inclined this evening."

Mercédès advanced towards Monte-Cristo, and asked, "Count, will you oblige me with your arm?"

The count almost staggered at these simple words; then he fixed his eyes on Mercédès. It was but the glance of a moment, but it seemed to the countess to have lasted for a century, so much was expressed in that one look. However, he offered his arm to her as she wished; she leaned upon it, or, rather, just touched it with her hand, and they, together, descended the steps, lined with rhododendrons and camelias. Behind them, by another outlet, a group of about twenty persons rushed into the garden with loud exclamations of delight.

Madame de Morcerf entered an archway of trees with her companion; it was a grove of limes, leading to a conservatory.

" It was too warm in the room, was it not, count ?" she asked.

" Yes, madame ; and it was an excellent idea of yours to open the doors and the blinds."

As he ceased speaking, the count felt her hand tremble.

" But you," he said, " with that light dress, and without any thing to cover you but that gauze scarf—perhaps you feel cold ?"

" Do you know where I am leading you ?" asked the countess, without replying to his question.

" No, madam," replied Monte-Cristo, " but you see I make no resistance."

" We are going to the green-house at the end of this grove."

He looked at her as if to interrogate her, but she continued walking in silence ; so on his side, Monte-Cristo also said nothing. They reached the building, filled with magnificent fruits, which ripen even in July, in the artificial temperature, which takes the place of the sun. The countess dropped the arm she held, and gathered a bunch of Muscatel grapes.

" See, count," she said, with a smile so sad in its expression, that he could almost see the tears on her eyelids, " our French grapes are not to be compared, I know, with yours of Sicily and Cyprus, but you will make allowance for our northern sun."

The count bowed, and stepped back.

" Do you refuse ?" said Mercédès, in a tremulous voice.

" Pray, excuse me, madam," replied Monte-Cristo, " but I never eat Muscatel grapes."

Mercédès let them fall and sighed. A magnificent peach was hanging against an adjoining wall, ripened by the same artificial heat. Mercédès drew near, and plucked the fruit.

" Take this peach, then," she said.

The count again refused.

" What, again !" she exclaimed, in so plaintive an accent that it seemed but to stifle a sob ; " really you pain me."

A long silence succeeded this scene ; the peach, like the grapes, was rolling on the ground.

" Count," added Mercédès, with a supplicating glance, " there is a beautiful Arabian custom, which makes eternal friends of those who have together eaten bread and salt beneath the same roof."

" I know it, madame," replied the count; "but we are in France, and not in Arabia ; and in France eternal friendships are as rare as the custom of dividing bread and salt with one another."

" But," said the countess, breathlessly, with her eyes fixed on Monte-Cristo, whose arm she convulsively pressed with both hands, " we are friends, are we not ? "

The count became pale as death, the blood rushed to his heart, and then, again rising, dyed his cheeks with crimson ; his eyes swam like those of a man suddenly dazzled.

" Certainly, we are friends," he replied ; " why should we not be ?"

The answer was so little like the one Mercédès desired, that she turned away to give vent to a sigh, which sounded more like a groan.

" Thank you," she said.

And they re-commenced walking. They went the whole length of the garden without uttering a word.

" Count," suddenly exclaimed the countess, after their walk had continued ten minutes in silence, " is it true that you have seen so much, travelled so far, and suffered so deeply ?"

" I have suffered deeply, madame," answered Monte-Cristo.

" But now you are happy ?"

" Doubtless," replied the count, " since no one hears me complain."

" And your present happiness, has it softened your heart ?"

" My present happiness equals my past misery," said the count.

" Are you not married ?" asked the countess.

" I, married !" exclaimed Monte-Cristo, shuddering, " who could have told you so ?"

" No one told me you were, but you have frequently been seen at the Opera with a young and lovely girl."

" She is a slave whom I bought at Constantinople, madame, the daughter of a prince. I have adopted her as my daughter, having no one else to love in the world."

" You live alone, then ?"

" I do."

" You have no sister—no son—no father ?"

" I have no one."

" How can you exist thus, without anyone to attach you to life ?"

" It is not my fault. At Malta, I loved a young girl.

18

was on the point of marrying her, when war came and carried me away. I thought she loved well enough to wait for me, and even to remain faithful to my grave. When I returned, she was married. This is the history of most men who have passed twenty years of age. Perhaps my heart was weaker than those of the generality, and I suffered more than they would have done in my place ; now you know all."

The countess stopped for a moment, as if gasping for breath.

" Yes," she said, " and you have still preserved this love in your heart—one can only love once—and did you ever see her again ?"

" Never !"

" Never ?"

" I never returned to the country where she lived."

" At Malta ?"

" Yes ; at Malta."

" She is, then, now at Malta ?"

" I think so."

" And have you forgiven her for all she has made you suffer ?"

" Yes, I have pardoned *her*."

" But only her ; do you, then, still hate those who separated you ?"

" I ! hate them ; not at all,—why should I ?"

The countess placed herself before Monte-Cristo, still holding in her hand a portion of the perfumed grapes.

"Take some," she said.

" I never eat Muscatel grapes," replied Monte-Cristo, as if the subject had not been mentioned before.

The countess dashed the grapes into the nearest thicket with a gesture of despair.

" Inflexible man !" she murmured.

Monte-Cristo remained as unmoved as if the reproach had not been addressed to him. Albert at this moment ran in.

"Oh, mother !" he exclaimed, "such a misfortune has happened ! M. de Villefort has come to fetch his wife and daughter because Madame de Saint-Méran has just arrived in Paris, bringing the news of M. de Saint-Méran's death, which took place on the first stage after he left Marseilles. Madame de Villefort, who was in very good spirits, would not believe the misfortune ; but Mademoiselle Valentine, at the first words, guessed the whole truth, notwithstanding all the precautions of her father."

"And how was M. de Saint-Méran related to Mademoiselle de Villefort?" said the count.

"He was her grandfather on the mother's side. He was coming here to hasten her marriage with Franz."

Mercédès took two or three steps forward. Monte-Cristo watched her with an air so thoughtful, and so full of affectionate admiration, that she returned, taking his hand; at the same time she grasped that of her son and joined them together.

"We are friends; are we not?" she asked.

"Oh, madame, I do not presume to call myself your friend, but at all times I am your most respectful servant."

The countess left with an indescribable pang in her heart, and before she had taken ten steps the count saw her raise her handkerchief to her eyes.

"Do not my mother and you agree?" asked Albert, astonished.

"On the contrary," replied the count, "did you not hear her declare that we were friends."

They re-entered the drawing-room, which Valentine and Madame de Villefort had just quitted. Monte-Cristo departed almost at the same time.

CHAPTER XXXIV

MADAME DE SAINT-MÉRAN

A GLOOMY scene had indeed just passed at the house of De Ville-fort. After the ladies had departed for the ball, whither all the entreaties of Madame de Villefort had failed in persuading him to accompany them, the procureur du roi had, as usual, shut himself up in his study, with a heap of papers calculated to alarm anyone else.

Presently he heard the noise of a carriage in the yard, then he heard the steps of an aged person ascending the stairs, followed by tears and lamentations, such as servants always assume when they wish to appear interested in their master's grief. He drew back the bolt of his door, and almost directly an old lady entered, unannounced, carrying her shawl on her arm and her bonnet in her hand. The white hair was thrown back from her yellow forehead, and her eyes, already sunken by the furrows of age, had now almost disappeared beneath the eyelids swollen with grief.

"Oh," she cried ; "what a misfortune ! I shall die of it ; oh ! yes ! I shall certainly die of it !"

And then falling upon the chair nearest the door, she burst into a paroxysm of sobs. The servants, standing in the door-way, not daring to approach nearer, were looking at Noirtier's old servant, who, having heard a noise in his master's room, had run there also, and remained behind the others. Villefort rose, and ran towards his mother-in-law.

"Why, what can have happened ?" he exclaimed, "what has thus disturbed you? Is M. de Méran with you ?"

"M. de Saint-Méran is dead !" answered the old marchioness, without preface, without expression ; she appeared stupefied.

Villefort drew back, and clasping his hands together, exclaimed,—

"Dead ! so suddenly ?"

"A week ago," continued Madame de Saint-Méran, "we went out together in the carriage after dinner. M. de Saint-Méran had been unwell for some days; still the idea of seeing our dear Valentine again inspired him with courage, and, notwithstanding his illness, he would leave; at six leagues from Marseilles, after having eaten some of the pastilles he is accustomed to take, he fell into such a deep sleep, that it appeared to me unnatural; still I hesitated to wake him. I fell asleep; I was soon awoke by a piercing shriek, as from a person suffering in his dreams, and he suddenly threw his head back. I stopped the postilion, I applied my smelling salts; but all was over, and I arrived at Aix by the side of a corpse."

Villefort stood with his mouth half-open, quite stupefied.

" Of course, you sent for a doctor ?"

" Immediately; but, as I have told you, it was too late."

" Yes; but then he could tell of what complaint the poor Marquis had died."

Villefort placed the arm of Madame de Saint-Méran within his own, and conducted her to his apartment.

" Rest yourself, mother," he said.

The marchioness raised her head at this word, and beholding the man who so forcibly reminded her of her deeply-regretted child who still lived for her in Valentine, she felt touched at the name of mother; and bursting into tears she fell on her knees before an arm-chair, where she buried her venerable head.

Villefort left her to the care of the women, while old Barrois ran half-scared to his master; for nothing frightens old men so much as when death relaxes its vigilance over them for a moment in order to strike some other.

Valentine on returning from the ball, was told the terrible news, but was not allowed to visit her grandmother.

The next morning she found her grandmother in bed; the fever had not abated; on the contrary, her eyes glistened and she appeared to be suffering from violent nervous irritability. After the young girl had wept her sympathy, Madame de Saint-Méran expressed an impatient desire to see her father.

Valentine durst not oppose her grandmother's wish, the cause of which she knew not, and an instant afterwards Villefort entered.

" Sir," said Madame de Saint-Méran, without using any circum-locution, and, as if she had no time to lose; " you wrote to me concerning the marriage of this child ?"

" Yes, madame," replied Villefort; " it is not only projected but arranged."

"Your intended son-in-law is named M. Franz d'Epinay. Is he not the son of General d'Epinay, who was on our side, and who was assassinated some days before the usurper returned from the Isle of Elba ?"

"The same."

"Does he not dislike the idea of marrying the grand-daughter of a Jacobin ?"

"Our civil dissensions are now happily extinguished, mother," said Villefort ; "M. d'Epinay was quite a child when his father died, he knows very little of M. Noirtier, and will meet him, if not with pleasure, at least with indifference."

During the whole of this conversation Valentine had remained silent.

"Well, sir," said Madame de Saint-Méran, after a few minutes' reflection, "I must hasten the marriage, for I have but a short time to live."

"You, madame !"   "You, dear grandmother !" exclaimed M. de Villefort and Valentine at the same time.

"I know what I am saying," continued the marchioness ; "I must hurry you, so that, having no mother, she may at least have a grandmother to bless her marriage.   I am all that is left to her belonging to poor Renée, whom you have so soon forgotten."

"Ah, madame," said Villefort, "you forget that I was obliged to give a mother to my child."

"A step-mother is never a mother, sir.   But this is not to the purpose, our business concerns Valentine ; let us leave the dead in peace."

All this was said with such exceeding rapidity, that there was something in the conversation that seemed like the commencement of delirium.

"When does M. d'Epinay return ?" said the Marchioness.

"We expect him every moment."

"It is well ; as soon as he arrives inform me.   We must be expeditious.   Then I also wish to see a notary, that I may be assured that all our property returns to Valentine."

"Ah, my grandmother !" murmured Valentine, pressing her lips on the burning brow of her grandmother, "do you wish to kill me ?   How feverish you are ! we must not send for a notary, but for a doctor !"

"A doctor !" said she shrugging her shoulders, "I am not ill ; I am thirsty—that is all."

" What are you drinking?"

" The same as usual, my dear, my glass is there on the table
—give it me, Valentine."

Valentine poured the orangeade standing on the table into a
glass, and gave it to her grandmother.

Then she kissed her, and left with her handkerchief to her
eyes; at the door she found the valet-de-chambre, who told her
the doctor, M. d'Avrigny, was waiting in the dining-room.
Valentine instantly ran down. The doctor was a friend of the
family, and at the same time one of the cleverest men of the
day; and very fond of Valentine, whose birth he had witnessed.
He had himself a daughter about her age; whose life was
one continued source of anxiety and fear to him from her mother
having been consumptive.

The doctor pressed Valentine's hand, and while he visited her
grandmother, she descended the steps into the garden. After
remaining for a short time in the *parterre* surrounding the house,
and gathering a rose to place in her waist or hair, she turned
into the dark avenue which led to the bank; then from the bank
she went to the gate. As she advanced she fancied she heard
a voice pronounce her name. She stopped astonished, then
the voice reached her ear more distinctly, and she recognised it
to be that of Maximilian.

It was indeed Maximilian Morrel, who had passed a wretched
existence since the previous day. With that instinct peculiar to
lovers he had anticipated, after the return of Madame de Saint-
Méran and the death of the marquis, that something would
occur at M. de Villefort's in connexion with his attachment for
Valentine. It was his uneasy forebodings which led him, pale
and trembling, to the gate under the chestnut-trees. Valentine
was ignorant of the cause of his sorrow and anxiety, and as it
was not his accustomed hour for visiting her, pure chance, or
rather a happy sympathy, had led her at the moment to that
spot.

" You here, at this hour?" said she.

" Yes, my darling," replied Morrel; " I come to bring and
to hear bad tidings."

" This is, indeed, a house of mourning!" said Valentine; " speak,
Maximilian; although the cup of sorrow seems already full."

" Dear Valentine," said Morrel, endeavouring to conceal his
own emotion, " listen, I entreat you, what I am about to say is
solemn. When are you to be married?"

" I will tell you all," said Valentine ; " from you I have nothing to conceal. This morning the subject was introduced, and my dear grandmother, on whom I depended as my only support, not only declared herself favourable to it, but is so anxious for it, that they only await the arrival of M. d'Epinay, and the following day the contract will be signed."

A deep sigh escaped the young man, who gazed long and mournfully at her he loved.

" Alas !" replied he, " it is dreadful thus to hear my condemnation from your own lips. The sentence is passed, and, in a few hours, will be executed. But, since you say nothing remains but for M. d'Epinay to arrive that the contract may be signed, and the following day you will be his, to-morrow you will be engaged to M. d'Epinay, for he came this morning to Paris."

Valentine uttered a cry.

" Tell me, Valentine," he cried, seizing her hands, " do you intend to struggle against our ill fortune ? For it is that I came to know."

Valentine trembled, and looked at him with amazement. The idea of resisting her father, her grandmother, and all the family, had never occurred to her.

" What do you say, Maximilian ?" asked Valentine. " What do you term a struggle ? Oh ! it would be sacrilege. I resist my father's order, and my dying grandmother's wish ? Impossible !"

" You are right," said Morrel, calmly.

" In what a tone you speak !" cried Valentine.

" I speak as one who admires you, mademoiselle."

" Mademoiselle !" cried Valentine ; " mademoiselle ! Oh, selfish man !—he sees me in despair and pretends he cannot understand me !"

" You mistake—I understand you perfectly. You will not oppose M. Villefort, you will not displease the marchioness, and to-morrow you will sign the contract which will bind you to your husband."

" But, tell me, how can I do otherwise ?"

" I am free," replied Maximilian, " and rich enough to support you. I swear to make you my lawful wife. I will take you to my sister, who is worthy also to be yours. We will embark for Algiers, for England, for America, or, if you prefer it, retire to the country, and only return to Paris when our friends have reconciled your family."

Valentine shook her head.

"You drive me to despair, Maximilian," said she. "What would you do, tell me, if your sister was in such a case?"

"Adieu, Valentine, adieu!" said Morrel, calmly passing through the gate.

"Where are you going?" cried the young girl, extending her hand through the opening, and seizing Maximilian by his coat, for she understood from her own agitated feelings that her lover's calmness could not be real; "where are you going?"

"I am going that I may not bring fresh trouble into your family."

Valentine trembled convulsively; she loosed her hold of the gate, her arms fell by her side, and two large tears rolled down her cheeks. The young man stood before her, sorrowful and resolute.

"Maximilian," cried she, "I will follow you, I will leave the paternal home, I will give up all. Oh! ungrateful girl that I am," cried Valentine, sobbing, "I will give up all, even my dear old grandfather, whom I had nearly forgotten."

"No," said Maximilian, "you shall not leave him. M. Noirtier has evinced, you say, a kind feeling towards me. Well! before you leave, tell him all; his consent will be your justification in God's sight. As soon as we are married, he shall come and live with us; instead of one child, he shall have two. You have told me how you talk to him, and how he answers you; I shall very soon learn that language by signs, Valentine; and I promise you solemnly, that instead of despair, it is happiness that awaits us."

"Oh! see Maximilian, see the power you have over me, you almost make me believe you; and yet, what you tell me is madness, for my father will curse me—he is inflexible—he will never pardon me. Now listen to me, Maximilian; if by artifice, by entreaty, by accident—in short, if by any means I can delay this marriage, will you wait?"

"Yes, I promise you, faithfully, if you will promise me, that this horrible marriage shall not take place, and that if you are dragged before a magistrate or a priest, you will refuse."

"Yes," said Valentine, "I will now acknowledge you are right, Maximilian; and now are you satisfied with your sweetheart?" said the young girl, sorrowfully.

"My adored Valentine, words cannot express one half of my satisfaction."

He kissed her, and Valentine fled back through the avenue. Morrel listened to catch the last sound of her dress brushing the branches, and of her footstep on the path, then raised his eyes with an ineffable smile of thankfulness. He returned home and waited all the evening and all the next day without hearing anything. It was only on the following day at about ten o'clock in the morning, as he was starting to call on M. Deschamps, the notary, that he received from the postman a note, which he knew to be from Valentine, although he had not before seen her writing. It was to this effect:—

"Tears, entreaties, prayers, have availed me nothing. Yesterday, for two hours, I was at the Church of St. Philipe du Roule, and for two hours I prayed most fervently. Heaven is as inflexible as man, and the signature of the contract is fixed for this evening at nine o'clock. I have but one promise and but one heart to give, that promise is pledged to you, that heart is also yours. This evening, then, at a quarter past nine, at the gate.

"Your betrothed,
"VALENTINE DE VILLEFORT.

"P.S.—My poor grandmother gets worse and worse; yesterday her fever amounted to delirium; to-day her delirium is almost madness. You will be very kind to me, will you not, Morrel, to make me forget my sorrow in leaving her thus? I think it is kept a secret from grandpapa Noirtier, that the contract is to be signed this evening."

When the hour approached at which he was to learn his fate, the young man concealed himself in the bushes near the gate. But instead of Valentine he saw approaching Villefort and Doctor d'Avrigny.

Seeing them approach, he drew back mechanically, until he found himself stopped by a sycamore-tree in the centre of the clump; there he was compelled to remain. Soon the two gentlemen stopped also.

"Ah, my dear doctor!" said the procureur. "My house is accursed! What a dreadful death!—what a blow! Seek not to console me! Alas! nothing can alleviate so great a sorrow—the wound is too deep and too fresh! She is dead!—she is dead!"

A cold dampness covered the young man's brow, and his teeth chattered. Who could be dead in that house which Villefort himself had called accursed ?

"My dear M. de Villefort," replied the doctor, with a tone which redoubled the terror of the young man, "I have not led you here to console you ; on the contrary——"

"What can you mean ?" asked the procureur, alarmed.

"I mean, that behind the misfortune which has just happened to you, there is another, perhaps still greater."

"Can it be possible ?" murmured Villefort, clasping his hands; "what are you going to tell me ?"

"I have a terrible secret to communicate to you," said the doctor. "Let us sit down."

Villefort fell rather than seated himself. The doctor stood before him, with one hand placed on his shoulder. Morrel, horrified, supported his head with one hand, and, with the other, pressed his heart, lest its beatings should be heard.

"Madame de Saint-Méran was, doubtless, advancing in years, but she enjoyed excellent health."

Morrel began again to breathe freely, which he had not done the last ten minutes.

"Grief has consumed her," said Villefort, "yes, grief, doctor ! After living forty years with the marquis——"

"It is not grief, my dear Villefort," said the doctor ; "grief may kill, although it rarely does, but never in a day, never in an hour, never in ten minutes. Did you notice the symptoms of the disease to which Madame de Saint-Méran has fallen a victim ?" he continued.

"I did. Madame de Saint-Méran had three successive attacks, at intervals of some minutes, each one more serious than the former. When you arrived, Madame de Saint-Méran had already been panting for breath some minutes ; she then had a fit, which I took to be simply a nervous attack, and it was only when I saw her raise herself in the bed, and her limbs and neck appear stiffened, that I became really alarmed. Then I understood from your face there was more to fear than I had thought. This crisis past, I endeavoured to catch your eye, but could not. You held her hand, you were feeling her pulse, and the second fit came on before you had turned towards me. This was more terrible than the first ; the same nervous movements were repeated, and the mouth contracted and turned purple."

"And at the third she expired."

"At the end of the first attack I discovered symptoms of tetanus ; you confirmed my opinion."

"The symptoms of tetanus and poisoning by vegetable substances are the same."

M. de Villefort started from his seat, then in a moment fell down again, silent and motionless.

Morrel knew not if he were dreaming or awake.

"Listen," said the doctor.   "I know the full importance of the statement I have just made, and the disposition of the man to whom I have made it."

"Do you speak to me as a magistrate or as a friend ?" asked Villefort.

"As a friend, and only as a friend, at this moment.   The similarity in the symptoms of tetanus and poisoning by vegetable substances is so great, that were I obliged to affirm by oath what I have now stated I should hesitate ; I therefore repeat to you, I speak not to a magistrate, but to a friend.   And to that friend I say, ' During the three quarters of an hour that the struggle continued, I watched the convulsions and the death of Madame de Saint-Méran, and am thoroughly convinced that not only did her death proceed from poison, but I could also specify the poison."

"Indeed, sir !—indeed !"

"The symptoms are marked—sleep disturbed by nervous fits, excitement of the brain, torpor of the system.   Madame de Saint-Méran has sunk under a violent dose of *brucine* or of *strychnine*, which—by some mistake, perhaps—has been given to her."

Villefort seized the doctor's hand.

"Oh, it is impossible !" said he ; "I must be dreaming ! It is frightful to hear such things from such a man as you ! Tell me, I entreat you, my dear doctor, that you may be deceived."

"I may, but it is not likely.   Had Madame de Saint-Méran any enemies ?"

"Not to my knowledge."

"Would her death affect any one's interests ?"

"It could not, indeed ; my daughter is her only heiress— Valentine alone.   Oh, if such a thought could present itself, I would stab myself to punish my heart for having for one instant harboured it."

"Indeed, my dear friend," said M. d'Avrigny, "I would not accuse any one ; I speak only of an accident, you understand ; of

a mistake : but whether accident or mistake, the fact is there ;
it speaks to my conscience, and compels me to speak aloud to
you.   Make inquiry."

"Of whom ?—how ?—of what ?"

"May not Barrois, the old servant, have made a mistake, and
have given Madame de Saint-Méran a dose prepared for his
master ?"

"For my father ?"

"Yes."

"But how could a dose prepared for M. Noirtier poison
Madame de Saint-Méran ?"

"Nothing is more simple.   You know poisons become
remedies in certain diseases, of which paralysis is one.   For
instance, having tried every other remedy to restore movement
and speech to M. Noirtier, I resolved to try one last means, and
for three months I have been giving him brucine ; so that in the
last dose I ordered for him there were six grains.   This quantity,
which it is perfectly safe to administer to the paralysed frame of
M. Noirtier, which has become gradually accustomed to it, would
be sufficient to kill another person."

" What do you propose to do, d'Avrigny ?" said Villefort, in
despair.

" My dear M. de Villefort," replied the doctor, " my first duty
is humanity.   I would have saved Madame de Saint-Méran if
science could have done it ; but she is dead, my duty regards the
living.   Let us bury this terrible secret in the deepest recesses of
our hearts ; I am willing, if any one should suspect this, that my
silence on this subject should be imputed to my ignorance.
Meanwhile, sir, watch always—watch carefully, for, perhaps, the
evil may not stop here.   And when you have found the culprit,
I will say to you, ' You are a magistrate, do as you will !' "

"I thank you doctor," said Villefort, with indescribable joy ;
"I never had a better friend than you." And as if he feared
Doctor d'Avrigny would recall his promise, he hurried him
towards the house.

When they were gone, Morrel ventured out from under the
trees, and the moon shone upon his face, which was so pale it
might have been taken for a phantom, but though what he had
heard agitated him indescribably, it was impossible for him to
take in the accusation implied against Valentine ; his mind was
incapable of harbouring such a suggestion.   He only felt a
desperate longing to see her.

Finding that Valentine did not come, he at length crossed the flower-garden, which, by the light of the moon, resembled a large white lake, and, having passed the rows of orange-trees which extended in front of the house, he reached the step, ran quickly up, and pushed the door, which opened without offering any resistance.

He found Valentine on the floor kneeling by a chair.

Valentine looked at the young man in astonishment; at that instant they heard the street door close; then M. de Villefort locked the garden-door, and returned up stairs. He stopped a moment in the ante-room, as if hesitating whether to turn to his own apartment or into Madame de Saint-Méran's; Morrel concealed himself behind a door; Valentine remained motionless, grief seemed to deprive her of all fear. M. de Villefort passed on to his own room.

"Ah," cried Valentine, "now you can neither go out by the front door nor by the garden, why did you come?"

Morrel looked at her with astonishment.

"There is but one way left you that is safe," said she; "it is through my grandfather's room." She rose; "Come," she added.

"Be careful, Valentine," said Morrel, hesitating to comply with the young girl's wishes; "I now see my error—I acted as a madman in coming in here. Are you sure you are more reasonable?"

"Yes," said Valentine.

She then crossed the corridor, and led the way down a narrow staircase to M. Noirtier's room; Morrel followed her on tiptoe; at the door they found the old servant.

"Barrois," said Valentine, "shut the door and let no one come in."

She passed first.

Noirtier, seated in his chair and listening to every sound, was watching the door; he saw Valentine, and his eye brightened. There was something grave and solemn in the approach of the young girl which struck the old man; and immediately his bright eye began to interrogate.

"Dear grandfather," said she hurriedly, "you know poor grandmamma died an hour since, and now I have no friend in the world but you."

His expressive eyes evinced the greatest tenderness.

"To you alone, then, may I confide my sorrows and my hopes?"

The paralytic motioned, " Yes."

Valentine took Maximilian's hand.

" Look attentively, then, at this gentleman."

The old man fixed his scrutinising gaze with slight astonishment on Morrel.

" It is M. Maximilian Morrel," said she; " the son of that good merchant of Marseilles whom you doubtless recollect."

" Yes," signed the old man.

" He bears an irreproachable name, which Maximilian is likely to render glorious, since at thirty years of age he is a captain, an officer of the Legion of Honour."

The old man signified that he recollected him.

" Well, grandpapa," said Valentine, kneeling before him, and pointing to Maximilian, " I love him, and will be only his; were I compelled to marry another, I would destroy myself."

The eyes of the paralytic expressed a multitude of tumultuous thoughts.

" You like M. Maximilian Morrel; do you not, grandpapa ?" asked Valentine.

" Yes."

" And you will protect us, who are your children, against the will of my father ?"

Noirtier cast an intelligent glance at Morrel, as if to say, " Perhaps I may."

Maximilian understood him.

" You thoroughly understand me, sir ? Pardon my eagerness, for my life depends on your answer. Will our help come from you ?"

" Yes."

There was so much firmness in the look which gave this answer, no one could, at any rate, doubt his will, if they did his power.

" Oh, thank you a thousand times ! But how, unless a miracle should restore your speech, your gesture, your movement, how can you, chained to that arm-chair, dumb and motionless, oppose this marriage ?"

A smile lit up the old man's face, a strange smile of the eyes in a paralysed face !

" Then I must wait ?" asked the young man.

" Yes."

" But the contract ?"

The same smile returned.

" Will you assure me it shall not be signed ?"

" Yes," said Noirtier.

"The contract shall not be signed," cried Morrel.   " Oh! pardon me, sir! I can scarcely realise so great a happiness. Will they not sign it ?"

" No," said the paralytic.

" Now," said Morrel, " do you wish me to retire ?"

" Yes."

He bowed deeply and retired.   He found the old servant outside the door, to whom Valentine had given directions ; he conducted Morrel along a dark passage, which led to a little door opening on the garden.

CHAPTER XXXV

Two days later the double funeral took place, and immediately on its conclusion M. de Villefort and Franz returned to the Faubourg Saint-Honoré. The procureur passed rapidly to his cabinet, where were his wife with her young son, and Valentine. He said:

"M. d'Epinay, allow me to remind you at this moment, which is, perhaps, not so ill chosen as at first sight may appear, for obedience to the wishes of the departed is the first offering which should be made at their tomb; allow me, then, to remind you of the wish expressed by Madame de Saint-Méran on her death-bed, that Valentine's wedding might not be deferred. You know the affairs of the deceased are in perfect order, and her will bequeaths to Valentine the entire property of the Saint-Méran family; the notary showed me the documents yesterday, which will enable us to draw up the contract immediately. You may call on the notary, M. Deschamps, Place Beauvau, Faubourg Saint-Honoré, and you have my authority to inspect those deeds."

"Sir," replied M. d'Epinay, "it is not, perhaps, the moment for Mademoiselle Valentine, who is in deep distress, to think of a husband; indeed, I fear——"

"Valentine will have no greater pleasure than that of fulfilling her grandmamma's last injunctions; there will be no obstacle from that quarter, I assure you."

"In that case," replied Franz, "as I shall raise none, you may make arrangements when you please; I have pledged my word, and shall feel pleasure and happiness in adhering to it."

"Then," said Villefort, "nothing further is required; the contract was to have been signed three days since; we shall find it all ready, and can sign it to-day."

"But the mourning?" said Franz, hesitating.

"Fear not," replied Villefort; "no ceremony will be neglected in my house. Mademoiselle de Villefort may retire during the prescribed three months to her estate of Saint-Méran ; I say hers, for she inherits it to-day. There, after a few days, if you like, the civil marriage shall be celebrated without pomp or ceremony. Madame de Saint-Méran wished her granddaughter to be married there. When that is over, you, sir, can return to Paris, while your wife passes the time of her mourning with her stepmother."

" Sir," said Franz, " I have one request to make."

" What is it ?"

" I wish Albert de Morcerf and Raoul de Château-Renaud to be present at this signature : you know they are my witnesses."

" Half an hour will suffice to apprise them ; will you go for them yourself, or will you send?"

" I prefer going, sir."

" I shall expect you, then, in half an hour, baron ; and Valentine will be ready."

M. de Villefort had scarcely said this, when the door opened and Barrois appeared.

" Gentlemen," said he, in a tone strangely firm for a servant speaking to his masters under such solemn circumstances, " Gentlemen, M. Noirtier de Villefort wishes to speak immediately to M. Franz de Quesnel, Baron d'Epinay."

Villefort started, Madame de Villefort let her son slip from her knees, Valentine rose, pale and dumb as a statue.

" Excuse me, sir," said Franz, " since M. Noirtier sent for me, I am ready to attend to his wish ; besides, I shall be happy to pay my respects to him, not having yet had the honour of doing so."

" Pray, sir," said Villefort, with marked uneasiness, " do not disturb yourself."

" Forgive me, sir," said Franz, in a resolute tone. " I would not lose this opportunity of proving to M. Noirtier how wrong it would be of him to encourage feelings of dislike to me, which I am determined to conquer, whatever they may be, by my devotion." And without listening to Villefort he rose, and followed Valentine, who was running down stairs with the joy of a shipwrecked mariner who finds a rock to cling to.

M. de Villefort followed them.

Noirtier was prepared to receive them dressed in black, and installed in his arm-chair. When the three persons he expected had entered, he looked at the door, which his valet immediately closed.

"Listen," whispered Villefort to Valentine, who could not conceal her joy; "if M. Noirtier wishes to communicate any thing which would delay your marriage I forbid you to understand him."

Valentine blushed, but did not answer. Villefort, approaching Noirtier,—

"Here is M. Franz d'Epinay," said he; "you requested to see him. We have all wished for this interview, and I trust it will convince you how ill formed are your objections to Valentine's marriage."

Noirtier answered only by a look, which made Villefort's blood run cold. He motioned to Valentine to approach. In a moment, thanks to her habit of conversing with her grandfather, she understood he asked for a key. Then his eye was fixed on the drawer of a small chest between the windows. She opened the drawer and found a key; and understanding that was what he wanted, again watched his eyes, which turned towards an old secrétaire, long since forgotten, and supposed to contain none but useless documents.

"Shall I open the secrétaire?" asked Valentine.

"Yes," signified the old man.

Valentine opened it and drew out a bundle of papers.

"Is that what you wish for?" asked she.

"Yes."

"Shall I give these papers to M. Franz d'Epinay?"

"Yes."

Franz, astonished, advanced a step.

"To me, sir?" said he.

Franz took them from Barrois, and, casting his eye on the cover, read :—

"To be given, after my death, to General Durand, who shall bequeath the packet to his son, with an injunction to preserve it as containing an important document."

"You understand, baron, my grandfather wishes you to read this paper," said Valentine.

Franz untied it, and in the midst of the most profound silence, read :—

"*Extract of the Procès-verbal of a meeting of the Bonapartist Club in the Rue Saint-Jacques, held February 5th, 1815.*"

Franz stopped.

"February 5th, 1815!" said he; "it is the day my father was murdered."

Franz read aloud the minutes of the meeting at which General d'Epinay was present. He read of the question the President put to him as to whether he was prepared to further the cause of Napoleon and his proud answer, given in defiance though finding himself unexpectedly in the midst of traitors. "I am a royalist, gentlemen; I have taken the oath of allegiance to King Louis XVIII."

Franz interrupted himself, and wiped the cold drops from his brow.

Valentine clasped her hands as if in prayer. Noirtier looked at Villefort with an almost sublime expression of contempt and pride.

Franz continued:—" When the meeting was ended the general was carried blindfold to a place chosen and there given the choice to fight for his life or be murdered.

"He chose to fight and his adversary was the president.

"It was a dark night. The ground from the steps to the river was covered with snow and hoar-frost, the water of the river looked black and deep. One of the seconds went for a lantern in a coal-barge near, and by its light they examined the arms.

"The president's sword was five inches shorter than the general's, and had no guard. The general proposed to cast lots for the swords, but the president said it was he who had given the provocation, and when he had given it he had supposed each would use his own arms. The witnesses endeavoured to insist, but the president bade them be silent.

"The lantern was placed on the ground, the two adversaries arranged themselves, and the duel commenced.

"The light made the two swords appear like flashes of lightning; as for the men they were scarce perceptible, the darkness was so great.

"M. le Général d'Epinay passed for one of the best swords-men in the army, but he was pressed so closely in the onset that he missed his aim and fell. The witnesses thought he was dead, but his adversary, who knew he had not struck him, offered him the assistance of his hand to rise. This circumstance irritated instead of calming the general, and he rushed on his adversary. But his opponent did not miss one stroke, receiving him on his sword, three times he made the general draw back, and he, finding himself foiled, returned to the charge. At the third he fell again. They thought he had slipped as at first, and the witnesses, seeing he did not move, approached and endeavoured to raise him, but the one who passed his arm round the body found it was moistened with blood; he was dangerously wounded. The general, who had almost fainted, revived.

"'Ah!' cried he, faintly, 'they have sent some fencing-master to fight with me.'

"The president, without answering, approached the witness who held the lantern, and raising his sleeve showed him two wounds he had received in his arm; then opening his coat, and unbuttoning his waistcoat, displayed his side, pierced with a third wound. Still he had not even uttered a sigh.

"The General d'Epinay died five minutes after."

Franz read these last words in a voice so choked that they were hardly audible, and then stopped, passing his hand over his eyes as if to dispel a cloud. But after a moment's silence, he continued :—

"The president went up the steps, after pushing his sword into his cane; a track of blood on the snow marked his course. He had scarcely arrived at the top when he heard a heavy splash in the water—it was the general's body, which the witnesses had just thrown into the river after ascertaining he was dead. The general fell, then, in a loyal duel, and not in ambush, as it might have been reported.

"In proof of this we have signed this paper to establish the truth of the facts, lest the moment should arrive when either of the actors in this terrible scene should be accused of premeditated murder or of infringement of the laws of honour.

"Signed, BEAUREPAIRE, DUCHAMPE, and LECHARPAL."

When Franz had finished reading this account, so dreadful for a son—when Valentine, pale with emotion, had wiped away a tear—when Villefort, trembling and crouching in a corner, had endeavoured to lessen the storm by supplicating glances at the implacable old man,—

"Sir," said d'Epinay to Noirtier, "since you are well acquainted with all these details, which are attested by honourable signa-tures,—since you appear to take some interest in me, although you have only manifested it hitherto by causing me sorrow, refuse me not one final satisfaction—tell me the name of the president of the club, that I may at least know who killed my father."

Noirtier looked at the dictionary. Franz took it, with a nervous trembling, and repeated the letters of the alphabet successively, until he came to M.

At that letter the old man signified " Yes."

" M ?" repeated Franz.

The young man's finger glided over the words, but at each one Noirtier answered by a negative sign.

Valentine hid her head between her hands.

At length Franz arrived at the word MYSELF.

" Yes !"

" You !" cried Franz, whose hair stood on end ; "you, M. Noirtier !—you killed my father ?"

" Yes !" replied Noirtier, fixing a majestic look on the young man.   Franz walked to the door and opened it, passing out without a word.

CHAPTER XXXVI

ALBERT AND HAYDÉE

A FEW days later Monte-Cristo's carriage containing himself and Albert de Morcerf stopped at the count's door. They both went into the house; the drawing-room was lighted up—they entered it.

"You will make tea for us, Baptistin," said the count.

Baptistin left the room without waiting to answer, and in two seconds reappeared, bringing on a waiter all that his master had ordered, ready prepared, and appearing to have sprung from the ground, like the repasts which we read of in fairy-tales.

"Really, my dear count," said Morcerf, "what I admire in you is, not so much your riches, for perhaps there are people even wealthier than yourself, nor is it only your wit, for Beaumarchais might have possessed as much,—but it is your manner of being served, without any questions, in a moment, in a second; it is as if they guessed what you wanted by your manner of ringing, and made a point of keeping everything you can possibly desire in constant readiness."

"What you say is perhaps true: they know my habits. For instance, you shall see; how do you wish to occupy yourself during tea-time?"

"*Ma foi!* I should like to smoke."

Monte-Cristo took the gong and struck it once. In about the space of a second a private door opened, and Ali appeared, bringing two chibouques filled with excellent latakia.

"It is quite wonderful!" said Albert.

"Oh, no; it is as simple as possible," replied Monte-Cristo. "Ali knows I generally smoke whilst I am taking my tea or coffee; he has heard that I ordered tea, and he also knows that I brought you home with me: when I summoned him he naturally guessed the reason of my doing so, and as he comes from a country where hospitality is especially manifested through the medium of smoking, he naturally concludes that we shall smoke in company—and now the mystery is solved."

"Certainly you give a most commonplace air to your explanation, but it is not the less true that you—— Ah! but what do I hear?" and Morcerf inclined his head towards the door, through which sounds issued resembling those of a guitar.

"*Ma foi!* my dear viscount, you are fated to hear music this evening; you have only escaped from the piano of Mademoiselle Danglars to be attacked by the guzla of Haydée."

"Haydée! what an adorable name! Are there, then, really women who bear the name of Haydée anywhere but in Byron's poems?"

"Certainly there are. Haydée is a very uncommon name in France, but it is common enough in Albania and Epirus; it is as if you said, for example, Chastity, Modesty, Innocence,—it is a kind of baptismal name, as you Parisians call it."

"Oh, that is charming!" said Albert; "how I should like to hear my countrywomen called Mademoiselle Goodness, Mademoiselle Silence, Mademoiselle Christian Charity! Only think, then, if Mademoiselle Danglars, instead of being called Claire-Marie-Eugénie, had been named Mademoiselle Chastity-Modesty-Innocence Danglars, what a fine effect that would have produced on the announcement of her marriage! Are there any more slaves to be had who bear this beautiful name!"

"Undoubtedly."

"Really, count, you do nothing, and have nothing, like other people. The slave of M. le Comte de Monte-Cristo! why, it is a rank of itself in France: and from the way in which you lavish money, it is a place that must be worth a hundred thousand francs a-year."

"A hundred thousand francs! the poor girl originally possessed much more than that; she was born to treasures, in comparison with which those recorded in the 'Thousand and One Nights' would seem but poverty."

"She must be a princess, then?"

"You know the history of the pacha of Yanina, do you not?"

"Of Ali Tebelen? oh! yes! it was in his service that my father made his fortune."

"Well! Haydée is his daughter."

"And your slave? But how did she become so?"

"Why, simply from my having bought her one day, as I was passing through the market at Constantinople."

"Wonderful! really my dear count, you seem to throw a sort of magic influence over all in which you are concerned; when

listening to you, existence no longer seems reality, but a waking
dream.   Now, I am perhaps going to make an impudent and
thoughtless request, but——"

"Say on."

"But, since you go out with Haydée, and sometimes even
take her to the Opera—present me to your princess."

"I will do so; on two conditions."

"I accept them at once."

"The first is, that you will never tell any one that I have
granted the interview."

"Very well," said Albert, extending his hand; "I swear I will
not."

"The second is, that you will not tell her that your father
ever served hers."

"I give you my oath that I will not."

"Enough, viscount; you will remember these two vows, will
you not?   But I know you to be a man of honour."

The count again struck the gong.   Ali reappeared.

"Tell Haydée," said he, "that I will take coffee with her, and
that I desire permission to present one of my friends to her."

Haydée was awaiting her visitors in the first room of her
suite of apartments, which was the drawing-room.   Her large
eyes were dilated with surprise and expectation, for it was the
first time that any man, except Monte-Cristo, had been accorded
entrance into her presence.   She was sitting on a sofa placed
in an angle of the room, with her legs crossed under her in the
Eastern fashion, and seemed to have made for herself a kind of
nest in the rich Indian silks which enveloped her.   Near her
was the instrument on which she had just been playing; it was
elegantly fashioned, and worthy of its mistress.   On perceiving
Monte-Cristo, she rose, and welcomed him with a smile
peculiar to herself, expressive at once of the most implicit
obedience and also of the deepest love.   Monte-Cristo advanced
towards her and extended his hand, which she, as usual, raised
to her lips.

Albert had proceeded no farther than the door, where he
remained rooted to the spot, being completely fascinated by the
sight of such surpassing beauty.

"Whom do you bring?" asked the young girl, in Romaic, of
Monte-Cristo; "is it a friend, a brother, a simple acquaintance,
or an enemy?"

"A friend," said Monte-Cristo, in the same language.

" What is his name ?"

" Count Albert; it is the same man whom I rescued from the hands of the banditti at Rome."

"In what language would you like me to converse with him ?"

Monte-Cristo reflected one instant.

" You will speak in Italian," said he.

Ali left the room.   The cups of coffee were all prepared with the addition of a sugar-glass, which had been brought for Albert.   Monte-Cristo and Haydée took the liquor in the original Arabian manner, that is to say, without sugar. Haydée took the porcelain cup in her little slender fingers, and conveyed it to her mouth with all the innocent *naïveté* of a child when eating or drinking something which it likes. At this moment two women entered, bringing salvers filled with ices and sherbet, which they placed on two small tables.

" My dear host, and you, signora," said Albert, in Italian, " excuse my apparent stupidity.   I am quite bewildered, and it is natural that it should be so.   Here I am in the heart of Paris ; but a moment ago I heard the rumbling of the omnibuses and the tinkling of the bells of the lemonade-sellers, and now I feel as if I were suddenly transported to the East; not such as I have seen it, but such as my dreams have painted it. Oh ! signora, if I could but speak Greek, your conversation, added to the fairy-scene which surrounds me, would furnish an evening of such delight as it would be impossible for me ever to forget."

" I speak sufficient Italian to enable me to converse with you, sir," said Haydée, quietly ; " and if you like what is Eastern, I will do my best to secure the gratification of your tastes while you are here."

" At what age did you leave Greece, signora ?" asked Albert.

" I left it when I was but five years old," replied Haydèe.

" Count," said Albert, in a low tone to Monte-Cristo, " do allow the signora to tell me something of her history.   You prohibited my mentioning my father's name to her, but, perhaps, she will allude to him of her own accord in the course of the recital, and you have no idea how delighted I should be to hear our name pronounced by such beautiful lips."

Monte-Cristo turned to Haydée, and with an expression of countenance which commanded her to pay the most implicit attention to his words, he said in Greek,—

" Tell us the fate of your father ; but neither the name of the traitor nor the treason."

Haydée sighed deeply, and a shade of sadness clouded her beautiful brow.

" What are you saying to her ?" said Morcerf, in an undertone.

"I again reminded her that you were a friend, and that she need not conceal any thing from you."

" Speak, speak, signora," said Albert, "I am listening with the most intense delight and interest to all you say."

Haydée answered his remark with a melancholy smile.

" Well ! I was but four years old, when one night I was suddenly awoke by my mother. We were in the palace of Yanina, she snatched me from the cushions on which I was sleeping, and on opening my eyes I saw hers were filled with tears. She took me away without speaking. When I saw her weeping I began to cry too. 'Silence, child !' said she. At other times in spite of maternal endearments or threats, I had, with a child's caprice, been accustomed to indulge my feelings of sorrow or anger by crying as much as I felt inclined ; but on this occasion there was an intonation of such extreme terror in my mother's voice when she enjoined me to silence, that I ceased crying as soon as her command was given. She bore me rapidly away. I saw then that we were descending a large staircase ; around us were all my mother's servants carrying trunks, bags, ornaments, jewels, purses of gold, etc., with which they were hurrying away in the greatest distraction. Behind the women came a guard of twenty men armed with long guns and pistols, and dressed in the costume which the Greeks have assumed since they have again become a nation. You may imagine there was something startling and ominous," said Haydée, shaking her head, and turning pale at the mere remembrance of the scene, " in this long file of slaves and women, only half aroused from sleep, or at least so they appeared to me, who was myself scarcely awake. Here and there, on the walls of the staircase, were reflected gigantic shadows, which trembled in the flickering light of the pine-torches, till they seemed to reach to the vaulted roof above.

" ' Quick !' said a voice at the end of the gallery. This voice made everyone bow before it, resembling in its effect the wind passing over a field of corn, by its superior strength forcing every ear to yield obeisance. As for me it made me tremble. This voice was that of my father. He marched the last, clothed in his splendid robes, and holding in his hand the carabine, with which your emperor presented him. He was leaning on the shoulder of his favourite Selim, and he drove us all before him, as a shepherd would his straggling flock. My father," said Haydée, raising her head, "was that illustrious man known in Europe under the name of Ali Tebelen, pacha of Yanina, before whom Turkey trembled."

Albert, without knowing why, started on hearing these words pronounced with such a haughty and dignified accent.

"We stepped into a boat and were rowed fast away. 'Why do we go so fast?' I asked my mother.

"'Silence, child!   Hush! we are flying.'

"I did not understand. Why should my father fly?—he, the all-powerful—he, before whom others were accustomed to fly,—he, who had taken for his device—

'THEY HATE ME, THEN THEY FEAR ME!'

"It was indeed a flight which my father was trying to effect. I have been told since, that the garrison of the castle of Yanina, fatigued with long service——"

Here Haydée cast a significant glance at Monte-Cristo, whose eyes had been riveted on her countenance during the whole course of her narrative.   The young girl then continued, speaking slowly like a person who is either inventing or suppressing some feature of the history which he is relating.

"Had treated with the Seraskier Kourchid, who had been sent by the sultan to gain possession of the person of my father ; it was then that Ali Tebelen took the resolution of retiring, after having sent to the sultan a French officer in whom he reposed great confidence, to the asylum, a kiosk, which he had long before prepared for himself."

"And this officer," asked Albert, "do you remember his name, signora?"

Monte-Cristo exchanged a rapid glance with the young girl, which was quite unperceived by Albert.

"No," said she, and continued : "It was towards this kiosk that we were rowing. The ground-floor, ornamented with arabesques, bathed its terraces in the water, and another floor, looking on the lake, was all which was visible to the eye.   But beneath the ground-floor, stretching out into the island, was a large subterraneous cavern, to which my mother, myself, and the women, were conducted.   In this place were together 60,000 purses and 200 barrels; the purses contained 25,000,000 of money in gold, and the barrels were filled with 30,000 pounds of gunpowder.

"Near these barrels stood Selim, my father's favourite. It was his duty to watch day and night a lance, at the end of which was a lighted match, and he had orders to blow up all—kiosk, guards, women, gold, and my father himself, at the first signal given by him. I remember well that the slaves, convinced that their lives hung by a thread, passed whole days and nights in praying, crying, and groaning. As for me, I can never forget the pale complexion and black eye of the young soldier, Selim; and whenever the Angel of Death summons me to another world, I am quite sure I shall recognise him. I cannot tell you how long we remained in this state, at that period I did not even know what time meant; sometimes, but very rarely, my father summoned me and my mother to the terrace of the palace; these were my hours of recreation; I who never saw any thing in the dismal cavern but the gloomy countenances of the slaves and the fiery lance of Selim. One day my father was endeavouring to pierce with his eager looks the remotest verge of the horizon, examining attentively every black speck which appeared on the lake, whilst my mother, reclining by his side, rested her head on his shoulder, and I played at his feet.

"He was watching the approach of some boats.

"'A boat!—two!—three!' murmured my father;—'four!'

"He then rose, seizing his arms and priming his pistols.

"'Vasiliki,' said he to my mother, trembling perceptibly, 'the instant approaches which will decide every thing. In the space of half an hour we shall know the emperor's answer. Go into the cavern with Haydée.'

"'Adieu! my lord,' murmured my mother, determining quietly to await the approach of death.

"During this time, in the kiosk, at the feet of my father, were seated twenty Palicares, concealed from view by an angle of the wall, and watching with eager eyes the arrival of the boats; they were armed with their long guns inlaid with mother-of-pearl and silver, and cartouches, in great numbers, were lying scattered on the floor; my father looked at his watch, and paced up and down with a countenance expressive of the greatest anguish. This was the scene which presented itself to my view when I quitted him after that last kiss. My mother and I traversed the gloomy passage leading to the cavern. Selim

was still at his post, and smiled sadly on us as we entered. We
fetched our cushions from the other end of the cavern, and sat
down by Selim. In great dangers the devoted ones cling to each
other; and young as I was, I quite understood that some immi-
nent danger was hanging over our heads."

Albert had often heard, not from his father, for he never
spoke on the subject, but from strangers, the description of the
last moments of the vizier of Yanina; he had read different
accounts of his death, but this history seemed to borrow new life
from the voice and expression of the young girl: the living
accent and the melancholy expression of countenance at once
charmed and horrified him.

" It was about four o'clock in the afternoon; and although
the day was brilliant out of doors, we were enveloped in the
gloomy darkness of the cavern. One single solitary light was
burning there, and it appeared like a star set in a heaven of
blackness; it was Selim's flaming lance. My mother was a
Christian and she prayed.

" Selim repeated from time to time these sacred words :—

" ' God is great !'

" My mother had still some hope. As she was coming
down, she thought she recognised the French officer who had
been sent to Constantinople, and in whom my father placed
so much confidence, for he knew that all the soldiers of the
French emperor were naturally noble and generous. She advanced some steps towards the staircase and listened.

" ' They are approaching,' said she ; ' perhaps they bring us
peace and liberty !'

" Then, whispering to Selim, she asked what were his master's
orders.

" ' If he send me his poniard, it will signify that the emperor's
intentions are not favourable, and I am to set fire to the powder;
if, on the contrary, he send me his ring, it will be a sign that
the emperor pardons him, and I may extinguish the match and
leave the magazine untouched.'

" ' My friend,' said my mother, ' when your master's order
arrives, if it is the poniard which he sends, instead of despatch-
ing us by that horrible death which we both so much dread, you
will mercifully kill us with this same poniard, will you not ?"

" ' Yes, Vasiliki,' replied Selim tranquilly.

" Suddenly we heard loud cries; we listened : they were
cries of joy ; the name of the French officer, who had been sent

to Constantinople, resounded on all sides amongst our Palicares; it was evident that he brought the answer of the emperor, and that it was favourable."

"And do you not remember the Frenchman's name?" said Morcerf, quite ready to aid the memory of the narrator.

Monte-Cristo made a sign to him to be silent.

"I do not recollect it," said Haydée.

"The noise increased, steps were heard approaching nearer and nearer; they were descending the stairs leading to the cavern.

"Selim made ready his lance.

"Soon a figure appeared in the grey twilight at the entrance of the cave, formed by the reflexion of the few rays of daylight which had found their way into this gloomy retreat.

"'Who are you?' cried Selim. 'Whoever you may be I charge you not to advance another step.'

"'Long live the emperor!' said the figure. 'He grants a full pardon to the Vizier Ali; and not only gives him his life, but restores to him his fortune and his possessions.'

"My mother uttered a cry of joy and clasped me to her bosom.

"'Stop!' said Selim, seeing that she was about to go out, 'you see I have not yet received the ring.

"'If you come from Ali himself,' said Selim to the stranger, 'you know what you were charged to remit to me?'

"'Yes,' said the messenger, 'and I bring you his ring.'

"At these words he raised his hand above his head to show the token, but it was too far off, and there was not light enough to enable Selim, where he was standing, to distinguish and recognise the object presented to his view.

"'I do not see what you have in your hand,' said Selim.

"'Approach, then,' said the messenger, 'or I will come nearer to you, if you prefer it.'

"'I will agree to neither one nor the other,' replied the young soldier; 'place the object which I desire to see in the ray of light which shines there, and retire whilst I examine it.'

"'Be it so,' said the envoy; and he retired after having first deposited the token agreed on in the place pointed out to him by Selim.

"Oh! how our hearts palpitated; for it did, indeed, seem to be a ring which was placed there. But was it my father's ring? that was the question.

"Selim still holding in his hand the lighted match, walked towards the opening in the cavern, and aided by the faint light which streamed in through the mouth of the cave, picked up the token.

"'It is well!' said he, kissing it; 'it is my master's ring!' And throwing the match on the ground he trampled on it and extinguished it.

"The messenger uttered a cry of joy, and clapped his hands. At this signal four soldiers of the Seraskier Kourchid suddenly appeared, and Selim fell pierced by five blows. Each man had stabbed him separately; and intoxicated by their crime, though still pale with fear, they sought all over the cavern to discover if there was any fear of fire, after which they amused themselves by rolling on the bags of gold.

"At this moment my mother seized me in her arms, and bounding lightly along numerous turnings and windings, known only to ourselves, she arrived at a private staircase of the kiosk, where was a scene of frightful tumult and confusion. The lower rooms were entirely filled with the Tchodoars of Kourchid, that is to say, with our enemies.

"At this crisis the whole flooring suddenly gave way. There was a whirlwind of fire and smoke kindled by these demons, which seemed like hell itself opening beneath our feet. I felt myself fall to the ground; my mother had fainted."

Haydée's arms fell by her side and she uttered a deep groan, at the same time looking towards the count as if to ask if he were satisfied with her obedience to his commands.

Presently she resumed: "When my mother recovered her senses we were before the Seraskier.

"'Kill me,' said she, 'but spare the honour of the widow of Ali.'

"'It is not me to whom you must address yourself, but,' said Kourchid, 'to your new master.'

"And Kourchid pointed out the traitor who had betrayed my father," said Haydée, in a tone of chastened anger.

"Then," said Albert, "you became the property of this man?"

"No," replied Haydée, "he did not dare to keep us, so we were sold to some slave merchants who were going to Constantinople. We traversed Greece and arrived, half dead, at the imperial gates. They were surrounded by a crowd of people, who opened a way for us to pass, when, suddenly, my mother having caught sight of the object which was attracting their attention, uttered a piercing cry and fell to the ground, pointing

as she did so to a head which was placed over the gates,
beneath which were inscribed these words,—

'THIS IS THE HEAD OF ALI TEBELEN, PACHA OF YANINA.'

"I cried bitterly, and tried to raise my mother from the earth,
but she was dead! I was taken to the slave market, and was
purchased by a rich Armenian. He caused me to be instructed,
gave me masters, and when I was thirteen years of age he sold
me to the Sultan Mahmoud."

"Of whom I bought her," said Monte-Cristo, "as I told you,
Albert, with the emerald which formed a match to the one I
had made into a box for the purpose of holding my pastilles of
hatchis."

"Oh! you are good! you are great! my lord!" said Haydée,
kissing the count's hand, "and I am very fortunate in belonging
to such a master."

Albert remained quite bewildered with all that he had seen
and heard.

"Come! finish your cup of coffee," said Monte-Cristo; "the
history is ended."

CHAPTER XXXVII

A NEWSPAPER PARAGRAPH

THE next morning, directly he awoke, Danglars asked for the newspapers, they were brought to him; he laid aside three or four, and at last fixed on "l'Impartial:" it was the paper of which Beauchamp was the chief editor. He hastily tore off the cover, opened the journal with nervous precipitation, passed contemptuously over *le premier Paris*, and arriving at the miscellaneous intelligence, stopped, with a malicious smile, at a paragraph headed "YANINA."

"Very good!" observed Danglars, after having read the paragraph; "here is a little article on Colonel Fernand."

At the same moment, that is at nine o'clock in the morning, Albert de Morcerf, dressed in a black coat buttoned up to his chin, might have been seen walking with a quick and agitated step in the direction of Monte-Cristo's house in the Champs Elysées. When he presented himself at the gate the porter informed him that the count had gone out about half an hour previously.

"Is M. le Comte shooting in the gallery?" said Morcerf.

"Yes, sir," replied the man.

Albert immediately drove to the shooting gallery. As he arrived, Monte-Cristo appeared on the threshold.

"I ask your pardon, my dear count," said Albert, "for following you here, but I have come to ask you a service. I am to fight to-day."

"What is the quarrel? people fight for all sorts of reasons you know."

"I fight in the cause of honour, will you be my second?"

"That is a serious matter, and we will not discuss it here; let us speak of nothing till we get home. Ali, bring me some water."

The count turned up his sleeves, and passed into the little vestibule where the gentlemen were accustomed to wash their hands after shooting.

" Come in, M. le Vicomte," said the marksman in a low tone'
" and I will show you something droll."

Morcerf entered, and instead of the usual mark he perceived
some playing-cards fixed against the wall. At a distance Albert
thought it was a complete suit, for he counted from the ace to
the ten.

" Ah! ah!" said Albert, " I see you were preparing for a
game of cards."

" No," said the count, " I was making a suit of cards."

" How ?" said Albert.

" Those are really aces and twos which you see, but my balls
have turned them into threes, fives, sevens, eights, nines, and
tens."

Albert approached.

In fact the balls had actually pierced the cards in the exact
places which the painted signs would otherwise have occupied,
the lines and distances being as regularly kept as if they had
been ruled with a pencil.

" Marvellous !" exclaimed Morcerf.

" What would you have, my dear viscount ?" said Monte-
Cristo, wiping his hands on the towel which Ali had brought
him ; " I must occupy my leisure moments in some way or other.
But come, I am waiting for you."

Both then entered Monte-Cristo's carriage, which in the course
of a few minutes deposited them safely at No. 30. Monte-Cristo
took Albert into his study, and pointing to a seat, placed another
for himself.

" Now, with whom are you going to fight ?" said the count.

" With Beauchamp."

" What has he done to you ?"

" There appeared in his journal last night—— But wait, read
for yourself."

And Albert handed over a paper to the count, who read as
follows :—

" A correspondent at Yanina informs us of a fact of which
until now we had remained in ignorance. The castle which
formed the protection of the town was given up to the Turks by
a French officer named Fernand, in whom the Grand Vizier, Ali
Tebelen, had reposed the greatest confidence."

" Well !" said Monte-Cristo, " what do you see in that to
annoy you ?"

" What do I see in it ?"

" Yes ; what does it signify to you if the castle of Yanina was given up by a French officer ?"

" It signifies to my father, the Count of Morcerf, whose Christian name is Fernand !"

" Did your father serve Ali Pacha ?"

" Yes ; that is to say, he fought for the independence of the Greeks, and they have fastened on to him that crime of the traitor of whom Haydée told us."

" Now just tell me, who the devil should know in France that the officer Fernand and the Count de Morcerf are one and the same person ? and who cares now about Yanina, which was taken as long ago as the year 1822 or 1823 ?"

" That just proves the blackness of the perfidy : they have allowed all this time to elapse, and then, all of a sudden, rake up events which have been forgotten, to furnish materials for scandal, in order to tarnish the lustre of our high position.   I inherit my father's name, and I do not choose that the shadow of disgrace should darken it.   I am going to Beauchamp, in whose journal this paragraph appears, and I shall insist on his retracting the assertion before two witnesses."

" Beauchamp will never retract, but he will tell you, what is very true, that perhaps there were fifty officers in the Greek army bearing the same name."

" We will fight, nevertheless.   I will efface that blot on my father's character.   My father, who was such a brave soldier, whose career was so brilliant——"

" Oh, well, he will add, ' We are warranted in believing that this Fernand is not the illustrious Count de Morcerf, who also bears the same Christian name.' "

" But if I am at last obliged to fight, will you not be my second ?"

" My dear viscount," said Monte-Cristo, gravely, " you must have seen before to-day that at all times and in all places I have been at your disposal, but the service which you have just demanded of me is one which it is out of my power to render you."

" Why ?"

" Perhaps you may know at some future period, and, in the meantime, I request you to excuse my declining to put you in possession of my reasons."

" Well, I will have Franz and Château-Renaud ; they will be

the very men for it." He left the count with the same haste with which he had sought him.

Beauchamp was in his office. It was one of those gloomy, dusty-looking apartments, such as journalists' offices have always been from time immemorial.

The servant announced M. Albert de Morcerf. Beauchamp repeated the name to himself, as though he could scarcely believe that he had heard right, and then gave orders for him to be admitted. Albert entered.

Beauchamp uttered an exclamation of surprise on seeing his friend leap over and trample under foot all the newspapers which were strewed about the room.

" Here! here! my dear Albert!" said he holding out his hand to the young man. " Are you out of your senses, or do you come peaceably to take breakfast with me ? Try and find a seat —there is one by that geranium, which is the only thing in the room to remind me that there are other leaves in the world besides leaves of paper."

" Beauchamp," said Albert, "it is of your journal that I come to speak."

"What is it ?" said Beauchamp, much surprised.

" It is an article headed Yanina."

Beauchamp took the paper, and read the article to which Albert pointed.

" You see it is a serious matter," said Morcerf when Beauchamp had finished the perusal of the paragraph.

" Is the officer alluded to a relation of yours, then ?" demanded the journalist.

" Yes," said Albert, blushing.

" Well, what do you wish me to do for you ?" said Beauchamp, mildly.

" My dear Beauchamp, I wish you to contradict this statement."

Beauchamp looked at Albert with a benevolent expression.

" Come," said he, " this matter will want a good deal of talking over; a retractation is always a serious thing, you know. Sit down, and I will read it again."

Having read it, he added : " You are irritated and vexed— tell me how this Fernand is related to you ?"

" He is merely my father," said Albert ; "M. Fernand Mondego, Count de Morcerf, an old soldier, who has fought in twenty battles, and whose honourable scars they would now denounce as badges of disgrace."

"Is it your father?" said Beauchamp; "that is quite another thing. Then I can well understand your indignation, my dear Albert. I will re-consider;" and he read the paragraph for the third time, laying a stress on each word as he proceeded. "But the paper nowhere identifies this Fernand with your father."

"No, but the connexion will be seen by others, and therefore I will have the article contradicted."

At the words *I will*, Beauchamp steadily raised his eyes to Albert, and then as gradually lowered them, and remained thoughtful for a few moments.

"You will retract the assertion, will you not, Beauchamp?" asked Albert, with increased, though stifled anger.

"Yes, when I am convinced that the statement is false," replied Beauchamp.

"But what is there to investigate, sir?" said Albert, enraged beyond measure. "If you do not believe that it is my father, say so immediately; and if, on the contrary, you believe it to be him, state your reason for doing so."

Beauchamp looked at Albert with the smile which was peculiar to him, and in its numerous modifications, served to express every varied feeling of his mind.

"Sir," replied he, "if you came to me with the idea of demanding satisfaction, you should have gone at once to the point, and not have entertained me with the idle conversation to which I have been patiently listening for the last half hour. Am I put to this construction on your visit?"

"Yes, if you will not consent to retract that infamous calumny."

"Wait a moment—no threats if you please, M. Albert Mondego, Vicomte de Morcerf; I never allow them from my enemies, and, therefore, shall not put up with them from my friends. You insist on my contradicting the article relating to General Fernand, an article in which, I assure you, on my word of honour, I have not taken the slightest share?"

"Yes, I insist on it!" said Albert, whose mind was beginning to get bewildered with the excitement of his feelings.

"And if I refuse to retract, you wish to fight, do you?" said Beauchamp, in a calm tone.

"Yes!" replied Albert, raising his voice.

"Well," said Beauchamp, "here is my answer, my dear sir.

The article was not inserted by me—I was not even aware of it ; but you have by the step which you have taken called my attention to the paragraph in question, and it will remain until it shall be either contradicted or confirmed by some one who has a right to do so."

" Sir," said Albert rising, " I will do myself the honour of sending my seconds to you, and you will be kind enough to arrange with them the place of meeting and the arms which we are to use; do you understand me ?"

" Certainly, my dear sir."

" And this evening, if you please, or to-morrow at the latest, we will meet."

" No ! no ! I will be on the ground at the proper time, but, in my opinion (and I have a right to dictate the preliminaries, as it is I who have received the provocation)—in my opinion, the time ought not to be yet. I know you to be well skilled in the management of the sword, whilst I am only moderately so ; I know, too, that you are a good marksman—there we are about equal. I know that a duel between us two would be a serious affair, because you are brave, and I am brave also. I do not therefore wish either to kill you, or to be killed myself, without a cause. Now I am going to put a question to you, and one very much to the purpose, too. Do you insist on this retractation so far as to kill me if I do not make it, although I have repeated more than once, and affirmed, on my honour, that I was ignorant of the thing with which you charge me, and although I still declare that it is impossible for anyone but you to recognize the Count de Morcerf under the name of Fernand ?"

" I maintain my original resolution."

" Very well, my dear sir, then I consent to cut throats with you ; but I require three weeks' preparation : at the end of that time I shall come and say to you, ' The assertion is false, and I retract it ;' or, ' The assertion is true,' when I shall immediately draw the sword from its sheath, or the pistols from the case, whichever you please."

" Three weeks !" cried Albert ; " they will pass as slowly as three centuries, when I am all the time suffering dishonour."

" Had you continued to remain on amicable terms with me, I should have said, ' Patience, my friend ;' but you have constituted yourself my enemy, therefore I say, ' What does that signify to me, sir ?'"

" Well, let it be three weeks, then," said Morcerf : " but

remember, at the expiration of that time, no delay or subterfuge will justify you in——"

" M. Albert de Morcerf," said Beauchamp, rising in his turn, " I cannot throw you out of the window for three weeks, that is to say, for twenty-one days to come, nor have you any right to split my skull open until that time has elapsed. To-day is the last of August, the 21st of September will, therefore, be the conclu-sion of the term agreed on, and till that time arrives—and it is the advice of a gentleman which I am about to give you—till then we will refrain from growling and barking like two dogs chained within sight of each other."

When he had concluded this speech, Beauchamp bowed coldly to Albert, turned his back upon him, and retired to his printing-office. Albert vented his anger on a pile of newspapers, which he sent flying all over the room by switching them violently with his stick ; after which ebullition he departed, not, however, without walking several times to the door of the printing-office, as if he had half a mind to enter it. Whilst Albert was lashing the front of his vehicle in the same manner that he had done to the newspapers which were the innocent agents of his discomfi-ture, he perceived Morrel, who was walking with a quick step and a bright eye. He was passing the Chinese Baths, and appeared to have come from the direction of the Porte Saint-Martin, and to be going towards the Magdalen.

" Ah !" said Morcerf, " there goes a happy man !"

And he was not mistaken in his opinion.

CHAPTER XXXVIII

THE LEMONADE

About two hours after the scene in M. Noirtier's room Villefort received the following letter :—

" After all the disclosures which were made this morning, M. Noirtier de Villefort must see the utter impossibility of any alliance being formed between his family and that of M. Franz d'Epinay. M. d'Epinay must say that he is shocked and astonished that M. de Villefort, who appeared to be aware of all the circumstances detailed this morning, should not have anticipated him in this announcement."

M. Noirtier, to whom his son sent this communication, sent for Morrel with the request that he would lose no time in coming to him—a command which Morrel obeyed to the letter, to the great discomfiture of Barrois who had been to fetch him.

On arriving at the house, Morrel was not even out of breath, for love lends wings to our desires, but Barrois, who had long forgotten what it was to love, was sorely fatigued by the expedition he had been constrained to use.

The old servant introduced Morrel by a private entrance, closed the door of the study, and soon the rustling of a dress announced the arrival of Valentine. She looked marvellously beautiful in her deep mourning-dress, and Morrel experienced such intense delight in gazing upon her, that he felt as if he could almost have dispensed with the conversation with her grandfather.

" M. Morrel," said Valentine to the young man, who was regarding her with the most intense interest, " my grandfather, M. Noirtier, had a thousand things to say, which he has already made me understand, and now he has sent for you, that I may repeat them to you : I will repeat them, then ; and since he has chosen me as his interpreter, I will be faithful to the trust, and will not alter a word of his intentions."

"My grandfather intends leaving this house," said she, "and Barrois is looking out suitable apartments for him in another. I shall not leave my grandfather, that is an understood thing between us. My apartment will be close to his. Now M. de Villefort must either give his consent to this plan or his refusal; in the first case, I shall leave directly; and in the second, I shall await my majority, which will be completed in about ten months. Then I shall be free, I shall have an independent fortune, and——"

"And what?" demanded Morrel.

"And with my grandfather's consent I shall fulfil the promise which I have made you."

Valentine pronounced these few last words in such a low tone, that nothing but Morrel's intense interest in what she was saying could have enabled him to hear them.

"Have I not explained your wishes, grandpapa?" said Valentine, addressing Noirtier.

"Yes," looked the old man.

"Oh!" cried Morrel, almost tempted to throw himself on his knees before Noirtier and Valentine, and to adore them as two superior beings, "what have I ever done in my life to merit such unbounded happiness?"

"Until that time," continued the young girl, in a calm and self-possessed tone of voice, "we will conform to circumstances, and be guided by the wishes of our friends, so long as those wishes do not tend finally to separate us; in one word, and I repeat it, because it expresses all I wish to convey—we will wait."

Morrel looked obedience to her commands. Noirtier regarded the lovers with a look of ineffable tenderness, whilst Barrois, who had remained in the room in the character of a man privileged to know every thing that passed, smiled on the youthful couple as he wiped the perspiration from his bald forehead.

"How hot you look, my good Barrois!" said Valentine.

"Ah! I have been running very fast, mademoiselle, but I must do M. Morrel the justice to say that he ran still faster."

Noirtier directed their attention to a tray, on which was placed a decanter containing lemonade and a glass. The decanter was nearly full, with the exception of a little, which had been already drunk by M. Noirtier.

"Come, Barrois," said the young girl, "take some of this lemonade; I see you are coveting a good draught of it."

"'The fact is, mademoiselle," said Barrois, "I am dying with thirst, and since you are so kind as to offer it me, I cannot say I should at all object to drinking your health in a glass of it."

"Take some, then, and come back immediately."

Barrois took away the tray, and hardly was he outside the door, which, in his haste, he forgot to shut, than they saw him throw back his head and empty to the very dregs the glass which Valentine had filled. Valentine and Morrel were exchanging their adieux in the presence of Noirtier when a ring was heard at the door-bell. It was the signal of a visit.

"Who rang?" asked Valentine.

"Doctor d'Avrigny," said Barrois, staggering into the room as if he would fall.

"What is the matter, Barrois?" said Valentine.

The old man did not answer, but looked at his master with wild staring eyes, whilst with his cramped hand he grasped a piece of furniture to enable him to stand upright.

"He is going to fall!" cried Morrel.

The trembling which had attacked Barrois gradually increased, the features of the face became quite altered, and the convulsive movement of the muscles appeared to indicate the approach of a most serious nervous disorder. Noirtier, seeing Barrois in this pitiable condition, showed by his looks all the various emotions of sorrow and sympathy which can animate the heart of man. Barrois made some steps towards his master.

Valentine uttered a cry of horror; Morrel took her in his arms, as if to defend her from some unknown danger.

"M. d'Avrigny! M. d'Avrigny!" cried she, in a stifled voice. "Help! help!"

Barrois turned round, and, with a great effort, stumbled a few steps, then fell at the feet of Noirtier, and resting his hand on the knee of the invalid, exclaimed, "My master! my good master!"

At this moment M. de Villefort, attracted by the noise, appeared on the threshold.

"Madam! madam!" cried Valentine, calling her step-mother, and running up-stairs to meet her; "come quick, quick! and bring your bottle of smelling-salts with you."

"What is the matter?" said Madame de Villefort, in a harsh and constrained tone.

Madame de Villefort now deliberately descended the staircase.

In one hand she held her handkerchief, with which she appeared to be wiping her face, and in the other a bottle of English smelling-salts. Her first look on entering the room was at Noirtier, whose face, independent of the emotion which such a scene could not fail to produce, proclaimed him to be in possession of his usual health ; her second glance was at the dying man. She turned pale, and her eye passed quickly from the servant and rested on the master.

" Madame," said De Villefort, " I ask, where is M. d'Avrigny ? In God's name answer me !"

" He is with Edward, who is not quite well," replied Madame de Villefort.

Villefort rushed up-stairs to fetch him himself.

" Take this," said Madame de Villefort, giving her smelling-bottle to Valentine. " They will, no doubt, bleed him, therefore I will retire, for I cannot endure the sight of blood ;" and she followed her husband up-stairs.

The doctor soon entered. Barrois was now showing signs of returning consciousness, the crisis seemed past, a low moaning was heard, and he raised himself on one knee. D'Avrigny and Villefort carried him into an adjoining room, and laid him on a couch.

The doctor hastily made up a draught of oil of turpentine and tartar emetic. " Drink," said he.

Barrois took the glass, and raising it to his purple lips, took about half of the liquid offered him.

" What have you eaten to-day ?"

" I have eaten nothing, I only drank a glass of my master's lemonade—that's all ;" and Barrois turned towards Noirtier, who, immovably fixed in his arm-chair, was contemplating this terrible scene without allowing a word or a movement to escape him.

" Where is this lemonade ? " asked the doctor, eagerly.

" Downstairs, in the decanter."

" Whereabouts downstairs ?"

" In the kitchen."

" Shall I go and fetch it, doctor ?" inquired Villefort.

" No, stay here, and try to make Barrois drink the rest of this glass of ether and water. I will go myself and fetch the lemonade."

D'Avrigny bounded towards the door, flew down the back stair-case, and almost knocked down Madame de Villefort, who was herself going down to the kitchen. D'Avrigny paid no attention to her; possessed with but one idea he cleared the last four steps with a bound, and rushed into the kitchen, where he saw the decanter about three parts empty still standing on the tray, where it had been left. He darted upon it as an eagle would seize upon its prey. Panting with loss of breath, he returned to the room he had just left. Madame de Villefort was slowly ascending the steps which led to her room.

He poured some drops of the lemonade into the palm of his hand, put his lips to it, and after having rinsed his mouth as a man does when he is tasting wine, he spat the liquor into the fire-place.

" Barrois," said the doctor, " can you speak ?"

Barrois muttered a few unintelligible words.

" Who made the lemonade ? "

" I did."

" Did you bring it to your master directly it was made ?"

" No, I left it in the pantry, because I was called away."

" Who brought it into this room, then ?"

" Mademoiselle Valentine."

D'Avrigny struck his forehead with his hand.

" My God, have mercy upon me !" said the unhappy man suddenly, and, uttering a fearful cry, Barrois fell back as if he had been struck by lightning.

D'Avrigny put his hand to his heart, and placed a glass before his lips.

Villefort drew back a few steps, and clasping his hands, exclaimed, with real amazement and sympathy,—

" Dead ! and so soon too !"

" Yes, it is very soon !" said the doctor looking at the corpse before him : " but that ought not to astonish you ; Monsieur and Madame de Saint-Méran died as soon. People die very suddenly in your house, M. de Villefort."

" What !" cried the magistrate, with an accent of horror and consternation, " are you still harping on that terrible idea ?"

" Still, sir ; and I shall always do so," replied D'Avrigny, " for it has never for one instant ceased to retain possession of my mind ; and that you may be quite sure I am not mistaken this time, listen well to what I am going to say, M. de Villefort."

The magistrate trembled convulsively.

" There is a poison which destroys life almost without leaving any perceptible traces. I know it well ; I have studied it in all its qualities and in the effects which it produces. I recognised the presence of this poison in the case of poor Barrois as well as in that of Madame de Saint-Méran. There is a way of detecting its presence. It restores the blue colour of litmus-paper reddened by an acid, and it turns syrup of violets green. We have no litmus-paper, but I have sent for the syrup of violets and here it comes."

The doctor was right; steps were heard in the passage. M. D'Avrigny opened the door, and took from the hands of the waiting maid a cup which contained two or three spoonsful of the syrup; he then carefully closed the door.

"Look!" said he to the procureur du roi, whose heart beat so loudly that it might almost be heard; "here in this cup is some syrup of violets, and this decanter contains the remainder of the lemonade of which M. Noirtier and Barrois partook. If the lemonade be pure and inoffensive, the syrup will colour; if, on the contrary, the lemonade be drugged with poison, the syrup will become green. Look well at it!"

The doctor then slowly poured some drops of the lemonade from the decanter into the cup, and, in an instant, a kind of light cloudy sediment began to form at the bottom of the cup; this sediment first took a blue shade, then from the colour of sapphire it passed to that of opal, and from opal to emerald. Arrived at this last hue, it changed no more. The result of the experiment left no doubt whatever on the mind.

"The unfortunate Barrois has been poisoned," said D'Avrigny; "and I will maintain this assertion before God and man!"

Villefort said nothing, but he clasped his hands, opened his haggard eyes, and, overcome with his emotion, sank into a chair.

"Listen," said the doctor, "the assassin first kills M. de Saint-Méran, then Madame de Saint-Méran—a double fortune to inherit."

Villefort wiped the perspiration from his forehead.

"M. Noirtier," resumed M. d'Avrigny, in the same pitiless tone,—"M. Noirtier was to be the next victim. His lemonade is poisoned but the unfortunate servant drank it before his master. To whom has M. Noirtier left his fortune?"

"Have mercy on my child, sir!" cried Villefort in agony.

"You see it is yourself who have first named her—you, her father!"

"Have pity on Valentine! Listen! it is impossible. I would

as willingly accuse myself! Valentine, whose heart is pure as a diamond or a lily."

"No pity, M. le procureur du roi; the crime is flagrant. Mademoiselle herself packed all the medicines which were sent to M. de Saint-Méran; and M. de Saint-Méran is dead. Mademoiselle de Villefort prepared all the cooling draughts which Madame de Saint-Méran took, and Madame de Saint-Méran is dead. Mademoiselle de Villefort took from the hands of Barrois, who was sent out, the lemonade which M. Noirtier has every morning, and he has escaped only by a miracle. Mademoiselle de Villefort is the culprit!—She is the poisoner M. le procureur du roi, denounce Mademoiselle de Villefort; do your duty."

"Doctor, I resist no longer; I can no longer defend myself! I believe you; but for pity's sake spare my life, my honour!"

"M. de Villefort," replied the doctor with increased vehemence, "if your daughter had committed only one crime, and I saw her meditating another, I would say, 'Warn her, punish her, let her pass the remainder of her life in a convent weeping and praying.' If she had committed two crimes, I would say, 'Here, M. de Villefort, is a poison that the prisoner is not acquainted with, one that has no known antidote, quick as thought, rapid as lightning, mortal as the thunderbolt; give her that poison, recommending her soul to God, and save your honour.' This is what I should say had she only killed two persons; but she has seen three deaths—has contemplated three murdered persons—has knelt by three corpses! To the scaffold with the poisoner!—to the scaffold! Do you talk of your honour? Do what I tell you!"

Villefort fell on his knees.

"Listen," said he, "I have not the strength of mind you have, or rather that which you would not have, if instead of my daughter Valentine, your daughter Madeleine were concerned."

The doctor turned pale.

"Listen!" continued the wretched father, "pity me,—help me! My daughter is not guilty. If you drag us both before a tribunal I will still say, 'No, my daughter is not guilty;—there is no crime in my house. I will not acknowledge a crime in my house.'—Are you a man?—Have you a heart?—No, you are a physician!—Well, I tell you I will not drag my daughter before a tribunal and give her up to the executioner! The bare idea would kill me! And if you were mistaken, doctor!—if it were not my daughter!—If I should come one day, pale as a spectre, and say to you, 'Assassin! you have killed my child!'"

"Well," said the doctor, after a moment's silence, "I will wait."

Villefort looked at him as if he had doubted his words

"Only," continued M. d'Avrigny, with a slow and solemn tone, "if any one falls ill in your house, if you feel yourself attacked, do not send for me, for I will come no more. I will consent to share this dreadful secret with you; but I will not allow shame and remorse to grow and increase in my conscience, as crime and misery will in your house."

"Then you abandon me, doctor?"

"Yes, for I can follow you no farther; and I only stop at the foot of the scaffold. Some further discovery will be made, which will bring this dreadful tragedy to a close. Adieu!"

"I entreat you, doctor!"

"All the horrors that disturb my thoughts make your house odious and fatal. Adieu, sir."

CHAPTER XXXIX

THE BURGLARY

THE day following, the Count of Monte-Cristo set out for his house at Auteuil, accompanied by Ali and several attendants, also taking with him some horses whose qualities he was desirous of ascertaining.

No sooner had he arrived than Baptistin brought him a letter on a silver salver.

The count opened the letter, and read:—

" M. de Monte-Cristo is apprised that this night a man will enter his house in the Champs-Elysées with the intention of carrying off some papers supposed to be in the secrétaire in the dressing-room. The count's well-known courage will render unnecessary the aid of the police, whose interference might seriously affect him who sends this advice. The count, by concealing himself in the dressing-room, would be able to defend his property himself. Many attendants or apparent precautions would prevent the attempt, and M. de Monte-Cristo would lose the opportunity of discovering an enemy."

The count's first idea was that this was an artifice—a gross deception, to draw his attention to a minor danger in order to expose him to a greater. He was on the point of sending the letter to the commissaire de police, notwithstanding the advice of his anonymous friend, or, perhaps, *because* of that advice, when suddenly the idea occurred to him that it might be some personal enemy, whom he alone should recognise, and over whom, if such were the case, he alone could gain any advantage.

The count had a vigorous and daring mind, denying any thing to be impossible, with that energy which marks the great man. From his past life, from his resolution to shrink from nothing, he had acquired an inconceivable relish for the contests in which he had engaged—sometimes against nature, sometimes against the world, which may pass for the devil.

"They do not want my papers," said Monte-Cristo, "they think I am there, and want to kill me; they are no robbers but assassins. I will not allow M. le Préfet de police to interfere with my private affairs. I am rich enough, forsooth, to dispute his authority on this occasion."

He allowed his servants, all except Ali, to think him still at Auteuil, but after dinner he returned to Paris.

He hastened to the side-door with Ali, entered precipitately, and, by the servants' staircase, of which he had the key, gained his bedroom without opening or disarranging a single curtain, without even the porter having the slightest suspicion that the house which he supposed empty contained its chief occupant.

Arrived in his bedroom, the count motioned to Ali to stop, then he passed into the dressing-room, which he examined : all was as usual—the precious secrétaire in its place, and the key in the secrétaire. He doubly locked it, took the key, returned to the bedroom door, removed the double staple of the bolt, and went in.

Meanwhile Ali had procured the arms the count required, namely, a short carbine and a pair of double-barrelled pistols, with which as sure an aim might be taken as with a single-barrelled one. Thus armed, the count held the life of five men in his hands.

It was about half-past nine; the count and Ali ate in haste a crust of bread and drank a glass of Spanish wine, then Monte-Cristo slipped aside one of the movable panels, which enabled him to see into the adjoining room. He had within his reach his pistols and his carbine, and Ali, standing near him, held one of those small Arabian hatchets, whose form has not varied since the crusades.

Through one of the windows of the bedroom, on a line with that in the dressing-room the count could see into the street.

Two hours passed thus. It was intensely dark ; still Ali, thanks to his wild nature, and the count, thanks, doubtless, to his long confinement, could distinguish in the darkness the slightest movement of the trees.

As the clock struck twelve, the count thought he heard a slight noise in the dressing-room; this first sound, or, rather, this first grinding, was followed by a second, then a third ; at the fourth the count knew what to expect. A firm and well-practised hand was engaged in cutting the four sides of a pane of glass with a diamond.

The window whence the noise proceeded was opposite the opening by which the count could see into the dressing-room. He fixed his eyes on that window, he distinguished a shadow in the darkness ; then one of the panes became quite opaque, as if a sheet of paper were stuck on the outside, then the square cracked without falling. Through the opening an arm was passed to find the fastening, then a second ; the window turned on its hinges, and a man entered. He was alone.

At that moment Ali touched his master slightly on the shoulder ; he turned. Ali pointed to the window of the room in which they were, facing the street. Monte-Cristo moved so as to gain a view from it.

"Good !" thought he, "there are two of them ; one acts while the other watches."

He made a sign to Ali not to lose sight of the man in the street, and returned to the one in the dressing-room.

The glass-cutter had entered, and was feeling his way, his arms stretched out before him. At last he appeared to have made himself familiar with all parts of it. There were two doors ; he bolted them both.

When he drew near to that of the bedroom Monte-Cristo expected he was coming in, and raised one of his pistols ; but he simply heard the sound of the bolts sliding in their copper rings. It was only a precaution. The nocturnal visitor, ignorant of the count's having removed the staples, might now think himself at home, and pursue his purpose with full security.

He touched a spring, and immediately a pale light, just bright enough to render objects distinct, was reflected on the hands and countenance of the man. Monte-Cristo started violently, for the face was known to him. Then he slipped back noiselessly, and returned transformed.

His tunic had disappeared under a long cassock, his hair under a priest's wig ; the three-cornered hat over this effectually transformed the count into an abbé.

The man had advanced straight to the secrétaire, the lock of which was beginning to crack under his instrument.

Monte-Cristo then drew a lighted taper from a closet, and when the thief was deeply engaged with his lock, silently opened the door, taking care that the light should shine directly on his face.

The door opened so quietly that the thief heard no sound. But, to his astonishment, the room was in a moment light. He turned.

"Good evening, dear M. Caderousse!" said Monte-Cristo; "what are you doing here at such an hour?"

"The Abbé Busoni!" exclaimed Caderousse; and, bewildered with terror at this strange apparition which had entered when he had bolted the doors, he let fall his bunch of keys, and remained motionless and stupefied.

The count placed himself between Caderousse and the window, thus cutting off from the thief his only chance of retreat.

"The Abbé Busoni!" repeated Caderousse, fixing his haggard gaze on the count.

"Yes, doubtless!—the Abbé Busoni himself," replied Monte-Cristo, "and I am very glad you recognise me, dear M. Caderousse; it proves you have a good memory, for it must be about ten years since we last met."

This calmness of Busoni, combined with his irony and boldness, staggered Caderousse.

"L'abbé! l'abbé!" murmured he, clenching his fists, and his teeth chattering.

"So you would rob the Count of Monte-Cristo," continued the false abbé.

"M. l'Abbé," murmured Caderousse, seeking to regain the window, which the count pitilessly intercepted,—"M. l'Abbé, I don't know—believe me—I take my oath——"

"A pane of glass out," continued the count, "a dark lantern, a bunch of false keys, a secrétaire half forced; it is tolerably evident——"

Caderousse was choking; he looked round for some corner to hide in—some way of escape.

"Come, come," continued the count, "I see you are still the same—an assassin."

"M. l'Abbé, since you know everything, you know it was not I, it was La Carconte; that was proved at the trial, since I was only condemned to the galleys."

"Is your time then expired, since I find you in a fair way to return there?"

"No, M. l'Abbé, I have been liberated by some one."

"That some one has done society a great kindness."

"Ah," said Caderousse, "I had promised ——"

"And you are breaking your promise!" interrupted Monte-Cristo.

"Alas, yes!" said Caderousse very uneasily.

"A bad relapse! That will lead you, if I mistake not, to the

Place de Grève. So much the worse—so much the worse, *diavolo!* as they say in my country."

" M. l'Abbé, I am impelled——"

" Every criminal says the same thing."

" Poverty—— "

"Pshaw!" said Busoni, disdainfully; "poverty may make a man beg, steal a loaf of bread at a baker's door, but not cause him to open a secrétaire in a house supposed to be inhabited. And when the jeweller Joannès paid you 45,000 francs for the diamond I had given you, and you killed him to get the diamond and the money both, was that also poverty?"

" Pardon, M. l'Abbé!" said Caderousse, " you know everything! You knew I was sent to the galleys and you know also why I was sent there!"

" Since you left Toulon what have you lived on? Answer me!"

" On what I could get. By Heaven!" cried Caderousse suddenly drawing from his waistcoat an open knife, and striking the count in the breast, " you shall not send me to the galleys again."

To Caderousse's great astonishment, the knife, instead of piercing the count's breast, flew back blunted.

At the same moment the count seized with his left hand the assassin's wrist, and wrung it with such strength that the knife fell from his stiffened fingers, and Caderousse uttered a cry of pain. But the count, disregarding his cry, continued to wring the bandit's wrist until, his arm being dislocated, he fell first on his knees, then flat on the floor.

The count then placed his foot on Caderousse's head, saying,—

" I know not what restrains me from crushing thy skull, rascal!"

" Ah, mercy—mercy!" cried Caderousse.

The count withdrew his foot.

" Rise!" said he.

Caderousse rose.

" What a wrist you have, M. l'Abbé!" said Caderousse, stroking his arm, all bruised by the fleshy pincers which had held it,—" what a wrist!"

" Silence! God gives me strength to overcome a wild beast like you; in the name of that God I act—remember that, wretch! Now, begone!"

" Which way?"

" The way you came."

"M. l'Abbé," said Caderousse, "are you going to give me one more chance—try me once more?"

"I will," said the count. "If you reach your home safely, and leave Paris, leave France; and wherever you may be, so long as you conduct yourself well, I will send you a small annuity; for, if you return home safely, then——"

"Then?" asked Caderousse, shuddering.

"Then I shall believe God has forgiven you, and I will forgive you too."

"As true as I am a Christian," stammered Caderousse, "you will make me die of fright!"

"Now, begone!" said the count, pointing to the window.

Caderousse, scarcely yet relying on this promise, put his legs out of the window and stood on the ladder. Monte-Cristo returned to his bedroom, and glancing rapidly from the garden to the street, he watched Caderousse, who, after walking to the end of the garden, fixed his ladder against the wall at a different place from where he came in.

Then Caderousse sat astride the coping, and, drawing up his ladder, passed it over the wall; he began to descend, or rather to slide down by the two stanchions, which he did with an ease which proved how accustomed he was to the exercise.

But, once he had started he could not stop. He saw a man spring from the shade when he was half way down—he saw an arm raised as he touched the ground, but he could not check his descent. Before he could defend himself that arm struck him so violently in the back that he let go the ladder, crying, "Help!"

A second blow struck him almost immediately in the side, and he fell, calling, "Help! murder!"

Then, as he rolled on the ground, his adversary seized him by the hair, and struck him a third blow in the chest. This time Caderousse endeavoured to call again, but he could only utter a groan, and he shuddered as the blood flowed from his three wounds. The assassin, finding he no longer cried, slipped his hands into his pockets and began a hasty search.

Then Caderousse, with a convulsive effort, raised himself on his elbow, and with a dying voice cried—

"Murder! I am dying! Help, M. l'Abbé—help!"

The door of the back staircase opened, then the side-gate of the garden, and Ali and his master were on the spot with lights, and the murderer fled.

Caderousse continued to call piteously—

" M. l'Abbé, help ! help !"

Ali and his master conveyed the wounded man into a room. Monte-Cristo motioned to Ali to undress him, and he then examined his dreadful wounds.

"My God!" he exclaimed, " Thy vengeance is sometimes delayed, but only that it may fall the more effectually."

Ali looked at his master for further instructions.

" Go, wake the porter, and send him for a surgeon."

Ali obeyed, leaving the abbé alone with Caderousse, who had not yet revived.

When the wretched man again opened his eyes, the count looked at him with a mournful expression of pity, and his lips moved as if in prayer.

" Did you recognise your murderer ?" he asked.

" Yes—it was my comrade. He gave me the plan of this house, hoping I should rob the count. He had doubtless planned from the first to waylay me, and murder me. He began to rifle my pockets but fled without discovering I had nothing, when he heard you coming."

"Remember my words—I said : ' If you return home safely, I shall believe God has forgiven you, and I will forgive you also.' "

" And you did not warn me !" cried Caderousse, raising himself on his elbows. " You knew I should be killed on leaving this house, and did not warn me !"

" No, for I saw God's justice placed in the hands of your comrade, and should have thought it sacrilege to oppose the designs of Providence."

" God's justice ! Speak not of it, M. l'Abbé. If God were just, you know many would be punished who now escape. Do you then believe in God ?"

" Had I been so unhappy as not to believe in Him until now," said Monte-Cristo, " I must believe on seeing you."

Caderousse raised his clenched hands towards heaven.

" Listen," said the abbé, extending his hand over the wounded man, as if to command him to believe ; " this is what the God in whom, on your death-bed you refuse to believe, has done for you : he gave you health, strength, regular employment, even friends—a life, in fact, which a man might enjoy with a calm conscience. Instead of approving these gifts, rarely granted so abundantly, this has been your course : you have given yourself up to sloth and drunkenness, and in a fit of intoxication have ruined your best friend.

"Listen," continued the abbé; "when you had betrayed your friend, God began not to strike, but to warn you; poverty overtook you; you had already passed half your life in coveting that which you might have honourably acquired, and already you contemplated crime under the excuse of want, when God worked a miracle in your behalf, sending you, by my hands, a fortune—brilliant, indeed, for you, who had never possessed any. But this unexpected, unhoped-for, unheard-of fortune sufficed you no longer when once you possessed it; you wished to double it; and how? by a murder! You succeeded, and then you were brought to justice. You see I have not lost sight of you but kept my eye on you throughout the intervening years since we met."

"It was not I who wished to kill the Jew who bought the stone," said Caderousse; "it was my wife."

"Yes," said Monte-Cristo, "and God, I cannot say in justice, for His justice would have slain you—but God, in His mercy, spared your life."

"*Pardieu!* to transport me for life; how merciful!"

"You thought it a mercy then, miserable wretch! The coward, who feared death, rejoiced at perpetual disgrace, for, like all galley-slaves, you said, 'I may escape from prison, I cannot from the grave.' And you said truly; the way was opened for you unexpectedly: then, wretched creature! then you tempted God again and you committed a third crime, without reason, without excuse. God is wearied, He has punished you."

Caderousse was fast sinking.

"Give me drink," said he; "I thirst—I burn!"

Monte-Cristo gave him a glass of water.

"I do not believe there is a God!" howled Caderousse; "you do not believe it: you lie—you lie!"

"Silence!" said the abbé. "What! you do not believe in God when He is striking you dead?—you will not believe in Him, who requires but a prayer, a word, a tear, and He will forgive?—God, who might have directed the assassin's dagger so as to end your career in a moment, has given you this quarter of an hour for repentance. Reflect then, wretched man, and repent."

"No," said Caderousse, "no; I will not repent: there is no God, there is no Providence—all comes by chance."

"There is a Providence, there is a God," said Monte-Cristo,

" of which you are a striking proof, as you lie in utter despair, denying Him ; while I stand before you, rich, happy, safe, and entreating that God in whom you endeavour not to believe, while in your heart you still believe in Him."

" But who are you, then ?" asked Caderousse, fixing his dying eyes on the count.

" Look well at me !" said Monte-Cristo, putting the light near his face.

" The abbé—the Abbé Busoni."

Monte-Cristo took off the wig which disfigured him, and uncovered his black hair, which added so much to the beauty of his pallid features.

" Oh !" said Caderousse, thunderstruck, "I have seen you before."

" Yes, Caderousse, you have seen me, you knew me once."

" Who, then, are you ?   And why, if you knew me, do you let me die ?"

" Because nothing can save you, your wounds are mortal. Had it been possible to save your life, I should have considered it another proof of God's mercy, and I would again have endeavoured to restore you, I swear by my father's grave."

" By your father's grave !" said Caderousse, half-raising himself to see more distinctly the man who had just taken this oath which all men hold sacred ; " who, then, are you ?"

The count had watched the approach of death. He knew this was the last struggle,—he approached the dying man, and leaning over him with a calm and melancholy look, he whispered,—

" I am—I am——"

And his almost closed lips uttered a name so low that he himself appeared afraid to hear it.

Caderousse, who had raised himself on his knees, and stretched out his arm, tried to draw back, then clasping his hands, and raising them with a desperate effort,—

" Oh! my God! my God!" said he, "pardon me for having denied Thee ; Thou dost exist ; Thou art, indeed, man's father in heaven, and his judge on earth. My God, my Lord, I have long despised Thee ! Pardon me, my God ; receive me, O my Lord!"

Caderousse sighed deeply, and fell back with a groan. The blood no longer flowed from his wounds. He was dead.

" *One !*" said the count, mysteriously, his eyes fixed on the wretch who had suffered so awful a death.

Ten minutes afterwards the surgeon arrived, and was received by the Abbé Busoni, who was praying by the side of the corpse.

CHAPTER XL

THE daring attempt to rob the count was the topic of conversation throughout Paris for the next fortnight : the dying man had signed a deposition declaring his comrade to be the assassin. The police had orders to make the strictest search for the murderer.

Caderousse's knife, dark lantern, bunch of keys, and clothing, excepting the waistcoat, which could not be found, were deposited at the registry ; the corpse was conveyed to La Morgue, The count told every one this adventure had happened during his absence at Auteuil, and that he only knew what was related by the Abbé Busoni, who that evening, by mere chance, had requested to pass the night in his house to examine some value able books in his library.

But three weeks had already passed, and the most diligent search had been unsuccessful ; the attempted robbery and the murder of the robber by his comrade were almost forgotten.

The delay demanded by Beauchamp had nearly expired. Morcerf appreciated the advice of Monte-Cristo to let things die away of their own accord ; no one had taken up the remark about the general, and no one had recognised in the officer who betrayed the castle of Yanina the noble count in the House of Peers.

Albert, however, felt no less insulted ; the few lines which had irritated him were certainly intended as an insult. Besides, the manner in which Beauchamp had closed the conference left a bitter recollection in his heart. He cherished the thought of the duel, hoping to conceal its true cause even from his seconds. Beauchamp had not been seen since the day he visited Albert ; and those of whom the latter inquired always told him he was away on a journey which would detain him some days. Where he was no one knew.

One morning Albert was awakened by his valet-de-chambre,

who announced Beauchamp. Albert rubbed his eyes, ordered his servant to introduce him into the small smoking-room on the ground floor, dressed himself quickly, and went down. Beauchamp was pacing the room; on perceiving Albert he stopped.

" Your arrival here, without waiting my visit at your house to-day, looks well, sir," said Albert. " Tell me, may I shake hands with you ? saying, ' Beauchamp, acknowledge you have injured me, and retain my friendship,' or must I simply propose to you a choice of arms ?"

" Albert," said Beauchamp, with a look of sorrow which stupefied the young man, " let us first sit down and talk."

" Rather, sir, before we sit down, I must demand your answer."

" Albert," said the journalist, " there are questions which it is difficult to answer."

" I will repeat the question, ' Will you, or will you not retract ?' "

" Morcerf, it is not enough to answer Yes or No to questions which concern the honour, the social interest, and the life of such a man as the lieutenant-general Count de Morcerf, peer of France."

" What must then be done ?"

"What I have done, Albert. I reasoned thus: Money, time, and fatigue, are nothing compared with the reputation and interests of a whole family; probabilities will not suffice, only facts will justify a deadly combat with a friend : if I strike with the sword, or discharge the contents of a pistol at a man with whom, for three years, I have been on terms of intimacy, I must, at least, know why I do so ; I must meet him with a heart at ease, and that quiet conscience which a man needs when his own arm must save his life."

" Well," asked Morcerf, impatiently, " what does all this mean ?"

" It means that I have just returned from Yanina. Here is my passport ; examine the *visa*,—Geneva, Milan, Venice, Trieste, Delvino, Yanina. Will you believe the government of a re-public, a kingdom, and an empire ?"

Albert cast his eyes on the passport, then raised them in astonishment to Beauchamp.

" Albert, had you been a stranger, a foreigner, I should not have taken this trouble; but I thought this mark of consideration due to you. I took a week to go, another to return, four days of quarantine, and forty-eight hours to stay there ; that makes three weeks. I returned last night ; and here I am."

" How long you are before you tell me what I most wish to know !"

" My friend," said Beauchamp, in the most affectionate tone, " I should gladly make an apology;—but alas ! The paragraph was correct. The traitor who surrendered the castle——"

" Was ?"

" Your father !"

A lbert advanced furiously towards Beauchamp ; but the latter rest rained him more by a mild look than by his extended hand.

" Here is a proof of it."

Albert opened the paper ; it was an attestation of four notable inhabitants of Yanina, proving that Colonel Fernand Mondego, in the service of Ali Tebelen, had surrendered the castle for two million crowns. The signatures were perfectly legal. Albert tottered and fell overpowered in a chair. It could no longer be doubted ; the family name was fully given. After a moment's mournful silence, his heart overflowed, and he gave way to a flood of tears.

Beauchamp, who had watched with sincere pity his paroxysm of grief, approached him.

" Now, Albert," said he, " you understand me ?—Do you not ? I wished to see all, and to judge of every thing for myself, hoping the explanation would be in your father's favour, and that I might do him justice. But, on the contrary, the particulars which are given prove that Fernand Mondego, raised by Ali Pacha to the rank of governor-general, is no other than Count Fernand de Morcerf ; so I saw nothing for it but to come straight to you and tell you frankly."

Albert, still extended on the chair, covered his face with both hands.

" I hastened to you," continued Beauchamp, " to tell you, Albert, in this changing age, the faults of a father cannot revert upon his children. Few have passed through this revolutionary period, in the midst of which we were born, without some stain of infamy or blood to soil the uniform of the soldier, the gown, or statesman. Now I have these proofs, Albert, and I am in your confidence, no human power can force me to a duel which your own conscience would reproach you with as criminal, but I come to offer you what you can no longer demand of me.

Do you wish these proofs, these attestations, which I alone possess, to be destroyed? Do you wish this frightful secret to remain with us? Confided to me, it shall never escape my lips; say, Albert, my friend, do you wish it?"

Albert raised his head.

"Ah! noble fellow!" cried he.

"Take these," said Beauchamp, presenting the papers.

Albert seized them with a convulsive hand, tore them in pieces; and, trembling lest the least vestige should escape, he approached the waxlight, always kept burning for cigars, and consumed every fragment.

"Let all be forgotten as a sorrowful dream," said Beauchamp; "let it vanish as the last sparks from the blackened paper, and disappear as the smoke from those silent ashes."

"Yes, yes," said Albert, "and may there remain only the eternal friendship which I promise you, which shall be transmitted to our children's children, and shall always remind me that I owe my life and the honour of my name, to you; for had this been known, oh! Beauchamp, I should have destroyed myself; or,—no, my poor mother! I could not have killed her by the same blow,—I should have fled from my country."

"Dear Albert!" said Beauchamp.

But this sudden and factitious joy soon forsook the young man, and was succeeded by still greater grief.

"Well," said Beauchamp, "what still oppresses you, my friend?"

"I am broken-hearted," said Albert. "Listen, Beauchamp! I cannot thus, in a moment, relinquish the respect, the confidence, and pride with which a father's untarnished name inspires a son. Oh! Beauchamp! Beauchamp! how shall I now approach mine! Shall I withhold my hand from his? I am the most wretched of men. Ah! my mother, my poor mother!" said Albert, gazing through his tears at his mother's portrait; "if you know this, how much must you suffer?"

"Come," said Beauchamp, taking both his hands, "take courage, my friend."

"But how came that first note to be inserted in your journal? Some unknown enemy has done this."

"The more must you fortify yourself, Albert. Let no trace of emotion be visible on your face. Go, my friend, reserve your strength for the moment when the crash shall come."

"You think, then, all is not over yet?" said Albert, horror-stricken.

"I think nothing, my friend; but all things are possible. Are you going to marry Mademoiselle Danglars?"

"No," said Albert; "the engagement is broken off."

"Well!" said Beauchamp. Then seeing the young man was about to relapse into melancholy, "Let us go out, Albert," said he; "a ride in the wood will refresh you; we will then return to breakfast, and you shall attend to your affairs, and I to mine."

"Willingly," said Albert; "but let us walk: I think a little exertion would do me good."

A week later there appeared in another paper the following paragraph:

"The French officer in the service of Ali, pacha of Yanina, alluded to three weeks since in the 'Impartial,' who not only surrendered the castle of Yanina but sold his benefactor to the Turks, styled himself truly at that time Fernand, as our honourable brother states; but he has since added to his Christian name a title of nobility and a family name. He now calls himself the Count of Morcerf, and ranks among the peers."

Thus this terrible secret, which Beauchamp had so generously destroyed, had appeared again; and another paper, cruelly informed, had published it broadcast. The same day, a great agitation was manifest in the House of Peers among the usually calm groups of the noble assembly. Every one had arrived before the usual hour, and was conversing on the melancholy event which was to concentrate their attention on one of their most illustrious members.

Some were perusing the article, others making comments, and recalling circumstances which substantiated the charges still more. The count was no favourite with his colleagues. Like all upstarts he had had recourse to a great deal of haughtiness to maintain his position. The true nobility laughed at him, the talented repelled him, and the honourable instinctively despised him.

The Count de Morcerf alone was ignorant of the news. He did not take in the paper in which it appeared, and had passed the morning in writing letters and in trying a horse. He arrived at the House of Peers at his usual hour, with a proud look and insolent demeanour; he alighted, passed through the corridors, and entered the house without observing the hesitation of the door-keepers or the coolness of his colleagues. Business had already been begun for half an hour when he entered.

Every one held the accusing paper, but, as usual, no one liked to take upon himself the responsibility of the attack. At length an honourable peer, Morcerf's acknowledged enemy, ascended the tribune with that solemnity which announced the expected moment had arrived.

There was an imposing silence; Morcerf alone knew not why such profound attention was given to an orator who was not always listened to with so much complacency. The count did not notice the introduction, in which the speaker announced that his communication would be of such vital importance that it demanded the undivided attention of the house; but, at the names Yanina and Colonel Fernand, he turned so awfully pale, that every member shuddered and fixed his eyes upon him. Moral wounds have this peculiarity, they conceal themselves but never close; always painful, always ready to bleed when touched, they remain fresh and open in the heart.

The article having been read during a painful silence, was only disturbed by a universal shudder. The orator stated his scruples and the difficulties of the case: it was the honour of M. de Morcerf, and that of the whole house, he proposed to defend, by provoking a debate on those personal questions always so warmly agitated. He concluded by calling for an examination, which might confound the calumnious report before it had time to spread, and to restore M. de Morcerf to the position he had long held in public opinion.

Morcerf was so completely overwhelmed by this enormous and unexpected calamity that he could scarcely stammer a few words as he looked round on the assembly. This timidity, which might proceed from the astonishment of innocence as well as the shame of guilt conciliated some in his favour; for men who are truly generous are always ready to be compassionate when the misfortune of their enemy surpasses the limits of their hatred.

The president put it to the vote, and it was decided the examination should take place. The count was asked what time he required to prepare his defence. Morcerf's courage had revived when he found himself alive after this horrible blow.

"My lords," answered he, "it is not by time I could repel the attack made on me by enemies unknown to me, and, doubtless, hidden in obscurity; it is immediately, and by a thunderbolt, I must repel the flash of lightning which for a moment, startled me.   Oh ! that I could instead of taking up this defence, shed my last drop of blood to prove to my noble colleagues that I am their equal in worth."

These words made a favourable impression on behalf of the accused.

" I demand, then, that the examination should take place as soon as possible, and I will furnish the house with all necessary information."

" What day do you fix ?" asked the president.

" To-day I am at your service," replied the count.

The president rang the bell.

" Does the house approve that the examination should take place to-day ?"

" Yes !" was the unanimous answer.

A committee of twelve members was chosen to examine the proofs brought forward by Morcerf.   The examination would commence at eight o'clock that evening in the committee-room, and, if it were necessary to postpone it, it would be resumed each evening at the same hour.   Morcerf asked leave to retire ; he had to collect the documents he had long been preparing against this storm, which his sagacity had foreseen.

At eight o'clock all were in their places, and M. de Morcerf entered at the last stroke.   He held some papers in his hand ; his countenance was calm and step firm, his dress particularly nice, and according to the ancient military costume, buttoned completely up to the chin.

" You are at liberty to speak, M. de Morcerf," said the president, as he unsealed the letter ; and the count began his defence, in a most eloquent and skilful manner.   He produced documents, proving that the vizier of Yanina had, to the last moment, honoured him with his entire confidence, since he had intrusted him with a negotiation of life and death with the emperor.   He produced the ring, his mark of authority, with which Ali Pacha generally sealed his letters, and which the latter had given him that he might, on his return at any hour of the day or night, or even in his harem, gain access to him.   Unfortunately, the negotiation failed, and when he returned to defend his benefactor, he was dead.   " But," said the count, "so great was Ali Pacha's confidence, that, on his death-bed, he resigned his wife and daughter to my care."

" Have you any idea what is become of them ?"

" Alas! no, sir," replied the count, " all those who surrounded the vizier, or who knew me at his court, are either dead or scattered; alone, I believe, of all my countrymen, I survived that dreadful war; I have only the letters of Ali Tebelen, which I have placed before you; the ring, a token of his good-will, which is here; and lastly, the most convincing proof I can offer, namely, the absence of all witness against my veracity and the purity of my military life."

A murmur of approbation ran through the assembly. It only remained to put it to the vote, when the president resumed :—

"Gentlemen, and you, M. le Comte, you will not be displeased, I presume, to listen to one who calls himself a very important witness, and who has just presented himself. He is, doubtless, come to prove the perfect innocence of our colleague. Here is a letter I have just received on the subject; shall it be read, or shall it be passed over ?"

" Mr. President,—I can furnish the committee of inquiry into the conduct of the Lieutenant-General Count de Morcerf in Epirus and in Macedonia with important particulars.

" I was on the spot at the death of Ali Pacha; I was present during his last moments; I know what is become of Vasiliki and Haydée: I am at the command of the committee, and claim the honour of being heard. I shall be in the lobby when this note is delivered to you."

The President called to the door-keeper to admit the visitor: all eyes were fixed on the door. To the astonishment of all behind the door-keeper walked a woman enveloped in a large veil, which completely concealed her. It was evident that she was young and elegant, but that was all. The president requested her to throw aside her veil, and it was then seen she was dressed in the Grecian costume, and was remarkably beautiful."

M. de Morcerf looked at her with surprise and terror.

" Madame," said the president when the flutter caused by this unexpected apparition had subsided, " you have engaged to furnish the committee with some important particulars respecting the affair at Yanina, and you have stated that you were an eyewitness of the events."

" I was indeed !" said the stranger with a tone of sweet melancholy, and with the sonorous voice peculiar to the East.

" But allow me to say, you must have been very young then."

"I was four years old; but as those events deeply concerned me, not a single particular has escaped my memory."

"In what manner could those events concern you? And who are you, that they should have made so deep an impression on you?"

"On them depended my father's life," replied she. "I am Haydée, the daughter of Ali Tebelen, pacha of Yanina, and of Vasiliki, his beloved wife."

The blush of mingled pride and modesty which suddenly suffused the cheeks of the young girl, the brilliancy of her eye, and her highly important communication, produced an inexpressible effect on the assembly. As for the count, he could not have been more overwhelmed if a thunderbolt had fallen at his feet.

"Madame," replied the president, bowing with profound respect, "allow me to ask one question, it shall be the last: Can you prove the authenticity of what you have now stated?"

"I can sir," said Haydée, drawing from under her veil a satin satchel highly perfumed; "for here is the register of my birth, signed by my father and his principal officers; and that of my baptism, my father having consented to my being brought up in my mother's faith; the latter has been sealed by the grand primate of Macedonia and Epirus; and lastly I have (and perhaps the most important), the record of the sale of my person and that of my mother to the Armenian merchant, El-Kobbir, by the French officer, who, in his infamous bargain with the Porte, had reserved for his part of the booty, the wife and daughter of his benefactor, whom he sold for the sum of four hundred thousand francs."

A greenish paleness spread over the count's cheeks and his eyes became blood-shot, at these terrible imputations, which were listened to by the assembly with an ominous silence.

A dreadful stillness succeeded the reading of the paper she handed over; the count could only look, and his gaze, fixed as if unconsciously on Haydée, seemed one of fire and blood.

"Madame," said the president, when he had scanned the papers, "I see the name of the Count of Monte-Cristo mentioned as your present guardian, may reference be made to the Count, who is now, I believe, in Paris?"

"Sir," replied Haydée, "the Count of Monte-Cristo, my other father, has been in Normandy the last three days."

"Who, then, has counselled you to take this step, one for

which the court is deeply indebted to you, and which is perfectly natural, considering your birth and your misfortunes ?"

" Sir," said Haydée, " I have been led to take this step from a feeling of respect and grief. Although a Christian, may God forgive me ! I have always sought to revenge my illustrious father. Since I set my foot in France, and knew the traitor lived in Paris, I have watched carefully. I live retired in the house of my noble protector, but I do it from choice ; I love retirement and silence, because I can live with my thoughts and recollections of past days. But M. le Comte de Monte-Cristo surrounds me with every paternal care, and I am ignorant of nothing which passes in the world."

" Then," remarked the president, " the Count of Monte-Cristo knows nothing of your present proceedings ?"

" He is quite unaware of them, and I have but one fear, which is, that he should disapprove of what I have done : but it is a glorious day for me," continued the young girl, raising her ardent gaze to heaven, " that on which I find at last an opportunity of revenging my father."

The count had not uttered one word the whole of this time ; his colleagues looked at him, and, doubtless, pitied his blighted prospects which sank under the breath of a woman ; his misery was depicted by sinister lines on his countenance.

" M. de Morcerf," said the president, " do you recognise this lady as the daughter of Ali Tebelen, pacha of Yanina ?"

" No," said Morcerf, attempting to rise, " it is a base plot, contrived by my enemies."

Haydée, whose eyes had been fixed upon the door as if expecting some one, turned hastily, and seeing the count standing, shrieked.

" You do not know me ?" said she ; " well, I fortunately recognise you ! You are Fernand Mondego, the French officer who led the troops of my noble father. It is you who surrendered the castle of Yanina ! It is you who, sent by him to Constantinople, to treat with the emperor for the life or death of your benefactor, brought back a false mandate granting full pardon ! It is you, who, with that mandate, obtained the pacha s ring, which gave you authority over Selim, the fire-keeper : It is you who stabbed Selim ! It is you who sold us, my mother and me, to the merchant, El-Kobbir ! Assassin ! assassin ! assassin ! you have still on your brow your master's blood ! Look, gentlemen, all !"

These words had been pronounced with such enthusiasm and evident truth, that every eye was fixed on the count's forehead, and he himself passed his hand across it, as if he felt Ali's blood still moist upon it.

" M. le Comte de Morcerf," said the president, " do not allow yourself to be depressed ; answer : the justice of the court is supreme and impartial as that of God ; it will not suffer you to be trampled on by your enemies without giving you an opportunity of defending yourself. Shall further inquiries be made ? Shall two members of the house be sent to Yanina ? Speak !"

" I have no reply to make," said the count in a low tone.

" Has the daughter of Ali Tebelen spoken the truth ?" asked the president. " Is she then the terrible witness to whose charge you dare not plead ' Not guilty '? Have you really committed the crimes of which you are accused ?"

The count looked round him with an expression which might have softened tigers, but which could not disarm his judges. Then he raised his eyes towards the ceiling, but withdrew them immediately, as if he feared the roof would open and reveal to his distressed view that second tribunal called heaven, and that other judge named God. Then, with a hasty movement, he tore open his coat, which seemed to stifle him, and flew from the room like a madman ; his footstep was heard one moment in the corridor, then came the rattling of his carriage-wheels, as he was driven rapidly away.

" Gentlemen," said the president, when silence was restored, " is M. le Comte de Morcerf convicted of felony, treason, and outrage ?"

" Yes," replied all the members of the committee of inquiry with an unanimous voice.

CHAPTER XLI

At eight o'clock next morning Albert arrived at Beauchamp's door. The valet-de-chambre had received orders to introduce him into the room of his master who was just then bathing.

"You know well why I am here," cried Albert.

"My poor friend," replied Beauchamp, "I expected you."

"You know then all that has happened? I never for one moment have doubted your good faith, but without losing time, tell me, have you the slightest idea whence this terrible blow proceeds?"

"I think I have some clue."

"What is the name of the traitor?"

"Danglars."

"He!" cried Albert; "yes, it is indeed he who has so long pursued my father with jealous hatred. He, the man who would be popular, cannot forgive the Count of Morcerf for being created a peer; and this marriage which has been broken off has angered him,—yes, it is all from the same cause."

"Inquire, Albert, but do not be angry without reason,—inquire, and if it is true——"

"Oh! yes; if it is true," cried the young man, "he shall pay me all I have suffered."

"Beware, Morcerf, he is already an old man."

"I will respect his age as he has respected the honour of my family; if my father had offended him, why did he not attack him personally? Oh! no, he was afraid to encounter him face to face."

"I do not condemn you, Albert: I only restrain you. Act prudently."

"Oh! do not fear; besides you will accompany me. Beauchamp, solemn transactions should be sanctioned by a witness. Before this day closes, if M. Danglars is guilty, he shall cease to live or I will die. *Pardieu!* Beauchamp, mine shall be a splendid funeral."

"When such resolutions are made, Albert, they should be promptly executed.   Do you wish to go to M. Danglars?"

They sent for a carriage.

When they arrived at M. Danglars' house, the servant announced the young men; but the banker, recollecting what had transpired the day before, did not wish them to be admitted.   It was, however, too late; Albert had followed the footman, and hearing the order given, forced the door open; and, followed by Beauchamp, found himself in the banker's study.

"Sir," cried the latter, "am I no longer at liberty to receive whom I choose in my house?   You appear to forget yourself sadly."

"No, sir," said Albert, coldly; "there are circumstances in which one cannot, except through cowardice,—I offer you that refuge,—refuse to admit certain persons at least."

"What is your errand, then, with me, sir?"

"I mean," said Albert, approaching, "I mean to propose a meeting in some retired corner where no one will interrupt us for ten minutes, that will be sufficient; where two men having met, one of them will remain on the ground."

"Sir," replied Danglars, pale with anger and fear, "I warn you, when I have the misfortune to meet with a mad dog I kill it; and far from thinking myself guilty of a crime, I believe I do society a kindness.   Now, if you are mad, and try to bite me, I will kill you without pity.   Is it my fault that your father has dishonoured himself?"

"Yes, miserable wretch!" cried Morcerf, "it is your fault."

Danglars retreated a few steps.

"My fault!" said he; "you must be mad! What do I know of Grecian history?   Have I travelled in that country?   Did I advise your father to sell the castle of Yanina—to betray——"

"Silence!" said Albert, with a thundering voice.   "No, it is not you who have directly made this exposure and brought this sorrow on us, but you have hypocritically provoked it."

"I?"

"Yes, you!   How came it to be known?"

"I suppose you read it in the paper in the account from Yanina?"

"Who wrote to Yanina?"

"To Yanina?"

"Yes.   Who wrote for particulars concerning my father?"

" I imagine any one may write to Yanina."

" But one person only wrote !"

" One only ?"

" Yes ; and that was you !"

"I, doubtless, wrote. It appears to me that when one's daughter has been insulted by the coolness of a young man supposed to be betrothed to her, one has a right to make what inquiries one pleases ; it is not only a right but a duty."

" You wrote, sir, knowing what answer you would receive."

"I, indeed ! I assure you," cried Danglars, with a confidence and security proceeding less from fear than from the interest he really felt for the young man, " I solemnly declare to you that I should never have thought of writing to Yanina, had I known anything of Ali Pacha's misfortunes."

" Who then urged you to write ?   Tell me."

" It was the most simple thing in the world.   I was speaking of your father's past history.   I said the origin of his fortune remained obscure.   The person to whom I addressed my scruples asked me where your father had acquired his property ?   I answered, 'In Greece.'   'Then,' said he, 'write to Yanina.'"

" And who thus advised you ?"

" No other than your friend Monte-Cristo."

Albert and Beauchamp looked at each other.

" Sir," said Beauchamp, who had not yet spoken, " you accuse the count, who is absent from Paris at this moment, but will be, I hear, present at the opera to-night."

"I accuse no one, sir," said Danglars ; " I relate, and I will repeat before the count what I have said to you."

" Does the count know what answer you received ?"

" Yes, I showed it to him."

" Did he know my father's Christian name was Fernand, and his family name Mondego."

" Yes, I had told him that long since ; and I did nothing more than any other would have done in my circumstances, and perhaps less."

Albert felt the colour mounting to his brow ; there was no doubt upon the subject, Danglars defended himself with the baseness, but at the same time with the assurance, of a man who speaks the truth at least in part, if not wholly—not for conscience' sake, but through fear.   Besides, what was Morcerf seeking ?   It was not whether Danglars or Monte-Cristo was more or less guilty ; it was a man who would answer for the offence, whether trifling or serious; it was a man who would fight, and it was evident Danglars would not fight.

And, in addition to this, every thing forgotten or unperceived before presented itself now to his recollection. Monte-Cristo knew every thing, as he had bought the daughter of Ali Pacha; and, knowing every thing, he had advised Danglars to write to Yanina. The answer known, he had yielded to Albert's wish to be introduced to Haydée, had allowed the conversation to turn on the death of Ali, and had not opposed Haydée's recital but had, doubtless, warned the young girl, in the few Romaic words he spoke to her, not to mention the name of Morcerf's father. Besides, had he not begged of Morcerf not to mention his father's name before Haydée? There could be no doubt that all had been calculated and previously arranged; Monte-Cristo then was in league with his father's enemies.

Albert took Beauchamp aside, and communicated these ideas to him.

"You are right," said the latter; "M. Danglars has only been a secondary agent in this sad affair; and it is of M. de Monte-Cristo that you must demand an explanation."

Albert turned.

"Sir," said he to Danglars, "understand that I do not take a final leave of you; I must ascertain if your insinuations are just, and am going now to inquire of the Count of Monte-Cristo." He bowed to the banker, and went out with Beauchamp. Danglars accompanied him to the door, where he again assured Albert no motive of personal hatred influenced him against the Count de Morcerf.

On his return home, Albert expressed his wish to Franz, Debray, and Morrel, to see them at the Opera that evening. Then he went to his mother, who, since the events of the day before, had refused to see any one, and had kept her room. He found her in bed, overwhelmed with grief at this public humiliation. The sight of Albert produced the effect which might naturally be expected on Mercédès; she pressed her son's hand and sobbed aloud; but her tears relieved her. Albert stood one moment speechless by the side of his mother's bed. It was evident, from his pale face and knit brows, that his resolution to revenge himself was growing weaker.

"My dear mother," said he, "do you know if M. de Morcerf has any enemy?"

Mercédès started; she noticed that the young man did not say my father.

"My son," she said, "persons in the count's situation have many secret enemies. Those who are known are not the most dangerous."

"I know it, and appeal to your penetration. Nothing escapes you."

"Why do you say so?"

"Because for instance, you noticed, on the evening of the ball we gave, M. de Monte-Cristo would eat nothing in our house."

Mercédès raised herself on her feverish arm.

"M. de Monte-Cristo!" she exclaimed; "and how is he connected with the question you asked me?"

"You know, my mother, M. de Monte-Cristo is almost an Oriental, and it is customary with Orientals to secure full liberty of revenge by not eating or drinking in the house of their enemies."

"Do you say M. de Monte-Cristo is our enemy?" replied Mercédès, becoming paler than the sheet which covered her. "Who told you so? Why, you are mad, Albert: M. de Monte-Cristo has only shown us kindness. M. de Monte-Cristo saved your life; you yourself presented him to us. Oh! I entreat you, my son, if you have entertained such an idea, dispel it; and my counsel to you—even more, my prayer, is, retain his friendship."

"My mother," replied the young man, "you have special reasons for telling me to conciliate that man."

"I!" said Mercédès, blushing as rapidly as she had turned pale, and again becoming paler than ever.

"Yes, doubtless; and is it not because he can never do us any harm?"

Mercédès shuddered, and, fixing on her son a scrutinising gaze,—

"You speak strangely," said she to Albert, "and you appear to have some singular prejudices. What has the count done?"

An ironical smile passed over Albert's lips. Mercédès saw it, and, with her double instinct of a woman and a mother, she guessed all, but prudent and strong-minded, she concealed both her sorrows and fears.

Albert was silent; an instant after the countess resumed. "You came to inquire after my health; I will candidly acknowledge I am not well. You should stay here and cheer my solitude. I do not wish to be left alone."

"My mother," said the young man, "you know how gladly I would obey your wish; but an urgent and important affair obliges me to leave you the whole evening."

"Well!" replied Mercédès, sighing; "go, Albert, I will not make you a slave to your filial piety."

Albert pretended he did not hear, bowed to his mother, and quitted her.

Scarcely had he shut her door than Mercédès called a confidential servant, and ordered him to follow Albert wherever he should go that evening, and to come and tell her immediately what he observed. Then she rang for her lady's maid, and, weak as she was, she dressed in order to be ready for whatever might happen.

The footman's mission was an easy one. Albert went to his room, and dressed with unusual care. At ten minutes to eight Beauchamp arrived; he had seen Château-Renaud, who had promised to be in the orchestra before the curtain was raised.

Both got into Albert's coupé, who, having no reason to conceal where he was going, he called aloud, "To the Opera!"

In his impatience, he arrived before the commencement of the performance.

Château-Renaud was at his post: apprised by Beauchamp of the circumstances, he required no explanation from Albert. The conduct of this son, seeking to avenge his father, was so natural, that Château-Renaud did not seek to dissuade him, and was content with renewing his assurances of friendship to Albert.

Debray was not yet come, but Albert knew he seldom lost a scene at the Opera. Albert wandered about the theatre until the curtain was drawn up. He hoped to meet with M. de Monte-Cristo either in the lobby or on the stairs. The bell summoned him to his seat, and he entered with Château-Renaud and Beauchamp. But his eyes scarcely quitted the box between the columns, which remained obstinately closed during the whole of the first act. At last, as Albert was looking at his watch about the hundredth time, at the commencement of the second act the door opened, and Monte-Cristo, dressed in black, entered, and leaning over the front of the box looked round the pit. Morrel followed him, and looked also for his sister and his brother-in-law; he soon discovered them in another box, and kissed his hand to them.

The count, in his survey of the pit, encountered a pale face and threatening eyes, which evidently sought to gain his attention. He recognised Albert, but thought it better not to notice him, as he looked so angry and discomposed. Without communicating his thoughts to his companion, he sat down, drew out his opera-glass, and looked another way. Although apparently not noticing Albert, he did not, however, lose sight of him; and when the curtain fell at the end of the second act, he saw him leave the orchestra with his two friends. Then his head was seen passing at the back of the boxes, and the count knew the approaching storm was intended to fall on him. He was at the moment conversing cheerfully with Morrel, but he was well prepared for what might happen. The door opened, and Monte-Cristo, turning round, saw Albert, pale and trembling, followed by Beauchamp and Château-Renaud.

"Well!" cried he, with that benevolent politeness which distinguished his salutation from the common civilities of the world, "Good-evening, M. de Morcerf."

His manner expressed the most perfect cordiality.

Morrel only then recollected the letter he had received from the viscount, in which, without assigning any reason, he begged him to go to the Opera, but he understood that something terrible was brooding.

"We are not come here, sir, to exchange hypocritical expressions of politeness or false professions of friendship," said Albert; "but to demand an explanation, count."

The trembling voice of the young man was scarcely audible.

"An explanation at the Opera?" said the count, with that calm tone and penetrating eye which characterises the man who knows his cause is good. "Little acquainted as I am with the habits of Parisians, I should not have thought this the place for such a demand."

"Still, if people will shut themselves up," said Albert, "and cannot be seen because they are bathing, dining, or asleep, we must avail ourselves of the opportunity whenever they are to be seen."

"I am not difficult of access, sir; for a few days ago, if my memory does not deceive me, you were at my house."

"I was at your house, sir," said the young man; "because then I knew not who you were."

In pronouncing these words Albert had raised his voice so as to be heard by those in the adjoining boxes and in the lobby. Thus the attention of many was attracted by this altercation.

"Where are you come from, sir? You do not appear to be in possession of your senses."

"Provided I understand your perfidy, sir, and succeed in making you understand that I will be revenged, I shall be reasonable enough," said Albert, furiously.

"I do not understand you, sir," replied Monte-Cristo; "and if I did, your tone is too high. I am at home here, and I alone have a right to raise my voice above another's. Leave the box, sir!" Monte-Cristo pointed towards the door with the most commanding dignity.

"Ah! I shall know how to make you leave your home!" replied Albert, clasping in his convulsed grasp his glove, which Monte-Cristo did not lose sight of.

"Well, well!" said Monte-Cristo, quietly, "I see you wish to quarrel with me; but I would give you one counsel, and do not forget it: it is a bad habit to make a display of a challenge. Display is not becoming to every one, M. de Morcerf."

At this name a murmur of astonishment passed round the group of spectators of this scene. They had talked of no one but Morcerf the whole day.

Albert understood the allusion in a moment, and was about to throw his glove at the count, when Morrel seized his hand, while Beauchamp and Château-Renaud, fearing the scene would surpass the limits of a challenge, held him back.

But Monte-Cristo, without rising, and leaning forward in his chair, merely extended his hand, and, taking the damp, crushed glove from the clenched hand of the young man,—

"Sir," said he, in a solemn tone, "I consider your glove thrown, and will return it you round a bullet. Now leave me, or I will summon my servants to throw you out at the door."

Wild, almost unconscious, and with eyes inflamed, Albert stepped back, and Morrel closed the door. Monte-Cristo took up his glass again as if nothing had happened: he certainly had a heart of brass and face of marble.

Morrel whispered, "What have you done to him?"

"I? nothing—at least personally," said Monte-Cristo.

"But there must be some cause for this strange scene."

"The Count de Morcerf's adventure exasperates the young man."

"Have you anything to do with it?"

"It was by Haydée the House was informed of his father's treason."

"Indeed!" said Morrel.   "I had been told, but would not credit it, that the Grecian slave I have seen with you here in this very box was the daughter of Ali Pacha."

"It is, notwithstanding, true."

"Then," said Morrel, "I understand it all, and this scene was premeditated."

"How so?"

"Yes.   Albert wrote to request me to come to the Opera, doubtless that I might be a witness of the insult he meant to offer you."

"Probably," said Monte-Cristo, with his imperturbable tranquillity.

"But what will you do with him?"

"With whom?"

"With Albert."

"What will I do with Albert?   As certainly, Maximilian, as I now press your hand, I will kill him before ten o'clock to-morrow morning."

Morrel in his turn took Monte-Cristo's hand in both of his, and he shuddered to feel how cold and steady it was.

"Ah! count," said he, "his father loves him so much!"

"Do not speak to me of that!" said Monte-Cristo, with the first movement of anger he had betrayed; "I will make him suffer."

Morrel, amazed, let fall Monte-Cristo's hand.

"Count! count!" said he.

"Dear Maximilian," interrupted the count; "listen how adorably Duprez is singing that line,—

"'O Mathilde! idole de mon âme!'

I was the first to discover Duprez at Naples, and the first to applaud him.   'Bravo! bravo!'"

Morrel saw it was useless to say more, and refrained.

The curtain, which had been drawn up during the scene with Albert, again fell, and a rap was heard at the door.

"Come in!" said Monte-Cristo, without his voice betraying the least emotion; and immediately Beauchamp appeared.

"Good-evening, M. Beauchamp," said Monte-Cristo, as if this was the first time he had seen the journalist that evening; "take a seat."

Beauchamp bowed, and sitting down,—

"Sir," said he, "I just now accompanied M. de Morcerf, as you saw."

"And that means," replied Monte-Cristo, laughing, "that you had probably just dined together. I am happy to see, M. Beauchamp, you are more sober than he was."

"Sir," said Beauchamp, "Albert was wrong, I acknowledge, to betray so much anger, and I come, on my own account, to apologise for him. And having done so, on my own account only you understand, M. le Comte, I would add that I believe you too gentlemanly to refuse giving him some explanation concerning your connexion with Yanina. Then I will add two words about the young Greek girl."

Monte-Cristo motioned to him to be silent.

"Come," said he, laughing, "there are all my hopes about to be destroyed."

"How so?" asked Beauchamp.

"Doubtless you wish to make me appear a very eccentric character; I am, in your opinion, a Lara, a Manfred, a Lord Ruthven: then, just as I am arriving at the climax, you defeat your own end, and seek to make a common man of me. You bring me down to your own level, and demand explanations! Indeed, M. Beauchamp, it is quite laughable."

"Yet," replied Beauchamp, haughtily, "there are occasions when probity commands——"

"M. Beauchamp," interrupted this strange man, "the Count of Monte-Cristo bows to none but the Count of Monte-Cristo himself. Say no more, I entreat you. I do what I please, M. Beauchamp, and it is always well done."

"Sir," replied the young man, "honest men are not to be paid with such coin. I require honourable guarantees."

"I am, sir, a living guarantee," replied Monte-Cristo, motionless, but with a threatening look ; "we have both blood in our veins which we wish to shed—that is our mutual guarantee. Tell the viscount so, and that to-morrow, before ten o'clock, I shall see what colour his is."

"Then I have only to make arrangements for the duel," said Beauchamp.

"It is quite immaterial to me," said Monte-Cristo, "and it was very unnecessary to disturb me at the Opera for such a trifle. In France people fight with the sword or pistol, in the colonies with the carbine, in Arabia with the dagger. Tell your client, that although I am the insulted party, in order to carry out my eccentricity, I leave him the choice of arms, and will accept without discussion, without dispute, any thing, even combat by drawing lots, which is always stupid, but with me different from other people, as I am sure to gain."

"Sure to gain!" repeated Beauchamp, looking with amazement at the count.

"Certainly," said Monte-Cristo, slightly shrugging up his shoulders, "otherwise I would not fight with M. de Morcerf. I shall kill him—I cannot help it. Only by a single line this evening at my house let me know the arms and the hour: I do not like to be kept waiting."

"Pistols, then, at eight o'clock, in the Bois de Vincennes," said Beauchamp, quite disconcerted, not knowing if he was dealing with an arrogant braggadocio or a supernatural being.

"Very well, sir," said Monte-Cristo. "Now all that is settled, do let me see the performance, and tell your friend Albert not to come any more this evening; he will hurt himself with all his ill-chosen barbarisms: let him go home and go to sleep."

Beauchamp left the box, perfectly amazed.

"Now," said Monte-Cristo, turning towards Morrel, "I may depend upon you, may I not?"

"Certainly," said Morrel, "I am at your service, count; still——"

"What?"

"It is desirable I should know the real cause."

"That is to say, you would rather not?"

"No."

"The young man himself is acting blindfolded, and knows not the true cause, which is known only to God and to me; but I give you my word, Morrel, that God who does know it will be on our side."

"Enough," said Morrel; "who is your second witness?"

"I know no one in Paris, Morrel, on whom I would confer that honour besides you and your brother Emmanuel. Do you think Emmanuel would oblige me?"

"I will answer for him, count."

"Well, that is all I require. To-morrow morning, at seven o'clock, you will be with me, will you not?"

"We will."

"Hush! the curtain is rising. Listen! I never lose a note of this opera if I can avoid it; the music of 'William Tell' is so sweet!"

CHAPTER XLII

THE NIGHT

M. DE MONTE-CRISTO waited, according to his usual custom, until Duprez had sung his famous " Suivez moi ;" then he rose, and went out.

Morrel took leave of him at the door, renewing his promise to be with him the next morning at seven o'clock and to bring Emmanuel with him.

Then he stepped into his *coupé*, calm and smiling, and was at home in five minutes. No one who knew the count could mistake his expression, when, on entering, he said,—

" Ali, bring me my pistols with an ivory cross."

Ali brought the box to his master, who examined his arms with a solicitude very natural to a man who is about to entrust his life to a little powder and shot.

These were particular pistols, which Monte-Cristo had had made to shoot at a target in his room. A cap was sufficient to drive out the ball, and from the adjoining room no one would have suspected the count was, as sportsmen would say, keeping his hand in. He was just taking one in his hand, and looking for the point to aim at, on a little iron plate, which served him as a target, when his cabinet door opened, and Baptistin entered.

Before he had spoken a word the count perceived in the next room a veiled woman, who had followed closely after Baptistin, and now seeing the count with a pistol in his hand and swords on the table, she rushed in.

Baptistin looked at his master, who made a sign to him, and he went out, closing the door after him.

" Who are you, madame ?" asked the count.

The stranger cast one look around her, to be certain they were quite alone, then bending, as if she would have knelt, and joining her hands, she said, with an accent of despair,—

" Edmond, you will not kill my son ?"

The count retreated a step, uttered a slight exclamation, and let fall the pistol he held.

352

"EDMUND, YOU WILL NOT KILL MY SON?"
Page 352.

" What name did you pronounce then, Madame de Morcerf?"
said he.

" Yours !" cried she, throwing back her veil,—" yours, which I
alone, perhaps, have not forgotten. Edmond, it is not Madame
de Morcerf who has come to you, it is Mercédès."

" Mercédès is dead," said Monte-Cristo ; " I know no one now
of that name."

" Mercédès lives, sir, and she remembers, for she alone
recognised you when she saw you, and even before she saw you,
by your voice, Edmond,—by the simple sound of your voice ;
and from that moment she has followed your steps, watched you,
feared you, and she needs not to enquire what hand has dealt the
blow which now strikes M. de Morcerf."

" Fernand do you mean?" replied Monte-Cristo, with bitter
irony ; " since we are recalling names, let us remember them all."

Monte-Cristo had pronounced the name of Fernand with such
an expression of hatred, that Mercédès felt a thrill of terror run
through every vein.

" You see, Edmond, I am not mistaken, and have cause to say,
' Spare my son !' "

" And who told you I have any hostile intentions against
your son ?"

" No one, in truth ; but a mother has a twofold sight. I
guessed all ; I followed him this evening to the Opera, and have
seen all."

" If you have seen all, madame, you know that the son of
Fernand has publicly insulted me," said Monte-Cristo, with awful
calmness.

" Oh for pity's sake !"

" You have seen that he would have thrown his glove in my
face if Morrel, one of my friends, had not stopped him."

" Listen to me: my son has also guessed who you are ; he
attributes his father's misfortunes to you."

" You are mistaken, they are not misfortunes,—it is a punishment. It is not I who strike M. de Morcerf ; it is Providence
which punishes him."

" And why do you represent Providence ?" cried Mercédès.
" Why do you remember when it forgets ? What are Yanina and
its vizier to you, Edmond ? What injury has Fernand Mondego
done you in betraying Ali Tebelen ?"

" And," replied Monte-Cristo, " all this is an affair between
the French captain and the daughter of Vasiliki. It does not

23

concern me, you are right; and if I have sworn to revenge myself, it is not on the French captain, nor on the Count de Morcerf, but on the fisherman Fernand, the husband of the Catalan Mercédès."

" Ah ! sir," cried the countess, " how terrible a vengeance for a fault which fatality made me commit ! for I am the only culprit, Edmond ; and if you owe revenge to anyone, it is to me, who had not fortitude to bear your absence and my solitude."

" But," exclaimed Monte-Cristo, " why was I absent? And why were you alone ?"

" Because you had been arrested, Edmond, and were a prisoner."

" And why was I arrested ? Why was I a prisoner ?"

" I do not know," said Mercédès.

" You do not; at least I hope not. But I will tell you. I was arrested and became a prisoner, because under the arbour of La Réserve, the day before I was to marry you, a man named Danglars wrote this letter which the fisherman Fernand himself posted."

Monte-Cristo went to a secrétaire, opened a drawer by a spring, from which he took a paper which had lost its original colour, and the ink of which had become a rusty hue : this he placed in the hands of Mercédès. It was Danglars' letter to the procureur du roi, which the Count of Monte-Cristo, disguised as a clerk from the house of Thomson and French, had taken from the bundle of Edmond Dantès, on the day he had paid the two hundred thousand francs to M. de Boville. Mercédès read with terror the following lines :—

" The procureur du roi is informed by a friend of the throne, and religion, that one, Edmond Dantès, mate of the ship, Pharaon, arrived this morning from Smyrna, after having touched at Naples and Porto-Ferrajo, has been entrusted by Murat with a letter for the usurper, and by the usurper with a letter for the Bonapartist committee in Paris.

" Proof of this crime will be found on arresting him, for the letter will be upon him or at his father's, or in his cabin on board the Pharaon."

" How dreadful !" said Mercédès, passing her hand across her brow moist with perspiration ; " and that letter——"

" I bought it for two hundred thousand francs," said Monte-

Cristo; " but that is a trifle, since it enables me to justify myself to you."

" And the result of that letter——"

" You well know that the result was my arrest ; but you do not know how long that arrest lasted. You do not know that I remained for fourteen years within a quarter of a league of you, in a dungeon in the Château d'If. You do not know that each day of those fourteen years I renewed the vow of vengeance which I had made the first day ; and yet I knew not you had married Fernand, my calumniator, and that my father had died of hunger !"

" Can it be ?" cried Mercédès, shuddering.

"That is what I heard on leaving my prison, fourteen years after I had entered it, and that is why, on account of the living Mercédès and my deceased father, I have sworn to revenge myself on Fernand, and—I have revenged myself."

" And you are sure the unhappy Fernand did that ?"

" I am satisfied that he did what I have told you ; besides that is not much more odious than a Frenchman, by adoption, having passed over to the English ; a Spaniard by birth, having fought against the Spaniards ; a stipendiary of Ali, having betrayed and murdered Ali. Compared with such things, what is the letter you have just read ? A lover's deception, which the woman who has married that man ought certainly to forgive, but not so the lover who was to have married her. Well ! the French did not avenge themselves on the traitor ; the Spaniards did not shoot the traitor ; Ali, in his tomb, left the traitor unpunished ; but I, betrayed, sacrificed, buried, have risen from my tomb, by the grace of God, to punish that man. He sends me for that purpose, and here I am."

The poor woman's head and arms dropped ; her legs bent under her ; and she fell on her knees.

" Forgive, Edmond, forgive for my sake, who love you still !"

Her forehead almost touched the carpet, when the count sprang forward and raised her. Then, seated on a chair, she looked at the manly countenance of Monte-Cristo, on which grief and hatred still impressed a threatening expression.

" Not crush that accursed race !" murmured he ; "abandon my purpose at the moment of its accomplishment ! Impossible, impossible !"

" Edmond," said the poor mother, who tried every means, " when I call you Edmond, why do you not call me Mercédès ?"

"Mercédès!" repeated Monte-Cristo: "Mercédès! Well! yes, you are right, that name has still its charms; and this is the first time for a long period that I have pronounced it so distinctly. O, Mercédès! I have uttered your name with the sigh of melancholy, with the groan of sorrow, with the last effort of despair; I have uttered it when frozen with cold, crouched on the straw in my dungeon; I have uttered it, consumed with heat, rolling on the stone floor of my prison. Mercédès, I must revenge myself, for I suffered fourteen years,—fourteen years I wept, I cursed; now I tell you, Mercédès, I must revenge myself!"

The count, fearing to yield to the entreaties of her he had so ardently loved, recalled his sufferings to the assistance of his hatred.

"Revenge yourself, then, Edmond," cried the poor mother; "but let your vengeance fall on the culprits; on him, on me, but not on my son!"

Monte-Cristo groaned, and thrust his hands through his hair.

"Edmond," continued Mercédès, with her arms extended towards him, "since I first knew you, I have adored your name, have respected your memory. Edmond, my friend, do not compel me to tarnish that noble and fine image reflected incessantly on the mirror of my heart. Edmond, if you knew all the prayers I have addressed to God for you while I thought you were living and since I have thought you must be dead! Yes, dead, alas! I thought your dead body was buried at the foot of some gloomy tower; I thought your corpse was precipitated to the bottom of one of those gulfs where gaolers roll their dead prisoners, and I wept! What could I do for you, Edmond, besides pray and weep? Listen; during ten years I dreamed each night the same dream. I had been told you had endeavoured to escape; that you had taken the place of another prisoner; that you had slipped into the winding-sheet of a dead body; that you had been precipitated alive from the top of the Château d'If; and the cry you uttered as you dashed upon the rocks first revealed to your gaolers that they were your murderers. Well! Edmond, I swear to you by the head of that son for whom I entreat your pity—during ten years I have seen every night men balancing something shapeless and unknown at the top of a rock; during ten years I have heard each night a terrible cry which has awoke me, shuddering and cold. And I, too, Edmond—oh! believe me—guilty as I was—oh! yes, I, too, have suffered much!"

"Have you felt your father die in your absence?" cried Monte-Cristo, again thrusting his hands in his hair; "have you seen the woman you loved giving her hand to your rival while you were perishing at the bottom of a dungeon?"

"No," interrupted Mercédès, "but I have seen him whom I loved on the point of murdering my son."

Mercédès pronounced these words with such deep anguish, with an accent of such intense despair, that Monte-Cristo could not restrain a sob. The lion was daunted; the avenger was conquered.

"What do you ask of me?" said he,—"your son's life? Well! he shall live!"

Mercédès uttered a cry which made the tears start from Monte-Cristo's eyes; but these tears disappeared almost instantaneously, for, doubtless, God had sent some angel to collect them; far more precious were they in his eyes than the richest pearls of Guzarat and of Ophir.

"Oh!" said she, seizing the count's hand, and raising it to her lips; "oh! thank you, thank you, Edmond! now you are exactly what I dreamt you were, such as I always loved you. Oh, now I may say so."

"So much the better," replied Monte-Cristo; "as that poor Edmond will not have long to be loved by you. Death is about to return to the tomb, the phantom to retire in darkness."

"What do you say, Edmond?"

"I say, since you command me, Mercédès, I must die."

"Die! and who told you so? who talks of dying? whence have you these ideas of death?"

"You do not suppose, that publicly outraged in the face of a whole theatre, in the presence of your friends and those of your son,—challenged by a boy, who will glory in my pardon as in a victory,—you do not suppose I can for one moment wish to live. What I most loved after you, Mercédès, was myself, my dignity, and that strength which rendered me superior to other men; that strength was my life. With one word you have crushed it, and I die."

"But the duel will not take place, Edmond, since you forgive?"

"It will take place," said Monte-Cristo, in a most solemn tone;

" but instead of your son's blood staining the ground, mine will flow."

Mercédès shrieked, and sprang towards Monte-Cristo, but suddenly stopping :—

" Edmond," said she ; " there is a God above us, since you live, since I have seen you again; I trust to Him from my heart. While waiting His assistance I trust to your word ; you have said my son should live, have you not ?"

" Yes, madam, he shall live," said Monte-Cristo, surprised that, without more emotion, Mercédès had accepted the heroic sacrifice he made for her.

Mercédès extended her hand to the count.

" Edmond," said she, and her eyes were wet with tears, " how noble it is of you, how great the action you have just performed ; how sublime to have taken pity on a poor woman who came to you with every chance against her ! Alas ! I am grown old with grief more than with years, and cannot now remind my Edmond by a smile, or by a look, of that Mercédès whom he once spent so many hours in contemplating. Ah ! believe me, Edmond, I told you, I too had suffered much ; I repeat it, it is melancholy to pass one's life without having one joy to recall, without preserving a single hope; but all is not yet over. No ! it is not finished, I feel it by what remains in my heart. Oh ! I repeat it, Edmond ; what you have just done is beautiful,—it is grand, it is sublime."

" Do you say so now, Mercédès, and what would you say, if you knew the extent of the sacrifice I make to you ? But, no, no, you cannot imagine what I lose in sacrificing my life at this moment."

Mercédès looked at the count with an air which depicted at the same time her astonishment, her admiration, and her gratitude.

Monte-Cristo pressed his forehead on his burning hands, as if his brain could no longer bear alone the weight of its thoughts.

"Edmond," said Mercédès, " I have but one word more to say to you."

The count smiled bitterly.

" Edmond," continued she, " though my face is pale, my eyes are dull, my beauty is gone ; though I am, in short, no longer my former self, yet my heart is still the same. Adieu, then, Edmond ; I have nothing more to ask of heaven—I have seen you again—and have found you as noble and as great as formerly you were. Adieu, Edmond, adieu, and thank you."

The count did not answer. Mercédès opened the door of the cabinet and had disappeared before he had recovered from the painful and profound reverie into which his thwarted vengeance had plunged him. The clock of the Invalides struck one as the carriage which conveyed Madame de Morcerf rolled away on the pavement of the Champs Elysées, and made Monte-Cristo raise his head.

"What a fool I was," said he, "not to tear my heart out on the day when I resolved to revenge myself!"

CHAPTER XLIII

AFTER Mercédès had left Monte-Cristo, a gloomy shadow seemed to overspread every thing. Around him and within him the flight of thought appeared stopped; his energetic mind slumbered as does the body after extreme fatigue.

" What!" said he to himself, while the lamp and the wax lights were nearly burnt out, and the servants were waiting impatiently in the ante-room; " what! this edifice which I have been so long preparing,—which I have reared with so much care and toil, is to be crumbled by a single touch, a word, even a slight breath! Yes, this self, of whom I thought so much, of whom I was so proud, which appeared so worthless in the dungeons of the Château d'If, but which I had succeeded in making so great, will be but a lump of clay to-morrow. Alas! it is not the death of the body I regret; for is not that destruction of the vital principle the rest to which every thing is tending, to which every unhappy being aspires, the repose of matter after which I so long sighed and which I was seeking to attain by the painful process of starvation when Faria appeared in my dungeon? What is death for me but one step more towards repose? No, it is not existence, then, that I regret, but the ruin of my projects, so slowly carried out, so laboriously framed. Providence is now opposed to them when I thought it would be most propitious. It is not God's will they should be accomplished. This burden, almost as heavy as a world, which I had raised, and had thought to bear to the end, was too great for my strength, and I am compelled to lay it down in the middle of my career. Oh! shall I then again become a fatalist, whom fourteen years of despair and ten of hope had rendered a believer in Providence? and all this, all this, because my heart, which I thought dead, was only sleeping—because it has awakened and has beaten again, because I have yielded to the pain of the emotion excited in my breast by a woman's voice. Yet," continued the count, becoming each moment more absorbed in the anticipation of the dreadful sacrifice for the morrow, which Mercédès had accepted, " yet it is impossible that so noble-minded a woman should thus, through selfishness, consent to my death when in the prime of life and strength ; it is impossible she can carry to such a point maternal love, or rather delirium. There are virtues which become crimes by exaggeration. No, she must have conceived some pathetic scene ; she will come and throw herself between us, and what would be sublime here will there appear ridiculous."

The blush of pride mounted to the count's forehead as this thought passed through his mind.

" Ridiculous !" repeated he ; " and the ridicule will fall on me. I ridiculous ; no, I would rather die."

By thus exaggerating to his own mind the anticipated ill-fortune of the next day, he went on to exclaim :—

" Folly ! folly ! folly ! to carry generosity so far as to place myself as a mark for that young man to aim at. He will never believe my death was a suicide ; and yet it is important for the honour of my memory (and this, surely, is not vanity, but a justifiable pride), it is important the world should know that I have consented by my free will to stay my arm, already raised to strike, and that with that arm, so powerful against others, I have struck myself. It must be, it shall be."

Seizing a pen, he drew a paper from a secret drawer in his bureau, and traced at the bottom of that paper, which was no other than his will, made since his arrival in Paris, a sort of codicil, clearly explaining the nature of his death.

" I do this, O my God !" said he, with his eyes raised to heaven, " as much for thy honour as for mine. I have during ten years considered myself the agent of thy vengeance ; and other wretches, a Morcerf, a Danglars, a Villefort, must not imagine that chance has freed them from their enemy. Let them know, on the contrary, that their punishment which had been decreed by Providence is only delayed by my present determination, that although they escape it in this world, it awaits them in another, and that they are only exchanging time for eternity."

While he was thus agitated by these gloomy uncertainties, these wretched waking dreams of grief, the first rays of twilight pierced his windows, and shone upon the pale blue paper on which he had just traced his justification of Providence. It was five o'clock in the morning, when a slight noise reached his ear, which appeared like a stifled sigh ; he turned his head, looked round him, and saw no one ; but the sound was repeated distinctly enough to convince him of its reality. He arose, and quietly opening the door of the drawing-room, saw Haydée, who had fallen on a chair with her arms hanging down, and her beautiful head thrown back. She had been standing at the door to prevent his going out without seeing her, until sleep, which the young cannot resist, had overpowered her frame, wearied as she was with watching so long. The noise of the door did not awaken her, and Monte-Cristo gazed at her with affectionate regret.

" Mercédès remembered she had a son," said he ; "and I forgot I had a daughter." Then shaking his head sorrowfully, " Poor Haydée !" said he ; " she wished to speak to me, as she has feared or guessed something. Oh ! I cannot go without taking leave of her ; I cannot die without confiding her to some one." He quietly regained his seat, and wrote under the other lines,—

" I bequeath to Maximilian Morrel, captain, and son of my former employer, Pierre Morrel, shipowner at Marseilles, the sum of twenty millions, a part of which may be offered to his sister Julia and brother-in-law Emmanuel, if he does not fear this increase of fortune may mar their happiness. These twenty millions are concealed in my grotto at Monte-Cristo, of which Bertuccio knows the secret. If his heart is free, and he will marry Haydée, the daughter of Ali, pacha of Yanina, whom I have brought up with the love of a father, and who has shown the love and tenderness of a daughter for me, he will thus accomplish my last wish.

" This will has already constituted Haydée heiress of the rest of my fortune ; consisting in lands, rents on England, Austria, and Holland, furniture in my different palaces and houses, and which, without the twenty millions, and the legacies to my servants, may still amount to sixty millions."

As he was finishing, the sound of a cabriolet entering the yard was heard. Monte-Cristo approached the window, and saw Maximilian and Emmanuel alight.

" Good !" said he ; it was time, and he sealed his will with three seals. One moment afterwards he heard a noise in the drawing-room, and went to open the door himself. Morrel was there, he had come twenty minutes before the time appointed.

"I am, perhaps, come too soon, count," said he ; " but I frankly acknowledge, I have not closed my eyes all night, nor has any one in my house. I required to see you strong in your courageous assurance to recover myself."

Monte-Cristo could not resist this proof of affection, he extended his hand to the young man.

"Morrel," said he ; " it is a happy day for me, to feel I am beloved by such a man as you. Good morning, Emmanuel ; you will come with me then, Maximilian ?"

"I watched you during the whole scene of that challenge yesterday ; I have been thinking of your firmness all this night, and I said, Justice must be on your side, or man's countenance is no longer to be relied on."

"But, Morrel, Albert is your friend ?"

"A simple acquaintance, sir."

"You met on the same day you first saw me ?"

"Truly, but I should not have recollected it had you not reminded me."

"Thank you, Morrel."

"My friend," exclaimed Morrel, " I may say to you what I would not to another.   Remember Albert has a mother."

"You are right," said Monte-Cristo, " and I have none."

"Break his arm—wound him—but do not kill him."

"I will tell you, Morrel," said the count, " that I need no entreaty to spare the life of M. de Morcerf ; he shall be so well spared, that he will return quietly with his two friends, while I shall be brought home."

"No, no ;" cried Maximilian, not knowing how to contain himself.

"As I told you, my dear Morrel, M. de Morcerf will kill me."
Morrel looked at him in utter unconsciousness.

"But what has happened then, since last evening, count ?"

"The same thing which happened to Brutus the night before the battle of Philippi ; I have seen a phantom."

"And that phantom——"

"Told me, Morrel, I had lived long enough."

Maximilian and Emmanuel looked at each other.

Monte-Cristo drew out his watch.

"Let us go," said he ; " it is five minutes past seven, and the appointment was for eight o'clock."

A carriage was in readiness at the door.   Monte-Cristo stepped into it with his two friends.

As the clock struck eight, they drove up to their place of meeting.

"We are the first," said Morrel, looking out of the window.

"No," said Emmanuel, "I perceive two young men down there, who are evidently waiting."

Morrel advanced towards Beauchamp and Château-Renaud, who, seeing his intention, came to meet him.

The three young people bowed to each other courteously, if not affably.

"Excuse me, gentlemen," said Morrel, "but I do not see M. de Morcerf."

"There is a carriage coming," said Château-Renaud.

It advanced rapidly along one of the avenues leading towards the open space where they were assembled.

"You are doubtless provided with pistols, gentlemen? M. de Monte-Cristo yields the right of using his."

"We had anticipated this kindness on the part of the count," said Beauchamp, "and I have brought some arms which I bought eight or ten days since, thinking I might want them on a similar occasion. They are quite new, and have not yet been used. Will you examine them?"

"Oh, M. Beauchamp, if you assure me M. de Morcerf does not know these arms, your word will be quite sufficient."

"Gentlemen," said Château-Renaud, "it is not Morcerf coming in that carriage ;—faith, it is Franz and Debray !"

The two young men he announced were indeed approaching.

"What chance brings you here, gentlemen?" said Château-Renaud, shaking hands with each of them.

"Because," said Debray, "Albert sent this morning to request us to come."

Beauchamp and Château-Renaud exchanged looks of astonishment.

"I think I understand his reason," said Morrel. "Yesterday afternoon I received a letter from M. de Morcerf, begging me to attend the Opera."

"And I," said Debray.

"And I, also," said Franz.

"And we, too," added Beauchamp and Château-Renaud. "Having wished you all to witness the challenge, he now wishes you to be present at the combat."

"But after all these arrangements, he does not come himself," said Château-Renaud ; "Albert is ten minutes behind time."

" There he comes !" said Beauchamp, " on horseback, at full gallop, followed by a servant."

" How imprudent," said Château-Renaud.

" And besides," said Beauchamp, " he has a collar above his cravat, an open coat and white waistcoat ! Why has he not painted a spot upon his heart ?—it would have been more simple."

Meanwhile Albert had arrived within ten paces of the group formed by the five young men. He jumped from his horse, threw the bridle on his servant's arm, and joined them. He was pale and his eyes were red and swollen ; it was evident he had not slept. A shade of melancholy gravity which was not natural to him overspread his countenance.

" I thank you, gentlemen," said he, " for having complied with my request ; I feel extremely grateful for this mark of friendship."

Morrel had stepped back as Morcerf approached, and remained at a short distance.

" And to you also, M. Morrel, my thanks are due. Come, there cannot be too many !"

" Sir," said Maximilian, " you are not perhaps aware I am M. de Monte-Cristo's friend ?"

" I was not sure, but I expected it. So much the better ; the more honourable men there are here the better I shall be satisfied."

" M. Morrel," said Château-Renaud, " will you apprise the Count of Monte-Cristo that M. de Morcerf is arrived, and we are at his command ?"

Morrel was preparing to fulfil his commission. Beauchamp had meanwhile drawn the box of pistols from the carriage.

" Stop, gentlemen !" said Albert ; " I have two words to say to the Count of Monte-Cristo."

" In private ?" asked Morrel.

" No sir ; before all who are here."

Albert's witnesses looked at each other ; Franz and Debray exchanged some words in a whisper ; and Morrel, rejoiced at this unexpected incident, went to fetch the count, who was walking in a retired path with Emmanuel.

" Ah " said Monte-Cristo, " I trust he is not going to tempt me by some fresh insult !"

The count advanced, accompanied by Maximilian and Emmanuel ; his calm and serene look formed a singular contrast to Albert's grief-stricken face.

When at three paces distant, Albert and the count stopped.

"Sir," said Albert, at first with a tremulous voice, which gradually became firmer; "I reproached you with exposing the conduct of M. de Morcerf in Epirus; for, guilty as I now know him to be, I thought you had no right to punish him; but I have since learned you have that right. It is not Fernand Mondego's treachery towards Ali Pacha which induces me so readily to excuse you, but the treachery of the fisherman Fernand towards you, and the almost unheard-of miseries which were its consequences; and I say, and proclaim it publicly, that you were justified in revenging yourself on my father; and I, his son, thank you for not using greater severity."

Had a thunderbolt fallen in the midst of the spectators of this unexpected scene, it would not have surprised them more than did Albert's declaration.

As for Monte-Cristo, his eyes slowly rose towards heaven with an expression of infinite gratitude. He could not understand how Albert's fiery nature had suddenly stooped to this humiliation. He recognised the influence of Mercédès, and saw why her noble heart had not opposed the sacrifice she knew beforehand would be useless.

"Now, sir," said Albert, "if you think my apology sufficient, pray give me your hand. Next to the merit of infallibility which you appear to possess, I rank that of candidly acknowledging a fault. But this confession concerns me only. I acted well as a man, but you have acted better than man. An angel alone could have saved one of us from death—that angel came from heaven, if not to make us friends (which, alas! fatality renders impossible), at least to make us esteem each other."

Monte-Cristo, with moistened eye, heaving breast, and lips half open, extended to Albert a hand, which the latter pressed with a sentiment resembling respectful fear.

"Gentlemen," said he, "M. de Monte-Cristo receives my apology. I had acted hastily towards him. Hasty actions are generally bad ones. Now my fault is repaired. I hope the world will not call me cowardly for acting as my conscience dictated. But if any one should entertain a false opinion of me," added he, drawing himself up as if he would challenge both friends and enemies, "I shall endeavour to correct his mistake."

"What has, then, happened during the night?" asked Beauchamp to Château-Renaud; "we appear to make a very sorry figure here."

"In truth, what Albert has just done is either very despicable or very noble," replied the young man.

"What can it mean?" said Debray to Franz. "The Count of Monte-Cristo acts dishonourably to M. de Morcerf, and is justified by his son! Had I ten Yaninas in my family, I should only consider myself the more bound to fight ten times."

As for Monte-Cristo, his head was bent down, his arms were powerless; bowing under the weight of twenty-four years' reminiscences, he thought not of Albert, of Beauchamp, of Château-Renaud, or of any of that group; but he thought of that courageous woman who had come to plead for her son's life, to whom he had offered his, and who had now saved it by the revelation of a dreadful family secret, capable of destroying for ever, in that young man's heart, every feeling of filial piety.

"Providence still!" murmured he; "now only am I fully convinced of being the emissary of God!"

The Count of Monte-Cristo bowed to the five young people with a melancholy and dignified smile, and got into his carriage with Maximilian and Emmanuel. Albert, Beauchamp, and Château-Renaud, remained alone. The young man's look at his two friends, without being timid, appeared to ask their opinion of what he had just done.

"Indeed, my dear friend," said Beauchamp, who had either the most feeling or the least dissimulation, "allow me to congratulate you: this is a very unhoped-for conclusion of a very disagreeable affair."

Albert remained silent and wrapped in thought. Château-Renaud contented himself with tapping his boot with his flexible cane.

"Are we not going?" said he, after an embarrassing silence.

"When you please," replied Beauchamp; "allow me only time to compliment M. de Morcerf, who has given proof to-day of such chivalric generosity, so rare!"

"Oh! yes," said Château-Renaud.

"It is magnificent," continued Beauchamp, "to be able to exercise so much self-control!"

"Assuredly; as for me, I should have been incapable of it," said Château-Renaud, with most significant coolness.

"Gentlemen," interrupted Albert, "I think you did not understand that something very serious had passed between M. de Monte-Cristo and myself."

"Possibly, possibly," said Beauchamp, immediately; "but

every simpleton would not be able to understand your heroism, and, sooner or later, you will find yourself compelled to explain it to them more energetically than would be convenient to your bodily health and the duration of your life. May I give you some friendly counsel? Set out for Naples, the Hague, or Saint Petersburg—calm countries, where the point of honour is better understood than among our hot-headed Parisians. Seek quietude and oblivion, so that you may return peaceably to France after a few years. Am I not right, M. de Château-Renaud?"

"That is quite my opinion," said the gentleman; "nothing induces serious duels so much as a fruitless one."

"Thank you, gentlemen," replied Albert, with a smile of indifference; "I shall follow your advice, not because you give it, but because I had before intended to quit France. I thank you equally for the service you have rendered me in being my seconds. It is deeply engraved on my heart, especially after what you have just said. I remember that only."

Château-Renaud and Beauchamp looked at each other, the impression was the same on both of them, and the tone in which Morcerf had just expressed his thanks was so determined, that the position would have become embarrassing for all if the conversation had continued.

"Farewell, Albert," said Beauchamp, suddenly, carelessly extending his hand to the young man, without the latter appearing to rouse from his lethargy; in fact he did not notice the offered hand.

"Farewell," said Château-Renaud in his turn, keeping the little cane in his left hand, and bowing.

Albert's lips scarcely whispered, "Farewell!" but his look was more explicit; it embraced a whole poem of restrained anger, proud disdain, and generous indignation. He preserved his melancholy and motionless position for some time after his two friends had regained their carriage; then, suddenly loosing his horse from the little tree to which his servant had fastened it, he sprang on it, and galloped off in the direction of Paris. In a quarter of an hour he was entering the mansion in the Rue du Helder.

The door was scarcely closed when Albert bent his steps to his mother's room; and no one being there to announce him, he advanced to her bed-room, and, distressed by what he saw and guessed, stopped for one moment at the door. Mercédès was in her apartments. Every thing was in order: laces, dresses, jewels, linen, money, all were arranged in the drawers, and the countess was carefully collecting the keys.

Albert saw all these preparations; he understood them, and exclaiming,—

"My mother!" he threw his arms round her neck. He was so overcome he could scarcely speak, "It is not the same with you and me—you cannot have made the same resolution I have, for I am come to warn you that I bid adieu to your house, and—and to you."

"I also," replied Mercédès, "am going, and I acknowledge I had depended on your accompanying me; have I deceived myself?"

"My mother," said Albert, with firmness, "I cannot make you share the fate I have planned for myself. I must live henceforth without rank and fortune, and to begin this hard apprenticeship I must borrow from a friend the loaf I shall eat until I have earned one. So my dear mother, I am going at once to ask Franz to lend me the small sum I shall require to supply my present wants."

"You, my poor child, suffer poverty and hunger! Oh! say not so, it will break my resolutions."

"But not mine, mother," replied Albert. "I am young and strong, I believe I am courageous, and since yesterday I have learned the power of will. From this moment I have done with the past, and accept nothing from it; not even a name, because you can understand your son cannot bear the name of a man who ought to blush before another."

"Albert, my child," said Mercédès, "if I had had a stronger heart, that is the counsel I would have given you! your conscience has spoken when my voice became too weak; listen to its dictates. You had friends, Albert; break off their acquaintance, but do not despair. You have life before you, my dear Albert, for you are yet scarcely twenty-two years old; and as a pure heart like yours wants a spotless name, take my father's; it was Herrera. I am sure, my Albert, whatever may be your career, you will soon render that name illustrious,"

"I will fulfil all your wishes, my dear mother," said the young man. "Let us act promptly. M. de Morcerf went out about half-an-hour since; the opportunity is favourable to avoid an explanation."

"I am ready, my son," said Mercédès.

Albert ran to fetch a hackney-coach; he recollected there

24

was a small furnished house to let in the Rue des Saints-Pères,
where his mother would find a humble but decent lodging;
and thither he intended conducting her. As the hackney-
coach stopped at the door, and Albert was alighting, a man
approached, and gave him a letter. Albert recognised the
bearer, it was Monte-Cristo's steward.

"From the count," said the man.

Albert took the letter, opened it, and read it; then looked
round for Bertuccio, but he was gone. He returned to Mercédès,
with tears in his eyes and heaving breast, and, without uttering
a word, he gave her the letter. Mercédès read :—

" Albert,—While showing you that I have discovered your
plans, I hope also to convince you of my delicacy. You are
free, you leave the count's house, and you take your mother to
your home; but reflect, Albert, you owe her more than your
poor noble heart can pay her. Keep the struggle for yourself,
bear all the suffering, but spare her the trial of poverty which
must accompany your first efforts ; for she deserves not even the
shadow of the misfortune which has this day fallen on her, and
Providence wills not the innocent should suffer for the guilty. I
know you are going to leave the Rue du Helder without taking
any thing with you ; do not seek to know how I discovered it—
I know it, that is sufficient. Now, listen, Albert. Twenty-four
years ago I returned proud and joyful to my country. I had a
betrothed, Albert, a lovely girl, whom I adored, and I was bringing to my betrothed a hundred and fifty louis, painfully amassed
by ceaseless toil. This money was for her, I destined it for her,
and knowing the treachery of the sea, I buried our treasure in
the little garden of the house my father lived in at Marseilles,
on the Allées de Meillan. Your mother, Albert, knows that
poor house well. A short time since I passed through Marseilles,
and went to see the old house, which revived so many painful
recollections, and in the evening I took a spade and dug in the
corner of the garden where I had concealed my treasure. The
iron box was there, no one had touched it ; it was under a
beautiful fig-tree my father had planted the day I was born,
which overshadowed the spot. Well, Albert, this money, which
was formerly designed to promote the comfort and tranquillity
of the woman I adored, may now, from a strange and painful
circumstance, be devoted to the same purpose. Oh ! feel for me,
who could offer millions to that poor woman, but who return

her only the piece of black bread, forgotten under my poor roof
since the day I was torn from her I loved. You are a generous
man, Albert, but, perhaps, you may be blinded by pride or
resentment; if you refuse me, if you ask another for what I have
a right to offer you, I will say it is ungenerous of you to refuse
the life of your mother at the hands of a man whose father was
allowed to die in all the horrors of poverty and despair by your
father."

Albert stood pale and motionless to hear what his mother
would decide after she had finished reading this letter.

Mercédès turned her eyes with an ineffable look towards
heaven.

"I accept it," said she : "he has a right to pay the dowry,
which I shall take with me to some convent !"

Putting the letter in her bosom, she took her son's arm, and
with a firmer step than she even herself expected, she went down
stairs.

CHAPTER XLIV

THE SUICIDE

WHEN Monte-Cristo had returned to town with Emmanuel and Maximilian they did not conceal their joy at having seen peace succeed to war, and acknowledged aloud his philanthropic tastes.

A moment after he had parted from them and entered his own house Baptistin announced the Count de Morcerf to M. de Monte-Cristo ; and the latter ordered the Count to be asked into the drawing-room. The general was pacing the room the third time, when, in turning, he perceived Monte-Cristo at the door.

"Eh ! it is M. de Morcerf," said Monte-Cristo, quietly; "I thought I had heard wrong."

"Yes, it is I," said the count, whom a frightful contraction of the lips prevented from articulating freely.

"May I know the cause which procures me the pleasure of seeing M. de Morcerf so early ?"

"Had you not a meeting with my son this morning ?" asked the general.

"I had," replied the count.

"And I know my son had good reasons to wish to fight with you, and to endeavour to kill you."

"Yes, sir, he had very good ones ; but you see, in spite of them, he has not killed me, and did not even fight."

"Yet he considered you the cause of his father's dishonour, the cause of the fearful ruin which has fallen on my house."

"Truly, sir," said Monte-Cristo, with his dreadful calmness, "a secondary cause, but not the principal."

"Doubtless you made, then, some apology or explanation ?"

"I explained nothing, and it is he who apologised to me."

"But to what do you attribute this conduct ?"

"To the conviction, probably, that there was someone more guilty than I am."

" And who was that ? "

" His father."

" That may be," said the count, turning pale ; " but, you know, the guilty do not like to find themselves convicted."

" I know it. And I expected this result."

" You expected my son would be a coward !" cried the count.

" M. Albert de Morcerf is no coward !" said Monte-Cristo.

" A man who holds a sword in his hand, and sees a mortal enemy within reach of that sword, and does not fight, is a coward ! Why is he not here, that I may tell him so ?"

" Sir," replied Monte-Cristo coldly, " I did not expect you had come here to relate to me your little family affairs. Go and tell M. Albert that, and he may know what to answer you."

" Oh, no, no !" said the general, smiling faintly, " I did not come for that purpose ; you are right ! I came to tell you that I also look upon you as my enemy ! I came to tell you I hate you instinctively ! That it seems as if I had always known you, and always hated you ; and, in short, since the young people of the present day will not fight, it remains for us to do it. Do you not think so, sir ?"

" Certainly. And when I told you I had foreseen the result, it is the honour of your visit I alluded to."

" So much the better. Are you prepared ?"

" Yes, sir."

" You know that we shall fight till one of us is dead !' said the general, whose teeth were clenched with rage.

" Until one of us dies," repeated Monte-Cristo, moving his head slightly up and down.

" Let us start, then ; we need no witnesses."

" Truly," said Monte-Cristo, " it is unnecessary, we know each other so well !"

" On the contrary," said the count, " we know so little of each other."

" Indeed !" said Monte-Cristo, with the same indomitable coolness ; " let us see. Are you not the soldier Fernand, who deserted on the eve of the battle of Waterloo ? Are you not the Lieutenant Fernand who served as guide and spy to the French army in Spain ? Are you not the Captain Fernand who betrayed, sold, and murdered his benefactor, Ali ? And have not all these Fernands, united, made the Lieutenant-General Count de Morcerf, peer of France ?"

" Oh !" cried the general, as if branded with a hot iron,

" wretch! to reproach me with my shame, when about, perhaps, to
kill me!   No, I did not say I was a stranger to you ; I know well,
demon, that you have penetrated into the darkness of the past,
and that you have read, by the light of what flambeau I know not,
every page of my life : but, perhaps, I may be more honourable
in my shame than you under your pompous coverings.   No—no,
I am aware you know me, but I know you not, adventurer, sewn
up in gold and jewellery.   You have called yourself, at Paris,
the Count of Monte-Cristo ; in Italy, Sinbad the Sailor; in Malta,
I forget what.   But it is your real name I want to know, in the
midst of your hundred names, that I may pronounce it when we
meet to fight, at the moment when I plunge my sword through
your heart."

The Count of Monte-Cristo turned dreadfully pale, his eye
seemed to burn with a devouring fire ; he bounded towards a
dressing-room, near his bed-room, and in less than a moment,
tearing off his cravat, his coat and waistcoat, he put on a sailor's
jacket and hat, from beneath which showed his long black hair.
He returned thus, formidable and implacable, advancing with his
arms crossed on his breast, towards the general, who could not
understand why he had disappeared : but who on seeing him
again, felt his teeth chatter and his legs sink under him, drew
back, and only stopped when he found a table to support his
clenched hand.

" Fernand," cried the Count, " of my hundred names I need
only tell you one to overwhelm you !   But you guess it now ; do
you not ?—or, rather, you remember it ?   For, notwithstanding
all my sorrows and my tortures, I show you to-day a face which
the happiness of revenge makes young again—a face you must
often have seen in your dreams since your marriage with
Mercédès, my betrothed !"

The general, with his head thrown back, hands extended, gaze
fixed, looked silently at this dreadful apparition ; then seeking
the wall to support him, he glided along close to it until he
reached the door, through which he went out backwards, uttering
this single mournful, lamentable, distressing cry,—

" Edmond Dantès !"

Then, with sighs which were unlike any human sound, he
dragged himself to the door, reeled across the court-yard, and
falling into the arms of his valet, he said, in a voice scarcely
intelligible,—

" Home! home !"

The fresh air, and the shame he felt at having exposed himself before his servants, partially recalled his senses; but the ride was short, and as he drew near his house all his wretchedness revived. He stopped at a short distance from the house and alighted. The door of the mansion was wide open, a hackney-coach was there in the middle of the yard—a strange sight. The count looked at it with terror, but, without daring to ask, he rushed towards his apartment. Two persons were coming down the stairs: he had only time to creep into a room to avoid them. It was Mercédès leaning on her son's arm and leaving the house. They passed close by the unhappy being, who, concealed behind the door, almost felt Mercédès' dress brush past him, and his son's warm breath pronouncing these words,—

"Courage, my mother! Come, this is no longer our home!"

The words died away, the steps were lost in the distance. The general drew himself up, clinging to the door; he uttered the most dreadful sob which ever escaped from the bosom of a father abandoned. He soon heard the clatter of the iron step of the hackney-coach, then the coachman's voice, and then the rolling of the heavy vehicle which shook the windows. He darted to his bedroom to see once more all he had loved in the world; but the hackney-coach drove on without the head of either Mercédès or her son appearing at the window to take a last look at the house or the deserted father or husband. And at the very moment when the wheels of that coach crossed the gateway a report was heard, and a thick smoke escaped through one of the panes of the window, which was broken by the explosion.

CHAPTER XLV

On leaving Monte-Cristo Morrel walked slowly towards Villefort's house; we say slowly, for Morrel had more than half-an-hour to spare to go five hundred steps, but he had hastened to take leave of Monte-Cristo because he wished to be alone with his thoughts. He knew his time well—the hour when Valentine was giving Noirtier his breakfast, and did not like to be disturbed in the performance of this duty. Noirtier and Valentine had given him leave to go twice a week, and he was now availing himself of that permission.

He arrived; Valentine was expecting him. Uneasy and almost wandering, she seized his hand and led him to her grandfather. This uneasiness, amounting almost to wildness, arose from the report Morcerf's adventure had made in the world; the affair of the Opera was generally known. No one at Villefort's doubted that a duel would ensue from it. Valentine, with her woman's instinct, guessed that Morrel would be Monte-Cristo's witness, and from the young man's well-known courage and his great affection for the count, she feared he would not content himself with the passive part assigned to him.

We may easily understand how eagerly the particulars were asked for, given, and received; and Morrel could read an indescribable joy in the eyes of his beloved, when she knew that the termination of this affair was as happy as it was unexpected.

"Now," said Valentine, motioning to Morrel to sit down near her grandfather, while she took her seat on his footstool, "now let us talk about our own affairs. You know, Maximilian, grandpapa once thought of leaving this house, and taking an apartment away from M. de Villefort's."

"Yes," said Maximilian, "I recollect this project, of which I highly approved."

"Well," said Valentine, "you may approve again, for grandpapa is again thinking of it.

"It is because I have not been very well," said Valentine. "And grandpapa is become my physician. He makes me swallow every morning a spoonful of the mixture prepared for him. When I say one spoonful, I began by one—now I take four. Grandpapa says it is a panacea.

"But listen! Do I not hear a carriage in the courtyard?" She opened Noirtier's door, ran to a window in the passage, and returned hastily. "Yes," said she, "it is Madame Danglars and her daughter, who are come to call on us. Good-bye! I must run away, for they would send here for me ; or rather, farewell till I see you again. Stay with grandpapa, Maximilian ; I promise you not to persuade them to stay."

When Valentine had greeted the guests she left her stepmother to entertain Madame Danglars, and herself taking Eugénie into a corner spoke to her in low tones.

She asked Eugénie timidly of her broken engagement, now known to all the world, and enquired if she were grieved.

"I!" replied Eugénie, with her usual candour. "Oh, not the least in the world! My wish was not to confine myself to domestic cares or the caprices of any man, but to be an artist, and, consequently, free in heart, in person, and in thought."

Eugénie pronounced these words with so firm a tone that the colour mounted to Valentine's cheeks. The timid girl could not understand that vigorous nature which appeared to have none of the timidities of woman.

"At any rate," said she, "I ought to be thankful to Providence for having released me from my engagement with M. Albert de Morcerf, or I should this day have been the wife of a dishonoured man."

Valentine, however, did not continue the conversation. She would, indeed, have found it impossible to repeat what had been said the last few minutes, when suddenly Madame Danglars' hand, pressed on her arm, aroused her from her lethargy.

"What is it?" said she, starting at Madame Danglars' touch as she would have done from an electric shock.

"It is, my dear Valentine," said the baroness, "that you are ill, look at yourself in that glass ; you have turned pale and red successively, three or four times in one minute."

Artless as she was, the young girl knew this was an opportunity to leave ; besides, Madame de Villefort came to her assistance.

"Retire, Valentine," said she ; "you are really suffering, and these ladies will excuse you; drink a glass of water, it will restore you."

Valentine kissed Eugénie, bowed to Madame Danglars, who had already risen to take her leave, and went out.

"That poor child," said Madame de Villefort when Valentine was gone, "she makes me very uneasy, and I should not be astonished if she had some serious illness."

Meanwhile, Valentine, in a sort of excitement which she could not quite understand, had crossed Edward's room without noticing some trick of the child's, and through her own had reached the little staircase. She was at the bottom excepting three steps; she already heard Morrel's voice, when suddenly a cloud passed over her eyes, her stiffened foot missed the step, her hands had no power to hold the baluster, and, falling against the wall, she rolled down these three steps rather than walked. Morrel bounded to the door, opened it, and found Valentine extended on the floor. Rapid as lightning he raised her in his arms and placed her in a chair. Valentine opened her eyes.

"Oh, what a clumsy thing I am!" said she, with feverish volubility; "I no longer know my way. I forgot there were three more steps before the landing."

"You have hurt yourself, perhaps," said Morrel. "What can I do for you, Valentine?"

Valentine looked round her; she saw the deepest terror depicted in Noirtier's eyes.

"Comfort yourself, dear grandpapa," said she, endeavouring to smile; "it is nothing,—it is nothing; I was giddy, that is all."

"Another giddiness!" said Morrel, clasping his hands. "Oh, attend to it Valentine, I entreat you!"

Valentine burst into a forced and melancholy laugh, her arms stiffened and twisted, her head fell back on her chair, and she remained motionless. The cry of terror which was stopped on Noirtier's lips, seemed to start from his eyes. Morrel understood it, he knew he must call assistance. The young man rang the bell violently, the housemaid who had been in Mademoiselle Valentine's room, and the servant who had replaced Barrois, ran in at the same moment. Valentine was so pale, so cold, so inanimate, that, without listening to what was said to them, they were seized with the fear which pervaded that house, and they flew into the passage crying for help.

Madame Danglars and Eugénie were going out at that moment; they heard the cause of the disturbance.

"I told you so!" cried Madame de Villefort. "Poor child!"

At the same moment M. de Villefort's voice was heard calling from his cabinet, "What is the matter?" Morrel consulted Noirtier's look, who had recovered his self-command, and with a glance indicated the closet. The young man had only time to get his hat, and throw himself breathless into the closet, when the procureur's footstep was heard in the passage. Villefort sprang into the room, ran to Valentine, and took her in his arms.

"A physician! a physician! M. d'Avrigny!" cried Villefort; "or rather I will go for him myself."

He flew from the apartment, and Morrel, at the same moment, darted out at the other door. He had been struck to the heart by a frightful recollection,—the conversation he had heard between the doctor and Villefort the night of Madame de Saint-Méran's death recurred to him; these symptoms, to a less alarming extent, were the same which had preceded the death of Barrois. At the same time Monte-Cristo's voice seemed to resound in his ear, he had said only two hours before, "Whatever you want, Morrel, come to me, I have great power." More rapidly than thought he darted down the Rue Matigon, and thence to the Avenue des Champs Elysées.

Meanwhile M. de Villefort arrived in a hired cab at M. d'Avrigny's door. He rang so violently, that the porter came alarmed. Villefort ran upstairs without saying a word. The porter knew him, and let him pass, only calling to him,—

"In his study, M. le Procureur du Roi,—in his study!"

Villefort pushed, or rather forced, the door open.

"Doctor," he cried, "you are right; my house is accursed!"

"What!" said the latter, with apparent coolness, but with deep inward emotion, "have you another invalid?"

"Yes, doctor," cried Villefort, seizing, with a convulsive grasp, a handful of hair, "yes!"

D'Avrigny's look implied, "I told you it would be so." Then he slowly uttered these words, "Who is now dying in your house? What new victim is going to accuse you of weakness before God?"

A mournful sob burst from Villefort's heart; he approached the doctor, and seizing his arm,—

"Valentine!" said he, "it is Valentine's turn!"

" Your daughter !" cried D'Avrigny, in amazement.

The same cab which had brought Villefort took them back at full speed, at the same moment when Morrel rapped at Monte-Cristo's door.

The count was in his cabinet, and was reading, with an angry look, something which Bertuccio had brought in haste.   Hearing Morrel announced, who had left him only two hours before, the count raised his head.   He, as well as the count, had evidently been much tried during those two hours, for he had left him smiling and returned with a disturbed air.   The count rose and sprang to meet him.

" What is the matter, Maximilian ?" asked he ; " you are pale, and the perspiration rolls from your forehead."

Morrel fell, rather than sat, down on a chair.

" Yes," said he, " I came quickly ; I wanted to speak to you."

" Is all your family well ?" asked the count, with an affectionate benevolence, whose sincerity no one could for a moment doubt.

" Thank you, count,—thank you," said the young man, evidently embarrassed how to tell his awful news, " yes, every one in my family is well."

" So much the better ; yet you have something to tell me?" replied the count, with increased anxiety.

" Yes," said Morrel, " it is true ; I have left a house where death has just entered to run to you."

" Are you then come from M. de Morcerf's ?" asked Monte-Cristo.

" No," gasped Morrel, " is some one dead there also ?"

" The general has just blown his brains out," replied Monte-Cristo, with great coolness.

" Oh, how dreadful !" cried Maximilian.

" Not for the countess, nor for Albert," said Monte-Cristo ; " a dead father or husband is better than a dishonoured one : blood washes out shame."

" Poor countess !" said Maximilian, " I pity her very much . she is so noble a woman !"

" Pity Albert also, Maximilian ; for, believe me, he is the worthy son of the countess.   But let us return to yourself : you have hastened to me ; can I be useful to you ?"

" Yes, I need your help ; that is, I thought, like a madman, you could lend me your assistance in a case where God alone can succour me, for this is a terrible thing," he cried, " Valentine de Villefort is dying."

Monte-Cristo shrugged his shoulders. "Three months since," said he coolly, "it was M. de Saint-Méran; two months since, Madame de Saint-Méran; the other day it was Barrois; to-day the old Noirtier or young Valentine."

"You knew it?" cried Morrel, in such a paroxysm of terror that Monte-Cristo started, he whom the falling heavens would have found unmoved; "you knew it, and said nothing?"

"And what is it to me?" replied Monte-Cristo, shrugging his shoulders: "Do I know those people?"

"But I," cried Morrel, groaning with sorrow,— "I love her!"

"You love!—whom?" cried Monte-Cristo, starting to his feet and seizing the two hands which Morrel was raising towards him.

"I love most fondly—I love madly—I love as a man who would give his life-blood to spare her a tear—I love Valentine de Villefort, who is dying at this moment! Do you understand me? I love her; and I ask you how I can save her?"

Monte-Cristo uttered a cry, which those only can conceive who have heard the roar of a wounded lion.

"Unhappy man!" cried he, wringing his hands in his turn; "you love Valentine!—that daughter of an accursed race!"

Never had Morrel witnessed such an expression,—never had so terrible an eye flashed before his face,—never had the genius of terror he had so often seen, either on the battle-field or in the murderous nights of Algeria, shaken around him more dreadful fires. He drew back terrified.

But the count quickly recovered himself. "You love her!" he echoed.

"Ah, for your sake I must save her! I tell you to hope. Do you understand me? Remember that I never utter a falsehood, and am never deceived. It is early, Maximilian; thank heaven that you came at noon rather than in the evening or to-morrow morning. Listen, Morrel!—It is noon; if Valentine is not now dead, she will not die."

"Oh! count, you overwhelm me with that coolness. Have you then power against death?—Are you superhuman?—Are you a spirit?"

And the young man, who had never shrunk from danger, shrank before Monte-Cristo with indescribable terror. But the count looked at him with so melancholy and sweet a smile that Maximilian felt the tears filling his eyes.

" I can do much for you, my friend," replied the count. " Go!
—I must be alone."

Morrel, subdued by the extraordinary ascendancy Monte-
Cristo exercised over everyone around him, did not endeavour
to resist it. He pressed the count's hand and left.

They had carried Valentine away : she had revived, but could
scarcely move or speak, so shaken was her frame by the attack.
She had, however, just power to give her grandfather one parting look ; and he, in losing her, seemed to be resigning his very
soul. D'Avrigny, after seeing the patient, wrote a prescription,
ordered Villefort to go in person to a chemist's to get the prescribed medicine, bring it himself, and wait for him in his
daughter's room.

CHAPTER XLVI

THE DEPARTURE FOR BELGIUM

BEFORE the news of Valentine's sudden illness had become generally known, two young girls were closeted together in the house of M. Danglars. They were his daughter Eugénie and her friend, Louise d'Armilly.

"Listen, Louise!" cried Eugénie, "I hate this life of the fashionable world, always ordered, measured, ruled like our music-paper. What I have always wished for, desired, and coveted, is the life of an artist, free and independent, relying only on my own resources, and accountable only to myself. Thus have I formed this plot to escape and persuaded you to be my accomplice. They tried to marry me to Albert de Morcerf, luckily my heart was not broken by his defection. My father has new projects for me to marry me elsewhere ; and to whom ?— To M. Debray, perhaps, as it was once proposed. No, Louise, no ! I did not seek a husband, I did not ask for one."

"How strong and courageous you are !" said the fair frail girl. "I have done everything you told me."

"The post-chaise——"

"Was happily bought three days since."

"Have you had it sent where we are to go for it ?"

"Yes."

"Our passport ?"

"Here it is !"

And Eugénie, with her usual decision, opened a printed paper, and read,—

"M. Léon d'Armilly, twenty years of age ; profession, artist ; hair black ; eyes black ; travelling with his sister."

"Capital ! How did you get this passport !"

"When I went to ask the friend I spoke of, for letters for the directors of the theatres of Rome and at Naples, I expressed my fears of travelling as a woman alone, he perfectly understood them, and undertook to procure for me a man's passport ; and two days after I received this, to which I have added with my own hand, ' travelling with his sister.'"

" Well," said Eugénie, cheerfully, " we have then only to pack up our trunks—that is all."

" Reflect well, Eugénie !"

" Oh, I have finished all my reflections !   I am tired of hearing only of reports, of the end of the month, of up and down, of Spanish funds, of Haïtian paper.   Instead of that, Louise—do you understand ?—Air, liberty, melody of birds, plains of Lombardy, Venetian canals, Roman Palaces, the bay of Naples! How much money have we ?"

Louise drew from an inlaid secrétaire a small portfolio with a lock, in which she counted twenty-three bank-notes.

" Twenty-three thousand francs," said she.

" And as much, at least, in pearls, diamonds, and jewels," said Eugénie.   " We are rich.   With forty-five thousand francs we have enough to live on as princesses during two years, and comfortably during four; but before six months—you with your music, and I with my voice—we shall double our capital.   Come, you shall take charge of the money, I of the jewel-box; so that if one of us had the misfortune to lose her treasure, the other would still have hers left.   Now, the portmanteau !—let us make haste—the portmanteau !"

" Stop !" said Louise, going to listen at Madame Danglars' door.

" The door is locked."

And the two young girls began to heap into a trunk all the things they thought they should require.

" There now !" said Eugénie, " while I change my costume do you lock the portmanteau."

Louise pressed with all the strength of her little hands on the top of the portmanteau.

" But I cannot," said she ; " I am not strong enough ; do you shut it."

" Ah you are right !" said Eugénie, laughing ; " I forgot I was Hercules, and you only the pale Amphale !"   And the young girl, kneeling on the top, pressed the two parts of the portmanteau together, while Mademoiselle d'Armilly passed the bolt of the padlock through.

When this was done, Eugénie opened a drawer, of which she kept the key, and took from it a wadded violet silk travelling cloak.

"Here," said she, "you see I have thought of every thing; with this cloak you will not be cold."

"But you?"

"Oh, I am never cold, you know! Besides, with those men's clothes——"

"Will you dress here?"

"Certainly. Come and help me."

From the same drawer she took a complete man's costume, from the boots to the coat, and also under-linen, where there was nothing superfluous but everything requisite.

Then, with a promptitude which indicated this was not the first time she had amused herself by adopting the garb of the opposite sex, Eugénie drew on the boots and pantaloons, tied her cravat, buttoned her waistcoat up to the throat, and put on a coat which admirably fitted her beautiful figure.

"Oh, that is very good!—indeed it is very good!" said Louise, looking at her with admiration; "but that beautiful black hair, those magnificent braids, will they go under a man's hat like the one that I see down there?"

"You shall see," said Eugénie.

And seizing with her left hand the thick mass, which her long fingers could scarcely grasp, she snatched with her right hand a pair of long scissors, and soon the steel met through the rich and splendid hair, which fell entire at the feet of the young girl, who leaned back to keep it from her coat. Then she passed to the front hair, which she also cut off, without expressing the least regret; on the contrary, her eyes sparkled with greater pleasure than usual under her eyebrows, black as ebony.

"Oh, the magnificent hair!" said Louise, with regret.

"And am I not a hundred times better thus?" cried Eugénie, smoothing the scattered curls of her hair, which had now quite a masculine appearance; "and do you not think me handsomer so?"

"Oh, you are beautiful—always beautiful!" cried Louise. "Now where are we going?"

"To Brussels, if you like; it is the nearest frontier. We can go to Brussels, Liège, Aix-la-Chapelle; then up the Rhine to Strassburg. We will cross Switzerland, and go down into Italy by Mount St. Gothard. Will that do?"

"Yes. I am looking at you; indeed you are adorable, like that! One would say you were carrying me off."

And the two young girls burst out laughing, as they cleared

25

away every visible trace of the disorder which had naturally accompanied the preparations for their escape. Then, having blown out the lights, with an inquiring eye, and listening ear, the two fugitives opened the door of a dressing-room which led by a side staircase down to the yard, Eugénie going first, and holding with one arm the portmanteau, which by the opposite handle Mademoiselle d'Armilly scarcely raised with both hands.

The yard was empty; the clock was striking twelve. The porter had not yet gone to bed. Eugénie approached softly, and saw the old man sleeping soundly in an arm-chair in his lodge. She returned to Louise, took up the portmanteau, which she had placed for a moment on the ground, and they reached the archway under the shadow of the wall.

Eugénie concealed Louise in an angle of the gateway, so that if the porter chanced to awake he might see but one person. Then placing herself in the full light of the lamp which lit the yard,—

"Gate!" cried she, with her finest contralto voice, rapping at the window.

The porter got up as Eugénie expected, and even advanced some steps to recognise the person who was going out, but seeing a young man striking his boot impatiently with his riding-whip, he opened it immediately.

Louise slid through the half-open gate like a snake, and bounded lightly forward. Eugénie, apparently calm, although her heart beat somewhat faster than usual, went out in her turn.

A porter was passing, they gave him the portmanteau, and told him to take it to No. 36 Rue de la Victoire; they themselves walked. They arrived at the appointed spot. Eugénie ordered the porter to put down the portmanteau, gave him some pieces of money, and, having rapped at the shutter, sent him away.

The shutter belonged to the laundress, who had been previously apprised, and was not yet gone to bed. She opened the door.

"Mademoiselle," said Eugénie, "let the porter get the post-chaise from the coach-house and fetch some post-horses from the hôtel. Here are five francs for his trouble."

The laundress looked on in astonishment, but as she had been promised twenty louis, she made no remark.

In a quarter of an hour the porter returned with a post-boy and horses, which were harnessed and put in the postchaise in a minute, while the porter fastened the portmanteau on with the assistance of a cord and a strap.

"Here is the passport," said the postilion; "which way are we going, young gentleman?"

"To Fontainebleau," replied Eugénie in a masculine voice.

"What did you say?" said Louise.

"I am providing against accidents," said Eugénie; "this woman to whom we have given twenty louis may betray us for forty; we will soon alter our direction."

And the young girl jumped into the vehicle, which was admirably arranged for sleeping in, scarcely touching the step.

A quarter of an hour afterwards the postilion, having been put in the right road, passed, cracking his whip, through the gateway of the Barrière Saint-Martin.

"Ah!" said Louise, breathing freely, "here we are out of Paris."

"Yes, my dear, and the escape is good and well effected," replied Eugénie.

"And without violence," said Louise.

These words were lost in the noise which the carriage made in rolling over the pavement of La Villette.

M. Danglars had lost his daughter.

CHAPTER XLVII

THE APPARITION

EVERY morning Morrel called on Noirtier to receive news of Valentine, and extraordinary as it seemed, each day found him less uneasy. Certainly, though Valentine still laboured under dreadful nervous excitement, she was better, and moreover Monte-Cristo had told him when, half-distracted, he had rushed to his house, that if she were not dead in two hours she was saved. Now four days had elapsed, and Valentine still lived.

Eleven o'clock had struck. The nurse, having placed the beverage prepared by the doctor within reach of the patient, and locked the door, went downstairs.

Ten minutes had elapsed since the nurse had left; Valentine, who for the last hour had been suffering from the fever which returned nightly. The night-lamp threw out countless rays, to her disordered imagination, each resolving itself into some strange form, when suddenly, by its flickering light, she thought that she saw a door in her room which was permanently closed, because it led into an uninhabited part of the house, open slowly. Behind the door a human figure appeared, but she was too familiar with such apparitions to be alarmed, and, therefore, only stared, hoping to recognise Morrel. The figure advanced towards the bed, and a ray of light glanced across his face.

" The Count of Monte-Cristo!" she murmured.

" Do not call any one—do not be alarmed," said the count,— " do not let a shade of suspicion or uneasiness remain in your breast; the man standing before you, Valentine, is nothing more than the tenderest father and the most respectful friend you could dream of."

Valentine was incapable of replying.

" Listen to me," said the count, " or, rather, look upon me; for four days I have not closed my eyes, for I have been constantly watching you, to protect and preserve you for Maximilian."

" Maximilian!" she exclaimed, and so sweet did the sound

appear to her, that she repeated it,—" Maximilian! Has he then owned all to you?"

" Everything."

" But you say you have watched," said Valentine, uneasily; " where have you been?—I have not seen you."

The count extended his hand towards the door. "I was hidden in the empty rooms beyond," he said.

" Drink some of this," he added, taking a bottle from his pocket containing a red liquid, of which he poured a few drops into the glass. " Drink this, and then take nothing more to-night."

Valentine smiled, and swallowed it.

" This is how you have lived during the last four nights, Valentine," said the count. " But, oh! the torture which I endured when I saw the deadly poison poured into your glass, and how I trembled lest you would drink it before I could find time to throw it away!"

" Sir," said Valentine feebly, " you say you endured tortures because you saw deadly poison poured into my glass; but who poured it?"

" Are you the first that this hand has stricken? Have you not seen M. de Saint-Méran, Madame de Saint-Méran, Barrois, all fall? Would not M. Noirtier also have fallen a victim, had not the treatment he has been pursuing for the last three years neutralised the effects of the poison?"

" Oh, heavens!" said Valentine; " is this the reason why grandfather has made me share all his beverages during the last month? But who, then, is this assassin—this murderer?"

" Valentine," said the count, "summon up all your courage, and feign to be asleep; then you will see. Good-bye for the present," he added, walking upon tip-toe towards the door by which he had entered, and smiling with an expression so sad and paternal, that the young girl's heart was filled with gratitude. Before closing the door he turned round once more, and said, " Not a movement,—not a word; let them think you asleep."

Hardly had he vanished than someone else entered by the usual door of the bedroom, and noiselessly approached the bed and drew back the curtains. Valentine summoned all her courage, and breathed with that regular respiration which announces tranquil sleep.

" Valentine!" said a low voice.

Then came the sound of some liquid being poured into the

glass which had just been emptied. Valentine ventured to peep cautiously over her extended arm. She saw a woman in a white dressing-gown pouring a liquor from a phial into her glass : it was Madame de Villefort.

Madame de Villefort, however, reassured by the silence, retired so gently that Valentine did not know when she had left the room.

The noiseless door of the empty rooms again turned on its hinges, and the Count of Monte-Cristo reappeared.

" Well," said he, " do you still doubt ?"

" Oh !" murmured the young girl.

" If you had taken that which Madame de Villefort has poured into your glass, Valentine, you would have been lost !"

" But," exclaimed the young girl, " what does it all mean ?"

" You are rich, Valentine ; you have 200,000 livres a year, and you prevent her son from enjoying these 200,000 livres."

" How so ? The fortune is inherited from my relations !"

"Certainly ; and this is why M. and Madame de Saint-Méran have died ; M. Noirtier was sentenced but escaped. However, this made little difference, once you are dead his money will come to his son undoubtedly. Therefore, you, in your turn, are to die : your father would inherit your property, and your brother, his only son, succeed to his."

" Edward ? Poor child ! are all these crimes committed on his account ? Tell me what am I to do ?"

Monte-Cristo gently laid his hand on the young girl's arm, drew the velvet coverlet close to her throat, and said, with a paternal smile,—

" My child, believe in my devotion to you as you believe in the goodness of Providence and the love of Maximilian."

Then he drew from his waistcoat-pocket the little emerald box, raised the golden lid, and took from it a pastille, about the size of a pea, which he placed in her hand. She took it and looked attentively at him ; there was an expression on his face which commanded her confidence. She carried the pastille to her mouth, and swallowed it.

" And now, my dear child, adieu for the present. I will try and gain a little sleep, for you are saved."

" Go," said Valentine ; "whatever happens, I promise you not to fear."

Monte-Cristo for some time kept his eyes fixed on the young girl, who gradually fell asleep, yielding to the effects of the narcotic he had given her. Then he took the glass, emptied three parts of the contents in the fireplace, that it might be supposed Valentine had taken it, and replaced it on the table. After that he disappeared, throwing a farewell glance on Valentine, who slept with the confidence and innocence of an angel.

The night-light continued to burn on the chimneypiece, exhausting the last drops of oil which floated on the surface of the water; the globe of the lamp appeared of a reddish hue, and the flame brightening before it expired, threw out those last flickerings which in an inanimate object have been so often compared with the last convulsions in a human frame. Madame de Villefort crept in to witness the effects of her draught. She drew aside the curtain, and leaning over the pillow, gazed intently on Valentine. The young girl no longer breathed, no breath issued through the half-closed teeth; the white lips no longer quivered; the eyes appeared floating in a bluish vapour, and the long black lashes rested on a cheek white as wax. There was no more to do in the room, so the poisoner retired stealthily. The darkness lasted two hours longer; then by degrees a cold light crept through the Venetian blinds, until at length it revealed the objects in the room. About this time the nurse's cough was heard on the stairs, and the woman entered the room with a cup in her hand.

She went to the fireplace and lit the fire, and although she had but just left her bed, she could not resist the temptation offered by Valentine's sleep, so she threw herself into an armchair to snatch a little more rest. The clock striking eight awoke her. Astonished at the prolonged sleep of the patient, and frightened to see that the arm was still hanging out of bed, she advanced towards Valentine, and for the first time noticed the white lips. She tried to replace the arm, but it moved with a frightful stiffness. She screamed aloud: then running to the door exclaimed,—

" Help ! help !"

" What do you mean ?" asked M. d'Avrigny, at the foot of the stairs, for it was the hour he usually visited the patient.

M. d'Avrigny ran to Valentine, and raised her in his arms.

" What ! this one, too !" he exclaimed. " Oh ! when will this cease ?"

Villefort rushed into the room.

" What are you saying, doctor ?" he exclaimed, raising his hands to heaven.

"I say that Valentine is dead!" replied D'Avrigny, in a voice terrible in its solemn calmness.

M. de Villefort staggered and buried his head in the bed. On the exclamation of the doctor and the cry of the father, the servants all fled with muttered imprecations; they were heard running down the stairs and through the long passages, then there was a rush in the court, afterwards all was still; they had, one and all, deserted the accursed house. Just then, Madame de Villefort, in the act of slipping on her dressing-gown, threw aside the drapery, and for a moment remained still, as though interrogating the occupants of the room, while she endeavoured to call up some rebellious tears.

"Mademoiselle de Villefort no longer requires help," said D'Avrigny, "since she is dead."

"Dead!—dead!" groaned forth Villefort, in a paroxysm of grief.

"Dead!" repeated a third voice.   "Who said Valentine was dead?"

The two men turned round, and saw Morrel standing at the door, pale and terror-stricken.

This is what had happened :— At the usual time, Morrel had presented himself at the little door leading to Noirtier's room which he visited every day to hear news of Valentine. Contrary to custom, the door was open, and, having no occasion to ring, he entered. He waited for a moment in the hall, and called for a servant to conduct him to M. Noirtier; but no one answered, the servants having deserted the house. Morrel had no particular reason for uneasiness : Monte-Cristo had promised him that Valentine should live ; and, until then, he had always fulfilled his word. Every night the count had given him news, which was the next morning confirmed by Noirtier. Still this extraordinary silence appeared strange to him, and he determined to go up.

In a minute he passed through several rooms, till, at length, he reached Valentine's. There was no necessity to push the door, it was wide open. A sob was the only sound he heard. He saw, as though in a mist, a black figure kneeling, buried in a confused mass of white drapery. A terrible fear transfixed him. It was then he heard a voice exclaim, "Valentine is dead!" and another voice which, like an echo, repeated,—

"Dead!—dead!"

Villefort rose, half ashamed of being surprised in such a

paroxysm of grief. The terrible office he had held for twenty-five years had succeeded in making him more or less than man. His glance, at first wandering, fixed itself upon Morrel.

"Who are you, sir," he asked, "who forget that this is not the manner to enter a house stricken with death? Go, sir, go!"

But Morrel remained motionless; he could not detach his eyes from that disordered bed, and the pale corpse of the young girl who was lying on it.

"Go!—do you hear?" said Villefort, while D'Avrigny advanced to lead Morrel out. Maximilian stared for a moment at the corpse, gazed all round the room, then upon the two men; he opened his mouth to speak, but finding it impossible to give utterance to the innumerable ideas that thronged his brain, he went out, thrusting his hands through his hair in such a manner, that Villefort and D'Avrigny, for a moment diverted from the engrossing topic, exchanged glances, which seemed to convey their idea that he was mad.

"Is there any particular priest you wish to pray with Valentine?" D'Avrigny asked the stricken father.

"No!" said Villefort; "fetch the nearest."

"The nearest," said the doctor, "is a good Italian abbé, who lives next door to you. Shall I call on him as I pass?"

"D'Avrigny," said Villefort, "be so kind as to do so. Here is the key of the door, so that you can go in and out as you please; you will bring the priest with you, and will oblige me by introducing him into my child's room."

"Do you wish to see him?"

"I only wish to be alone. You will excuse me, will you not? A priest can understand a father's grief." And M. de Villefort, giving the key to D'Avrigny, retired to his study, where he began to work. For some temperaments work is a remedy for all afflictions.

As D'Avrigny entered the street, he saw a man in a cassock standing on the threshold of the next door.

"Sir," he said, "are you disposed to confer a great obligation on an unhappy father who has just lost his daughter? I mean M. de Villefort, the procureur du roi."

"Ah!" said the priest, in a marked Italian accent: "yes; I have heard that death is in that house."

"Then I need not tell you what kind of service he requires of you."

" I was about to offer myself, sir," said the priest ; "it is our mission to forestall our duties."

" It is a young girl."

" I know it, sir ; the servants who fled from the house informed me. I also know that her name is Valentine, and I have already prayed for her."

" Thank you, sir," said D'Avrigny ; "since you have commenced your sacred office, deign to continue it. Come and watch by the dead, and all the wretched family will be grateful to you."

" I am going, sir, and I do not hesitate to say that no prayers will be more fervent than mine."

D'Avrigny took the priest's hand, and without meeting Villefort, who was engaged in his study, they reached Valentine's room, which on the following night was to be occupied by the undertakers. On entering the room they found that Noirtier had been wheeled there by his attendant who had replaced Barrois, and who had afterwards fled like the rest. Noirtier's eyes met those of the abbé, and no doubt he read some particular expression in them, for he remained in the room. D'Avrigny recommended the attention of the priest to the living as well as to the dead, and the abbé promised to devote his prayers to Valentine and his attentions to Noirtier. In order, doubtless, that he might not be disturbed while fulfilling his sacred mission, the priest, as soon as D'Avrigny departed, rose and bolted the door through which the doctor had just left.

CHAPTER XLVIII

THE next morning rose sad and cloudy. Monte-Cristo was to be seen driving slowly towards the Rue de la Chaussée d'Antin to call on M. Danglars. The banker saw the carriage of the count enter the court-yard, and advanced to meet him with a sad though affable smile.

"Well!" said he, extending his hand to Monte-Cristo, "I suppose you have come to sympathise with me, for indeed misfortune has taken possession of my house. When I perceived you, I was just asking myself whether in wishing harm towards those poor Morcerfs, I have justified the proverb of ' He who wishes misfortunes to happen to others experiences them himself.' Well! on my word of honour, I answered, ' No!' I wished no ill to Morcerf ; he was a little proud, perhaps, for a man who, like myself, had risen from nothing ; but we all have our faults. Do you know, count, that persons of our time of life—not that you belong to the class, you are still a young man, but, as I was saying, persons of our time of life—have been very unfortunate this year. For example, look at the Puritanical procureur du roi, who has just lost his daughter. And in fact nearly all his family in so singular a manner ; Morcerf dishonoured and dead ; and then myself having lost my daughter, who has run away. Oh, how happy you must be in not having either wife or children !"

"Still, baron," said Monte-Cristo, "family griefs, or indeed any other affliction which would crush a man whose child was his only treasure, are endurable to a millionaire. Philosophers may well say, and practical men will always support the opinion, that money mitigates many trials ; and if you admit the efficacy of this sovereign balm, you ought to be very easily consoled ; you, the king of finance, who form the intersecting point of all the powers in Europe, nay, the world !"

Danglars looked at him obliquely, as though to ascertain whether he spoke seriously.

" Yes," he answered, " if a fortune brings consolation, I ought to be consoled ; I am rich."

" So rich, dear sir, that your fortune resembles the Pyramids : if you wish to demolish them, you could not ; if it were possible, you would not dare !"

Danglars smiled at the good-natured pleasantry of the count.

" That reminds me," he said, " that when you entered, I was on the point of signing five little bonds ; I have already signed two, will you allow me to do the same to the others ?"

" Pray do so."

There was a moment's silence, during which the noise of the banker's pen alone was heard, while Monte-Cristo examined the gilt mouldings of the ceiling.

" Are they Spanish, Haytian, or Neapolitan bonds ?" he asked presently.

" Neither," said Danglars, smiling ; " they are bonds on the Bank of France, payable to the bearer. Stay," he added, " count, you who may be called the emperor, if I claim the title of king of finance, have you many pieces of paper of this size, each worth a million ?"

The count took the papers which Danglars had so proudly presented to him, into his hands, and read :—

" To the Governor of the Bank.   Please to pay to my order from the funds deposited by me, the sum of a million.

" BARON DANGLARS."

" One, two, three, four, five," said Monte-Cristo ; " five millions ! why, what a Crœsus you are !   Payable at sight ?"

" Yes indeed," said Danglars.

" It is a fine thing to have such credit ; really, it is only in France these things are done.   Five millions on five little scraps of paper !— it must be seen to be believed."

" You do not doubt it ?"

" No !"

" You say so with an accent——Stay, you shall be convinced ; take my clerk to the bank, and you will see him leave it with an order on the Treasury for the same sum."

" No !" said Monte-Cristo, folding the five notes, " most decidedly not ; the thing is so curious, I will make the experiment myself.   I am credited to you for six millions.   I have drawn nine hundred thousand francs, you therefore still owe me five millions and a hundred thousand francs.   I will take the five scraps of paper that I now hold as bonds, with your signature alone, and here is a receipt in full for the six millions between us. I had prepared it beforehand, for I am much in want of money to-day."

And Monte-Cristo placed the bonds in his pocket with one hand, while with the other he held out the receipt to Danglars.

If a thunderbolt had fallen at the banker's feet, he could not have experienced greater terror.

"What!" he stammered, "do you mean to take that money? Excuse me, excuse me, but I owe this money to the hospital,— a deposit which I promised to pay this morning."

"Oh! well, then," said Monte-Cristo, "I am not particular about these five notes, pay me in a different form; I wished, from curiosity, to take these, that I might be able to say, that without any advice or preparation the house of Danglars had paid me five millions without a minute's delay: it would have been so remarkable. But here are your bonds, pay me differently;" and he held the bonds towards Danglars, who seized them like a vulture extending its claws to grab the food wrested from it. Suddenly he rallied, made a violent offort to restrain himself, and then a smile gradually widened the features of his disturbed countenance.

"Certainly," he said, "your receipt is money."

"Oh dear, yes; and if you were at Rome, the house of Thomson and French would make no more difficulty about paying the money on my receipt than you have just done."

"Pardon me, count, pardon me."

"Then I may keep this money?"

"Yes," said Danglars, while the perspiration started from the roots of his hair. "Yes, keep it—keep it."

Monte-Cristo replaced the notes in his pocket with that indescribable expression which seemed to say, "Come, reflect; if you repent there is still time."

"No," said Danglars, "no, decidedly no; keep my signatures. But you know none are so formal as bankers in transacting business; I intended this money for the hospitals, and I seemed to be robbing them if I did not pay them with these precise bonds. How absurd! as if one crown were not as good as another. Excuse me;" and he began to laugh loudly, but nervously.

"Certainly, I excuse you," said Monte-Cristo, graciously, "and pocket them." And he placed the bonds in his pocket-book.

"But," said Danglars, "there is still a sum of one hundred thousand francs?"

"Oh! a mere nothing," said Monte-Cristo. "The balance would come to about that sum; but keep it, and we shall be quits."

"Count," said Danglars, "are you speaking seriously?"

"I never joke with bankers," said Monte-Cristo, in a freezing manner, which repelled impertinence; and he turned towards the door, just as the valet-de-chambre announced,—

"M. de Boville, receiver-general of the hospitals."

"Ma foi!" said Monte-Cristo; "I think I arrived just in time to obtain your signatures, or they would have been disputed with me."

Danglars again became pale, and hastened to conduct the count out. Monte-Cristo exchanged a ceremonious bow with M. de Boville, who was standing in the waiting-room, and who was introduced into Danglars' room as soon as the count had left. The count's sad face was illumined by a faint smile, as he noticed the portfolio which the receiver-general held in his hand. At the door he found his carriage, and was immediately driven to the bank. Meanwhile Danglars, repressing all emotion, advanced to meet the receiver-general. We need not say that a smile of condescension was stamped upon his lips.

"Good morning, creditor!" said he; "for I wager any thing it is the creditor who visits me."

"You are right, baron," answered M. de Boville; "the hospitals present themselves to you through me; the widows and orphans depute me to receive alms to the amount of five millions from you."

"And yet they say orphans are to be pitied," said Danglars, wishing to prolong the jest. "Poor things!"

"I have brought my receipt."

"My dear M. Boville, your widows and orphans must oblige me by waitingtwe nty-four hours, since M. de Monte-Cristo, whom you just saw leaving here—you did see him, I think? Well, M. de Monte-Cristo has just carried off their five millions."

"How so?"

"The count had unlimited credit upon me; a credit opened by Thomson and French of Rome: he came to demand five millions at once, which I paid him with cheques on the bank; my funds are deposited there; and you can understand that if I draw out ten millions on the same day, it will appear rather strange to the governor. Two days will be a different thing," said Danglars, smiling.

"Here is his receipt. Believe your own eyes."

M. de Boville took the paper Danglars presented him, and read:

"Received of Baron Danglars the sum of five millions one hundred thousand francs; which will be repaid whenever he pleases by the house of Thomson and French, of Rome."

"It is really true," said De Boville.

"His charities alone amount to 20,000 francs per month."

"It is magnificent! I will set before him the example of Madame de Morcerf and her son, who gave all their fortune to the hospitals. The mother retires into the country, and the son enters the army."

"Certainly," said Danglars, in the most natural tone in the world. "The receipt of M. de Monte-Cristo is as good as money; take it to Rothschild's or Lafitte's, and they will take it of you directly."

"What, though payable at Rome?"

"Certainly; it will only cost you a discount of 5 or 6000 francs."

The receiver started back.

"Then it will be to-morrow? Send to-morrow at twelve, and the bank shall be informed."

"I will come myself."

"Better still, since it will afford me the pleasure of seeing you."

They shook hands.

M. de Boville had scarcely left before Danglars, enclosing Monte-Cristo's receipt in a little pocket-book, exclaimed:

"Yes, come at twelve o'clock; I shall then be far away!"

He double-locked his door; emptied all his drawers, collected about fifty thousand francs in bank-notes, burned several papers, left others exposed to view, and then commenced writing a letter which he addressed:—

"To Madame la Baronne Danglars."

"I will place it on her table myself to-night," he murmured.

Taking a passport from his drawer, he said,—

"Good! it is available for two months longer."

CHAPTER XLIX

THE CEMETERY OF PÈRE-LA-CHAISE

M. DE BOVILLE had met the funeral procession which conducted Valentine to her last home on earth. The weather was dull and stormy, a cold wind shook the few remaining yellow leaves from the boughs of the trees, and scattered them amongst the crowd which filled the Boulevards. M. de Villefort, a true Parisian, considered the cemetery of Père-la-Chaise alone worthy of receiving the mortal remains of a Parisian family ; there alone the corpses belonging to him would be surrounded by worthy associates. More than fifty private carriages followed the twenty mourning-coaches, and behind them more than five hundred persons joined the procession on foot.

As they left Paris, an equipage with four horses, at full speed, was seen to draw up suddenly : it contained Monte-Cristo. The count left the carriage and mingled in the crowd, who followed on foot. Château-Renaud perceived him ; and immediately alighting from his coupé, joined him. The count looked attentively through every opening in the crowd ; he was evidently watching for some one, but his search ended in disappointment.

" Where is Morrel ?" he asked : " do either of these gentlemen know where he is ?"

"We have already asked that question," said Château-Renaud, " for none of us have seen him."

The count was silent, but continued to gaze around him.

At length they arrived at the cemetery. The piercing eye of Monte-Cristo glanced through clusters of bushes and trees, and was soon relieved from all anxiety, for he saw a shadow glide between the yew-trees, and recognised him whom he sought.

Everything was conducted in the usual manner.

The funeral being over, the guests returned to Paris. Château-Renaud looked for a moment for Morrel ; but while watching the departure of the count, Morrel had quitted his post, and Château-Renaud failing in his search, joined Debray and Beauchamp.

"YES, COME AT TWELVE O'CLOCK; I SHALL THEN BE FAR AWAY!"
Page 400.

Monte-Cristo concealed himself behind a large tomb, and watched Morrel, who, by degrees, approached the tomb and knelt down; he bent his head till it touched the stone, then clutching the grating with both hands, he murmured,—

"Oh! Valentine!"

Thus he remained for a long time, then he rose, brushed the dust from his knees, and turned towards Paris, without once looking back. He walked slowly down the Rue de la Roguette. The count followed him about a hundred paces behind. Maximilian crossed the canal, and entered the Rue Meslay by the Boulevards.

The count still followed him; on arrival at the house he insisted on entrance and followed the young man to his room. As he had expected, Morrel had laid his pistols on the table beside him.

"Listen to me one instant," said Monte-Cristo, "I am the only man in the world having the right to say to you,—'Morrel, your father's son shall not die to day;'" and Monte-Cristo, with an expression of majesty and sublimity, advanced with his arms folded towards the young man, who involuntarily recoiled a step.

"Why do you mention my father?" stammered he; "why do you mingle a recollection of him with the affairs of to-day?"

"Because I am he who saved your father's life when he wished to destroy himself, as you do to-day,—because I am the man who sent the purse to your young sister, and the Pharaon to old Morrel,—because I am the Edmond Dantès who nursed you, a child, on my knees."

Morrel made another step back, staggering, breathless, crushed. Then his nature underwent a complete and sudden revulsion; he rose, bounded out of the room, and rushed to the stairs, exclaiming energetically,

"Julie! Julie! Emmanuel! Emmanuel!"

Monte-Cristo endeavoured also to leave, but Maximilian would have died rather than relax his hold of the handle of the door, which he closed upon the count. Julie, Emmanuel, and some of the servants, ran up in alarm on hearing the cries. Morrel seized their hands, and opening the door, exclaimed in a voice choked with sobs,—

"On your knees! on your knees! he is our benefactor! the saviour of our father! He is——"

He would have added "Edmond Dantès," but the count seized his arm and prevented him. Julie threw herself into the arms of the count; Emmanuel embraced him as a guardian angel; Morrel again fell on his knees, and struck the ground with his forehead. Then the iron-hearted man felt his heart swell in his breast; a flame seemed to rush from his throat to his eyes, he bent his head and wept. Meanwhile, Emmanuel, in a broken voice, said to the count,—

"Oh! count, how could you, hearing us so often speak of our unknown benefactor, seeing us pay such homage of gratitude and adoration to his memory, how could you continue so long without discovering yourself to us? Oh, it was cruel to us, and—dare I say it?—to you also."

"Listen, my friend," said the count—"I may call you so, since we have really been friends for the last eleven years; the discovery of this secret has been occasioned by a great event of which you must never know. I wished to bury it during my whole life in my own bosom, but your brother, Maximilian, wrested it from me by a violence he repents of now, I am sure." Then turning round, and seeing that Morrel had thrown himself into an arm-chair, he added in a low voice, pressing Emmanuel's hand significantly,—

"Watch over him."

Julie had rushed from the room and returned, holding in her hands the silken purse, while tears of joy rolled down her cheeks.

"Here is the relic," she said; "do not think it will be less dear to us now we are acquainted with our benefactor!"

"My child," said Monte-Cristo, colouring, "allow me to take back that purse: since you now know my face, I wish to be remembered alone through the affection I hope you will grant me.

"My kind friends," he added, "leave me alone with Maximilian."

When they had gone he turned to the young man.

"My friend," he said, with an expression of melancholy equal to his own, "listen to me; one day, in a moment of despair like yours, since it led to a similar resolution, I, like you, wished to kill myself: one day, your father, equally desperate, wished to kill himself too. If any one had said to your father at the moment he raised the pistol to his head—if any one had told me, when in my prison I pushed back the food I had not tasted for three days—if any one had said to either of us then, 'Live.

the day will come when you will be happy, and will bless life ';
no matter whose voice had spoken, we should have heard him
with the smile of doubt, or the anguish of incredulity ; and yet
how many times has your father blessed life while embracing
you ! how often have I myself——"

" Ah !" exclaimed Morrel, interrupting the count, " you had
only lost your liberty, my father had only lost his fortune, but
I have lost Valentine."

" Look at me," said Monte-Cristo, with that expression
which sometimes made him so eloquent and persuasive,—" look
at me, there are no tears in my eyes, nor is there fever in my
veins, yet I see you suffer—you, Maximilian, whom I love as my
own son. Well, does not this tell you that in grief, as in life,
there is always something to look forward to beyond ? Now, if
I entreat, if I order you to live, Morrel, it is in the conviction
that one day you will thank me for having preserved your life."

" Have pity on me, count !"

" I feel so much pity towards you, Maximilian, that—listen
to me attentively—if I do not cure you in a month, to the day,
to the very hour, mark my words, Morrel, I will place loaded
pistols before you, and a cup full of the deadliest Italian poison—
a poison, more sure and prompt than that which has killed
Valentine."

" In a month, then, on your honour, if I am not consoled,
you will let me take my life in my own hands, and whatever
may happen, you will not call me ungrateful ?"

" In a month to the day ; the very hour and the date is
a sacred one, Maximilian. I do not know whether you remember that this is the 5th of September ; it is ten years to-day
since I saved the life of your father who wished to die."

Morrel seized the count's hand and kissed it.

" And now," the count said, "after to-day, you will come and
live with me ; you can occupy Haydée's apartment, and my
daughter will at least be replaced by my son."

" Haydée ?" said Morrel ; " what has become of her ?"

" She departed last night."

" To leave you ?"

" To wait for me. Hold yourself ready then to join me at
the Champs Elysées, and let me out of this house without any
one seeing my departure."

Maximilian hung his head, and obeyed with childlike
reverence.

CHAPTER L

THE day after the conversation between M. Danglars and
Monte-Cristo, Lucien Debray called as usual on Madame
Danglars.

"Lucien! a great event has happened!" said the lady,
glancing inquiringly at him,—"M. Danglars left last night!"

"What do you mean? Does he not intend to return?"

"Certainly not; at ten o'clock at night his horses took him
to the barrier of Charenton ; there a postchaise was waiting for
him—he entered it with his valet-de-chambre, saying that he
was going to Fontainebleau ; he left a letter for me."

And she handed him a letter.

It ran as follows :

"Madame and most faithful wife.

"When you receive this, you will no longer have a husband ! Oh ! you need not be alarmed, you will only have lost him
as you have lost your daughter ; I mean that I shall be travelling
on one of the thirty or forty roads leading out of France. I this
morning received five millions which I paid away; almost
directly afterwards another demand for the same sum was
presented to me ; I postponed this creditor till to-morrow, and I
intend leaving to-day to escape that to-morrow, which would be
rather too unpleasant for me to endure. You understand this,
do you not, my most precious wife? So long as I hoped we
were working for the good of our house and for the fortune of
our daughter, I philosophically closed my eyes and struggled on,
now she has gone I care to stay no longer. You were rich
when I married you, but little respected. I have augmented our
fortune, and it has continued to increase during the last fifteen
years, till extraordinary and unexpected catastrophes have
suddenly overturned it, without any fault of mine, I can
honestly declare. You, madam, have only sought to increase

404

your own, and I am convinced you have succeeded. I leave you, therefore, as I took you, rich, but little respected. Adieu! I also intend from this time to work on my own account. I shall not return to you.

" Your very devoted husband,
"BARON DANGLARS."

The baroness had watched Debray while reading this long and painful letter, and saw him, notwithstanding his self-control, change colour once or twice. When he had ended, he folded the letter, and resumed his pensive attitude.

" Oh Lucien," she cried, " I ask your advice."

" Then if you wish to take my advice," said the young man, coldly, " I would recommend you to travel."

"; To travel !" she murmured.

" Certainly ; as M. Danglars says, you are rich and perfectly free. In my opinion, a withdrawal from Paris is absolutely necessary after the double catastrophe of Mademoiselle Danglars' and M. Danglars' disappearance. The world will think you abandoned and poor, for the wife of a bankrupt would never be forgiven were she to keep up the appearance of opulence. You have only to remain in Paris for about a fort-night, telling the world you are abandoned, and relating the details of this desertion to your best friends, who will soon spread the report. Then you can quit your house, leaving your jewels, and giving up your jointure, and every one's mouth will be filled with praises of your disinterestedness. They will know you are deserted, and think you also poor : for I alone know your real financial position, and am quite ready to give up my accounts as an honest partner."

The dread with which the baroness, pale and motionless, listened to this, was equalled by the calm indifference with which Debray had spoken.

" Deserted !" she repeated ; " ah, yes, I am, indeed, deserted ! You are right, sir, and no one can doubt my position."

These were the only words uttered by the proud and violent woman.

" But then you are rich,—very rich, indeed," continued Debray, taking out some papers from his pocket-book, which he spread upon the table.

Madame Danglars saw them not ; she was fully engaged in stilling the beatings of her heart, and restraining the tears which were ready to gush forth.   At length a sense of dignity prevailed, and if she did not entirely master her agitation, she at least succeeded in preventing the fall of a single tear.

"Madame," said Debray, "it is nearly six months since we have been associated.   You furnished a principal of 100,000 francs.   Our partnership began in the month of April.   In May we commenced operations, and in the course of the month gained 450,000 francs.   In June the profit amounted to 900,000. In July we added 1,700,000 francs : it was, you know, the month of the Spanish bonds.   In August we lost 300,000 francs at the beginning of the month, but on the 13th we made up for it, and we now find that our accounts, reckoning from the first day of partnership up to yesterday, when I closed them, showed a capital of 2,400,000 francs, that is 1,200,000 francs for each of us.   Now, madame," said Debray, delivering up his accounts in the methodical manner of a stockbroker, "there are still 80,000 francs, the interest of this money, in my hands."

"But," said the baroness, "I thought you never put the money out to interest ?"

"Excuse me," said Debray, coldly, "I had your permission to do so, and I have made use of it.   There are then 40,000 francs for your share, besides the 100,000 you furnished me to begin with, making, in all, 1,340,000 francs for your portion.   I took the precaution of drawing out your money the day before yesterday.   There it is, half in bank-notes, the other half in a cheque payable to the bearer.

Madame Danglars mechanically took the cheque and the heap of bank-notes.   This enormous fortune made no great appearance on the table.   Madame Danglars, with tearless eyes, but with her breast heaving with concealed emotion, placed the bank-notes in her bag, put the cheque into her pocket-book, and then, standing pale and mute, awaited one kind word of consolation. But she waited in vain.

"Now, madame," said Debray, "you have a splendid fortune, an income of about 60,000 livres a-year, which is enormous for a woman who cannot keep an establishment here for a year at least. You will be able to indulge all your fancies ; besides, should you find your income insufficient, you can, for the sake of the past, make use of mine; and I am ready to offer you all I possess on loan."

"Thank you, sir,—thank you," replied the baroness; "you forget that what you have just paid me is much more than a poor woman requires, who intends for some time, at least, to retire from the world."

Debray was, for a moment, surprised, but immediately recovering himself, he bowed with an air which seemed to convey,—

"As you please."

Madame Danglars had, until then, perhaps hoped for something : but when she saw the careless bow of Debray and the glance by which it was accompanied, together with his significant silence, she raised her head, and, without passion, or violence, or even hesitation, ran down stairs, disdaining to address a last farewell to one who could thus part from her.

Not far off the room in which Debray had been dividing two millions and a half with Madame Danglars was another, inhabited by persons who have played a prominent part in the incidents related.

Mercédès and Albert were in that room.

Madame Morcerf had lived there since leaving her home ; but the continual silence of the spot oppressed her. Albert, too, was ill at ease : the remains of luxury prevented his sinking into his actual position. If he wished to go out without gloves, his hands appeared too white ; if he wished to walk through the town, his boots seemed too highly polished. Yet these two noble and intelligent creatures, united by the indissoluble ties of maternal and filial love, had succeeded in tacitly understanding one another, and economising their stores.

"Mother!" exclaimed Albert to Madame de Morcerf, just as Madame Danglars was descending the stairs, "let us reckon our riches, if you please ; I need capital to build my plans upon."

"Capital—nothing!" replied Mercédès, with a mournful smile.

"No, mother—capital, 3,000 francs. And I have an idea of our leading a delightful life upon this 3,000 francs."

Albert then took a pen and wrote :

	Frs.
"Coupé, thirty-five francs	35
From Chalons to Lyons you will go on by the steam-boat—six francs	6
From Lyons to Avignon (still by steam-boat), sixteen francs	16
From Avignon to Marseilles, seven francs .	7
Expenses on the road, about fifty francs .	50
Total	114 frs."

"Well, be it so.   But these 200 francs?"

"Here they are, and 200 more besides.   See, I have sold my watch for 100 francs, and the guard and seals for 300.   How fortunate the ornaments were worth more than the watch. Now I think we are rich, since, besides the 114 francs we require for the journey, we find ourselves in possession of 286."

"But we owe something in this house?"

"Thirty francs; but I pay that out of my 286 francs; that is understood.   But that is not all.   What do you say to this, mother?"

And Albert took out of a little pocket-book with golden clasps, a remnant of his old fancies, or perhaps a tender *souvenir* —a note of 1000 francs.

"What is this?" asked Mercédès.

"A thousand francs."

"But whence have you obtained them?"

Albert, rising, kissed his mother on both cheeks, then stood looking at her.

"Mother dearest, it is decided that you are to live at Marseilles, and that I am to leave for Africa, where I will earn for myself the right to use the name I now bear instead of the one I have thrown aside."

Mercédès sighed.

"Well, mother! I yesterday engaged myself in the Spahis," added the young man, lowering his eyes with a certain feeling of shame.   "I thought my body was my own, and that I might sell it.   I yesterday took the place of another.   I sold myself for more than I thought I was worth," he added, attempting to smile; "I fetched 2000 francs."

"Then these 1000 francs——" said Mercédès, shuddering—

"Are the half of the sum, mother; the half will be paid in a year."

Mercédès raised her eyes to heaven with an expression it would be impossible to describe, and tears, which had hitherto been restrained, now ran down her cheeks.

"Well! now you understand, mother," continued Albert; "here are more than 1000 francs settled on you, there is also the money that the count spoke of, in the garden of the little house at Marseilles, that is 3000 francs more; upon these you can live for a while."

"I shall live! then you will not leave me, Albert?"

"Mother, I must go," said Albert in a firm, calm voice; "you love me too well to wish me to remain useless and idle with you; besides, I have signed."

Albert gathered up his papers hastily, rang the bell to pay the thirty francs he owed to the landlord, and, offering his arm to his mother, they descended the stairs. As they passed into the street some one was walking before them, and hearing the rustling of a silk dress, he turned round.

"Debray!" muttered Albert.

"You, Morcerf!" replied the secretary, resting on the stairs. It was, indeed, strange to find the young man whose misfortunes had made so much noise in Paris.

"Morcerf!" repeated Debray.

Then, noticing, in the dim light, the still youthful and veiled figure of Madame de Morcerf :—

"Pardon me!" he added with a smile.

Albert understood his thoughts.

"Mother," he said, turning towards Mercédès, "this is M. Debray, secretary of the minister for the interior, once a friend of mine.'

"How, once!" stammered Debray; "what do you mean ?"

"I say so, M. Debray, because I have no friends now, and I ought not to have any. I thank you, for having recognised me."

Debray stepped forward and cordially pressed his hand.

"Believe me, dear Albert," he said, with all the emotion he was capable of feeling, "believe me, I feel deeply for your misfortunes, and if, in any way, I can serve you, I am yours."

"Thank you," said Albert, smiling. "In the midst of our misfortunes we are still rich enough not to require assistance from any one. We are leaving Paris, and when our journey is paid we shall have 4000 francs left."

The blood mounted to the temples of Debray, who held a million in his pocket-book; he muttered a few words of general civility, and parted from them in confusion.

CHAPTER LI

It must be recalled that the Abbé Busoni had remained alone with Noirtier in the chamber of death, and that the old man and the priest were the sole guardians of the young girl's body. Perhaps it was the Christian exhortations of the abbé, perhaps his kind charity, perhaps his persuasive words, which had restored the courage of Noirtier; for ever since he had conversed with the priest his violent despair had yielded to a calm resignation, which surprised all who knew his excessive affection for Valentine.

M. de Villefort had not seen his father since the morning of the death. The whole establishment had been changed; another valet-de-chambre was engaged for himself, a new servant for Noirtier; two women had entered Madame de Villefort's service; in fact, everywhere there were new faces.

The assizes were about to commence. Villefort with his papers under his arm and hat in hand, before going out, directed his steps towards his wife's room. At the door he paused for a moment to wipe his damp pale brow.

Madame de Villefort was sitting on an ottoman, and impatiently turning over the leaves of some newspapers and pamphlets which young Edward, by way of amusing himself, was tearing in pieces before his mother could finish reading them. She was dressed to go out, her hat was placed beside her on a chair, and her gloves were on her hands.

"Ah! here you are, sir," she said, in her naturally calm voice; "but how pale you are! Have you been working all night? Why did you not come down to breakfast?"

Madame de Villefort had multiplied her questions in order to gain one answer, but to all her inquiries M. de Villefort remained mute and cold as a statue.

"Edward!" said Villefort, fixing an imperious glance on the child, "go and play in the drawing-room, my dear: I wish to speak to your mamma."

Madame de Villefort shuddered at the sight of that cold countenance, that resolute tone, and the strange preliminaries. Edward raised his head, looked at his mother, and then, finding that she did not confirm the order, began cutting off the heads of his leaden soldiers.

"Edward!" cried M. de Villefort, so harshly that the child started on the carpet, "do you hear me?—Go!"

The child, unaccustomed to such treatment, rose, pale and trembling; it would be difficult to say whether his emotion were caused by fear or passion. His father went up to him, took him in his arms, and kissed his forehead.

"Go," he said, "go my child!"

Edward ran out. M. de Villefort went to the door, which he closed behind the child, and bolted it.

"Madame, where do you keep the poison you generally use?" said the magistrate, without any introduction, placing himself between his wife and the door.

Madame de Villefort experienced something of the sensation of a bird, which, looking up, sees the murderous spring closed over its head. A hoarse, broken tone, which was neither a cry nor a sigh, escaped from her, while she became deadly pale.

"Sir," she said, "I—I do not understand you." And, as in her first paroxysm of terror, she had raised herself from the sofa, in the next, stronger than the other, she fell down again on the cushions.

"I asked you," continued Villefort, in a perfectly calm tone, "where you conceal the poison by the aid of which you have killed my father-in-law, M. de Saint-Méran, my mother-in-law, Madame de Saint-Méran, Barrois, and my daughter, Valentine."

"Ah, sir!" exclaimed Madame de Villefort, clasping her hands, "what do you say?"

"It is not for you to interrogate, but to answer."

"Is it to the judge or to the husband?" stammered Madame de Villefort.

"To the judge,—to the judge, madame!"

It was terrible to behold the frightful pallor of that woman, the anguish of her look, the trembling of her whole frame.

"And you cannot deny it," added Villefort, extending his hand towards her, as though to seize her in the name of justice. "You have accomplished these different crimes with impudent address, which could only deceive those whose affection for you blinded them. Since the death of Madame de Saint-Méran I

have known that a poisoner lived in my house. M. d'Avrigny
warned me of it. After the death of Barrois my suspicions
were directed towards an angel : but after the death of Valentine,
there has been no doubt in my mind, and not only in mine, but
in those of others : thus your crime, known by two persons,
suspected by many, will soon become public ; and, as I told you
just now, you no longer speak to the husband but to the
judge."

The young woman hid her face in her hands.

"Oh, sir !" she stammered, "I beseech you, do not believe
appearances."

"Are you, then, a coward ?" cried Villefort, in a contemp-
tuous voice. "But I have always remarked that poisoners were
cowards. Can you be a coward, you who have had the courage
to witness the death of two old men and a young girl murdered
by you ?"

"Sir ! sir !"

"Can you be a coward," continued Villefort, with increasing
excitement, "you who could count, one by one, the minutes of
four death-agonies ?"

Madame de Villefort stretched out her hands, and fell on her
knees.

"I understand," he said, "you confess ; but a confession made
to the judges, a confession made at the last moment, extorted
when the crime cannot be denied, diminishes not the punishment
inflicted on the guilty !"

"The punishment !" stammered Madame de Villefort.

"Certainly. Did you hope to escape it, because you were four
times guilty ? Did you think the punishment would be withheld
because you are the wife of him who pronounces it ?—No!
madame, no ! the scaffold awaits the poisoner, whoever she may
be, unless, as I just said, the poisoner has taken the precaution of
keeping for herself a few drops of her deadliest poison."

Madame de Villefort uttered a wild cry, and a hideous and
uncontrollable terror spread over her distorted features.

"Oh ! do not fear the scaffold," said the magistrate, "I will
not dishonour you, since that would be to dishonour myself :
no ! if you have heard me distinctly, you will understand that
you are not to die on the scaffold. The wife of the first magistrate in the capital shall not, by her infamy, soil an unblemished
name ; she shall not, with one blow, dishonour her husband and
her child."

"Oh, heavens . oh, heavens !" and she rose, with her hair dishevelled and her lips foaming.

"Have you answered the question I put to you on entering the room : Where do you keep the poison you generally use, madame ?"

Madame de Villefort raised her arms to heaven, and convulsively struck one hand against the other.

"Oh, mercy, mercy, sir !"

"What I require is, that justice be done. I am on the earth to punish," he added, with a flaming glance; "any other woman, were it the queen herself, I would send to the executioner; but to you I shall be merciful. To you I will say, Have you not put aside some of the surest, deadliest, most speedy poison ?"

"In the name of our child ! Ah, for the sake of our child, let me live !"

"No! no ! no ! I tell you ; one day, if I allow you to live, you will, perhaps, kill him as you have the others !"

"I!—I kill my boy!" cried the distracted mother, rushing towards Villefort; "I kill my son! Ha! ha! ha!" and a frightful, demoniac laugh finished the sentence, which was lost in a hoarse rattle.

She fell at her husband's feet. He approached her.

"Think it over," he said ; "if on my return justice has not been satisfied, I will denounce you with my own mouth and arrest you with my own hands!"

She listened, panting, overwhelmed, crushed, her eye alone lived and glared horribly.

"Do you understand me ?" he said. "I am going down there to pronounce the sentence of death against a murderer. If I find you alive on my return, you shall sleep to-night in the Conciergerie."

Madame de Villefort sighed ; her nerves gave way, and she sank on the carpet.

The procureur du roi seemed to experience a sensation of pity, he looked upon her less severely, and bowing to her, said, slowly,—

"Farewell, farewell !"

That farewell struck Madame de Villefort like the executioner's knife. She fainted.

The procureur du roi went out, after having double-locked the door.

At last the assizes were over and the procureur du roi could return to his home.

The carriage stopped at the door of the house. Villefort leaped out of the carriage, and saw his servants surprised at his early return ; he could read no other expression on their features. Neither of them spoke to him, they merely stood aside to let him pass by as usual, nothing more. As he passed by M. Noirtier's room, he perceived, through the half-open door, two figures ; but he experienced no curiosity to know who was visiting his father ; anxiety carried him on farther.

" Come," he said, as he ascended the stairs leading to his wife's room, " nothing is changed here."

He then closed the door of the landing.

He entered the little room in which Edward slept ; for though the child went to school during the day, his mother could not allow him to be separated from her at night. With a single glance Villefort's eye ran through the room.

" Not here," he said ; " doubtless she is in her bed-room."

He rushed towards the door ; it was bolted ; he stopped, shuddering. " Heloïse!" he cried. He fancied he heard the sound of a piece of furniture being removed. " Heloïse !" he repeated.

No one answered. Villefort burst the door open with a violent blow.

At the entrance of the room which led to her boudoir, Madame de Villefort was standing erect, pale, her features contracted, and her eyes glaring horribly.

She extended her stiff white hand towards him.

" It is done, sir," she said with a rattling which seemed to tear her throat. " What more do you want ?" and she fell on the floor.

Villefort ran to her and seized her hand, which convulsively clasped a crystal bottle with a golden stopper. Madame de Villefort was dead.

Villefort stepped back to the threshold of the door, fixing his eyes on the corpse. Then he exclaimed suddenly, " Where is my son ?—Edward, Edward !" and he rushed out of the room still crying, " Edward, Edward !" The name was pronounced in such a tone of anguish that the servants ran up.

" Where is my son ?" asked Villefort ; " let hi m be removed from the house."

"Master Edward is not downstairs, sir," replied the valet-de-chambre.

"Then he must be playing in the garden ; go and see."

"No, sir ; Madame de Villefort sent for him half an hour ago ; he went into her room, and has not been downstairs since."

A cold perspiration burst out on Villefort's brow ; his legs trembled, and his brain filled with a confused mass of ideas.

"In Madame de Villefort's room ?" he murmured, and slowly returned, with one hand wiping his forehead, and with the other supporting himself against the wall. To enter the room, he must again see the body of his unhappy wife.

"Edward !" he stammered, "Edward !" but the child did not answer. Where, then, could he be, if he had entered his mother's room and not since returned ? He stepped forward. Through the open door a portion of the boudoir was visible, containing an upright piano and a blue satin couch. Villefort stepped forward two or three paces, and beheld his child lying—no doubt asleep on the sofa. The unhappy man uttered an exclamation of joy ; a ray of light seemed to penetrate the abyss of despair and darkness. He had only to step over the corpse, enter the boudoir, take the child in his arms, and flee far, far away.

Villefort no longer presented a type of civilised man : he more resembled a tiger wounded to death. He leaped over the corpse as though it had been a furnace. He took the child in his arms, pressed him, shook him, called him, but the child replied not. He pressed his burning lips to the cheeks, but they were icy cold and pale ; he felt his stiffened limbs ; he pressed his hand upon the heart, but it no longer beat : the child was dead. A folded paper fell from Edward's breast.

Villefort, thunderstruck, fell upon his knees. He picked up the paper, and recognising his wife's writing, ran his eyes rapidly over its contents : they were as follows :—

"You know that I was a good mother, since it was for my son's sake I became a criminal. A good mother cannot depart without her son."

Villefort could not believe his eyes,—he could not believe his reason. Then a piercing cry escaped from his breast, and he cried, "Still the hand of God." He now rose, his head bent beneath the weight of grief, and shaking his damp hair,—he who had never felt compassion for any one, determined to seek his father, that he might have some one to whom he could relate his misfortunes,—some one by whose side he might weep. He descended the little stairs and entered Noirtier's room.

The old man appeared to be listening attentively and as affectionately as his infirmities would allow to the Abbé Busoni, who looked cold and calm, as usual.

Villefort, perceiving the abbé, passed his hand across his brow. He recollected the visit the abbé had paid to his house on the day of Valentine's death.

" You here, sir !" he exclaimed.

Busoni turned round, and perceiving the excitement depicted on the magistrate's face, the savage lustre of his eyes, he understood that something frightful had happened, and he said in a tone of coldest condemnation :

" I come to tell you that you have sufficiently repaid your debt, and that from this moment I will pray to God to forgive you as I do."

" Good heavens !" exclaimed Villefort, stepping back fearfully, " surely that is not the voice of the Abbé Busoni !"

" No !" the abbé threw off his false tonsure, shook his head, and his hair, no longer confined, fell in black masses around his manly face.

" It is the face of the Count of Monte-Cristo !" exclaimed the procureur du roi, with a haggard expression.

" You are not exactly right, M. le Procureur du roi; you must go farther back."

" That voice ! that voice !—where did I first hear it ?"

" You heard it for the first time at Marseilles, twenty-three years ago, the day of your marriage with Mademoiselle de Saint-Méran. Refer to your papers."

" You are not Busoni ?—you are not Monte-Cristo ? Oh, heavens ! you are then some concealed, implacable, and mortal enemy ! I must have wronged you in some way at Marseilles ! Oh ! woe to me !"

" Yes ; you are, indeed, right, " said the count, crossing his arms over his broad chest ; " search ! search !"

" But what have I done to you ?" exclaimed Villefort, whose mind was balancing between reason and insanity, " what have I done to you ? Tell me, then ! Speak !"

" You condemned me to a horrible, tedious death,—you killed my father,—you deprived me of liberty, of love, and happiness. "

" Who are you, then ? Who are you ?"

" I am the spectre of a wretch you buried in the dungeons of

the Château d'If. The form of the Count of Monte-Cristo was
given to that spectre when he at length issued from his tomb,
enriched with gold and diamonds!"

"Ah! I recognise you! I recognise you!" exclaimed the procureur du roi; "you are——"

"I am Edmond Dantès!"

"You are Edmond Dantès!" cried Villefort, seizing the count
by the wrist, "then come here!" And he dragged Monte-
Cristo up the stairs. "Hold! Edmond Dantès!" he said, pointing to the bodies of his wife and child. "See! are you well
revenged?"

Monte-Cristo became pale at this horrible sight; he felt he
had passed beyond the bounds of vengeance, and that he could
no longer say, "God is for and with me." With an expression
of indescribable anguish he threw himself upon the body of the
child, reopened its eyes, felt its pulse, and then rushed with him
into Valentine's room, of which he locked the door.

"My child!" cried Villefort. "He carries away the body of
my child! Oh! curses, woe, death to you!" and he tried to
follow Monte-Cristo; but, as though in a dream, he was transfixed to the spot.

A quarter of an hour afterwards, the door of Valentine's
room opened, and Monte-Cristo reappeared. Pale, with a dull
eye and heavy heart, all the noble features of that face, usually
so calm and serene, appeared overwhelmed by grief. In his arms
he held the child, whom no skill had been able to recall to life.
Bending on one knee, he placed it reverently by the side of its
mother, with its head upon her breast. Then, rising, he went
out, and meeting a servant on the stairs, he asked,—

"Where is M. de Villefort?"

The servant, instead of answering, pointed to the garden.
Monte-Cristo ran down the steps, and, advancing towards the
spot designated, beheld Villefort, encircled by his servants, with
a spade in his hand, and digging the earth with fury.

"I will make a grave for him," he cried. "But not here!"
And then he moved farther on, and recommenced digging.

Monte-Cristo approached him, and said, in a low voice, with
an expression almost humble,—

"Sir, you have indeed lost a son; but——"

Villefort interrupted him; he had neither listened nor heard.

"Oh!" cried the count, "he is mad. This has unseated his
reason!" And as though he feared that the walls of the

27

accursed house would crumble around him, he rushed into the street, for the first time doubting whether he had the right to do as he had done.

On entering his own house he met Morrel, who wandered about like a ghost.

"Prepare yourself, Maximilian," he said, with a smile; "we leave Paris to-morrow."

"Have you nothing more to do there?" asked Morrel.

"No," replied Monte-Cristo, "God grant I may not have done too much already!"

The next day they indeed left, accompanied only by Baptistin. Haydée had taken away Ali, and Bertuccio remained with Noirtier.

CHAPTER LII

THE DEPARTURE

THE recent events formed the theme of conversation throughout all Paris. The following evening Emmanuel and his wife conversed with natural astonishment in their little apartment in the Rue-Meslay upon the three successive sudden and most unexpected castastrophes of Morcerf, Danglars, and Villefort. Maximilian, who was paying them a visit, listened to their conversation, or rather was present at it, plunged in his customary state of apathy.

At that instant, the door of the room was opened, and the Count of Monte-Cristo appeared on the threshold. The young people uttered a cry of joy, while Maximilian raised his head but let it fall again immediately.

"Maximilian," said the count, without appearing to notice the different impressions which his presence produced on the little circle, "I come to seek you."

"I am ready," said Maximilian, "I came expressly to wish them farewell."

"Whither are you going, count?" asked Julie.

"In the first instance to Marseilles."

"To Marseilles!" exclaimed the young couple.

"I have a passport, and my clothes are ready packed," said Morrel in his tranquil, but mournful manner.

"Good!" said Monte-Cristo, smiling, "in these prompt arrangements we recognise the order of a well-disciplined soldier."

"And you quit us thus?" said Julie, "at a moment's warning, you do not give us a day—no, not even an hour before your departure?"

"My carriage is at the door, and I must be in Rome in five days."

"Farewell, my dear sister; Emmanuel, adieu!" Morrel repeated.

"His carelessness and indifference touch me to the heart," said Julie. "Oh! Maximilian, Maximilian, you are certainly concealing something from us."

"Pshaw!" said Monte-Cristo, "you will see him return to you gay, smiling, and joyful."

Maximilian cast a look of disdain, almost of anger, on the count.

"We must leave you," said Monte-Cristo.

"Before you quit us, count," said Julie, "will you permit us to express to you all that the other day——"

"Julie," interrupted the count, taking her two hands in his, "all that you could say in words would never express that which I read in your eyes; the thoughts of your heart are fully understood by mine. I should have left you without seeing you again; but because I am a weak and vain man, fond of the tender, kind, and thankful glances of my fellow-creatures, I carry my egotism so far as to say, 'Do not forget me, my kind friends, for probably you will never see me again.'"

"Never see you again!" exclaimed Emmanuel, whilst two large tears rolled down Julie's cheeks; "never behold you again! It is not a man then, but some angel that leaves us, and this angel is on the point of returning to heaven after having appeared on earth to do good."

"Say not so," quickly returned Monte-Cristo,—"say not so, my friends; angels never err, fate is not more powerful than they; it is they who, on the contrary, overcome fate. No! Emmanuel, I am but a man, and your admiration is as unmerited as your words are sacrilegious."

And pressing his lips on the hand of Julie, he extended his other hand to Emmanuel; then tearing himself from this house, the abode of peace and happiness, he made a sign to Maximilian, who followed him passively with the indifference which was perceptible in him ever since the death of Valentine had stunned him.

The next moment the carriage was on its road; and the feet of the horses struck a shower of sparks from the pavement. Maximilian settled himself in his corner without uttering a word. Half an hour had fled, when the carriage stopped suddenly; for the count had just pulled the silken check-string, which was fastened to Ali's finger. The Nubian immediately descended, and opened the carriage-door. It was a lovely starlight night— they had just reached the top of the hill of Villejuif, the plat form from whence Paris, like some dark sea, is seen to agitate its millions of lights, resembling phosphoric waves,—waves indeed, more noisy, more passionate, more changeable, more furious, more greedy, than those of the tempestuous ocean,—waves which never lie calm, like those of the vast sea,—waves ever destructive, ever foaming, and ever restless.

The count stepped out, and on a sign from his hand, the carriage advanced some steps. He contemplated for some time, with his arms crossed, the vast city. When he had fixed his piercing look on this modern Babylon—

"Great city!" murmured he, inclining his head and joining his hands as if in prayer, "less than six months have elapsed since first I entered thy gates. God only knows that I retire from thee without pride or hatred, but not without many regrets; He only knows that the power confided to me has never been made subservient to my personal good or any useless cause. Oh! great city! it is in thy palpitating bosom that I have found that which I sought; like a patient miner, I have dug deep into thy very entrails to root out evil thence; now my work is accomplished, my mission is terminated, now thou canst neither afford me pain nor pleasure. Adieu, Paris! adieu!"

His look wandered over the vast plain like that of some genius of the night; he passed his hand over his brow, and, getting into the carriage, the door was closed on him, and the vehicle quickly disappeared on the other side of the hill in a cloud of dust and noise.

The journey was performed with that marvellous rapidity which the unlimited power of the count ever commanded, towns fled from them like shadows on their path, and trees shaken by the first winds of autumn seemed like giants madly rushing on to meet them, and retreating as rapidly when once reached. The following morning they arrived at Châlons, where the count's steam-boat was waiting for them; without an instant being lost, the carriage was placed on board, and the two travellers embarked without delay. The boat was built for speed; her two paddle-wheels resembled two wings with which she skimmed the water like a bird. As the distance increased between the travellers and Paris, an almost superhuman serenity appeared to surround the count; he might have been taken for an exile about to revisit his native land.

Ere long Marseilles presented herself to view. Marseilles, full of life and energy. Powerful memories were stirred within them by the sight of that round tower, that fort Saint-Nicholas, that port with its quays of brick, where they had both gambolled as children; and it was with one accord that they stopped on the Cannebière. A vessel was setting sail for Algiers, and on board the bustle usually attending departure prevailed. The passengers and their relations crowded on the deck, friends taking a tender, but sorrowful, leave of each other, some weeping, others noisy in their grief, formed a spectacle, exciting even to those who witnessed similar ones daily, but which had not the power to disturb the current of thought that had taken possession of the mind of Maximilian from the moment he had set foot on the broad pavement of the quay.

" Here," said he, leaning heavily on the arm of Monte-Cristo, " here is the spot where my father stopped, when the Pharaon entered the port; it was here that the good old man, whom you saved from death and dishonour, threw himself into my arms. I yet feel his warm tears on my face, and his were not the only tears shed, for many who witnessed our meeting wept also."

Monte-Cristo gently smiled and said,—

" I was there;" at the same time pointing to the corner of a street. As he spoke, and in the very direction he indicated, a groan, expressive of bitter grief, was heard; and a woman was seen waving her hand to a passenger on board the vessel about to sail. Monte-Cristo looked at her with an emotion that must have been remarked by Morrel had not his eyes been fixed on the vessel.

" Oh! heavens!" exclaimed Morrel, " I do not deceive myself —that young man who is waving his hat, that youth in the uniform of a lieutenant, is Albert de Morcerf!"

" Yes," said Monte-Cristo, " I recognised him."

" How so?—you were looking the other way."

The count smiled, as he was in the habit of doing when he did not wish to make any reply, and he again turned his look towards the veiled woman who soon disappeared at the corner of the street. Turning to his friend,—

" Dear Maximilian," said the count, " have you anything you wish to do in this city?"

" I wish to visit the grave of my father," replied Morrel in a broken voice.

" Well, then, go,—wait for me there, and I will soon join you."

Morrel bent his steps to the east of the city. Monte-Cristo

walked slowly towards the Allées de Meillan. It was covered by an immense vine, which spread its aged and blackened branches over the stone front, burnt yellow by the ardent sun of the south. Two stone steps, worn away by the friction of the feet, led to the door, made of three planks, which, owing to their never having made acquaintance with paint or varnish, parted annually to reunite again when the damp season arrived. This house, with all its crumbling antiquity and apparent misery, was yet cheerful and picturesque, and was the same that old Dantès formerly inhabited—the only difference being that the old man occupied merely the garret, while the whole house was now placed at the disposal of Mercédès by the count.

At the end of a passage, paved with bricks, was seen a little garden, bathed in sunshine, and rich in warmth and light—it was in this garden that Mercédès found, in the place Monte-Cristo had indicated, the sum of money which he, through a sense of delicacy, intimated had been placed there four-and-twenty years previously. The trees of the garden were easily seen from the steps of the street-door. Monte-Cristo, on stepping into the house, heard a sigh, almost resembling a deep sob ; he looked in the direction whence it came, and there, under an arbour of Virginian jessamine, with its thick foliage, and beautiful long purple flowers, he perceived Mercédès seated, with her head bowed, and weeping bitterly. She had raised her veil, and with her face hidden by her hands, was giving free scope to those sighs and tears which had been so long restrained by the presence of her son. Monte-Cristo advanced a few paces, and his steps were heard on the gravel. Mercédès raised her head, and uttered a cry of terror on beholding a man before her.

" Mercédès," said the count, " it is no longer in my power to restore you to happiness, but I offer you consolation ; will you accept it as coming from a friend ?"

" I am, indeed, most wretched," replied Mercédès. " Alone in the world, I had but my son, and he has left me !"

" He possesses a noble heart," replied the count, " and he has acted rightly."

" Oh !" said the wretched woman, mournfully shaking her head. " You have acted kindly, count, in bringing me back to the place where I have enjoyed so much bliss. I ought to be ready to meet death on the same spot where happiness was once all my own."

" Alas !" said Monte-Cristo, " your words sear and embitter

my heart, the more so as you have every reason to hate me ; I have been the cause of all your misfortunes ; but why do you pity, instead of blame me ? You render me still more unhappy——"

"Hate you,—blame you,—*you*, Edmond! Hate—reproach the man that has spared my son's life!"

The count looked up, and fixed his eyes on her, while she, partly rising from her seat, extended both her hands towards him.

"Oh! look at me," continued she, with a feeling of profound melancholy; "my eyes no longer dazzle by their brilliancy, for the time has long fled since I used to smile on Edmond Dantès, who anxiously looked out for me from the window of yonder garret. Years of grief have created an abyss between those days and the present.—I neither reproach you nor hate you, my friend! Oh, no, Edmond, it is myself that I blame,—myself that I hate!"

Monte-Cristo approached her, and silently took her hand.

"No," said she, withdrawing it gently, "no, my friend, touch me not. You have spared me, yet of all those who have fallen under your vengeance I was the most guilty. They were influenced by hatred, by avarice, and by self-love; but I was base, and, for want of courage, acted against my judgment. Nay, do not press my hand, Edmond!"

As Mercédès spoke, the tears chased each other down her worn cheeks; the unhappy woman's heart was breaking, as memory recalled the changeful events of her life. Monte-Cristo, however, took her hand, and imprinted a kiss on it, but she herself felt that it was with no greater warmth than he would have respectfully bestowed one on the hand of some marble statue of a saint.

"It often happens," continued she, "that a first fault destroys the prospects of a whole life. I believed you dead; why did I survive you? What good has it done me to mourn for you eternally in the secret recesses of my heart? Only to make a woman of nine-and-thirty look like one of fifty years of age. Why, having recognised you, why was I able to save my son alone?"

"Mercédès," said Monte-Cristo, "you judge yourself with too much severity. You are a noble-minded woman, and it was your grief that disarmed me. Still I was but an agent, led on by an invisible and offended Deity, who chose not to withhold the fatal blow that I was destined to hurl. Examine the past and then say whether I am not a Divine instrument."

"Enough," said Mercédès, "enough, Edmond! Believe me that she who alone recognised you has been the only one to comprehend you. And had she crossed your path, and you had crushed her like a frail glass, still, still she must have admired you! Like the gulf between me and the past, there is an abyss between you and the rest of mankind; and I tell you freely that the comparison I draw between you and other men will ever be one of my greatest tortures. No! there is nothing in the world to resemble you in worth and goodness! But we must say farewell, Edmond; and let us part!"

"Before I leave you, Mercédès, have you no request to make?" said the count.

"I desire but one thing in this world, Edmond—the happiness of my son."

"But have you no request to make for yourself, Mercédès?"

"For myself I want nothing. I live, as it were, between two graves. The one that of Edmond Dantès—lost to me long, long since. He had my love! That word ill becomes me now, but it is a memory dear to my heart, and one that I would not lose for all that the world contains. The other grave is that of the man who met his death from the hand of Edmond Dantès. I approve of the deed, but I must pray for the dead."

"Yes, your son shall be happy, Mercédès," repeated the count.

"Then I shall enjoy as much happiness as this world can possibly confer."

"But what are your intentions?"

"To say that I shall live here, like the Mercédès of other times, gaining my bread by labour, would not be true nor would you believe me. I have no longer the strength to do any thing but to spend my days in prayer. However, I shall have no occasion to work, for the little sum of money buried by you, which I found in the place you mentioned, will be sufficient to maintain me."

"Mercédès," said the count, "I do not say it to blame you, but you made an unnecessary sacrifice in relinquishing the whole of the fortune amassed by M. de Morcerf; half of it, at least, by right belonged to you, in virtue of your vigilance and economy."

"I perceive what you are intending to propose to me; but I cannot accept it, Edmond—my son would not permit it."

"Nothing shall be done without the full approbation of Albert de Morcerf. But if he be willing to accept my offer, will you oppose them?"

"You well know, Edmond, that I am no longer a reasoning creature. I have no will. If succour be sent to me I will accept it."

Monte-Cristo dropped his head and shrank from the vehemence of her grief.

"Will you not even say you will see me again?" he asked.

"On the contrary, we shall meet again," said Mercédès, pointing to heaven with solemnity. "I tell you so to prove to you that I still hope." And after pressing her own trembling hand upon that of the count, Mercédès rushed up the stairs and disappeared.

Monte-Cristo slowly left the house and turned toward the quay. But Mercédès did not see his departure, though she was seated at the little window of the room which had been occupied by old Dantès. Her eyes were straining to see the ship which was carrying her son over the vast sea. But still her voice involuntarily murmured softly—

"Edmond! Edmond! Edmond!"

The count departed with a sad heart from the house in which he had left her, for he would probably never behold her again.

Since the death of little Edward a great change had taken place in Monte-Cristo. Having reached the summit of his vengeance by a long and tortuous path, he saw an abyss of doubt on the other side of the mountain. More than this, the conversation which had just taken place between Mercédès and himself had awakened so many recollections in his heart that he felt it necessary to fight them down.

As he reasoned with himself, Monte-Cristo walked down the Rue de la Caisserie. It was the same through which, twenty-four years ago, he had been conducted by a silent and nocturnal guard; the houses, to-day so smiling and animated, were on that night dark, mute, and closed.

He proceeded towards the quay by the Rue Saint-Laurent, and advanced to the Consigne; it was the point where he had embarked. A pleasure-boat was passing, with its striped awning; Monte-Cristo called the owner, who immediately rowed up to him, with the eagerness of a boatman hoping for a good fare.

The weather was magnificent. The sun, red and flaming, was sinking into the water, which embraced it as it approached.

But notwithstanding that serene sky, the graceful boats, and the golden light in which the whole scene was bathed, the Count of Monte-Cristo, wrapped in his cloak, could think only of his

The Departure 427

terrible voyage, the details of which were, one by one, recalled
to his memory. The solitary light burning at the Catalans—
the first sight of the Château d'If, which told him whither they
were leading him, the struggle with the gendarmes when he
wished to throw himself overboard, his despair when he found
himself vanquished, and the cold sensation of the end of the
carbine touching his forehead—all these were brought before
him in vivid and frightful reality. As they reached the shore
overhung by the massive masonry of the Château d'If, the count
instinctively shrank back while the owner called out—

" Sir, we have reached the shore."

Monte-Cristo remembered that on that very spot, on the same
rock, he had been violently dragged up by the guards, who forced
him to ascend the slope at the points of their bayonets. The
journey had seemed very long to Dantès, but Monte-Cristo
found it equally short.

There had been no prisoners confined in the Château d'If
since the revolution of July ; it was only inhabited by a guard
placed for the prevention of smuggling. A concierge waited at
the door to exhibit this monument of terror to visitors.

The count inquired whether any of the ancient gaolers were
still there, but they had all been pensioned, or had passed on to
some other employment. The concierge who conducted him had
only been there since 1830.

He visited his own dungeon. He again beheld the dull light
vainly endeavouring to penetrate the narrow opening. His eyes
rested upon the spot where his bed, since then removed, had
stood, and, behind the bed, the new stones indicated where the
breach made by the Abbé Faria had been.

Monte-Cristo felt his limbs tremble ; he seated himself upon
a log of wood.

" Are there any stories connected with this prison ?" he
asked.

" Yes, sir ; indeed the gaoler Antoine told me one connected
with this very dungeon."

Monte-Cristo shuddered ; Antoine had been his gaoler. He
had almost forgotten his name and face, but on hearing the
former pronounced, memory recalled his person as he used to
see it, wearing a brown jacket, with the bunch of keys, the
jingling of which he still seemed to hear. The count turned
round, and fancied he saw him in the corridor, rendered still
darker by the torch carried by the concierge.

"This dungeon," continued the concierge, "was, it appears, some time ago occupied by a very dangerous prisoner, the more so since he was full of industry. Another person was confined in the Château at the same time, but he was not wicked, he was only a poor mad priest."

"Ah, indeed!—mad!" repeated Monte-Cristo; "and what was his mania?"

"He offered millions to any one who would set him at liberty."

"Could the prisoners see each other?" he asked.

"Oh, no, sir, it was expressly forbidden; but they eluded the vigilance of the guards, and made a passage from one dungeon to the other."

"And which of them made this passage?"

"Oh, it must have been the young man, certainly, for he was strong and industrious, while the abbé was aged and weak; besides, his mind was too vacillating to allow him to carry out an idea."

"Blind fools!" murmured the count.

"The result was, the two men communicated together; how long they did so nobody knows. One day the old man fell ill and died. Now guess what the young one did?"

"Tell me."

"He carried off the corpse, which he placed in his own bed with its face to the wall; then he entered the empty dungeon, closed the entrance, and slid himself into the sack which had contained the dead body—he fancied they buried the dead at the Château d'If, and imagining they would not expend much labour on the grave of a prisoner, he calculated upon raising the earth with his shoulders; but, unfortunately for him, their arrangements at the Château frustrated his projects: they never buried their dead; they merely attached a heavy cannon-ball to the feet, and then threw them into the sea. This is what was done. The young man was thrown from the top of the rock; the corpse was found on the bed next day, and the whole truth was guessed: for the men who performed the office then mentioned what they had not dared to speak of before, namely, that at the moment the corpse was thrown into the deep, they heard a shriek, which was almost immediately stifled by the water in which it disappeared."

The count breathed with difficulty; the cold drops ran down his forehead, and his heart was full of anguish.

"No," he muttered, "the doubt I felt was but the commencement of forgetfulness; but here the wound reopens, and the heart again thirsts for vengeance. And the prisoner," he continued aloud, " was he ever heard of afterwards ?"

" Oh! no; of course not. You can understand that one of two things must have happened : he must either have fallen flat, in which case the blow, from a height of ninety feet, must have killed him instantly, or he must have fallen upright, and then the weight would have dragged him to the bottom, where he remained,—poor fellow! He was a naval officer who had been confined for plotting with the Buonapartists."

The count asked, " Was his name ever known ?"

" Oh! yes; but only as No. 34."

" I want to see the poor abbé's room."

" Ah! No. 27."

" Yes; No. 27," repeated the count, who seemed to hear the voice of the abbé answering him in those very words through the wall when asked his name.

" Stop," said the guide; " I have forgotten the other key."

" Go and fetch it."

The guide carried away the torch. Scarcely had a few seconds elapsed, ere the count saw everything as distinctly as by daylight. He looked around him, and really recognised his dungeon.

" Yes," he said, " there is the stone upon which I used to sit; there is the impression made by my shoulders on the wall; there is the mark of my blood made when I, one day, dashed my head against the wall. Oh! those figures! how well I remember them! I made them one day to calculate the age of my father, that I might know whether I should find him still living, and that of Mercédès, to know if I should find her still free. After finishing that calculation, I had a minute's hope. I did not reckon upon hunger and infidelity!" and a bitter laugh escaped him. He saw in fancy the burial of his father and the marriage of Mercédès. On the other side of the dungeon, he perceived an inscription, the white letters of which were still visible on the green wall. ' Oh! God,' he read, ' preserve my memory.' " Oh! yes," he cried, " that was my only prayer at last; I no longer begged for liberty but memory; I dreaded to become mad and forgetful. O God! thou hast preserved my memory; I thank Thee! I thank Thee!"

At this moment the light of the torch was reflected on the wall; the guide was advancing; Monte-Cristo went to meet him.

"Follow me, sir;" and without ascending the stairs, the guide conducted him by a subterranean passage to another entrance. There again Monte-Cristo was assailed by a crowd of thoughts. The first thing that met his eye was the meridian, drawn by the abbé on the wall, by which he calculated the time; then he saw the remains of the bed on which the poor prisoner had died. The sight of this, instead of exciting the anguish experienced in his own dungeon, filled his heart with a soft and grateful sentiment, and tears fell from his eyes.

"This is where the mad abbé was kept, sir, and that is where the young man entered;" and the guide pointed to the opening which had remained unclosed. "From the appearance of the stone," he continued, "a learned gentleman discovered that the prisoners might have communicated together for ten years. Poor things! they must have been ten weary years."

Dantès took some louis from his pocket, and gave them to the man who had twice unconsciously pitied him. The guide took them, thinking them merely a few pieces of little value; but the light of the torch revealed their true worth.

"Sir," he said, "you have made a mistake; you have given me gold."

"I know it."

The concierge looked at him with surprise.

"Sir, since you are so liberal, I ought to offer you something. One day I discovered a hollow sound against the head of the bed and under the hearth I raised the stones, and found——"

"A rope-ladder and some tools?"

"How do you know that?" asked the guide, in astonishment.

"I do not know—I only guess it, because this sort of things are generally found in prisoners' cells."

"Yes, sir, a rope-ladder and tools. I sold them to visitors, who considered them great curiosities; but I have still something left. A sort of book, written upon strips of cloth."

"Go and fetch it my good fellow."

The guide went out.

Then the count knelt down by the side of the bed, which death had converted into an altar. "O, second father!" he exclaimed, "thou who hast given me liberty, knowledge, riches; thou who, like beings of a superior order to ourselves, couldest understand the science of good and evil; if in the depths of the tomb there still remains something within us which can respond to the voice of those who are left on earth ; if after death the soul ever revisit the places where we have lived and suffered, then, noble heart !—sublime soul ! then I conjure thee, by the paternal love thou didst bear me, by the filial obedience I vowed to thee, grant me some sign, some revelation ! Remove from me the remains of a doubt, which, if it change not to conviction, must become remorse !" The count bowed his head, and clasped his hands together.

" Here, sir," said a voice behind him.

Monte-Cristo shuddered and rose. The concierge held out the strips of cloth upon which the Abbé Faria had spread the stores of his mind. The manuscript was the great work of the Abbé Faria upon the kingdoms of Italy. The count seized it hastily, and his eyes immediately fell upon the epigraph, and he read, " Thou shalt tear out the dragons' teeth, and shalt trample the lions under foot, saith the Lord."

" Ah !" he exclaimed, " here is my answer. Thanks, father, thanks !" And feeling in his pocket, he took thence a small pocket-book, which contained ten bank-notes, each of 1000 francs.

" Here," he said, " take this pocket-book ; but only on condition that you will not open it till I am gone ;" and placing the treasure he had just found in his breast, more valuable to him than the richest jewel, he hastened out of the passage, and reaching his boat, cried, " To Marseilles !" Then, as he departed, he fixed his eyes upon the gloomy prison.

" Woe," he cried, "to those who confined me in that wretched prison ; and woe to those who forgot that I was there !"

On landing, the count turned towards the cemetery, where he felt sure of finding Morrel.

Morrel was leaning against a cypress-tree, mechanically fixing his eyes on the grave. His grief was so profound, he was nearly unconscious.

" Maximilian," said the count, " you should not look on the grave, but there ;" and he pointed upwards.

" Who can be more wretched than the man who has lost all he loved and desired in the world ?"

" Listen, Morrel, and pay attention to what I am about to tell you. I knew a man who, like you, had fixed all his hopes of happiness upon a woman. He was young, he had an old father whom he loved, a betrothed bride whom he adored. He was about to marry her when one of those caprices of fate—which would almost make us doubt the goodness of Providence, if that Providence did not afterwards reveal itself by proving that all is but a means conducting to an end,—one of those caprices deprived him of his betrothed, of the future of which he had dreamed, and plunged him into a dungeon."

" Ah !" said Morrel, " one quits a dungeon in a week, a month, or a year."

" He remained there fourteen years, Morrel," said the count, placing his hand on the young man's shoulder.

Maximilian shuddered.

" Well ! at the height of his despair God assisted him through human means ; at first, perhaps, he did not recognise the infinite mercy of the Lord, but at last he took patience and waited. One day he miraculously left the prison, transformed, rich, powerful. His first cry was for his father ; but that father was dead ! He was, then, a more unhappy son than you, Morrel, for he could not even find his father's grave !"

" But then he had the woman he loved still remaining ?"

" You are deceived, Morrel, that woman was faithless, and had married one of the persecutors of her betrothed. You see, then, Morrel, that he was a more unhappy lover than you."

" And does he ever expect to be happy ?"

" He hopes so, Maximilian."

The young man's head fell on his breast.

" You have my promise," he said, after a minute's pause, extending his hand to Monte-Cristo. " Only remember——"

" On the 5th of October, Morrel, I shall expect you at the island of Monte-Cristo. On the 4th a yacht will wait for you in the port of Bastia, it will be called the Eurus. You will give your name to the captain, who will bring you to me. It is understood—is it not ?"

" But, count, do you remember that the 5th of October——"

" Child !" replied the count, " not to know the value of a man's word ! I have told you twenty times that if you wish to die on that day I will assist you. Morrel, farewell ! I have business in Italy. The steamer waits, and in an hour I shall be far from you. Will you accompany me to the harbour, Maximilian ?"

" I am entirely yours, count."

Morrel accompanied the count to the harbour ; the white steam was ascending like a plume of feathers from the black chimney of the vessel. The steamer soon disappeared, and in an hour afterwards, as the count had said, was scarcely distinguishable in the horizon amidst the fogs of the night.

CHAPTER LIII

THE FIFTH OF OCTOBER

It was about six o'clock in the evening ; an opal-coloured light, through which an autumnal sun shed its golden rays, descended on the blue sea. The heat of the day had gradually decreased, and a light breeze arose, like the respiration of nature on awaking from the burning siesta of the south; a delicious zephyr played along the coasts of the Mediterranean, and wafted from shore to shore the sweet perfume of plants, mingled with the fresh smell of the sea.

A light yacht was gliding amidst the first dews of night over the immense lake, extending from Gibraltar to the Dardanelles, and from Tunis to Venice. The motion resembled that of a swan with its wings opened towards the wind, gliding on the water. It advanced, at the same time, swiftly and gracefully, leaving behind it a glittering track. Standing on the prow, was a tall man, of a dark complexion, who saw with dilating eyes that they were approaching a dark mass of land in the shape of a cone, rising from the midst of the waves, like the hat of a Catalan.

" Is that Monte-Cristo ?" asked the traveller, to whose orders the yacht was for the time submitted, in a melancholy voice.

" Yes, your excellency," said the captain, " we have reached it."

Ten minutes afterwards, the sails were furled, and they cast anchor about one hundred paces from the little harbour. The boat was already in the sea, loaded with four rowers and the steersman. The traveller descended, and instead of sitting down at the stern of the boat, which had been decorated with a blue carpet for his accommodation, stood up with his arms crossed. The rowers waited, their oars half lifted out of the water, like birds drying their wings.

" Proceed !" said the traveller. The eight oars fell into the sea simultaneously without splashing a drop of water, and the boat, yielding to the pressure, glided forward. In an instant they found them. elves in a little harbour, formed by a natural creek; the boat touched the fine sand.

"Will your excellency be so good as to mount the shoulders of two of our men, who will carry you ashore?"

The young man answered this invitation with a gesture of indifference, and stepped out of the boat, whereupon the sea immediately rose to his waist.

"Ah! your excellency," murmured the steersman, "you should not have done so; our master will scold us for it."

The young man continued to advance, following the sailors, who chose a firm footing. After about thirty paces they landed; as he stamped on the ground to shake off the wet, he looked round for some one to show him his road, for it was quite dark. Just as he turned, a hand rested on his shoulder, and a voice which made him quiver, exclaimed,—

"Good evening, Maximilian! you are punctual, thank you!"

"Ah! is it you, count?" said the young man, in an almost joyful accent, pressing Monte-Cristo's hand with both his own.

"Yes; you see I am as exact as you are. But you are dripping, my dear fellow; you must change your clothes. Come, I have a lodging prepared for you, in which you will soon forget fatigue and cold."

Morrel saw with surprise that the men who had brought him had left without being paid or uttering a word. Already the sound of their oars might be heard as they returned to the yacht.

"Oh, yes," said the count, seeing him look round, "you are looking for the sailors."

"Yes; I paid them nothing, and yet they are gone."

"Never mind that, Maximilian," said Monte-Cristo, smiling. "I have made an agreement with the navy, that the access to my island shall be free of all charge."

Morrel looked at the count with surprise.

"Count," he said, "you are not the same here as in Paris."

"How so?"

"Here you laugh."

The count's brow became clouded.

"You are right to recall me to myself, Maximilian," he said; "I was delighted to see you again, and forgot for the moment that all happiness is fleeting."

"Oh, no, no! count," cried Maximilian, seizing Monte-Cristo's hands, "pray, laugh; be happy, and prove to me, by your indifference, that life is endurable to sufferers. Oh! how charitable, kind, and good you are; you affect this gaiety to inspire me with courage."

"You are wrong, Morrel; I was really happy."

Morrel mechanically followed the count, and they had entered the grotto before he perceived it. He felt a carpet under his feet, a door opened, perfumes surrounded him, and a brilliant light dazzled his eyes. Morrel hesitated to advance, he dreaded the enervating effect of all that he saw. Monte-Cristo drew him in gently.

"Maximilian," he said, "you know I have no relation in the world. I have accustomed myself to regard you as my son; well, then, to save my son, I will sacrifice my life, nay even my fortune."

"What do you mean?"

"I mean, that you wish to quit life because you do not understand all the enjoyments which are the fruits of a large fortune. Morrel, I possess nearly a hundred millions, I give them to you; with such a fortune you can attain every wish. Are you ambitious? every career is open to you. Overturn the world, change its character, yield to mad ideas, be even criminal,—but live."

"Count, I have your word," said Morrel, coldly, then taking out his watch, he added, "It is half-past eleven."

"Morrel, can you intend it, in my house, beneath my eyes?"

"Then let me go," said Maximilian, "or I shall think you did not love me for my own sake, but for yours;" and he rose.

"It is well," said Monte-Cristo, whose countenance brightened at these words; "you wish it, you are inflexible; yes, as you said, you are indeed wretched, and a miracle alone can cure you; sit down, Morrel, and wait."

Morrel obeyed; the count rose and unlocking a cabinet with a key suspended from his gold chain, took from it a little silver casket, beautifully carved and chased; the corners of which represented four bending figures, similar to the Caryatides. He placed the casket on the table; then opening it, took out a little golden box, the top of which flew open when touched by a secret spring. This box contained an unctuous substance, partly solid. It was a mixed mass of blue, red, and gold. He took out a small quantity of this with a gilt spoon, and offered it to Morrel, fixing a long steadfast glance upon him.

"This is what you asked for," he said, "and what I promised to give you."

"I thank you from the depths of my heart," said the young man, taking the spoon into his hands.

And slowly, though without any hesitation, he swallowed the mysterious substance. Then they were both silent. Ali, mute and attentive, brought the pipes and coffee, and disappeared. By degrees the lamps gradually faded in the hands of the marble statues which held them, and the perfumes appeared less powerful to Morrel. An overpowering sadness took possession of the young man; his hands relaxed their hold; the objects in the room gradually lost their form and colour; and his disturbed vision seemed to perceive doors and curtains open in the wall.

"Friend," he cried, "I feel that I am dying; thanks!" He made a last effort to extend his hand, but it fell powerless beside him. Then it appeared to him that Monte-Cristo smiled, not with that strange and fearful expression, which had sometimes revealed to him the secrets of his heart, but with the benevolent kindness of a father for a child. At the same time the count appeared to increase in stature; his form, nearly double its usual height, stood out in relief against the red tapestry, his black hair was thrown back, and he stood in the attitude of a menacing angel.

A brilliant light shone from the next room. In it he saw a woman of marvellous beauty appear on the threshold of the door separating the two rooms. Pale, and sweetly smiling, she looked like an angel of mercy conjuring the angel of vengeance.

"Is it heaven that opens before me?" thought the dying man, "that angel resembles the one I have lost."

Monte-Cristo made a sign with his hand, and the new-comer advanced with a smile upon her lips.

"Valentine! Valentine!" Maximilian mentally ejaculated, but his lips uttered no sound; and as though all his strength was centred in that eternal emotion, he sighed and closed his eyes.

Valentine rushed towards him; his lips again moved.

"He is calling you," said the count, "he to whom you have confided your destiny, he from whom death would have separated you, calls you to him. Happily I vanquished death, as I told you, he is but momentarily unconscious. Henceforth, Valentine, you need never doubt him, since he has rushed into what he believed to be death to find you. Without me you would both have died. May God accept my atonement of these two existences!"

Valentine seized the count's hand, and in her irresistible impulse of joy carried it to her lips.

"Oh! thank me again!" said the count, "tell me till you are weary that I have restored you to happiness; you do not know how much I require this assurance."

"Oh! yes, yes, I thank you with all my heart," said Valentine; "and if you doubt the sincerity of my gratitude, then! ask Haydée, ask my beloved sister Haydée, who ever since our departure from France, has enabled me to wait patiently for this happy day, by talking to me of you."

"You then love Haydée?" asked Monte-Cristo, with an emotion he in vain endeavoured to dissimulate.

"Oh, yes! with all my soul."

"You have called Haydée your sister; let her become so indeed, Valentine; render to her all the gratitude you fancy you owe me; protect her, for (his voice was hoarse with emotion) henceforth she will be alone in the world."

"Alone in the world!" repeated a voice behind the count, "and why?"

Monte-Cristo turned round, Haydée was standing pale and motionless, looking at him with an expression of fearful amazement.

"Because to-morrow, Haydée, you will be free; you will then assume your proper position in society, for I will not allow my destiny to overshadow yours. Daughter of a prince! I restore to you the riches and name of your father."

Haydée became pale, and lifting her transparent hands to heaven, exclaimed in a voice hoarse with tears—

"Then you leave me, my lord?"

"Haydée, Haydée! you are young and beautiful, forget even my name, and be happy!"

"It is well," said Haydée, "your order shall be executed, my lord; I will forget even your name, and be happy." And she stepped back.

"Oh heavens!" exclaimed Valentine, who was supporting the head of Morrel on her shoulder, "do you not see how pale she is? Do you not see how she suffers?"

Haydée answered with a heart-rending expression.

"Why should he understand this, my sister? He is my master, and I am his slave; he has a right to notice nothing."

The count shuddered at the tones of a voice which penetrated the inmost recesses of his heart; his eyes met those of the young girl, and he could not bear their brilliancy.

"Haydée, would it please you to remain with me?" he exclaimed.

"I am young," gently replied Haydée, "I love the life you have made so sweet to me, and should regret to die."

"You mean then that if I leave you Haydée——"

"I should die; yes, my lord."

"Do you then love me?"

"Oh Valentine! he asks if I love him. Valentine, tell him if you love Maximilian."

The count felt his heart dilate and throb; he opened his arms, and Haydée, uttering a cry, sprang into them.

"Oh, yes!" she cried, "I do love you! I love you as one loves a father, brother, husband! I love you as my life, for you are the best, the noblest of created beings!"

"Let it be, then, as you wish; God has sustained me in my struggle with my enemies, and has given me this victory; he will not let me end my triumph with this penance; I wished to punish myself, but he has pardoned me! Love me then, Haydée! Who knows? perhaps your love will make me forget all I wish not to remember."

"What do you mean, my lord?"

"I mean that one word from you has enlightened me more than twenty years of slow experience; I have but you in the world, Haydée; through you I again connect myself with life, through you I shall suffer, through you rejoice!"

"Do you hear him, Valentine?" exclaimed Haydée, "he says my life for his."

The count looked at her strangely for a moment.

"Have I discovered the truth?" he cried; "but whether it be for recompense or punishment, I accept my fate. Come, Haydée, come!" and throwing his arm round the young girl's waist, he disappeared.

An hour had nearly passed, during which Valentine, breathless and motionless, watched steadfastly over Morrel. At length she felt his heart beat, a faint breath played upon his lips, and a slight shudder, announcing the return of life, passed through the young man's frame. At length his eyes opened, but they were at first fixed and expressionless; then sight returned, and with it feeling and grief.

"Oh!" he cried, in an accent of despair, " the count has deceived me; I am yet living," and extending his hand towards the table, he seized a knife.

"Dearest!" exclaimed Valentine, with her adorable smile, "awake."

Morrel uttered a loud exclamation, and frantic, doubtful, dazzled as though by a celestial vision, he fell upon his knees.

*　　*　　*　　*　　*

The next morning, at daybreak, Valentine and Morrel were walking arm-in-arm on the sea-shore, Valentine relating how Monte-Cristo had appeared in her room; how he had unveiled everything; how he had revealed the crime; and, finally, how he had saved her life by allowing her to seem dead. They had found the door of the grotto open, and went forth, the few remaining stars yet pressing through the morning light. Morrel soon perceived a man standing amidst the group of rocks, who was awaiting a sign from them to advance; he pointed him out to Valentine.

"Ah! it is Jacopo," she said, " the captain of the yacht;" and she beckoned him towards them.

"Do you wish to speak to us?" asked Morrel.

"I have a letter to give you from the count."

"From the count!" murmured the two young people.

"Yes; read it."

Morrel opened the letter and read;—

"My dear Maximilian,

"There is a vessel for you at anchor. Jacopo will conduct you to Leghorn, where M. Noirtier waits his grand-daughter, whom he wishes to bless before you lead her to the altar. All that is in this grotto, my friend, my house in the Champs-Elysées, and my château at Tréport, are the marriage gifts bestowed by Edmond Dantès upon the son of his old master, Morrel. Mademoiselle de Villefort will share them with you; for I entreat her to give to the poor the immense fortune reverting to her from her father, now a madman, and her brother, who died last September with his mother. Tell the angel who will watch over your future destiny, Morrel, to pray sometimes for a man, who, like Satan, thought himself, for an instant, equal to God; but who now acknowledges, with Christian humility, that God alone possesses supreme power and infinite wisdom. Perhaps those prayers may soften the remorse he feels in his heart. There is neither happiness nor misery in the world; there is only the comparison of one state with another, nothing more. He who has felt the deepest grief is best able to experience supreme happiness. We must have felt what it is to die, Morrel, that we may appreciate the enjoyments of life.

"Live, then, and be happy, beloved children of my heart! and never forget, that until the day when God will deign to reveal the future to man, all human wisdom is contained in these two words,—' *Wait and hope.*'

"Your friend,

"EDMOND DANTÈS,
"Count of Monte-Cristo."

During the perusal of this letter, which informed Valentine, for the first time, of the madness of her father and the death of her brother, she became pale, a heavy sigh escaped her, and tears, not the less painful because they were silent, ran down her cheeks; her happiness cost her very dear. Morrel looked round uneasily.

"But," he said, "the count's generosity is too overwhelming; Valentine, you will be satisfied with my humble fortune. Where is the count, friend? Lead me to him."

Jacopo pointed towards the horizon.

"What do you mean?" asked Valentine. "Where is the count?—where is Haydée?"

"Look!" said Jacopo.

The eyes of both were fixed upon the spot indicated by the sailor, and on the blue line separating the sky from the Mediterranean Sea they perceived a large white sail.

"Gone!" said Morrel: "Gone!—Adieu, my friend!—adieu, my father!"

"Gone!" murmured Valentine: "Adieu, my friend!—adieu, my sister!"

"Who can say whether we shall ever see them again?" said Morrel with tearful eyes.

"Maximilian," replied Valentine, "has not the count just told us that all human wisdom was contained in these two words,— ' *Wait and hope.*' "

THE END.

JACOPO POINTED TOWARDS THE HORIZON.
Page 440.